An Indian Freedom Fighter in Japan

An Indian Freedom Fighter in Japan

Memoirs of A. M. Nair

Written by A. M. Nair

Japan Publishing Industry Foundation for Culture

Publisher's Note
This book follows the Hepburn system of romanization. In line with the original English edition, Japanese, Chinese, and Korean names are given by first name followed by family name.

This edition is supplemented with a new preface adapted by permission from "Aisuru naki chichi o omoinagara," in *Shirarezaru Indo dokuritsu sensō: A. M. Nairu kaisōroku* (Tokyo: Futoh-sha, 2008), translated by Alex G. K. Pulsford. All images courtesy of Futoh-sha / G. M. Nair.

An Indian Freedom Fighter in Japan: Memoirs of A. M. Nair
A. M. Nair.

Published by
Japan Publishing Industry Foundation for Culture (JPIC)
2-2-30 Kanda-Jinbocho, Chiyoda-ku, Tokyo 101-0051, Japan

First edition: March 2025

© 1982 G. M. Nair
English translation of the Foreword © 2025 Japan Publishing Industry Foundation for Culture
All rights reserved.

This publication is the result of a collaborative effort between the Japan Institute of International Affairs (JIIA) and Japan Publishing Industry Foundation for Culture (JPIC).

This book was first published as *An Indian Freedom Fighter in Japan: Memoirs of A. M. Nair* (Orient Longman Limited, 1982).
Publishing rights arranged with the copyright holder.

Book design: Niall Biser
Jacket and cover photos: Courtesy of G. M. Nair

Printed in Japan
hardcover ISBN 978-4-86658-261-0
ebook (ePub) ISBN 978-4-86658-262-7
ebook (PDF) ISBN 978-4-86658-263-4
https://www.jpicinternational.com/

To my Mother

Throughout the ages geography has made us one great land, history has made us one land, the common culture has made us one land and our common aspirations, our common hopes and fears, victories and defeats, have made us one. That is the past. In the present, by our common labours, common sacrifices and common struggles, we gained the freedom of India.... The past and present have provided a common ground to us. So also must the future be common to us, the future that we are striving to attain, the future of millions of our people, their welfare. In whatever region we may live, this calls for unity of purpose, unity of endeavour and sacrifice.

Jawaharlal Nehru

TABLE OF CONTENTS

Foreword: In Loving Memory 9
Preface 17

1. My Home State 23
2. Early Years 29
3. A Turning Point 36
4. Social Reforms Movement 43
5. At the Crossroads 48
6. Departure for Japan 57
7. At Kyoto University 64
8. Meeting Rash Behari Bose 72
9. The Emperor's Coronation Day 80
10. Student Days in Kyoto 87
11. 1932–33, A New Turning Point 98
12. In Manchukuo 108
13. In Mongolia and Sinkiang 123
14. Visit to Tokyo 138
15. To Mongolia Again: My "Economic War" with Britain . . 144
16. Manchukuo Again 154
17. My Marriage 160
18. Last Spell in Manchukuo 165
19. The Second World War and the IIL in Southeast Asia . . 176

20.	The Tokyo Conference of the IIL	190
21.	The Bangkok Conference	199
22.	The Indian National Army	213
23.	The IIL's Move from Bangkok to Singapore	223
24.	The Subhas Era and the Second INA	229
25.	The Imphal Campaign	251
26.	The Close of the Subhas Era	258
27.	The Surrender of Japan	272
28.	The Disappearance of Subhas Chandra Bose	279
29.	India and Postwar Japan	291
30.	The India-Japan Peace Treaty	301
	Epilogue	315

Appendices

1.	Explanatory Notes	325
2.	Rash Behari Bose's Presidential Address at the Inauguration of the Bangkok Conference (June 15, 1942)	328
3.	Brief Life Sketches of Justice (Dr.) Radhabinod Pal and Yasaburo Shimonaka	337
4.	The Treaty Of Peace Between the Governments of India and Japan (June 9, 1952)	340

About the Author 346

Foreword: In Loving Memory

This text was originally written by G. M. Nair, the son of author A. M. Nair, for the publication of the revised Japanese edition by Futoh-sha in 2008. For the reissue of this English edition, the original has been partially revised and reproduced following an interview with G. M. Nair.

I was born in 1944 in Ibaraki, where my family had evacuated, one year before the end of the war. My parents had originally lived in the town of Ogawa in Manchuria. However, my father, well aware of the worsening war situation and sensing that Japan's defeat was imminent, urged my mother, then pregnant with me, to return to Japan with my five-year-old brother. Through a connection, my mother found refuge in Ibaraki. Years later, she told me of their perilous journey across the sea from the Chinese mainland to Japan. During the voyage, my brother developed a high fever, prompting officials to deny them passage on the ship on the grounds that they "could not take a sick child aboard." As a result, my mother and brother had to board a different vessel. The ship they had initially been scheduled to take was later attacked and sunk in the Genkai Sea—a twist of fate that ensured their survival. I was eventually born in our evacuation home.

Unfortunately, my memories of Ibaraki are sparse. A few years later, we moved to a house in Bunkyo Ward, Tokyo. There, I vividly recall visits from members of the General Headquarters (GHQ). They frequently came to question my father about wartime matters, including investigations into the infamous Ishii Unit[*] in Manchuria. My father, however, remained resolutely

---

[*] Unit 731 was a secret biological warfare research unit in Manchuria led by Surgeon General Shiro Ishii.

tight-lipped. "I won't speak," he would insist, refusing to compromise his principles. Despite these tense encounters, my father often took me on outings. One striking memory is meeting Prime Minister Shigeru Yoshida as a child. My father brought me to the Industry Club in Marunouchi, Tokyo, where a long table dominated the room. I played underneath it until Yoshida sternly scolded me: "Young man, you mustn't do that."

In 1947, three years after my birth, India realized its long-cherished dream of independence. The following year saw the end of the Tokyo Trial, and by 1952, the San Francisco Peace Treaty was signed, along with the Treaty of Peace Between Japan and India. During the Tokyo Trial, my father stayed at the Imperial Hotel with Dr. Radhabinod Pal, the Indian judge, helping him gather information and prepare documents. He did more than simply act as a translator; he taught Dr. Pal, who was not well-versed in Japanese thought and customs, many essential things. He also worked tirelessly behind the scenes to facilitate the signing of the Japan-India treaty.

This memoir also recounts my brother's extended stay at Dr. Pal's residence in Calcutta in 1958, a visit I would later repeat. Accompanied by my father on my first visit, I traveled alone during my final year of high school. At the time, my father's disdain for English meant we never spoke it at home, leaving me with only the basics I had learned at school. Communicating in India was a challenge, but the experience was deeply formative. It was an era when flying was a novelty and overseas travel even rarer. Among the many vivid memories of my time there, one stands out: the warmth with which Dr. Pal embraced me upon my arrival, a gesture of profound kindness I will never forget.

I remember my father as being fully absorbed in his work, yet what stands out in my recollections of him is not his intensity but his gentle, kind smile. It was only later, each time I held this book in my hands, that I realized the deep connection between my father's calm demeanor and the fierce, protracted battle for the independence of India, Japan, and other Asian countries that was etched into his being.

This book presents the events my father saw with his own eyes, heard with his own ears, and experienced in the flesh, told from an objective and impartial standpoint, both as an insider and an outsider. I believe it provides a fresh perspective on a history we think we know—one that sheds new light not only on India's struggle but also on Japan and other Asian countries before and after World War II.

In addition to the goal of revealing historical truths to a broader audience, this book carries another important wish: that the true contributors to India's independence receive the recognition they deserve. While many studies of India's independence have focused on Subhas Chandra Bose as president of the Indian Independence League (IIL), it was Rash Behari Bose who laid the foundation for the movement, along with my father.

All the activities of Rash Behari Bose and my father were guided by the philosophy of *anasakta karma*—action without attachment, or deeds done without attachment for their fruits. They sought no reward, be it wealth, fame, or status. Their only desire was the independence of their beloved homeland, and they devoted themselves entirely to that cause. This is what I respect most about my father.

My father never sought recognition for himself. His deepest wish was that Rash Behari Bose and the other pioneers of the independence movement receive the credit they deserved, as he took pride in remaining "nameless." Whether working with Rash Behari Bose or later when Subhas Chandra Bose took over as his successor, my father's stance remained unchanged. Yet, reading through episodes of him traveling through Mongolia disguised as a Buddhist monk or a Muslim and being attacked by bandits, his incredible courage, spirit of adventure, and boundless curiosity emanate from the pages. I believe readers will come to appreciate the strength he possessed, comparable to that of the most renowned freedom fighters in history.

Is it merely a son's bias to think my father's work deserves its rightful place as a great contribution to India's independence? I leave that judgment to you, the reader, as you finish this book.

* * *

In 1928, my father entered Kyoto Imperial University's Faculty of Engineering, thanks to the strong encouragement and support of his older brother, Narayanan, who had graduated from Hokkaido Imperial University and was already the director of the Indian Fisheries Department. It was no easy feat for an Indian, then under British colonial rule, to study abroad. Even those who could afford it usually went to British universities, like Gandhi and Nehru. That my family could send two brothers to study in Japan reflected their wealth, but more than that, it showed the family's deep commitment to education, as they recognized Japan's high academic standards and sought to give their sons the best possible knowledge.

Moreover, Japan's victory in the Russo-Japanese War (1894–1895), where

General Nogi defeated General Stoessel at 203-Meter Hill and Admiral Togo crushed the Baltic Fleet, was a landmark event: the East had triumphed over the West. It's not hard to imagine how this stirred admiration and respect for Japan among Indians struggling under British rule.

From what my father told me, few in Japan's countryside had even heard of India at that time, but when he mentioned "Tenjiku"* (the ancient Japanese word for India), people would finally understand. After all, he was said to be the only Indian student in Japan at that time.

The Japanese language skills and deep understanding of Japanese people and culture that my father cultivated during his time at Kyoto Imperial University became invaluable tools for him later in life. He often said, "Kyoto is the finest city in Japan," and, even in his later years, he insisted on attending alumni reunions, no matter what, as those years were some of the most important of his life.

My father was tireless in his efforts. He worked assiduously to learn the foreign language and culture of Japan as quickly as possible. What he was most fortunate in, however, was meeting many people who supported his endeavors. He was a linguistic genius, as I mentioned earlier, but his talent for building networks was equally remarkable.

Although I call it fortune, I believe it was inevitable. My father's uncompromising beliefs and his ability to express precise and forthright opinions won people's trust. Unfortunately, such strong convictions also drew prejudice at times, but those who trusted him connected him with others, and so his network grew, transcending nationalities and generations.

As a side note, most of my father's personal photographs show him dressed in Japanese clothing. He disliked wearing a Western suit and tie, saying they were for Westerners. He maintained this belief even after Japan's defeat in the war.

* * *

In the autumn of 1938, while in Tokyo on business from Manchuria, my father attended a dinner hosted by his old friend Risuke Fuwa, where he met my mother, Fuwa's sister-in-law. As this book recounts, it was, to all appearances, love at first sight. Thanks to the strong support of friends, as well as financial

---

* Buddhism has deep roots in Japan, where it is widely known that the homeland of Buddha, as described in Buddhist scriptures, is "Tenjiku," or India.

backing from prominent figures like General Seishiro Itagaki, then war minister, and my father's close friend, Lee Kai-ten, a leader in the Korean independence movement, my parents were married in February of the following year.

At the time, international marriages were almost unheard of. For a daughter of a prominent family in Saitama to marry a foreigner would have naturally met with opposition. In fact, there were objections from my maternal grandfather, Imagoro Asami, but he recognized my father's character and sympathized with his cause. My mother shared that view.

Later in life, my mother said, "If he had been a run-of-the-mill curry shop owner, I wouldn't have married him." She had an unusual interest in political movements for a woman of her time, and it was her admiration for my father's passion for his work that led her to marry a foreigner over ten years her senior. She was a courageous and intelligent woman.

While my mother didn't speak much about it, her steadfast support behind the scenes was extraordinary. After the war, my father would frequently say, "I'm a man already dead." Perhaps this reflected a sense of distance he felt from post-war India, which had embraced a path of nonviolence, unlike his revolutionary activism before independence. During this period of despondency, it was my mother who took the lead, declaring, "I'll provide for the family," and establishing what is now the long-standing Nair Restaurant in Ginza, Tokyo.* My mother, who had never run a business before, drew upon the culinary skills she had acquired in Manchuria, where Indian neighbors had taught her to cook Indian dishes for my father. With her old-fashioned sense of spousal devotion, she told him, "You just sit by the cash register," and took on the full responsibility of managing the restaurant.

In its early days, the Nair Restaurant was frequented by GHQ personnel, as Indian cuisine was still unfamiliar and considered luxurious for most Japanese in the post-war years. My mother worked tirelessly to support the family, telling others, "Someone who could walk freely into the Army Ministry and General Staff Headquarters before the war should not have to do menial tasks," thus preserving my father's dignity as a revolutionary.

For my father, however, the restaurant was largely a means of survival. When I decided to take over, he told me to "do something else," and rarely involved himself in its operation. Nonetheless, he supported it quietly in the background. In 1970, during the Osaka Expo, the Indian Embassy approached him, seeking someone fluent in Japanese, English, and Hindi who could assist with restaurant operations. My father sent me, then freshly graduated

---

* The Nair restaurant in Tokyo's Ginza district—Tokyo's most prestigious and upscale shopping and entertainment area—is well known as a pioneer of Indian cuisine in Japan.

from university, to Osaka. There, I trained for a year surrounded by India's top chefs, an invaluable experience that later greatly benefited the Nair Restaurant.

As mentioned in the main text of this book, my father, during his time as a visiting professor at Kenkoku University in Manchuria, would often invite students of various ethnic backgrounds to his home, sharing his vision of a united Asia in which all peoples would one day achieve independence. When these countries gained independence after the war, he was overjoyed. His joy extended even beyond Asia; upon hearing news of African nations achieving independence, he would tremble with emotion, saying, "This is wonderful." I believe his love for other peoples was genuine. His deep and lasting friendships with many people from Korea and Mongolia were no doubt made possible by my mother's hospitality in welcoming these students into their home so soon after their marriage.

I also remember my mother helping translate my father's documents. She would translate his English into Japanese, and he would translate her Japanese into English. Or sometimes, they would work together to craft the best possible text. My mother never involved herself publicly in his political activities, but in everything she fully supported him, with the same spirit of *anasakta karma*—action without attachment.

* * *

My father loved both India and Japan deeply. He would often criticize India to the Japanese and Japan to the Indians. Those who didn't know him well would label him "anti-Japan" or "anti-India," but those who understood him knew that these words came from his love for each country and his desire to see them improve.

My mother, my brother, my two sons, and I all hold Indian citizenship. My father often said to us, "You are blessed to have two homelands: Father India and Mother Japan." Even in those turbulent times, we could take pride in that sentiment.

An episode regarding the career paths of my brother and me illustrates my father's postwar connection to India. My brother pursued fisheries science at university and went on to earn a PhD in Science from Kyoto University. I studied agriculture at university and gained practical agricultural knowledge. These choices were strongly influenced by my father's guidance. He believed that among India's industries, agriculture and fisheries were the most underdeveloped. It seems he wanted his two sons to gain expertise in these fields so they could contribute to India's development when they returned.

The ties between India and Japan go back to ancient times, with the transmission of Buddhism (allowing for China's part in the process). During India's independence movement, figures like the Pan-Asian nationalist Mitsuru Toyama and Dr. Shumei Okawa, who spread awareness of India's plight in Japan, provided invaluable support. This forged a relationship of deep mutual trust. In modern times, the economic exchange between India and Japan has further deepened, with both nations growing into major powers in Asia. I believe that this deep bond between India and Japan will endure forever and must be preserved. While I cannot endorse the actions of the Japanese military during the war, it is an undeniable fact that the war hastened the independence of many Asian countries. I hope that through this book, more people will come to understand how the twists and turns of history have shaped the present.

Today, India's international presence is rising. Now is the time for India and Japan, as fellow Asian nations, to join hands and increase their influence in the global arena. My father's experiences will undoubtedly offer valuable lessons for this effort. Writing this book was an arduous task. With no records from the time to rely on, my father had no choice but to draw entirely from memory. I remember him spending several months sequestered away, immersed in his writing. When the original edition of this memoir was published, my father said he felt as though a great weight had been lifted from his shoulders. I believe he would have been pleased to see this memoir being republished in English today.

Finally, I am deeply grateful to my father for leaving me the legacy of Nair Restaurant, which he established with the slogan "India-Japan friendship begins in the kitchen," as he shifted from political activism to fostering citizen-level exchanges. I feel truly blessed that I have been able to pass this legacy on to the next generation.

I would like to extend my heartfelt thanks to all those who assisted in the republication of this book, and to all the readers who have picked it up.

G. M. Nair
Chiba
October 2024

PREFACE

The first half of this century witnessed some of the most momentous military and political developments in the history of modern times. In the space of less than one generation it went through two world wars, the second one marked by the American use against Japan of the deadliest killer science had discovered till 1945: the atom bomb. There were two major political revolutions. The emergence of military superpowers vying with each other in a nuclear arms race has posed the threat of not only mutual annihilation but destruction of the whole world.

During this period, Japan became the most powerful Asian country. It set out on an expansionist course, borrowing a few lessons from the examples previously shown by Western colonial powers. In 1941, it overreached itself by challenging the combined might of America and Britain besides Chiang Kai-shek's China with which it was already at war. After some spectacular initial successes, the country suffered its first-ever defeat and alien occupation of its homeland. Then, within a short span of less than a decade, it made an incredible and miraculous recovery the likes of which the world had never known, not only regaining its position as an Asian giant but going on to become one of the world's economic superpowers.

The rise and fall of Japan practically coincided with the beginning of the end of the biggest and the mightiest colonial empire ever known: the British Raj. India, which had remained enslaved by it for two centuries, ultimately freed herself from bondage in August 1947. Winston Churchill's prediction in 1931 that the loss of India would reduce Britain to a minor power almost came true. Following India's independence, other erstwhile colonies in Asia and Africa emerged to freedom one after another.

I was born in the first decade of this century and have, together with others of my generation, either lived through or closely observed much of these and other events of global significance. For me personally, the greatest event was the fulfilment of India's "tryst with destiny" and her emergence to freedom. This was so particularly because, although the great struggle had a sweep of two hundred years, its most poignant and dramatic phase was contemporaneous with the most active years of my own political career in the independence movement.

The story of that period is one of great tragedy and tears on the one hand, and of unique heroism and sacrifice on the other. Most of the patriots fought from Indian soil but many did so from outside. For the most part, I belonged to the latter group.

After a brief coverage of my early years in India, the first few chapters of this book relate to my activities as an Indian freedom fighter in Japan, China, Inner Mongolia and the erstwhile state of Manchukuo prior to Japan's entry into the so-called Greater East Asia War in the Pacific. The later portions primarily deal with my work with the Indian Independence League in East and Southeast Asia cofounded by the legendary Indian revolutionary patriot Rash Behari Bose and myself. When Rash Behari fell seriously ill in the early part of 1943 he himself arranged, with my close support, to have Subhas brought over from Germany to take over as his successor in the leadership of the movement represented by the Indian Independence League.

In the closing years of the Allied Occupation of Japan, I was privileged to fulfil an official assignment as adviser to the ambassador of India in Japan primarily in relation to the negotiation of the bilateral peace treaty between Japan and India. After 1952, just as many other things changed, including the course of Japan's history, I embarked on a new career as a businessman, inviting in the process the jocular though well-intentioned observation from friends that I had "lowered" my position by one notch, from the status of a samurai or a ronin, to that of a mere merchant.

The focus of these reminiscences is primarily on my political life. After the conclusion of the India Japan Peace treaty, I continued (and still do) to be actively associated with several organizations engaged in the promotion of goodwill and friendship between the two countries, especially in my capacity as president of the Indian Association in Tokyo, but I have not considered the humdrum preoccupation of a contemporary business career important enough to merit elaboration in this book.

PREFACE

Many friends had been urging me to write my memoirs. Their reason was that I, as perhaps the oldest surviving Indian who was most vitally associated with the Independence struggle of our country in East and Southeast Asia, should leave behind for posterity the legacy of an authentic story of a most important though turbulent epoch in the history of the movement. But the opportunity for me to do so came only recently, and that too through what was literally an accident.

When visiting a friend in Trivandrum in 1980, I happened to slip on the polished mosaic floor of his house and sustained a serious back injury which entailed my hospitalization in Tokyo for several weeks. To relieve the tedium of the enforced bed rest, I got hold of a tape recorder and began dictating into it my recollections of my life and work. What was begun as a means of mental release grew into the raw material for this narrative.

After my discharge from hospital, I immediately returned to my earlier routine, and the recorded tapes remained as they were in a locker for the next one year. In the middle of 1981, when I was on another brief visit to Kerala on a vacation, I took them out and put myself to the task of editing them and verifying some of the recollections against historical records in order to ensure accuracy. It is as the outcome of that work that my memoirs have taken the shape of this book which, in all modesty, I now present before the public.

Much has been written about Japan and World War II by authors, including Indians, who have also published a plethora of works on the Indian Independence League and the role of the INA and Subhas Chandra Bose in Southeast Asia. Unhappily, a good deal of all these has been put out by writers who were never even anywhere near the scenes of the incidents they have sought to describe. In a number of cases the facts are wrong, either through genuine ignorance, or due to manipulations by vested interests.

One of the purposes of this book is to reveal the events of a crucial period of India's freedom struggle in their true perspective. Wherever I have given my own interpretations and assessments, I have taken care to be completely objective and honest. For everything I have said, I assume full personal responsibility because every one of the experiences recounted herein has behind it either my own personal knowledge as a participant or my observation as an impartial eyewitness from as close a range as anyone could get to. I had the privilege of being a cofounder of the Indian Independence League together with the great Rash Behari Bose and to function as the closest link between the League and the Japanese government. There was some change in the situation under the Subhas regime, but I was nevertheless always on the scene till the very end.

PREFACE

Portrait of the author in 1983. (Photograph by Michio Kamijo)

Readers will find in my narrative a number of instances of departure from what they may have read elsewhere. My assessments may even raise the eyebrows of those who had been led to rely on propaganda and political publicity motivated by bias. For instance, whereas Subhas Chandra Bose was undoubtedly a great leader and an ardent freedom fighter and patriot, a higher place in the roll of honor in the cause of Indian independence must be assigned to Rash Behari Bose. I have tried to explain why in these memoirs. I invite the readers to make their own judgment after cool deliberation devoid of emotional overtones.

There are other distortions also which I have tried to rectify. Among them is the wholly false notion that the Indian National Army was "raised" by Captain Mohan Singh. He has obviously done a great deal of self-propaganda. But the truth, in my view, is that it was Mohan Singh, self-styled "general," with recognition as such by none excepting a Japanese major, who wrecked the organization and caused utter confusion among the Indian POWs by choosing to pick a wholly unwarranted quarrel with Rash Behari.

Another misconception which seems to be widely prevalent is that after Mohan Singh had destroyed the INA, it was Subhas who rebuilt it. The fact is that the rebuilding process was done by Rash Behari Bose who handed over the edifice to Subhas intact as an efficient and coherent establishment. Although with the best of intentions from his own point of view, Subhas eventually threw the INA into a battle for India as a small appendage of Japanese forces, with the disastrous consequences which everyone who has cared to study the course of the history of the episode surely knows very well.

These and other differences in my perceptions are not intended in any way to deny or even minimize the great patriotic struggle on the part of Subhas and the INA. What I say is only that the events have to be viewed in proper perspective and not in isolation from other factors, particularly the most indefatigable and pioneering work of Rash Behari and his compatriots. They must not be forgotten but be given the historical recognition they rightly deserve. Indian independence was not the result of the work of just one or two persons or organizations, but the culmination of a colossal effort by a vast number of people, under the leadership of many stalwarts and aided by a variety of circumstances.

In fact in the last category can be included the Greater East Asia War started by Japan, regardless of its consequences as they turned out for that particular country itself. Japan, no doubt, suffered a great defeat, but no less a person than the noted British historian, Sir Arnold Toynbee, has observed that the war which Japan waged against the West had the wide-ranging effect of changing the whole tide of history of the world, especially the relationship between East and West. The latter could no longer take the former for granted.

When fighting against colonial Britain I was admittedly motivated by much anger against Englishmen as a group although not as individuals. After my country became independent, I have no rancor against either any groups or individuals, of whatever race or complexion they may be. I count among my friends not only Indians and Japanese but persons of every other nationality, whether they be Americans, Englishmen, or any others. In recalling my experiences and presenting them in these memoirs, I have malice towards none.

I thank all those who have helped me by sharing with me their own experiences and impressions of a great period in history and offering very useful suggestions.

A. M. Nair
Tokyo
December 1, 1981

CHAPTER ONE
My Home State

Trivandrum (present Thiruvananthapuram), my birthplace, is the capital city of Kerala, one of the smaller states of independent India. During British rule it was the headquarters of the princely state of Travancore. After independence Travancore was initially merged with Cochin, another princely state adjoining it on the north. When the Indian states were reorganized on linguistic lines in 1956, Travancore, Cochin, and the Malabar district of the erstwhile Madras Presidency were combined into one administrative entity under the name Kerala. The common language of this area is Malayalam.

Tucked away in the southwestern corner of India, Kerala is a narrow strip of land accounting only for a little over one percent of India's area. In density of population (over 550 per sq km), however, it ranks highest in the country. Washed on its west coast by the sparkling waters of the Arabian Sea and ranged on the east by the craggy hills of the Western Ghats with valleys abounding in verdant forests, Kerala is one of the most beautiful regions of the Indian subcontinent. Golden beaches and placid lagoons dotting its coastline mingle with lush green rice fields and luxuriant coconut groves. Country boats glide along gracefully on the backwaters as though skating lightly on the wooded banks. Kovalam, a sheltered beach near Trivandrum, is among the world's most magnificent seaside resorts. Its crescent-shaped and crystal-clear swimming bay, caressing its delicately contoured shores of sheer greenery, presents a panorama of exquisite charm. Overlooking it all from a hillock is the beautiful Kovalam Ashok Hotel, built near an artistic mansion which a former maharaja had constructed as his holiday palace.

Kerala attracted world attention in 1957, when its communist party won a majority of seats in the general elections and formed a government in the state. That was the first occasion in any part of the globe when communists were voted into power through a democratic and parliamentary process. It was essentially a culmination of the people's frustration aroused by a gross inadequacy of economic growth to match the high rate of educational progress. They gambled on the theory that since nothing could perhaps be worse, radicalism might as well be given a trial. But the people were soon disenchanted with communist motives, and the government fell from power in about two years. After 1959, except for short periods of direct presidential rule from New Delhi, the state has been administered by coalition governments with leftist parties' participation but no communist majority.

The origin of the region is shrouded in legend. The tradition is that it was created by a mighty god, Parasurama. He waged a series of severe wars against the kshatriyas, the martial caste of the Hindus who ruled the land, and conquered them, but was later saddened by the slaughter he had wrought in the process. In atonement, he did grave penance on the mountains and, in the end, flung his battleaxe into the ocean with a hefty heave. The waters receded up to the point where the axe had come down, and thus emerged the land crust of Kerala. While this of course is pure fantasy, there is enough scientific evidence that the southwestern part of India was at one time below the sea. In any case, the belief that Kerala is a sea-gifted land prevails fairly widely among the Hindus. Some of them, finding life a little too difficult, seriously hope that Parasurama, wherever he may be now, would come once again, this time to use his axe to send the whole state back to the bottom of the sea and thus put a rapid end to all their troubles!

Kerala has a maritime history stretching back to well over thirty centuries, beginning with the adventures of the Phoenicians. In the tenth century before Christ, King Solomon sent out trading ships to India where they berthed at Ophir, which has been identified as the small village of Poovar near Trivandrum. After Alexander's conquest of Egypt, the Greeks did some commerce with India, centered in Kerala. In course of time Arab merchants came on the scene and emerged as the dominant element in the region's overseas trade. They virtually monopolized it until the advent of Western colonial powers, commencing with the arrival of the Portuguese explorer and adventurer Vasco da Gama. He came in search of oriental spices and landed in Calicut in 1498. There was a trade agreement between him and the local chief, called the zamorin. The Portuguese were followed, among others, by Britain, which eventually annexed the whole of India to its empire.

The population is predominantly Hindu. Shankaracharya, (788–820), the most venerated Indian sage after Gautama Buddha, and the supreme exponent of *advaita* (nondualism), which is one of the profoundest contributions to human thought and philosophy, was born in Kerala. But Christianity and Islam coexisted with Hinduism. The first conversions of Indians to Christianity were done in Kerala by St. Thomas in the first century, and to those can be traced the origin of the Syrian Christian church and community who form an enlightened and important segment of the state's people. The Moplahs of Malabar, believed to be the first permanent Muslim settlers in the country, are descendants of Arab merchants who married Kerala women. There was even a Jewish community, primarily in Cochin, some of whom were probably among the earliest of the Hebrew people anywhere in the world. They are said to have arrived with King Solomon's ships.

Despite such alien contacts, Kerala has retained an identity distinctly its own. Foreign influences were assimilated but the indigenous culture remained intact. India as a whole has a diversity of cultural traditions; yet a strong strand of common heritage runs through all of them, to which Kerala's contribution outweighs the share of any other state of comparable size. Its religious and cultural sweep covers, besides Hinduism, Christianity and Islam, Buddhism and Jainism as well, although the last two did not leave a permanent imprint. The integrated ethos which remains its own, however synthesizes the Aryan and the Dravidian, the northern and the southern. Whereas the identity of each component has been preserved, a homogeneity of character has also been established, which has enriched the totality of Indian civilization.

The state has also played a vital role in the growth of the oldest of the Indo-Aryan languages, Sanskrit, and its great and many-sided literature, from at least around the eighth century. Its contribution not only to philosophy but to the sciences of astronomy, mathematics and astrology has been of a high order. Aryabhata's famous works on astronomy were summarized in a simple form by Bhaskara I of Kerala as early as the seventh century. The six-volume *Keraliya Samskrita Sahityacaritram* (History of Sanskrit Literature in Kerala) by Vadakkumkur Rajaraja Varma is a monumental work. Besides numerous litterateurs from academic circles, several members of the ruling families were patrons of learning; some of them were great scholars themselves—like Rama Varma I (r. 1758–1798) and Swathi Thirunal (r. 1829–1847) of Travancore, and Rama Varma XV (r. 1895–1914) of Cochin. The Sanskrit college established in Trivandrum during the time of Raja Srimoolam Thirunal (r. 1885–1924) and the one in Thrippunithura in Cochin founded by Raja Rama Varma XV were among the best in India. Rama Varma Parikshit Thampuran, the last raja of Cochin, was among the foremost Sanskrit scholars of modern India.

The sum total of Kerala's contribution to Sanskrit writings is phenomenal, a fact which is sometimes overlooked due to the fact that here it was mostly taught, learned and written in the Malayalam script instead of Devanagari, as in the north.

The Nairs of Kerala traditionally belonged to the martial class and were the strong arm of the kings: the power behind the throne. Known for their courage, they were great sticklers for chivalry and honor. Their relationship with their kings was not very different from that of the samurai of Japan with the daimyo and the shogun. Kerala's ballads are replete with beautiful stories of swashbuckling and romantic Nair heroes whose code of honor resembled the Japanese *bushido* ("way of the warrior"). The Kalari system of physical conditioning, which prepared them for both defense and attack, was a highly skilled art like the jujitsu of Japan. It is also on record that the principality of Valluvanad had mobilized, during its wars with the Cholas, several battalions of Chaver (suicide squad) Nairs who volunteered to sacrifice themselves in land warfare, just as Japan's kamikaze pilots did in the air during the Second World War.

The power of the Kerala chieftains used to be judged by the size of their Nair armies. The zamorin of Calicut had at one time a force of 160,000 men, and the raja of Cochin mobilized 140,000. Travancore had an even larger number. In the eighteenth century and early nineteenth, these armies were disbanded, but Travancore and Cochin continued to maintain certain Nair brigades modelled on the British pattern, until the time of India's independence in 1947.

But this does not mean that all Nairs were soldiers. They were prominent in a wide spectrum of activities. Among the many distinguished public men in recent history is Sir Chettur Sankaran Nair, an eminent jurist who was president of the Indian National Congress in 1897. Although appointed to the Viceroy's Executive Council in 1915, he was a nationalist to the core and resigned from the council in protest against British repressions in the Punjab in the wake of the Amritsar tragedy.

Vappala Pangunni Menon, the closest confidant of Vallabhbhai Patel and Lord Louis Mountbatten (the last viceroy and British governor-general of India), conducted what many had thought would be an impossible task; that is, integrating some 560 princely states into the Indian Union after the partition of India. And no one can forget that V. K. Krishna Menon, who was leader of the Indian Independence Movement in England for many years until 1947, was one-time editor of Pelican Books, and became independent India's first high commissioner to Great Britain. He led the Indian delegations to the United Nations over a period of almost fifteen years and was a great champion of the cause of the underdeveloped countries. A personal friend of Jawaharlal Nehru and defense minister in Nehru's cabinet from 1957–62, he was, during that period, considered the "second most powerful man in India." Although he had to resign following India's debacle in the Chinese invasion of 1962, he continued to enjoy Nehru's personal affection. On his death in 1974, he bequeathed all his private property to the nation. The third world will long remember him as one of their staunchest supporters.

The old social structure of the Nair community has evoked much curiosity among foreign observers, particularly sociologists and anthropologists. The society was organized into joint family units called *tharavads* which followed the matrilineal system. Basically, it meant that lineal descent was traced through the mother's side instead of the father's. Each *tharavad* would be under the control of the eldest male member called the *karanavan*, but the women always enjoyed an important place in the system. The properties of a *tharavad* would be owned collectively by its members descended from a common mother or other ancestress. A father's wealth would go, not to his sons or daughters, but to the children of his sisters. If he had no sisters, he would ordinarily adopt one or two in order to have nephews to whom his worldly belongings could go after his time. In the states of Travancore and Cochin, successors to the rulers as heirs to the throne were not their sons but their eldest nephews.

The reason behind this seemingly strange practice among the Nairs was that the menfolk among them were often away from their homes on military duty for long periods and had to leave the management of domestic affairs to the women. This enhanced the importance and prestige of the women. Anthropologists have observed a remarkable equality of sex in the old Nair society.

There is a theory that because the Japanese monarchy is believed to have descended from the sun goddess, the original social setup in Japan was matrilineal where the women must have occupied a position of influence. The male-dominated pattern of Japanese society could have evolved much later through external contacts.

More or less as a byproduct of matriliny was polyandry, another peculiar feature of the old Nair families. But with the passage of time, both of the customs became anachronisms. Changes had begun in practice by the beginning of the current century, gathering momentum by the 1920s. By 1925, legislation was introduced in Travancore (and somewhat later in what was then called British Malabar) abolishing matriliny. Simultaneously, hypergamy also became illegal.

CHAPTER TWO
Early Years

My ancestral house was the joint family called Oottichakkonath Valiya Veedu in the small town of Neyyattinkara, about twenty kilometers from Trivandrum. It was one of the aristocratic households in the area and, as its name suggests, was large in size. My mother, Lakshmi Amma, lived there until she was about seventeen years of age, when she married my father in the year 1874. Hers was an intercaste marriage. My father, Aramuda Ayyangar, was a high caste brahmin from Kumbakonam, which was then in the Madras province, now known as Tamil Nadu.

Under the joint family system among the Nairs, the *karanavan* generally insisted on the women marrying at a young age. Moreover, the bridegroom would be chosen by the girl's parents or, more often, by her uncles, with the girl seldom having any say in such "arranged" marriages. Where intercaste weddings were concerned, if a Nair woman married a man of a "lower caste" it would at once be regarded as a transgression of custom. But if she were married to a brahmin or a kshatriya, it would be an honor both to her and her family. In the case of my mother's marriage, not only the family but the township as a whole felt proud because my father was not only a high caste brahmin but was widely regarded as a genius in the prestigious engineering profession. He had come to Travancore in response to a joint invitation from the then ruler, Ayilyam Thirunal, and his dewan (chief minister), Sir Tanjore Madhava Rao. Both the ruler and his principal minister were enlightened persons dedicated to the progress of the state and the welfare of the people. Public works received their high-priority attention. My father, who rose to the position of chief engineer within a short period, was the kingpin of all the building activity.

The progressive policies of Ayilyam Thirunal and Sir T. Madhava Rao were continued by their successors, Visakham Thirunal and Nanu Pillai respectively. Both of them gave my father a free hand, which helped him to implement a large number of projects in record time. Among the many works which bear testimony to his dynamic leadership are the buildings housing Trivandrum's general museum and the Museum of Fine Arts, the city's public library, a wide network of road communications throughout the state, the central jail building, which bears an artistic aspect unusual for prisons, and the famous Varkala backwater canal.

Soon after their marriage, my parents moved to a new house which my father had built in Trivandrum. It was a large one, paradoxically called "Kunju Veedu," which literally means "little house." My father also acquired several acres of paddy field and coconut groves as sources of substantial income for the family. My parents had ten children, of whom I was the last. I was born on the fourth day of the second month (*kanni*) of the Malayalam year 1081, corresponding to September 18, 1905. A talking point in the neighborhood was that my astrological star, Rohini, was the same as that of the god Krishna! Whether that had any particular significance or not, I would never know. What I did come to know, with much sorrow, was that four of the children had died before I was born. I have recollections therefore of only two brothers and three sisters.

From all accounts, my father was personally kindhearted, but was an unrelenting taskmaster, and a stickler for perfection. He was well-known for his innovative mind and practical methods. For instance, to test the standard of construction of roads, I have seen him adopting the unorthodox means of plying his horse-driven coach up and down a number of times on newly laid macadam stretches. If the wheels of the carriage showed any excessive depression at any place, he would order the section to be rebuilt. I remember very well several roads constructed during my father's time: their quality was distinctly superior to those built nowadays. It is not that our engineers have in any way become less competent; in fact, we have today men (and even women) with higher technical qualifications. We also have sophisticated machines which were unknown in India during my young days. Yet the standard of work seems to have fallen because supervision is lax and pride in performance appears to be at a low ebb.

EARLY YEARS

* * *

When I was on a visit to Trivandrum in April 1980, a newspaper reporter sought my impressions of the Kerala of my early years and asked for my opinion on the current state of affairs. For a moment, I wished that he had not put me the question, because the thoughts it provoked were not pleasant. But having been asked, I decided to give my honest views.

I said that I was highly disappointed. Many of us had worked hard, and sacrificed much, to contribute to the attainment of freedom. At the dawn of independence, we envisioned the glory of building our motherland as a great and rich nation that would be an example to the rest of the world. But after more than three decades of freedom, what did I see in reality? There was indeed progress, but why so little and why so slow? We seemed to have let ourselves down in many ways by not using our talents to the best purpose. The politicians spent more time in squabbling among themselves than in working for the progress of the country. The bureaucracy pleaded helplessness against the doings of their political masters.

Our civic sense seemed to have practically vanished. In addition to tolerating air pollution, we appeared to be determined to spread "sound pollution." Loudspeakers blared away nonstop in busy areas for days and nights on end, preventing everyone from working or sleeping. Many persons might have become deaf already; others would probably become so before long unless this infliction was curbed. And in our temples, our gods were subjected to the same kind of punishment. We also indulged in poisoning the devotional songs offered to them with mixtures of rock 'n' roll. Our public health services were in a terrible state. The list of things as they should not be would become very long if I were to attempt to enumerate more items.

During a public meeting in Trivandrum in the 1920s, Gandhiji had observed that he was impressed by the cleanliness of our state, and that the white dress of our people and our tidy environment reflected the purity of our minds and our habit of simple living and high thinking. I wondered what Gandhiji would feel if he were able to visit us now and see the state of hygiene in our cities. Could it be that after independence our minds had turned dirty? It required no great sacrifice from anyone to keep our state, indeed the whole country, clean, healthy, and beautiful. But our municipalities must function. Let the authorities take a look at some places outside our country; for example, Singapore, a very crowded place but maintained spotlessly clean. Why was it that our administrators did not appear to care?

These, I told my interviewer, were my impressions. I was not proud of them. As an overseas Indian, I offered to contribute whatever little might lie within my means to keep our cities clean, if the government had any plan to invite collaboration from their countrymen abroad. If the government agencies had the will to work hard and the ability to enlist the cooperation of our people, we could make our state a "paradise on earth."

* * *

To come back to the theme of my early life: My father retired from Travancore government service prematurely and worked in various other centers. For a number of years, he was chief engineer to the state of Baroda (present Vadodara). Wherever he went, he took the whole family with him. In addition, several of my uncles and other relations would accompany him. Everywhere, therefore, he had practically a whole *tharavad* to take care of, and the house was like a large *oottupura* (common dining hall). My eldest brother, Kumaran Nair, was a problem for our father. He was a fine sportsman, but also a particularly uncontrollable and naughty young man with a great propensity to get into various types of trouble with boys of his age and even with those older than him. To keep him in check, my father would, to the extent possible, take him along with him during his tours. Many of his journeys had to be on horseback. By the side of my father's big horse, there would be a little one carrying "Chellappan" (my brother's pet name), so that he would remain within our father's sight and therefore away from mischief.

My boyhood was spent wholly in Trivandrum. My father, who was frequently on the move, would come to see us and stay with us whenever he could, but due to frequent touring he was unable to devote as much of his time to me as my older brothers and sisters had been fortunate enough to receive. My early life was therefore mostly centered on my mother. She became the greatest influence on me, and my mental makeup and character were shaped almost entirely by her. I remember her as a person of extraordinary courage and poise. Her own upbringing had been according to Hindu traditions, where religious, philosophical, and moral values held the uppermost place in education. She was highly proficient in Sanskrit and Malayalam literature, including, naturally, the two great epics, the Ramayana and Mahabharata, besides the Puranas. Whatever were her other pressing domestic responsibilities, she would never fail to do everything necessary to inculcate in her children the deep interest in learning which she had developed herself. My mother belonged to the old school, but always thought and acted ahead of her time.

The author's mother, Lakshmi Amma.

Our home was a venue for frequent philosophical and religious discussions. The audience each time would number some fifty or sixty, and it was a strict rule that everyone should be served sumptuous refreshments at the end of the meetings. All the Hindu festivals would be observed, but with no less regularity there would also be visits by Christian nuns coming to sing the hymns and explain passages from the Bible, and by Muslim religious men to recite the Koran and offer commentaries on the teachings of Islam. I used to enjoy this medley, particularly watching the assembled audience. There were among them many who were genuinely attracted to the discourses, but the main interest of some lay in the direction of the eatables.

Some visitors appreciated our house for its dignity and decorum; others viewed it as a convenient place for free board. There were also certain sections of the neighborhood who looked at my mother's unorthodox practices with open hostility or displeasure. They thought that by entertaining preachers from other religions, we were lowering our caste prestige. But my mother always did what she thought was right, regardless of praise or deprecation. Her courage of conviction never faltered. I believe that those days have left a permanent imprint on my mind. Although I say it myself, it is remarkable that in my later life, when on several occasions I had to go through situations of grave peril, I hardly ever felt anything amounting to fear. If such a trait is a virtue, I must have inherited it from my mother.

My early school days were not different from those of boys from any other upper middle-class home in Travancore of the time. As usual, I had nearly two years of initial education, partly at home and partly in a nearby children's school. In 1913, when I was about eight years old, I was admitted to Government Model High School in Trivandrum. Founded in 1911 under the auspices of Maharaja Sri Moolam Thirunal Rama Varma, it was one of the best schools in the state. It had a similar reputation in the whole of India as well. C. F. Clarke, a Scotsman, was the first headmaster.

My teachers were able and highly dedicated men. They enforced discipline with an iron hand; at the same time, they treated the students as members of their own families. Those were days when the traditional *guru-shishya* (teacher-student) relationship subsisted in its finest form. My first six years at school were uneventful: I did my lessons and went through the usual class rhythm like any other "good boy." In sports, I was a keen footballer and captained the junior boys' team. From the time I was about fourteen years old and had reached the high school, the debating society was my main extracurricular attraction. Together with a few close friends, I would hold forth there on a wide range of subjects. The teachers generally encouraged discussions on academic and even social issues, but not on political subjects. Since I and a few other students were prone to transgress into the last category and to speak out against the inequity of foreign rule in India, we would often get pulled up by some of the teachers. But there was also a section of the staff who gave us silent encouragement by turning their ears the other way.

Government Model High School is now seventy years old. I was in the second or third batch of its students, who then totaled about eight hundred, spread over eleven classes. I had occasion to visit the school when I was on a brief vacation in Trivandrum in April 1981 and to meet the headmaster, Madhavan Pillai, and some of his colleagues. They were very kind and took me round to see the entire campus, including the hostel, which is a relatively recent addition. With no significant expansion of accommodation facilities since its inception, the school has now about 2800 students. It was a wonder how, in spite of the severe handicaps, the management was upholding the school's high reputation for excellence. There was hardly any year in which the school did not win numerous trophies, testifying to its students' high standards of performance.

I had completed my lower secondary term when I was about thirteen years old and was enrolled for the first year of matriculation in Government Model High School itself, in 1919. That year, however, marked a turning point in my career, as it did in the history of Travancore itself.

CHAPTER THREE
A Turning Point

The struggle for India's freedom from British rule had begun in various parts of the country as early as the middle of the eighteenth century, but except for a few isolated cases of resistance, Travancore had remained rather remote and aloof from the independence movement until the early part of the current century. This was indeed generally true of the princely states as a group, because many of the princes, for obvious reasons, saw their interest differently from the aspirations of the mass of people in the rest of the country. The nominal rulers of these states, and under their influence their subjects too, generally took the British Empire for granted. Many of them were staunch supporters of the colonial regime because it suited their personal interests and pleasures, which the British were careful to pamper. Even those persons in these "native" states who spoke against British exploitation mostly did so without much fervor. The situation was not very different in Travancore.

But the national awakening that gripped most of the nation towards the end of the First World War, and the intense patriotic spirit of the masses aroused under the leadership of Gandhiji after his return from South Africa in 1915, could no longer fail to permeate the state. A major impetus to this was provided by the establishment of a branch of the Indian National Congress in Trivandrum in 1919 to coordinate and enlarge the movements for both political emancipation and social reforms. The latter claimed first priority because it was only after setting one's own house in order that sufficient strength could be mustered for campaigning effectively for the former.

Under the auspices of the new organization, an action committee was set up to chalk out programs to combat social injustices. Uppermost among overdue reforms was the need to eliminate the evil of untouchability practiced by the higher-caste Hindus against the so-called lower castes. Many of the other social and economic inequities were its corollaries.

The caste system among Hindus was a curse all over India, but nowhere was it perhaps more complex than in Kerala. It was bad enough anywhere that a high caste person should consider himself "polluted" by contact with any member of the low castes, but Kerala practiced a particularly obnoxious type of untouchability which some anthropologists call "distance pollution." A member of a high caste could be polluted by a low caste person, for example a Pulaya, if the latter even came within a certain distance of the former. A more vicious custom was difficult to imagine.

The teachings of a number of eminent men like Sree Narayana Guru and the poet Kumaran Asan, as well as the work of certain organizations like the Nair Service Society, had begun to rouse the people's conscience, but a concerted campaign against this and other evil practices under the caste system gathered momentum mainly after the Indian National Congress had moved in and a number of distinguished leaders had come forward to carry it further. In the forefront were such men as C. Krishnan and T. K. Madhavan, editors of the *Mithavadi* and the *Deshabhimani* newspapers respectively, George Joseph, a close disciple of Gandhiji, Mannath Padmanabha Pillai, Changanesseri Parameswaran Pillai, K. P. Kesava Menon, M. N. Nair, C. V. Kunjiraman, Alummoottil Govindan Channar, K. Kelappan, Krishnaswamy Iyer, and numerous others.

These developments had a deep impact on my mind. Conditioned by the religious liberalism of our own home under my mother's inspiration, I had already begun to feel revolted by caste prejudices wherever I saw them. The same was the case with a number of my friends. Although too young as yet for any leadership roles in public campaigns, we felt highly restive and were keen to lend our support to the reforms movement as best as we could. We would often help the leaders by volunteering our services to look after visitors, organize public conventions and to assist them in their multifarious tasks. Many non-brahmins encouraged us, but the brahmin-dominated establishments, which included the government machinery generally, viewed our activities with open displeasure.

CHAPTER THREE

For my nonacademic preoccupations, I had to pay an unexpected price. Without my realizing it, my involvement in social activities had come in the way of my giving adequate attention to my classroom work. In the first year high school examination, I failed in some of the subjects. The sudden setback to my image as a good student naturally was something of a shock to me, but what hurt most was the thought that my performance at school had disappointed my mother, even though she had the forbearance not to show it. I did not really regret any of my extramural doings, but surely I was embarrassed. As an escape, I decided to leave Government Model High School and go to another institution where I could turn over a new leaf. I joined Srimoolavilasam School at Vanchiyoor, commonly known merely as Vanchiyoor School.

It is futile to seek any alibi for my failure, and I do not propose to do so. Yet, in long retrospect, I recall that after the middle school stage, I had really become out of tune with the Government Model High School environment. The reason lay in just one source: the style of behavior of the headmaster, and my reflex reaction against it, unexpressed but strong. Mr. Clarke had in him the same kind of haughtiness which the typical white man generally exhibited against Indians. It was not any case of individual victimization, nor even specific provocation, but rather an undisguised general superciliousness and an attitude of racial superiority. Mr. Clarke seemed to run the school like a part of the colonial empire, and I seemed to react against it involuntarily with a sense of resentment.

In contrast, the atmosphere at Vanchiyoor was informal and refreshingly friendly. It helped to restore my depressed morale, and I even consoled myself with the thought that perhaps it was preordained that I should have a change of school. My initial discomfiture soon wore off and gave place to a buoyancy of spirit. Not only did I feel equal to my classwork, but I was eager to be associated even more than before with social work.

While social pressures were building up on a broad base gradually under the leadership of the congress organization, a new situation developed rather precipitately among the youth. That was the students' strike of 1922, in which some of my close associates and I happened to have the leading role.

* * *

The first two decades of the present century witnessed a strange incongruity in Travancore. On the one hand there was Maharaja Sri Moolam Thirunal Rama Varma, who favored the introduction of reforms to the maximum extent wherever possible; on the other, two dewans of his were narrow-minded and reactionary semi-autocrats. The first was P. Rajagopalachari, who was power hungry. He would brook no kind of criticism from any quarter. Some of his actions reflected the same kind of attitude that the colonial rulers showed towards the so-called natives. He was intolerant of anything that appeared to be expressions of patriotism. K. Ramakrishna Pillai, editor of the nationalist newspaper *Swadeshabhimani*, wrote an article criticizing the dewan's policies. Rajagopalachari retaliated by ordering Pillai's deportation out of Travancore and closure of the newspaper's offices.

Undaunted by such high-handedness, and in spite of his long period of illness, Ramakrishna Pillai maintained his opposition to the dewan's arbitrary measures right through until his death in Cannanore (Kannur) in North Malabar in 1916. I remember the episode with a personal touch of poignancy because, at a later stage, Ramakrishna Pillai's closest associate and confidant, C. P. Govinda Pillai, married one of my sisters. Although he was spared the ordeal of expulsion, he was naturally deeply aggrieved at the treatment meted out to his friend. Govinda Pillai was a reputed teacher of Malayalam at the Vanchiyoor school and was the author of several works, including a collection of ancient Malayalam songs. During the time of Ramakrishna Pillai's expulsion, he was also with the Editorial Department of *Swadeshabhimani*.

The simmering discontent of the people was aggravated by the ham-handed administration of Dewan Raghavaiah. The student community had been asking for an enlargement of educational facilities and a reduction of tuition costs in order to help more boys and girls, particularly from the weaker sections. Instead of showing any sympathy for the popular demand, Raghavaiah announced in 1922 an *increase* in college tuition fees. Many of us viewed this as an affront to the student community as a whole and decided to oppose it. On the eve of the date set for the fee raise, four of my student friends and I gathered near the tank called Manjalikkolam on the Thambanoor Road. It was a recreational venue where we often met to play card games. (The tank was subsequently reclaimed and is today a playground.) We talked a great deal about the forthcoming fee increase, and, before leaving, decided that Raghavaiah's move be prevented at any cost.

As agreed amongst us, we went to our school the next morning one hour before the scheduled opening time. After evicting the peons (they offered no resistance) we closed the entrance gate and took charge of the campus. Forming ourselves into a picket, we began explaining to the approaching students why we were boycotting the classes and asking them to join the agitation. The response was wholly in our favor, and absentation from school was total. Thus came about what was reported as the first students' strike in India. Some observers thought that it was probably also the first student agitation of its kind in the world.

From Vanchiyoor, almost all the students marched to St. Joseph's School. After some feeble resistance the authorities of that school gave in, and soon there was a large procession of students from both schools proceeding to the Maharaja's College. There it was a case of instant cooperation with us. By that time the procession had assumed massive proportions. Its next destination was Government Model High School from where I had checked out the year before. As some of us had anticipated, trouble arose there when the arrogant headmaster, Mr. Clarke, tried to stop the procession by merely placing himself between it and the school entrance. It was an absurd and vainglorious exhibition of bravado, for which he paid heavily. Despite the efforts of myself and my fellow leaders, Mr. Clarke was badly thrashed by some of the students. Fortunately, a school peon managed to carry him away to safety.

News of the agitation in Trivandrum spread rapidly and educational institutions all over Travancore joined in and staged a sympathetic strike. Instead of negotiating a reconciliation, Raghavaiah unleashed severe repressive measures, which led to several confrontations between the students and the police and a number of casualties on both sides. Stray cases of attacks on Englishmen on the roads tended to give the agitation an anti-British complexion. At one stage, the deputy resident, an Englishman endowed with the same kind of arrogance as Mr. Clarke, thought that he could "teach the students a lesson" singlehanded. He came with a horsewhip to the vicinity of Government Model High School where trouble had continued and began lashing out at the demonstrators. In a trice, he was knocked down by stones pelted by the agitators. A tremendous thrashing followed which would have killed him but for his timely removal from the scene by some of the students, under my instructions. Other violent incidents followed, disrupting normal life in Trivandrum and several other towns for a number of days. Eventually the government succeeded in crushing the agitation through brute force.

Raghavaiah wanted the police to get hold of me, but his effort failed because, at the insistence of my family, I took shelter in my elder brother Kumaran Nair's house. My brother, who was a medical officer in the army, had his residence within the military headquarters area, which was not accessible to the police. Later the government entrusted the task of instituting legal proceedings against me and my fellow leaders to the public prosecutor—Mannuvila Achuthan Pillai. Ironically, he was a relative of mine, a nephew of my eldest brother-in-law. His mother and mine were also friends, and the two ladies used to be associated with several activities connected with the Padmanabhaswamy Temple, the most famous place in Hindu worship in Trivandrum, of which the chief patron was the maharaja himself. Against such a background, one would have thought that the public prosecutor would be kind to me, but events turned out otherwise. For no fault of mine at all, Achuthan Pillai harbored a suspicion against me.

Achuthan Pillai's first wife, who died prematurely, had been closely related to my *tharavad*. I used to call Pillai "uncle," and believed that I was one of his favorites. Even after his remarriage (his second wife was from a family bv name Charuvila which was also friendly to ours) we got on well, just as before. Trouble started only during the students' strike, and that too under a total misunderstanding on Pillai's part. One night, when he was walking from his home to his new wife's residence, he was waylaid, possibly by some student who had a grudge against him. His hurricane lantern was knocked from his hand when he was turning a corner near the Amman Kovil (a temple by that name) of Thambanoor, and he was hit badly from behind.

I had absolutely no part in the attack, but, for some inexplicable reason Achuthan Pillai thought that I was his assailant. Against the background of our old connections, this was an irrational suspicion, and all that I could conclude was that for no ostensible cause, some persons could suddenly go mad. The net result was that the top executives of the government, plus the public prosecutor, were now after my blood. I was expecting an arrest warrant any time but, strangely, it did not come. I failed to understand why but gathered much later that it was not due to any kindness on the part of the resident, dewan, or public prosecutor, but owing to some legal hitch pointed out by the Political Department of the government of India in New Delhi. Having failed to establish any ordinarily cognizable case against me in connection with the students' strike or any other incident, Raghavaiah and the resident sought the government of India's permission to hold me and some of my friends in preventive detention as politically undesirable and dangerous persons. But the Political Department in New Delhi demurred. Therefore, the government in Trivandrum quietly dropped the proceedings.

Meanwhile, the foolhardy adventure of the deputy resident who had tried to quell the students' demonstrations with his horsewhip had provoked much anti-British sentiment among the people. And news of various atrocious measures adopted elsewhere in the country by the colonial rulers to suppress the nationalist movement, created an ever-increasing sense of resentment against the agents of the empire.

CHAPTER FOUR
Social Reforms Movement

As the trauma of the students' strike gradually faded and educational institutions regained normalcy, the congress-sponsored campaign against untouchability was growing stronger. In 1924, Travancore witnessed one of the most tenacious of agitations in this respect, the Vaikom Satyagraha* around which are gathered some of my vivid memories of my young days.

Vaikom, a small town in central Travancore, was noted for its famous Shiva temple. Under an offensive practice introduced by a section of the local brahmin community and connived at by the Nairs, the access roads to this temple had been declared closed to the so-called lower castes. Some of my student friends and I had joined issue from time to time with a number of prominent brahmins, but with practically no success. Only organized agitation on a large scale could be expected to make a dent in the wicked practice that had become strongly entrenched.

Accordingly, the congress took up the matter and decided to launch a wide-ranging campaign. A special committee was formed, including leaders like A. K. Pillai, Hassan Koya Mullah, Kurur Neelakandan Namboodiripad, and K. P. Kesava Menon. This group arrived in Vaikom in February 1924 and held meetings to mobilize public opinion in favor of the movement that was to

---

* A Sanskrit word denoting "reliance on truth." The concept became current with Mahatma Gandhi's policy of nonviolent resistance to British rule. It is now used to describe any nonviolent moevement to ventilate grievances.

begin soon. Kesava Menon was the principal speaker on these occasions. A few fellow students and I made it a point to attend these meetings, missing our classes. The audience at these gatherings was larger than any that Travancore had witnessed at any time before. At one of the meetings, the decision was openly taken to launch a satyagraha movement to press the temple authorities to allow all Hindus, regardless of caste, not only the right of use of the access roads, but the freedom to worship in the temple.

The next month (March 1924), three *satyagrahis*—Kunjappi, who was a Pulaya, Bahuleya who belonged to the Ezhava community, and Govinda Panikkar, a Nair—led a large procession towards the temple. Vast numbers of people had collected all along the way, and the government had deployed a strong police force to control the crowd. The procession halted before reaching the "restricted area," but the three *satyagrahis* moved forward to cross into it. The police announced that while the Nair member was free to proceed, the other two must stop. Panikkar protested and told the police that the three formed a group that would not separate. That meant confrontation. There was tension, but the crowd remained entirely nonviolent. Soon all the three *satyagrahis* were arrested on the ground of causing public disorder and imprisoned after a farcical trial.

There was public anger but, thanks to the patience and tact of the organizers of the campaign, the agitation remained peaceful. After about two weeks, T. K. Madhavan and K. P. Kesava Menon were arrested on a charge of inciting "untouchables" to violate the ban on entry into the temple roads. They were taken to Trivandrum and sentenced to six months' imprisonment in the central jail. In the next few days, several others were also incarcerated. Bitter memories of these events have always lingered in my mind, and the bitterness becomes even sharper whenever I visit Trivandrum, because my house there, Janaki Vilas (named after my wife), is not far from the hillock housing the jail where Kesava Menon and other great nationalists had suffered much for demanding elementary human rights for their fellow men. It is a strange irony that this jail was one of the buildings constructed under the supervision of my father when he was chief engineer in Travancore.

Instead of weakening the campaign, the punishment meted out to the leaders served to strengthen it. Public opinion was irresistibly building up behind the satyagraha movement. Meanwhile, Sri Moolam Thirunal passed away, and Rani Sethu Lakshmi Bayi became regent. As a mark of respect for the departed ruler's memory, all political prisoners were released, among them Madhavan and Kesava Menon. Sethu Lakshmi Bayi was sympathetic to the agitation against untouchability.

The movement however gained its greatest strength when Gandhiji visited Vaikom during the same year. At Sethu Lakshmi Bayi's insistence, Gandhiji was welcomed as a state guest. The British rulers were shocked, but the people were jubilant. Following discussions between Gandhiji and several cross sections of the people, a compromise was reached: for the time being all caste discrimination on the temple roads would be abolished, but the demand for the right of entry for all castes into the temple would be deferred for a while. The latter issue would form part of a statewide agitation covering all the temples.

At long last, after several years of struggle by leaders like Changanassery Parameswaran Pillai, Mannath Padmanabha Pillai, and several others, Maharaja Sree Chithira Thirunal issued a proclamation on November 12, 1936, legally prohibiting untouchability and granting to every member of the Hindu faith, irrespective of caste or creed, full freedom to worship at all the Hindu temples in Travancore. Gandhiji hailed this as a "modern miracle."

But it is curious how every good thing often has some aspects that fit ill with the rest of it. I am told that under the numerous classifications now prevalent for the purpose of reservation of jobs under the government, and for certain other material advantages, the Ezhavas are treated as "backward." This has apparently been the result of some manipulations by vested interests. There are several sections of Hindus who surely still need special protection to elevate them socially and economically, but Ezhavas are no longer backward. Such a downgrading as they seem to have accepted for the purpose of certain special benefits is hardly complimentary to them because today they are as progressive as any of the "forward" communities.

* * *

While untouchability had for long been the worst curse of the Hindu society in Kerala, the matrilineal and joint family system of the Nairs was also an aspect of the social structure where reform was necessary. The system had so degenerated over the years as to lead virtually to a situation of anarchy. The *karanavans* were losing control of the affairs of the households; properties jointly held were being frittered away by malpractices resulting from indiscipline. Several joint families had begun to break up in practice, but the anomalies of matriliny and its byproducts could be removed fully only by abolishing the system through legislation.

CHAPTER FOUR

The incongruity of the system was particularly glaring where relationships between the high caste brahmins and the Nairs were concerned. The former, particularly the Nambudiris, followed the custom of primogeniture, meaning briefly that only the eldest male member of their families would marry women of their own caste; the others would either wed, or merely have *sambandham* (liaison) with Nair women, with no legal obligation to support them or the children if any. It was clearly an anachronistic and unjust practice. I and some likeminded students turned our attention to this peculiar feature of the social setup and started a propaganda campaign, mostly through the process of lecture meetings, to mobilize support for the termination of the matrilineal practice and changing the Nair society to the patriarchal pattern.

One of the obstacles to the acceptance of such a change was opposition from the ruling families themselves. Some of my readers will have heard of the story of the Ettuveetil Pillamar, the group of eight Nair military men who were the pride of Travancore's army some 250 years ago. The ruler during the period, Rama Varma (r. 1721–29), who was the uncle of King Marthanda Varma, had two sons from his marriage to a Nair lady. On Raja Rama Varma's death, these sons, by name Padmanabhan Thampi and Raman Thampi, laid claim to the throne in preference to Marthanda Varma. The eight Nair leaders supported the bid, and thus became the first ever important group to rebel against the matrilineal system. They were able to mobilize help from a number of quarters, but Marthanda Varma and his followers were too canny for them. They charged the Ettuveetil Pillamar with sedition and put all of them to death. According to legend, the spirits of these eight heroes began to haunt the ruling families and had to be propitiated by containing them in copper vessels with the help of brahmin priests and installing them in Changanassery, one of the strongholds of the Nair community.

During my boyhood years, it was an offence to speak in support of the Ettuveetil Pillamar, but gradually the social mood changed as more and more Nair families switched over to patriliny voluntarily. In the 1920s, public pressure for legislation to enforce the change gathered momentum. The movement spearheaded by the younger groups of people, including students like me, was a supporting factor which served to hasten the enactment by the Sree Moolam Popular Assembly, in 1925, of the Nair Act which abolished matriliny, thus ending all remnants of the old feudal practices. And it is of interest to note that in October 1980 the Kerala government recognized the Ettuveetil Pillamar as courageous revolutionary heroes, instead of traitors as had been declared by Marthanda Varma, and has taken over the copper vessels believed to contain their spirits, to be enshrined as archaeological monuments.

A special mention must be made here, of the period during which the Nair Act was enacted, because it witnessed the management of the state by Rani Sethu Lakshmi Bayi, an enlightened lady with superb administrative ability and zeal for social reforms.

When the Nair Act was promulgated, I was just twenty. To practice what I had been preaching, I asked for the partition of our joint family at Neyyattinkara. My mother was initially rather disturbed because she, as the eldest member of the family, was not happy to preside over the liquidation of the *tharavad*. But before long she agreed that with the changed times, joint families had lost their purpose. Both of us accordingly went to Neyyattinkara and completed the formalities for the apportionment of the properties. The process of dividing the assets of joint families was always tedious. There would be numerous complaints because it was impossible to satisfy everyone. Litigation could be avoided only through a spirit of give and take. I took over the partition work and recall my relief when it was completed with the least acrimony. I thought that this was good administrative training.

I had however one serious regret. There were two Pulaya families who had been dependent on our *tharavad* for a long time. I wanted them to be given some piece of land each, on par with the regular members of our household. My uncles objected, and since I could derive no support from the legal provisions, I was dispirited and had to give up the idea. But as some atonement for my failure, I organized a Pulaya *sangam* (an association of Pulayas) in Neyyattinkara. There was much consternation among the elders in the area who viewed me as a troublemaker, but my mother did not raise any objection. She was, as I have said before, ahead of her times, and always favored any social activity that was progressive. The *sangam* met frequently. At the end of one of the meetings, I organized a big lunch at which I sat with the Pulayas and shared their food. It became the talk of the township. I incurred still more displeasure from the conservative groups but was pleased that there were several other sections lauding my action.

CHAPTER FIVE
At the Crossroads

The year 1924 was an important landmark in the socioeconomic history of Travancore, but it happened to be a tragic one in the life of my family. To everyone's distress, my parents separated after nearly fifty years of happy married life. It transpired that my father had allowed himself to be "trapped" by another woman who undoubtedly had her eyes hitched to his position, prestige, and wealth. In the social milieu of the time, such episodes were not unknown and did not attract any particular stigma. Many women might have taken them in their stride; but my mother, distraught in the extreme, could not brook the rejection. She looked upon it with a sense of great humiliation.

Although our home could never be the same again, my father continued to be beneficent to all the children. He would visit us on important occasions to enquire about our welfare and would bring us many gifts. The breakup of his marriage to my mother was beyond our comprehension and must remain in the category of such facts of life as are utterly inscrutable.

My father remained active, both in body and mind, throughout his long life. After his retirement from active professional work, he became a keen observer of the progress of the nationalist movement, with which he was in full sympathy. He often derided Britain's exploitation of India and, on several occasions, declared publicly that the white rulers were stultifying the scientific talents of many bright young Indians by denying them necessary facilities for advanced technical education within the country.

When India's independence was proclaimed on August 15, 1947, he was overwhelmed with emotion, and forgetting the handicap of old age, he undertook a long march at the head of a large procession, carrying an outsized national flag, to celebrate the historic event. Immediately on returning home, he collapsed and passed away. He was 98 years old. It was as though he was just waiting for the dawn of Indian freedom before leaving the earth.

It was also in 1924 that I graduated from high school. For a while, I toyed with the idea of joining the university but felt a greater compulsion to be part of the political and social activities that had assumed much vigor in many parts of the country. I decided that I had to outgrow the confines of the college campus in order to be able to involve myself adequately with national movements. I was also anxious to assume a leadership role in those movements, instead of being merely a passive follower, but was still searching for the means by which I could expect to do so.

After the partition of our joint family in 1925, I tried my hand for some time at agriculture, but soon learned that, due to fragmentation of land holdings, what was feasible on my own would not be economically viable. There was a suggestion that I might go to the hill tracts, acquire and clear some extensive areas of virgin forest, and start large-scale farming of cash crops such as tea, cardamom, rubber and so on. Most of such plantations were the preserve of Englishmen who had exploited Indian labor and carted away large profits for themselves. I visited a number of their establishments to acquire the technical know-how, which they were ordinarily unwilling to share with Indians.

Although my ideas of management of such estates were different from the Englishmen's, something worthwhile might have fructified if I had pressed on with my plans, but I had to abandon them under strong opposition from my mother. According to her, it was inadvisable for me to live in mountain terrain and be constantly exposed to hazards like malaria, poisonous snakes, and wild beasts. I myself had no such anxieties, but decided not to go against my mother's wishes, particularly since in the wake of her bitter experience of a shattered marriage she needed all the help and comfort her children could give her. I was thus back at the same mental crossroads from where I had started.

Once again, I found myself drawn towards the political field; at the same time, it was clearer than before that to be able to play an effective role in it, I had to acquire greater experience. The first requisite was to know more than I did about the history of the freedom movement as such, and particularly to be in touch with happenings elsewhere in the country where noncooperation campaigns and other freedom struggles were strong as compared to the still

CHAPTER FIVE

lukewarm atmosphere in the princely states, including Travancore.

My contacts with the congress leaders, and the extracurricular reading which I had been doing, had already given me some idea of the distortions that the British educationists had painstakingly implanted in the school curriculum. Much of the material contained in the textbooks on Indian history was unreliable and inaccurate; they had been tailored to suit the purposes of the empire. Several important facts were suppressed and many others grossly misrepresented. In the classrooms, students were heavily fed on the glories of British rule in India, but nothing was said about the people's resistance to it in various forms from time to time, nor about the wave of opposition which was surely and steadily gathering strength in the country as a whole.

We had not been told anything about our own heroes in Kerala who had fought against imperialism. For instance, there was no account in any of the prescribed textbooks about the rebellion spearheaded against the British by Kerala Varma Pazhassi Raja, a historic struggle in which he sacrificed his life in 1805. About the same time, the Nair battalions in Travancore under the leadership of Dewan Velu Thampi had rebelled against the repressive policies of the British resident, but Vincent Smith's *Oxford History of India*, which was the school textbook on Indian history, dismissed the event as a "mutiny of officers." The truth was that it was an uprising against the imposition of a new treaty of subsidiary alliance by the British, on the state. The patriotic dewan, Velu Thampi, strongly resisted and put up a valiant fight. He lost because the British had superior weapons, but he had roused the nationalist spirit of the people to a high pitch. In atonement for his defeat, Velu Thampi committed suicide in 1809, to the great sorrow of all his surviving supporters. Vincent Smith's book disposed of the whole incident in one tendentious statement: it was "a mad rebellion."

Such was the state of brainwashing in vogue in schools. It was clear to me that to get at the true picture of events, one had to unlearn much of what one had been taught and learn afresh from other sources.

* * *

Indian opposition to British colonialism in India had in fact begun almost simultaneously with the process of annexation of the country to the empire, started by Robert Clive with the Battle of Plassey in 1757. Revolts spread over some 150 years had taken place in several regions: Bengal, Bihar, Orissa (present Odisha), Gujarat, Maharashtra, the Deccan, etc. I have mentioned two important instances in respect of Kerala itself. The mass rebellion of Indian soldiers in 1857 was a clear expression of anti-British feelings which ran high almost throughout the country, even though biased English historians sought to explain it away as merely a "sepoy mutiny."

The galaxy of illustrious leaders who were at the forefront of the freedom movement that gathered momentum over the next few decades was very large. Among them, to mention only a very few, were Gopal Krishna Gokhale, Bal Gangadhar Tilak, Aurobindo Ghose (Sri Aurobindo), Lala Lajpat Rai, Surendranath Banerjea, and Madan Mohan Malaviya. They had kindled the torch of emotional nationalism which shone bright in most Indian hearts. Tilak had stirred the nation's conscience as early as 1906 by his famous slogan "*swaraj* (freedom) is my birthright." Aurobindo's message was no less thrilling. Rabindranath Tagore, the many-splendored genius, roused Indian nationalism to a high degree through his unique and patriotic poetry and prose. Bankim Chandra Chatterjee electrified the people with his soul-stirring poem in his novel *Anandamath* with the magic words "Vande Mataram" ("Hail Thee, Mother"; or, "Hail, Motherland, I bow to Thee"), to which millions rallied in defiance of the ban imposed by the British on its use.

When Gandhiji arrived on the national scene after his return from South Africa (1915), the wave of nationalism gathered irresistible power. British repression was severe, and the crusaders for Indian independence went through untold suffering. Among the numerous self-sacrificing stalwarts were Motilal Nehru, Jawaharlal Nehru, C. R. Das, Vallabhbhai Patel, C. Rajagopalachari, Srinivasa Ayyangar, Subhas Chandra Bose, and countless others. Some of them had different views from those of Gandhiji regarding the modus operandi for the attainment of freedom, but in their objective there was complete unanimity. The Muslim community did not lag behind; they had among them the indomitable Ali brothers, Mohammad and Shaukat, Abul Kalam Azad, Abdul Ghaffar Khan (affectionately called the "Frontier Gandhi"), and others. Mohammad Ali Jinnah was also initially with the congress but unfortunately broke away to lead the Muslim League and eventually to cause the partition of India as the bitter culmination of the British policy of "divide and rule."

During and after Curzon's time as viceroy (r. 1899–1905), anti-British agitations in Bengal and elsewhere in Eastern India and in several parts of the north and west tended to be channelized through revolutionary activities. Most of them were carried on from underground bases due to repressions launched against public demonstrations. Several news journals with strong nationalistic views had come into circulation. The force and vigor of the writings of many patriots matched the ruthlessness of the bureaucratic offensive. Some of them turned out material from their presses, like molten lava from a volcano. Magistrates prohibited the use of the words "Vande Mataram," which sounded like the death knell of imperialism in Bengal and elsewhere, but the British did not succeed much in suppressing the people's patriotic fervor that Bankim Chandra had aroused.

The cult of violence against the British rulers was being propagated by a secret organization of terrorists, some of whom took pains to learn the technique of producing bombs. Several leaders of this movement were apprehended and victimized by the government authorities. One of the few who succeeded in maintaining their cover in spite of the efforts of the British to find them was Rash Behari Bose. But eventually he found himself in danger and therefore left for Japan to continue his freedom struggle for India from there. In later years, I was destined to be intimately associated with him in the common cause, as will be narrated later in this book.

During the first two decades of the present century, there were also pioneering attempts by a number of enterprising young Indians to work for Indian freedom from bases abroad. They had centers in the USA, Europe, China, Burma, Southeast Asia, Japan, etc. Among the more notable of the organizations overseas was the Ghadr Party in America, formed by a few Indian students of the University of Berkeley, California, in 1907. It was started under the enterprise of Tarak Nath Das from Bengal and strengthened by the dynamic Lala Har Dayal from the Punjab. The Sikh emigrants to the USA and Canada had a particularly important role in the freedom movement from outside.

The discriminatory nature of the Asiatic Immigration Act of 1909 caused much grievance among the Indian community in America, many of whom found in it justification for intensifying their revolutionary campaign. Their efforts gradually led to the creation of the Pacific Coast Hindustan Association, the Indian Independence League of America, the Berlin Indian Independence Committee in Germany, and other similar organizations which commenced operations in several countries and kept in touch with one another. They also served as fillips to underground revolutionary activities within India itself, especially in Bengal and the Punjab. Among the prominent overseas leaders were Krishna Varma, Virendra Chattopadhyaya (brother of Sarojini Naidu), Chempakaraman Pillai and Barkatullah in Europe, Mahmud Hasan in the Ottoman Empire, and Ubaidullah Sindhi and Mahendra Pratap in Afghanistan.

In America and Canada, the freedom fighters had to undergo much hardship and suffering as a result of repressive measures launched against them at Britain's instigation. A dark chapter in Canadian history is the event of 1914 known as the *Komagata Maru* episode. The Sikh community in Vancouver, through an agent in Hong Kong, had chartered the Japanese ship *Komagata Maru* to bring a number of their compatriots from the Punjab into Canada. But Canadian immigration refused permission for the ship to dock at any of their ports and, after a number of ugly incidents, the vessel was sent back to Calcutta via Singapore under outrageous conditions of hardship to the passengers. The British authorities added much to the sufferings of these passengers. Some of their agents in Singapore nearly riddled them with bullets in a bid to expedite their disembarkation for transshipment to India. British callousness was of the most reprehensible kind.

* * *

In the First World War, India was actively supporting Britain's war effort, and Indian soldiers were fighting and dying in various theaters of war for the victory of their colonial masters. Some 800,000 Indians were serving in various war fronts and elsewhere. About 70,000 of them were killed in action, a terrible toll extracted by an imperialist and colonial power from a subject nation. At the very least, India expected that the hopes held out by Britain initially in order to enlist Indian support would not go unrecognized; but after the initial enthusiasm to placate Indian sentiment and mobilize it on their side, Britain gave enough evidence of its indifference to the cause of India's freedom. Intense frustration against what appeared as a betrayal of good faith brought up anti-British feelings in India to full fury. Revolutionary groups in various parts of the country began actively challenging British authority.

Yet generally, the people's demands, represented by the voice of the congress, remained peaceful. They desired a settlement through cooperation and negotiation, but the colonial rulers let loose a series of repressive measures in a bid to curb the growing agitations. First came the Rowlatt Act, giving sweeping powers for preventive detention of suspected political activists, implicitly calculated to be used against demonstrations in the Punjab. Gandhiji, describing it as a "black Bill," challenged it and asked the viceroy to withhold his assent. When his plea was unheeded, he organized defiance of it by proclaiming a *hartal* (suspension of business) on April 6, 1919.

CHAPTER FIVE

Soon afterwards, on April 10, occurred what came to be known as the Amritsar tragedy. Two respected congress leaders, Dr. Kitchlew and Dr. Satyapal, were detained by the district magistrate of Amritsar for no ostensible reason. When word spread of the arrest, crowds marched to the police and civil authorities' headquarters to demand their release. While the police barred their route, skirmishes occurred and there were casualties among the opposing groups. Five Englishmen were killed. Similar instances occurred elsewhere also within a short time, leading to the clamping of curfew in some parts of Amritsar. The Sikhs were inflamed. To cap it all, on April 13, the Hindu New Year Day that year, public sentiment in the Punjab and virtually the whole of India was set ablaze by what is probably the blackest event in the history of British atrocities in India: the barbarity commonly known as the Jallianwala Bagh Massacre.

Some 20,000 people had gathered in the public park called Jallianwala Bagh, which had only one entrance-cum-exit, and that was just large enough to allow a few persons at a time to pass through. All of a sudden, some two hundred soldiers appeared on the scene under the command of Brigadier R. E. H. Dyer who ordered them to fire on the crowd, which had been given no warning at all to disperse and could not have dispersed easily even if they had been so ordered, because the exit was so small and had been blocked by the soldiers. A volley of bullets killed about 400 innocent unarmed Indians and seriously wounded over 1,200. According to the bloodthirsty Dyer, he "wanted to produce a moral effect throughout the Punjab," and the only reason why there were not more casualties was that he had run out of ammunition! The atrocity was one of indescribable cruelty. Even Winston Churchill, no friend of India, called the Jallianwala Bagh Massacre "a monstrous event, the greatest blot that has been placed upon English history since the days gone by when we burned down Joan of Arc."

The Amritsar tragedy evoked throughout India the bitterest condemnation of British rule. Jawaharlal Nehru was afire with indignation. Rabindranath Tagore renounced the knighthood which the British king had conferred on him. There was a strong demand not only for severe punishment of Brigadier Dyer, but for the recall of the Punjab lieutenant governor Michael O'Dwyer and the viceroy, Lord Chelmsford. Eminent leaders like Vithalbhai Patel, Surendranath Banerjea, Srinivasa Sastri, Tej Bahadur Sapru, Annie Besant, and others asked for an urgent enquiry. But the government was unresponsive to the public anger and anguish. The martial law administration proclaimed earlier was continued. In protest against such a ruthless policy, Sir C. Sankaran Nair, as I have mentioned earlier, resigned from the viceroy's executive council.

The emotional tension created by the Jallianwala tragedy was still in full wind when another unexpected development took place: the Khilafat movement of 1921. It began as a religious protest from the Indian Muslims following the defeat of the Ottoman Empire in the First World War. In the aftermath, the British decided to abolish the office of khalif, the highest religious institution in the Muslim world, and to break up the Ottoman Empire. Muslims everywhere regarded these actions as an insult to them, and in India the Muslim leaders set in motion a strong campaign against the British. The Indian National Congress supported the movement, and so did the Hindu community, resulting in a combined Hindu-Muslim move against the British.

But unfortunately, the jubilation which prevailed on this count was short-lived. The communal amity proved all too soon to be fragile and unreal. Things turned topsy-turvy in respect to the agitation in India, when Kemal Ataturk took control in Istanbul and news got round that the khalifate was going to be abolished under a new secular dispensation. The Indian Muslims suddenly came to the conclusion that there was no longer any point in their agitating or retaining the newly formed alliance with the Hindus. In a backlash which ensued, communal differences raised their heads once again.

In the Malabar district, many clashes became violent and led to what is known as the Moplah Rebellion (1921). Some of the atrocities committed were such as should have made both parties hang their heads in shame. The Madras government sent thousands of troops, including a number of Gurkha soldiers, to quell the communal riots. Even official estimates of the casualties on the two sides together were staggering: about 2,400 killed, 1,600 wounded, and 39,000 "captured as prisoners," of whom 24,000 were convicted of various crimes. The unfortunate episode bore the aspects of a full-scale military operation, and the bitterness of it lingered for quite a while before it finally blew over.

Fortunately, the tragic denouement of the Khilafat movement hardly affected the Travancore-Cochin regions of Kerala. There, the socioeconomic reforms work continued without any religious or communal overtones. In fact, there was a remarkable sense of unity among the members of all the faiths. As one of the prominent youth leaders, I can confidently say that the student community played a very positive role in maintaining such harmony. Neither the students' strike of 1922 nor the Vaikom Satyagraha of 1924 were tainted by any communal feelings. When Malabar was in the grip of the Moplah Rebellion, Travancore was preparing for an increased tempo of civil disobedience of the foreign rule and for stronger campaigns of boycotts against British goods. In both, the student leaders worked hand in hand with the elders.

CHAPTER FIVE

In the organization of picketing of shops dealing in British goods, I and a number of fellow students had the most prominent part. The boycott culminated in the huge bonfire witnessed on the Trivandrum beach in 1925, soon after Gandhiji's visit to Travancore. It was virtually achieved through student leadership. Bundles after bundles of British clothing wound up on the beach in an almost never-ending human conveyor line, comprising Hindus, Muslims, Christians, the old and the young, men, women, and children, each vying with the other in feeding the flame which had been lit by Gandhiji's son, Devadas. It was a lesson in what the people could do if properly motivated, without any consideration of creed and caste.

CHAPTER SIX
Departure for Japan

My eldest brother, Dr. Kumaran Nair, was about fourteen years older than me. The whole family deeply respected him. Besides his medical work with the army, he had a flourishing practice at private clinics and hospitals and enjoyed a high reputation. But his professional preoccupations left him very little time for personal affairs. There was no doubt that he had much affection for all of us, but with a wife and three children to look after, he could naturally not devote to his brothers and sisters as much attention as he would have liked.

It so happened, therefore, that the brother to whom I was most closely attached was Narayanan Nair, five years my senior. He was a brilliant student, with a flair for the sciences. When he completed his matriculation in 1920, my father decided that he should take up a technical line, which would be more or less new in India. To the surprise of many friends, his choice fell on fisheries—a surprise because it was not usual for a high caste brahmin, vowed to vegetarianism, to think of developing fish or meat food resources even for others. But my father had the vision to see Kerala's high potential for a fishing industry and he judged it best, therefore, that my brother should be trained to be a fisheries expert. I remember his telling me that as far as he knew, the best institution during those days which offered a degree course in fishery science was the Japanese Imperial University of Sapporo in Hokkaido. He wrote to the principal of the university and secured admission there for my brother,

CHAPTER SIX

for the BSc degree course beginning in 1921.

Those were days when my parents' domestic life was happy. My father arranged to send my brother to Hokkaido and met all the expenses until the time he obtained his degree. By then, unfortunately, the rift between my parents had taken place, and my father did not send my brother any money for his return journey. Funds for it, therefore, about 2,000 rupees, were remitted by my eldest brother Kumaran Nair, but the circumstances in which he did so evoked much adverse criticism against him. It came to be known that he had obtained the money from a friend after striking a bargain with him promising, quid pro quo, that Narayanan Nair, on his return, would marry the friend's daughter.

Although I respected my eldest brother, I felt that his action in this matter was unethical and unfair to Narayanan Nair, whom he had not consulted before making the commitment. Such "deals" were not particularly uncommon at the time, but I viewed them with strong dislike. Apart from the wrong morality involved, it was not necessary even from a pecuniary viewpoint for Kumaran Nair to "mortgage" his brother in this fashion. Narayanan Nair, after graduation, was earning enough as a part-time research scholar in his own university to be able to finance his return voyage. He was not pleased by what our eldest brother had done, but gracefully concurred so as to preserve the family's "prestige." He had sufficient philosophy to adjust to the situation and make a success of the "forced" marriage.

On his return, he joined the Travancore government's Agricultural Department as an inspector of fisheries. Subsequently, when a new department of fisheries was created, he was appointed its director. After a while he went to Canada and obtained a master's degree in bacteriology related to fish culture, and in his days was acknowledged one of the topmost scientists in the world in his field of work.

Meanwhile, my family was anxious about my own future. My activities at school had already got me on the wrong side of the authorities, and if I took to full-time political work, as many thought I was intending to do, it would perhaps not be long before I wound up in jail as an anti-British agitator. My brother Narayanan Nair, therefore, took upon himself the responsibility to prevent me from drifting into politics. He decided, in 1927, that the best means of saving me from moving into an area of certain trouble would be to ask me to take up higher studies. He picked engineering as the best subject in which I might obtain a degree, since that was guaranteed to start me off on a secure job, just as fishery science had helped to do in his own case. And because of his connections in Japan and the high standard of education available there, he thought it best that I should undertake further study in that country. There was also the precedent of the case of Neelakanta Pillai, a distant relation of mine, who had graduated from Kyoto University in 1915 as an engineer and obtained a high position in the Travancore government. With such ideas in mind, my brother corresponded with Kyoto University and secured a seat for me in its engineering degree course beginning in 1928.

I had very much wanted to join the Indian freedom movement actively under the congress, and therefore thought about the new proposal with much mental reservation. Ultimately my affection for my brother and respect for his wishes outweighed my personal preference. I was reconciled, at least for once, to the decision handed down to me, and mentally prepared myself for a technical profession.

I found that I had to learn mathematics of a higher level than I had done in high school, and therefore sought the help of a well-known tutor who had a master's degree in the subject. After I had acquired requisite proficiency in it, my brother finalized arrangements for my journey to Japan. I was scheduled to travel from Colombo on February 18, 1928, by the Japanese ship *Suwa Maru*. In the second week of the month, I left for Ceylon (Sri Lanka), together with Narayanan Nair who insisted on seeing me off onboard.

There my brother introduced me to the captain of the vessel. A long conversation ensued between them in the Japanese language. It sounded strange to me, but noticing the captain's attitude of respect, it was obvious that my brother had a high degree of fluency in that language. Later he gave me a translation of what he had said to the captain. He had told him, "This is my dear brother; he is going to study in Japan. Will you please see that he is served only Japanese meals during the voyage so that he will get accustomed to them and will not face the kind of food problems that I initially had?" He was also urging the captain to take personal care of me in the event of any particular need.

The captain assured him on both scores, and indeed was true to his word. Under his personal supervision, I was initiated into Japanese cuisine, to the exclusion of any other food. He even went out of his way to give me frequent briefings on Japanese customs and way of life. I also managed to pick up a smattering of the new language so that I could at least find my way around on disembarkation.

On board as a first-class passenger was Dr. Fukuda, a reputed professor of medicine from Kanagawa Prefecture. He was returning to Japan after attending an international medical conference in Calcutta. My brother had spoken to him also about me, and the good doctor was kind enough to treat me like a younger brother of his and to make me feel as much at home as possible in the circumstances. As regards my food, I was served rice, miso (soya bean) soup and other typical Japanese preparations, all of which I found in the beginning to be far from tasty. I was also plagued by seasickness and suffered occasional bouts of vomiting. There were times when I thought that it would be better to return to India but of course that was not feasible, and I had necessarily to put up with my problems. Also, on reflection, I would tell myself that to turn back, even if it were possible, would be cowardice. Moreover, it was unthinkable that I should disappoint my brother who had taken so much trouble for my sake.

* * *

During the voyage I had hardly any source of news from India or anywhere else. Worldwide broadcasting had not yet developed fully; in any case, the *Suwa Maru*'s wireless sets were not powerful enough to receive shortwave broadcasts from countries far away.

A little before my leaving India, many unfortunate incidents had taken place in Bengal and in some provinces in the north, involving Hindu-Muslim clashes that were an outgrowth of the seeds of communal dissension sown by the British. On the national front, the congress was preparing for another showdown with the viceroy and the British government. In its session held in Madras in December 1927, a resolution introduced by Jawaharlal Nehru declaring *purna swaraj* (complete independence) as the goal of Indians, had been adopted. Sensing the growing mood of anger of the people, Britain had announced, in November 1927, the appointment of a statutory commission to propose certain reforms, hopefully to placate the growing public outcry against the alien domination of the country. It was called the Simon Commission, after the name of its chairman, Sir John Simon, a constitutional jurist and a member of the British Liberal Party in the House of Commons.

The manner in which it was constituted, however, showed no genuine intention on the part of Britain to give up any of its substantive powers. Its membership was confined to members of the British parliament. Indian leadership at once reacted sharply against the exclusion of Indian participation. It could not accept the position that the parliament in London was to be the sole instrument to decide the destiny of the Indian people. On February 18, 1928, a resolution for the boycott of the Simon Commission was introduced in the legislative assembly in Delhi by Lala Lajpat Rai and was carried amidst tumultuous scenes. By a strange coincidence, that was the date on which my ship left Colombo!

As I learned later, the members of the commission travelled extensively in India for long periods, but everywhere they were greeted with black flags carried by hostile demonstrators. Eight years were to pass before anything concrete materialized from their deliberations. And eventually, when the results were embodied in the Government of India Act of 1935, the product of the commission's labors was found to be merely certain half-hearted decisions on provincial autonomy as an "experiment." Even this was riddled with many difficulties and marked by a serious deterioration of intercommunal relations. When the Second World War broke out in 1939, Britain found it convenient to push constitutional reforms in India to the background and to encourage the separatist activities of the Muslim League. It was only after another eight agonizing years that India became independent; and that too accompanied by the tragedy of the dismemberment of the subcontinent by the creation of Pakistan.

The *Suwa Maru* berthed at Kobe on March 12, 1928. The immigration officers were rather puzzled about the entry in my passport under the heading "national status." I was described there as "Citizen of Travancore—British protected person." There was some hurried consultation among the officers. One of the Japanese co-passengers who knew English told me quietly what he had overheard. Some of the immigration staff had no knowledge of a "country" called Travancore. One of them was smart enough to remember that it was "some place in India," but was nevertheless bewildered as to how I could be a "citizen" of a place in India rather than of India itself; it would be like calling a Japanese national a "citizen" of Saitama or Gunma Prefectures.

Apparently, none of the immigration personnel had made such a deep study of history as to know that the British had created 601 small Indias within India. They called them "princely states" (or, often, "native states") and had made special treaties which gave their rulers certain special privileges in return for their pledge of loyalty. It needed a special type of mind, which Kobe immigration did not seem to possess, to comprehend the devious modes of political skullduggery the British rulers practiced in India to tighten their colonial grip on the country. However, eventually the chief of immigration ruled that since I looked thoroughly Indian, I must be one, and that the entry in my passport must be some kind of mistake. During all these deliberations I kept mum, on the principle that where silence was golden, it would be folly to be wise. Then suddenly I was cleared for landing. I was told, again by my English-knowing Japanese co-passenger, that the authorities decided to overlook the "mistake" because I had a letter from Kyoto University granting me admission there, which they evaluated as more important and convincing than my passport.

In later years a friend told me that if I had that passport of mine now, I would be quite a VIP. Probably I could have even sold that unique document to an antique collector for a fabulous amount. Alas, I lost that precious document either in Japan or somewhere in Southeast Asia during the last world war. Not realizing its potential value in the long run, I had not taken much care to preserve it either. And, frankly, I do not regret the loss.

* * *

I proceeded to Kyoto by train the same day. By the time I checked into a Japanese inn, I had exhausted all my Japanese vocabulary acquired during the voyage. It was clear that I had not learned much. For a while I pressed sign language into service, to the amusement of everyone subjected to it, but before long told myself that without learning Japanese properly I could not expect to get very far with my studies or anything else in a country where most of the people knew only their own language.

My first main meal at the inn was net-broiled bream served with rice. Net-broiled bream is just that: bream broiled in a net. Frankly, the first time I tasted it, I did not like it. However, I wanted to be polite and pretended that it was excellent, that I enjoyed it. But soon I quietly slipped out of the inn, went to a nearby shop, bought some *anpan* (Japanese red bean-jam bread) and ate it to my heart's content, right in the open, unmindful of the passersby. They must have felt horrified because they were not accustomed to seeing anyone standing on the road and consuming food so voraciously. But it is only fair to add that in course of time I developed a taste for Japanese food in its general range, *and* a strong preference for net-broiled bream. It became one of my favorite dishes.

The Japanese do not eat with their hands or fingers as we do; they use a pair of chopsticks (or *hashi*, in Japanese). I had started practicing the use of it during my voyage and had difficulty in the beginning. A Japanese waiter on the ship, taking pity on me, brought out forks and spoons and knives and the rest of the paraphernalia of western table settings for my benefit; but since I was not accustomed to those either, I said to myself: "Let me try the *hashi* and see what happens; after all, I must familiarize myself with them." Over time, I found them easy to handle and as efficient as one's fingers or even knives and forks. It is surprising how the *hashi*, skillfully used, can do anything that cutlery can, including shredding the meat portion off the bones of chicken or other meat pieces. Of course, it took me considerable practice to attain that standard of proficiency; but considering that in the early stages I had trouble even while trying to handle udon (thick wheat noodles) and eggs, with *hashi*, my perseverance was worthwhile.

CHAPTER SEVEN
At Kyoto University

After an overnight stay at the inn, I reported to Kyoto University the following morning. My introduction was first of all to Dr. Takahashi, professor of bridge engineering who had apparently the additional responsibility of taking care of the admission of foreign students. I was struck by the dignity of the professor. He had a serene face, but his deep-set eyes were sharp and clear, and appeared to penetrate me as though to discover what was located inside! I formed an impression of him as a kindly person, but one to be respected and never taken for granted. I had heard that he held a PhD from a German university, was a highly competent teacher, and was one of the world-renowned scientists in his field.

After the usual preliminaries relating to admission, I asked Dr. Takahashi what I should do next. He said that first of all one or two things had to be done *for me*: I must be provided accommodation in an environment congenial to study, and arrangements should be made immediately for me to learn the Japanese language. He spoke briefly to Assistant Professor Taguchi who came over and joined us. It was at once decided that I would be a house guest of the Taguchis. I was overwhelmed by the generous gesture and thanked these fine gentlemen as well as I could.

In the afternoon of the same day, I had a different kind of experience—almost an anticlimax to that of the morning. After taking leave of Dr. Takahashi, I decided to return to my inn to arrange for my move to Professor

Taguchi's house. Although it was springtime, it had snowed in the morning and the weather was quite cold. Therefore, I put on my overcoat outside Dr. Takahashi's room and started off for the nearest point from where I could catch a tram to reach my inn. While still within the campus, I suddenly felt someone tapping me on my shoulder from behind. Turning round, I saw a tall, elderly man with a raincoat and umbrella. "Come with me," he said in perfect English, and in a tone that had an unmistakable ring of authority. I felt a little odd at this abrupt command but decided not to start any argument: at least not just yet. The tall man took me to a large room in a nearby building in the university and, seating himself behind an impressive desk, asked me to sit down in a chair directly opposite to his. For two or three minutes he did nothing but look at me, hardly batting his eyelids. Then suddenly he raised his right hand, pointed a finger at me and sharply shot out the question: "Are you a spy?"

That was something I was least prepared for, but somehow, I managed to retain my composure and replied calmly: "No, I am not a spy. I am a student here."

Perhaps there was something he noticed in the way I answered him, or something else I had no idea about. His severity seemed to melt suddenly and a gentle smile appeared on his face. In a totally different tone, mild this time, he said almost casually: "You are from India, but from which part of it?" I kept looking straight into his face without demur, trying to control a certain resentment that was welling up in me but which I knew would be imprudent to exhibit. I said, "Trivandrum." Then came a quick-fire question which again I had not expected: "How is Ganapati Sastri?"

I did not quite know what to think of this old gentleman who first had asked me whether I was a spy and was now enquiring about Ganapati Sastri. I knew of course who Ganapathy Shastry was: he was professor of Sanskrit at the Maharaja's College (present University College Thiruvananthapuram), Trivandrum. I used to see him occasionally on the road to the college, but never cared much for him. In fact, privately I had a vague kind of grudge against him. In retrospect I think it was irrational, but at the same time my grouse probably arose from a feeling that he was a competitor to my brother-in-law, C. P. Govinda Pillai, who was the professor of Malayalam. Both these teachers were well-known scholars and authors. There was no obvious reason why I should have cold-shouldered Sastri, but prejudices are sometimes inexplicable and unreasonable. I suppose I had felt the way I did only because I loved my brother-in-law and therefore subconsciously harbored a sense of jealousy against his colleague. Preoccupied with thoughts of this kind

I fumbled for an answer, and the man behind the desk repeated his question with a touch of annoyance in his voice.

"How is he?"

Again I was hesitant and, perhaps in an involuntary attempt to evade the question, merely murmured: "How is he . . ." At this the gentleman threw up his hands with a gesture of surprise and despair.

"What? You do not know how Ganapati Sastri is? You have not heard of him? Don't you know that he is the greatest Sanskrit scholar in India and one of the three greatest in the world?"

Needless to say, I was embarrassed and felt awkward. Of course, I knew something about Ganapati Sastri, but had not realized that he was what the person in front of me had just said. It was good to know that here was someone in Kyoto University who admired Sastri and for a moment I forgot my petty jealousy and even felt rather proud. Later, I was to know that one of the other two among the "greatest three scholars" was a European (I forget whether he was German or French, and his name also escapes my mind) and the remaining person was none other than my interrogator: Dr. Sakakibara, senior professor of Indology and Indian philosophy and Sanskrit at Kyoto University.

To say that I felt rather small and out of sorts would be an understatement. I also gathered subsequently that Professor Sakakibara was one of the kindliest of persons and that he was simply conducting a psychological test on me to see what kind of person I was. It was of course not the occasion for me to ask him whether I had come up to his expectations, but what followed was proof enough that I had passed his test. The famous professor was soon a changed man and was the picture of compassion.

"What is it that has brought you here?" he asked.

I said, "I have come as a student to study civil engineering."

He smiled gently. "How do you think you can study engineering without first learning the Japanese language? You had better come to me every evening. I shall teach you Japanese."

For a moment I felt a sensation that could only be described as weird. I wondered whether what had just happened was all real or merely a dream. Or was it a kind of miracle? So much had occurred in one day: I was to be the house guest of an assistant professor; I was then asked whether I was a spy and put through a minor sort of inquisition as part of a psychological test administered by the famous Sanskrit scholar and Indologist Sakakibara, and eventually the same professor offered to be my Japanese teacher. It was somewhat confusing to me in the beginning, but I was only laboring the obvious when, at the end of it all, I told myself that I was rather fortunate.

I shifted my residence the same evening to the home of Professor and Mrs. Taguchi, where I was warmly welcomed by them both. They treated me as a member of their own family. They were a most lovable couple whose kindness I can never forget.

My Japanese language tuition under Professor Sakakibara commenced without delay. The professor was a great teacher. He was doing me an honor, not so much because I was a student in Kyoto University but because he had the highest respect for India, also because I was coming from the same place as that of Ganapati Sastri whom he admired. This was the first real feel I had of the type of consideration which a Japanese professor was capable of extending to fellow scholars elsewhere.

While Sakakibara was my chief language teacher, my hosts, the Taguchis, also took great pains to give me supplementary coaching. And the way they did so was remarkable. Both Professor and Mrs. Taguchi belonged to Kyoto and were naturally accustomed to the Kansai style of Japanese, which is somewhat different from the Kanto dialect of Tokyo. Tokyo being the capital and the seat of the imperial household, the manner of speech used there is treated as standard Japanese. The case is more or less like that of "Oxford English" being the standard for "Queen's English." The Taguchis were anxious to ensure that, as a foreign student, I should learn "Tokyo (or Kanto) Japanese." It is rather tiresome for a Kansai speaker to switch over suddenly from his habitual way of speech to the Kanto style, but my wonderful hosts took all the trouble to do so for my sake. They decided that in my presence they would use only the Kanto style. It was a touching gesture on their part.

My hosts were equally solicitous about my food. They would do everything possible to cater to what they felt would suit me. It was an odd situation: whereas I would want to get used to traditional Japanese food, the Taguchis would go out of their way to attempt cooking for me in the Indian style, the result being that the product would be neither the one nor the other. For instance, my hosts would serve me large bowls of rice mixed with red ginger in large quantities of *shoyu* (soy sauce). In Japan it is unusual to mix *shoyu* or *shoyu*-soaked side dishes with rice; rice and the other items are eaten separately, unlike in India where we mix a variety of curries and other subsidiaries with rice. Mrs. Taguchi would often prepare *oyakodonburi* (rice with chicken and eggs) for me in a special way; she would season it with a dash of sugar and a sprinkling of *shoyu* to make it extra tasty and good-humoredly call it "Mr. A. M. Nair's patent."

We would sometimes discuss the use of spices in the preparation of curry, and also experiment with them to see the results which, I must say, were generally quite satisfactory. In India, as everyone knows, curry powder comes in various types and combinations, the formula varying in accordance with the tastes catered for. Our food habits vary considerably as between different regions of the country: for instance, the southerner uses more spice than his comrade in the north, the North Indian would like more ghee (refined butter) than the South Indian, and so on. In contrast, Japanese food is relatively simple and yet nourishing. Regional variations are not many. Although the typical Japanese meal does not use much of spice, the Japanese people do enjoy curries with authentic Indian spices. In the Taguchi home, after a period of fairly wide-ranging trials, we eventually settled down to wholly Japanese style food. Whenever we wanted a change, there was no difficulty because Indian style (at least something near to it) curry and rice had become popular in several city hotels and restaurants in Japan from the 1920s, together with certain typical Western food items like cornflakes and tomato ketchup. In fact, "curry rice" had become part of Japanese vocabulary, as *kareraisu*.

During my time, there was a well-known restaurant called Cherry near Kyoto University; I am not sure whether it exists still. The canteen within the campus had a certain version of *kareraisu*, but what we got at Cherry tasted better. One of my teachers who was particularly informal used to take me there occasionally for lunch. He had his own favorite dishes that he would order for himself but would tell the waiter with much flourish and a serious gesture: "A curry and rice for Mr. Nair." Another professor, Dr. Kobayashi (who, incidentally, was yet one more kindly soul who took much interest in teaching me Japanese), occasionally entertained me to *kareraisu* at a medium-level eating-house elsewhere, but I hardly relished the preparation. Perhaps quietly noticing my discomfiture, he did not take me there again but would ask me out to high-grade restaurants, somewhat to my embarrassment because they were so expensive. In course of time, I discovered several "joints" which served rice and curry, but some of them used strange mixtures of spices that did not taste good because they were not Indian. However, nowhere in those days was food very expensive. In my time, a plate of curry and rice in our university canteen cost five sen (about 10 paise)—something that will now sound incredible.

I took my studies seriously and worked hard on my lessons. I was in a new country, spending my family's money, and was anxious to get the most benefit possible. Japan had become a world power and its standard of education was high. Thanks to the special mathematics tuition I had before leaving for Kyoto, I found no serious difficulty with my university curriculum in the engineering faculty and was therefore able to devote all the necessary attention to achieve advanced proficiency in the Japanese language. For students, especially of technical subjects, the range of vocabulary had to be much wider than for some others (for example, businessmen) who could manage with a relatively limited acquaintance with conversational Japanese.

During his time at Kyoto Imperial University. The author is seated fourth from the left.

Both my teachers and I were quite pleased with my rapid progress in mastering the language. Besides those I have mentioned, there were several teachers who helped me from time to time to resolve any difficulties I faced, and my fellow students were equally cooperative. Being of a gregarious nature, I was keen to associate with the rest of the students at my university and found it a most rewarding exercise. On the one hand, the knowledge of the language I had already acquired helped me to mix with them freely and thereby develop a feeling of belonging instead of isolation which could lead to frustration. On the other, by being constantly in the milieu, my proficiency in the language improved rapidly. Social contacts also became much easier. I found that the Japanese people, although characteristically reserved and taciturn, were warmhearted and extremely friendly once you got to know them well, and especially if you spoke their language with ease and refinement.

CHAPTER SEVEN

Foreign students, almost everywhere, usually have the tendency to form themselves into groups of their own, which I have always thought is not quite the right thing to do. Whereas they should always retain their own cultural values, they can well do so without giving the impression of incompatibility with the main body of the institution. In my case, there was the fortuitous circumstance that I was the only Indian university student in Kyoto or elsewhere in Japan during my time, and so there was no question of my getting into any "group" other than that of my fellow Japanese students.

I got to like Kyoto very much. It is one of the most beautiful cities of Japan and is popularly adored even today as the nation's cultural capital. It was built in 794, after which the seat of the imperial family was moved there from the nearby city of Nara. In the course of its history, Kyoto suffered much damage from time to time from fire and earthquakes, besides internal wars. It was almost wholly destroyed during the early second half of the fifteenth century as a result of the Onin War, but was rebuilt towards the end of the sixteenth century by Toyotomi Hideyoshi. Hideyoshi was the military commander under whose leadership political and administrative unity was restored to the country after some one hundred years of continual civil strife. The emperors resided in Kyoto for about eleven centuries. It was after the Meiji Restoration of 1868 that the capital was officially moved to Tokyo. At one time Kyoto was known as "Heian-kyo," literally signifying a center of peace and tranquility, a description which fits even today.

Traditionally a fountainhead of religion, education, and art, Kyoto houses some three thousand Buddhist temples and Shinto shrines. Among its marvelous buildings and numerous castles is the Golden Pavilion, which was originally the residence of Shogun Ashikaga Yoshimitsu and was converted, after his death, into a Buddhist temple.

Kyoto University, one of the most prestigious of the country's elite educational institutions, was founded in 1897. The national museum of the city is rated among the best in the world. Altogether, Kyoto has a unique personality and owns a highly delicate and exalted order of aesthetic refinement. The landscape is a picture of timeless natural beauty. The city is set against a backdrop of gently undulating hills covered by pines, cypresses, willows, and a variety of other magnificent trees. Japanese gardens are invariably things of beauty, but in Kyoto they present the universally acknowledged artistic taste of the Japanese at its best. During spring, which is the season for the famous cherry blossoms, the whole place takes on the aspect of an exquisite dream world.

Several sensitive poets and prose writers have written profusely about the beauty of the Japanese country, and every region has its own special charm. One piece of "prose poetry" by the famous nineteenth-century Japanese writer Hirotari Nakajima runs as below:

> 木々紅葉むらむら染めわたして尾花が神も人持ち顔に打ちまねく山路のいとおもしろきに女郎花蘭などのやうやううらがれ行く中より今吹きはじめたる菊の露もとをたなびき出でたる物よりことに目に立ちていとなつかしうおぼゆ。

Here and there the leaves of the trees are deeply dyed with yellow and crimson, the pampas-grass waving as though beckoning someone, with long sleeves,—in such a mountain-path of beauty, from the gradually withering midst of maiden-flower and orchid, the chrysanthemums now beginning to bloom, their branches bowed with dew, sway out, and, more than all else, touch us with their grace and loveliness.

I cannot say which particular landscape Hirotari was describing, but I think that his pen-picture could well apply to Kyoto.

It was fortunate for Japan that Kyoto was spared from bombardment during the last world war, when most other Japanese cities were razed to the ground by the American air force.

CHAPTER EIGHT
Meeting Rash Behari Bose

Early in April 1928, I visited Tokyo briefly. I wanted to see the university there, but had also another purpose which was equally, if not indeed more, important. The famous Indian revolutionary Rash Behari Bose was living in self-exile in Tokyo. I had heard much about him and his work in India and also of his continued activities in Japan in the cause of Indian freedom. I was keen to meet him as early as possible, and called on him at Nakamuraya, the store operated by him and his family, in Shinjuku.

Welcoming me warmly, Rash Behari Bose entertained me to a good meal of curry and rice. I was struck by his bearing, which was both kindly and forceful. Although he was some twenty-five years older than me, I could easily sense his magnetic personality. He was happy to see me, especially as I was the only Indian student in Japan at that time

I have written briefly earlier about the anti-British agitations in India in the early decades of this century and how the political ferment sometimes took a revolutionary and terroristic aspect. Those who were inclined to the cult of violence as a means to attain freedom from the imperialist yoke, met with brute repression from the all-powerful and efficient police. Many terrorists were either executed or jailed after sham trials in courts. Most of them made no attempt to escape and undauntedly faced the sentences. Rash Behari was an exception. He would not give up his struggle, and in order to continue it, he must naturally remain alive. He had the unique distinction of making the British dragnet look foolish by giving it the slip, achieving a daring getaway from India and eventually settling in Japan to carry on his activities in furtherance of the cause of Indian freedom under a new strategy.

Rash Behari Bose had begun his adult life as a clerk at the Forest Research Institute in Dehradun but managed to devote most of his time to secret revolutionary political work. He kept in frequent touch with prominent left-wing leaders in Bengal, and also learned how to make bombs. He was instrumental in bringing about secret contacts between the revolutionaries in North India, particularly the Punjab, and those in Bengal and eventually became the organizational mainspring of the terrorist activity of the extremists. He believed that only through terrorism could the masses in India be awakened to the reality that they were living under slavery. When so aroused, he was sure, they would rise in revolt.

He enlisted a band of followers who were seized with a degree of cold courage and loyalty that equipped them to face any kind of hardship and even to risk their lives. They in turn influenced others, so that the extremists dedicated to the cause of dislodging British power in India through violent means increased in number both in Bengal, the Punjab, and other North Indian provinces. There were a number of bomb attacks on Englishmen. A secret campaign for clandestine circulation of revolutionary newspapers was also successfully launched and carried on with remarkable efficiency. The government was of course not slow to react and meted out harsh punishment not only to those suspected of violent action but to those found to possess "seditious" literature. Many were imprisoned for long periods. The most important target of the police was the person whom they believed was responsible for unleashing a spirit of revolt, Rash Behari Bose, but all their efforts to find him failed.

In 1912, the British government decided to shift the seat of the viceroy's office from Calcutta to New Delhi, which was to be built up as the country's new capital. The viceroy, Lord Hardinge, arrived at the Delhi railway station on December 23. Mounting a caparisoned elephant,

Rash Behari Bose, 1942.

he started for the new viceregal mansion, some six miles away, at the head of a colorful and pompous procession. About a mile from the railway station, while the large crowds were still cheering, a bomb burst behind the viceroy's seat on the elephant, seriously injuring an army officer sitting behind him and inflicting multiple wounds on the viceroy himself.

There are different versions as to who exactly hurled the bomb; there are some who attribute the action to Rash Behari himself, but reasonable doubt exists in this regard. It was unlikely that Rash Behari would expose himself so publicly when the possibility of his being apprehended was great. He himself is not known to have confided the truth of this to anyone, but the best circumstantial evidence gathered so far seems to suggest that he had entrusted the action to one Basant Kumar Biswas, a close lieutenant. Biswas had, it is said, disguised himself as a girl and mixed with the women standing in one section of the crowd watching the procession. At one point he managed to distract the attention of the women around him, flung the bomb, and quietly slipped back and got lost in the same section again nonchalantly.

The daring attack baffled all investigations for several months until the police caught up with the secret organization distributing revolutionary literature and began concentrating on those involved in it. Eventually, in what came to be known as the Delhi conspiracy case, eleven suspects including Biswas were arrested and indicted for possession of explosives, murder, etc. Biswas and three others were executed on May 11, 1915. But Rash Behari Bose, who was on the primary list of those accused, was missing.

The government announced a prize of 5,000 rupees to anyone who could provide clues leading to his capture, but the offer went a-begging. Rash Behari had many disguises and moved about quite publicly for some time when the police were searching supposedly secret hideouts for him. He lived dangerously. Among his rare qualities were a gift for languages, a great talent for quick grasp of any situation in its perspective and, above all, sheer courage and an inflexible resolve to see India free from colonial rule, whatever the cost. His associates usually called him Satish Chandra or merely Fat Babu. Few even among them knew his real name.

He had scheduled a massive general uprising to take place on February 21, 1915, but some fifth columns had leaked the secret and the plan failed. Several of his compatriots were arrested but he himself could not be located. When the police hunt became furiously intensive, his friends felt that it was no longer safe for him to stay in India and persuaded him to leave the country. He agreed reluctantly, but with the determination to continue the struggle from elsewhere. The poet Rabindranath Tagore had been scheduled to visit Japan around the middle of 1915, and Rash Behari hit upon the brilliant idea of a perfect disguise as a certain P. N. Tagore, supposedly a secretary proceeding ahead to make preliminary arrangements connected with the visit.

There is some doubt as to the ship by which he left Calcutta. According to one version, he boarded a "neutral" vessel because the police were constantly watching every Japanese ship on the assumption that he might try to get on to one of them. But the common belief is that "P. N. Tagore," who looked every inch a secretary to the great poet, had no difficulty in boarding the Japanese liner *Shanuki Maru* which left Calcutta for Japan on May 12, 1915, right under the nose of the ever-vigilant police.

It is unlikely that the two reports can ever be verified, and perhaps any attempt to do so will hardly be relevant. The important thing is that Rash Behari was able to evade the police by his remarkable ingenuity. Whether he was briefly in Shanghai before or after reaching Japan, it was a fact that he visited that city and contacted certain German agents with whose help he exported a consignment of firearms to Bengal for use by the terrorists there. Unfortunately for him, the shipment did not get to its destination because the British Intelligence agents got wind of it and managed to confiscate it before it reached Calcutta.

It may surprise many that the exact details of Rash Behari's part in the bomb attack on Lord Hardinge and of his voyage to Japan remain shrouded in some mystery, despite all the deep research that has been done about his life and work. The reason seems to be that Rash Behari hardly ever talked about himself and of his exploits. Although an extrovert who could even be humorous at times, he kept a tight lid on his own past activities. And, to the best of my knowledge, no one ever felt bold enough to ask him. Hence, he was a rare phenomenon of a man who even succeeded in foiling history to an extent.

For Rash Behari, those things which he did not wish to tell others, were unimportant for the cause for which he lived and fought. He was a great believer in the message of the Bhagavad Gita, the great epic chapter in the Mahabharata epitomizing the best in Hindu philosophy. He carried a copy of it wherever he went. What was important to him was only *action* according to his conscience, not the fruits of it. In other words, he practiced the tenets of *nishkama* (or *anasakta*) *karma*, meaning action without the taint of attachment or desire for any reward:

> Your duty is but to act, never to be concerned with results; let not the fruit of action be your motive; do not let yourself be drawn into the path of nonaction.

CHAPTER EIGHT

That, briefly, was his strongest faith, and if I have known any Indian, or anyone else for that matter, other than Gandhiji whose action came to the same level of that which he preached, it was Rash Behari.

* * *

Rash Behari arrived in Japan in June 1915, and before long got in touch with two other famous revolutionaries to whom Japan had granted asylum: one was Lala Lajpat Rai from India, who later left for the United States of America, and the other Sun Yat-sen of China. But British intelligence in India and East Asia, particularly in Japan, had not been idle. Its network in Japan was a strong and efficient one, and soon discovered that Rash Behari was in Japan, although it did not know his exact whereabouts in the country. Rash Behari was too clever for them and kept changing his address frequently. Yet the strain became too much, and he feared apprehension by the police at any time. The British embassy in Japan approached the Japanese government to try and locate him through a nationwide manhunt and extradite him to India.

There were many in the higher echelons of the government and in the public life of Japan who were sympathetic to Bose, one of them being the prime minister, Count Shigenobu Okuma himself. But the Anglo-Japanese Alliance of 1902 was still in force, and Britain was therefore able to bring strong pressure to bear on the Ministry of Foreign Affairs. An extradition order against Bose was actually issued and a date fixed for his deportation to India via Shanghai. The intention of the British government was that once they could get him to Shanghai, they could have him arrested there because in Shanghai they had certain extraterritorial rights. But before the extradition order could be executed, Rash Behari had the good fortune to be introduced by Sun Yat-sen to Mitsuru Toyama, who headed an extreme right-wing nationalist group in Japan.

Toyama was an enormously powerful man, with much influence down the line from the palace to the peasant. He was greatly impressed by Rash Behari's fervent patriotism and decided to arrange for his safe asylum in Japan. One day when Rash Behari was at Toyama's house, the Japanese police were reported to be waiting outside to get him when he came out (they dared not enter the house). Toyama knew this and arranged for Bose's exit from his house by the back door. No one else knew where Rash Behari had gone. What had happened was that under Toyama's advice, a most remarkable couple,

Aizo Soma and his wife Kokko, owners of Nakamuraya in Shinjuku, had agreed to shelter Rash Behari secretly in their house. They took a big risk. If the British Secret Service had got scent of the address, not only Rash Behari but his benefactors as well could be in serious trouble. But the secret remained well guarded.

Meanwhile, Toyama advised the Japanese government that they should not oblige the British by trying to trace the Indian patriot, who would be hanged if he were ever handed over to his hunters. It also so happened that in the wake of the war in Europe, Japan's policy towards both China and Britain began to change. Japanese interests in China clashed with those of Britain in the area, and Anglo-Japanese relations came under strain. Therefore, although the Japanese government eventually came to know where Rash Behari was, they did not trouble him. They kept the British guessing and fooled them with empty promises to do everything possible to get hold of the man they wanted. In fact, as I heard later, the police official who had been "ordered" to book him used to be Rash Behari's frequent swimming partner at Chiba beach. Mitsuru Toyama had ensured that Rash Behari would be free from harm.

Mitsuru Toyama of the Kokuryukai (Black Dragon Society).

The British had sent a senior police officer, an Englishman, from India to Japan to "help" the Japanese authorities locate Rash Behari. According to the information which that officer "gathered" with much effort and reported to the government of India in 1915, Rash Behari was living in the compound of the lord chamberlain to the emperor. That was incredible naïveté on the part of the British Secret Service. Moreover, as though to decelerate British diplomacy's influence in Japan, an incident occurred in the South China Sea where a British patrol party raided a Japanese ship and arrested its personnel, including several Indians. An upsurge of indignation in Japan followed, and the foreign office in Tokyo cancelled the extradition order on Rash Behari in

April 1916. But, although he was thus technically a free man, danger to him had not passed, because British secret agents were still operating all over Japan and they might well have attempted a kidnap.

Therefore, Rash Behari continued to be on his guard and kept changing house. He, however, remained secretly in touch with the Somas, whose help he needed in various ways. The channel of such contact was Toshiko, the eldest daughter of Aizo and Kokko Soma, a remarkable woman unafraid of the great risks to which she was exposing herself. Reflecting on the situation, it occurred to Mitsuru Toyama that if the two parties had no objection, it might be a good thing if the Somas could give Toshiko in marriage to Rash Behari Bose so that his life could be a little less unbearable. The parents left the decision to their daughter. Toshiko, who thought the matter over for a month, decided that she would be happy to marry Rash Behari. The latter, for his part, loved Toshiko, but was initially in a quandary because he had regarded her parents like his own; in fact, he was accustomed to calling them "father" and "mother." But Toshiko settled the problem by announcing to her parents her own decision. She and Rash Behari were married in 1917.

It was a rare event: there were not many instances of Japanese girls being given away in wedlock to foreigners. And in the present case the foreigner was one who carried a big price on his head. But this marriage turned out to be a successful one. The great-hearted Toshiko showed admirable courage. The devotion which subsisted between Rash Behari and Toshiko constitutes one of the most heartwarming of human stories.

They had two children: the elder was a son and the younger a daughter. The son, Masahide Bose, who also had the Indian name Asoka, was unfortunately killed in action in Okinawa during the Second World War. The daughter, Tetsuko, now around fifty-nine years of age, is happily married to Mr. Higuchi, a successful engineer. She herself has never visited India, but her eldest daughter did so in January 1969. She had at one time thought of studying in Delhi, but eventually had to give up the idea because of language difficulties and the problems of adjustment to a totally different environment.

Toshiko Bose unfortunately passed away in 1925, eight years after her marriage. She was then only twenty-eight years old. Rash Behari, whose courage as a revolutionary was legendary, was heartbroken but kept up his spirits through hard work in a variety of ways, in the cause of Indian freedom. Meanwhile, again at the insistence of Mitsuru Toyama, the Japanese government had granted him naturalized citizenship of their country in 1923, which enabled him to intensify his activities with the confidence of a free man. He engaged himself in a ceaseless schedule of meeting dignitaries and lobbying for India, lecturing and organizing pro-India associations in Japan and all over Southeast Asia. He mastered the Japanese language so well that he could not only lecture in it but translate English, Bengali, and Hindi books into it with facility. Among his Japanese translations is Sunderland's *India In Bondage*. He was the originator of an organized movement in Japan to promote the struggle for the liberation of India.

I have had the good fortune to know the great Somas of Nakamuraya, and the Higuchi family and my family have maintained a warm and affectionate relationship for long. When I was a student in Kyoto, my association with Rash Behari was limited to occasional meetings, but from the time Japan entered the Second World War (I was then in Manchukuo) our relationship was constant and intimate. I shall return to this subject later in this book but should like to record in the context of this chapter that although technically a naturalized Japanese citizen, and also perfectly adjusted to the Japanese way of life, he was, in his innermost heart, as strong an Indian patriot as he was even before coming to Japan. Until his last breath, he worked for the cause of Indian independence. Often, during his lectures on Hindu philosophy or the Gita, he would announce that his only wish, after India's liberation, was to live either on Mount Fuji or in the Himalayas.

After meeting Rash Behari, I returned to Kyoto with the feeling that I had gone on a pilgrimage and stood before a holy presence. It never ceased to inspire me.

CHAPTER NINE
The Emperor's Coronation Day

The course of my life at the university was briefly ruffled by an unpleasant interlude, ironically in the midst of a great national celebration in Kyoto: the coronation of Emperor Hirohito.

Even after the nation's capital was shifted from Kyoto to Tokyo during the Meiji era, tradition required (and still does because the rules have not been changed) that the enthronement ceremony of every new emperor should be conducted at the imperial palace in Kyoto. When Emperor Taisho passed away on December 25, 1926, the regent and crown prince, Hirohito, immediately succeeded to the throne, but his formal coronation had necessarily to wait until ceremonial arrangements could be made in Kyoto. These arrangements had to be such that would befit Japan's prestige as a world power and were naturally time-consuming. Heads of state from all over the world had to be invited and suitable logistics organized for the occasion. Everything had to be done to perfection to uphold the dignity of the event. Above all, security measures must be foolproof. The memory was still fresh of the attempt on the regent's life in December 1923, by Daisuke Namba at Toranomon near the palace in Tokyo, when tragedy was narrowly averted by the lucky circumstance that the bullet missed the intended mark.

The auspicious event was ultimately scheduled to take place at 4:00 p.m. on November 10, 1928. From about 9:00 p.m. the previous evening, great stretches of roadway were crowded with people gathered to secure standing space along the route of the grand procession leading to the palace. The people wanted to see their emperor who would lead the procession in his horse-driven chariot, followed by an interminably long motorcade.

Occasions of this nature have certain inherent difficulties which even the most thoroughgoing official machinery cannot resolve fully on its own. For instance, when hundreds of thousands of people collect along the road and remain there for nearly a whole day, normal systems can possibly not cope with the needs arising from the calls of nature. The problem at this juncture was basically twofold: one relating to the bowels, the other to the kidneys, and the question was how to tackle the output from these organs without defiling the roadsides or creating health hazards.

The people had the answers ready. The bowels would simply be held for the duration: the discomfort would be bearable. But the kidneys would not brook so much delay for relief, especially when the weather was cold, as it was during November. So, a way had necessarily to be invented. Everyone would carry either a rubber bladder or an empty bottle, use it to ease the urinary pressure as and when required, cork it up when done and hold on to it until the function ended. These receptacles would thereafter be deposited in prescribed collection centers and hygienically disposed of. Where there was a will, there was surely a way.

Not wanting to miss the celebrations, I equipped myself with an empty bottle, and late in the evening of November 8 got ready to do what everyone else was going to do. But at once I found myself in a peculiar situation. As soon as I had positioned myself along the road, a few security guards advanced towards me. After bowing according to the typical Japanese custom, one of them frisked me all over, again and again, as though to be doubly sure that there was no lethal article hidden on my person. Of course they did not find any. My urine bottle was like anyone else's and therefore could not be harmful. Yet, some of the guards remained standing by my side all the time. As far as I could see, no one else was being given such special attention. I thought it strange that I should be singled out as an odd man, and altogether felt weary. I said, partly to myself, partly for the benefit of the guards, that I did not wish to see the procession from the road: perhaps I could do so in a cinema house in due course. With a sour mind, I went home and slept.

But the matter did not end there. The next day I learned that the plain-clothes wing of the police had sought the university authorities' permission to keep a watch over my movements. The authorities refused to allow any such action within the campus, but had naturally nothing to say about what the police might do outside. Since I was living in Professor Taguchi's house, a police officer approached him and asked for his consent to keep me under surveillance. He told a surprised Taguchi that the Secret Service had instructions to watch me because I could be a security risk to the Duke of Gloucester, who was in Kyoto representing the British Crown at the coronation ceremony.

My hosts were naturally disturbed beyond words. As though to mollify them, the captain of the surveillance squad told them that he and his men would not embarrass them; they would watch me unobtrusively from the rooftop of the house and from outside the gate. Professor Taguchi was far from happy but saw no way to object. He suggested, however, that it would only be fair to tell me what all this was about.

The officer came to me and after bowing politely showed me his identification card. He was even respectful, which I had not quite expected, especially since I was only a student. "Mr. Nair," he said, "Let us be friends: we shall take you to a cinema, or anywhere you may wish to go, but we have to be with you." When I enquired what for, he replied, "The Duke of Gloucester will be passing by; we are told that you are a dangerous man and might try to harm him. If so we shall all be in big trouble, so we have to watch you."

It was an amazingly open declaration of something which anyone would normally expect a security force to regard as a secret—whether there was any truth in it or not. However, that did not make me any the less annoyed. I retorted, quite angrily, "Why do you think so?" With the perfect composure of an iceberg, the police officer answered, "Because we have received information from India. The British police want us to watch you, so you must be a dangerous man."

Although outraged, I tried to remain calm, and said with as much poise as I could muster, "I am not a dangerous man; I am only a student here in Kyoto University." But the man would not leave me in peace. "No," he continued, in the same vein as before. "According to the British, you are dangerous." Losing my temper after all, I said brusquely, "Look, my friend, this is your country; you go ahead and do your duty as long as you do not bother me. I am a duly enrolled Indian student in your university here, and I do not see why I should be harassed by you and your men." The way the officer kept his cool perhaps irritated me all the more. "Of course we shall not harm you," he said casually. "We shall wear students' dress if you like, but we must stay with you wherever you go."

"How can you wear students' dress when you are policemen and must be in your own uniform?" I enquired.

"Oh," he replied. "No problem. We are not ordinary police but special police; we can wear any kind of dress."

I thought it was pointless to continue this hopeless discussion, and said in frustration, "You are paid by your government to obey their orders: do what you like."

I did not doubt the officer's claim that he was acting under orders. Obviously, the British intelligence in Japan and the police in India must have made some request which the Japanese authorities were implementing. I had heard that the British Secret Service was an octopus organization and it must naturally have been in contact with India as well as other countries. I was undoubtedly in the bad books of the Travancore police, but it was news to me that anyone had asked the Japanese police to watch me because I was "dangerous" and the Duke of Gloucester had to be protected from me. Surely there was something wrong, but I did not know what exactly it was, and it seemed that I could do nothing about it except to feel terribly bitter.

The Duke of Gloucester was in Kyoto for one week; throughout that period, the special police followed me everywhere like my own shadow, even when I used the toilet or the bathroom. I must however give them credit for their behavior which was invariably courteous. One of the officers told me that he was sorry for what he had to do to a student like me. He said that I could go anywhere except places near the duke's presence; elsewhere, all I had to put up with was his men "being with me." One day when the duke left his suite in the Miyako Hotel on a sightseeing tour, they decided that I would like to see a film, and therefore took me to one. Later I wished to go to Kobe to see a friend, and they came with me. When I was trying to purchase my ticket, the officer said, "There's no need, you may travel free." At that point I felt insulted and told him so. He said he did not mean any offense and was only trying to save me the journey expense. I replied that I did not want any charity. But the constant company of the police was something I could not avoid. It was the thought of the duress I was placed under without any ostensible reason, rather than the manner of its operation, that was difficult to tolerate.

**

Soon after the Duke of Gloucester and the other foreign dignitaries had departed, the good police officer and some of his men brought me a box of cake and offered it to me. They apologized for what they had to do during the past week. They wanted that I should not misunderstand them for doing their duty. Although smarting under the humiliation inflicted on me by whoever was really responsible for it, I told them that as far as they were concerned, I understood their position and that I had no personal ill will. On the contrary, I appreciated their having been so good in their conduct. It was someone else whom I had to be angry with. They went away cheerfully.

But I did not feel satisfied. I wrote a strongly worded letter to the governor of Kyoto, bitterly complaining that I had been insulted. An Asian student of goodwill towards Japan and studying at Kyoto University had been insulted. Was that the right way for the most advanced country in Asia to deal with persons from other parts of Asia? I really let myself go, in my letter, and went to the extent of asking the governor whether Japan was a "puppet of Britain."

The governor must surely have been surprised. Probably he could have ignored my letter, but he did not. I learned that he called his number two officer, the superintendent, and said, "We must do something." The superintendent came to my residence, took me to his own house, entertained me to a good meal, and said, "We are sorry, but please do not misunderstand. We know that you are a good man; we think you are a patriot and that is why the British do not like you. But we had the responsibility for full security precautions for our state guests."

I thought this was not much of an explanation and asked him why I was singled out as a "dangerous man." If it was a question of watching anti-British individuals, why shadow only me and not anyone else—for instance, Rash Behari Bose?

The superintendent appeared pricked when I mentioned Rash Behari's name. He was confused and seemed at a loss for words for a while, but eventually said something to the effect that since Mr. Bose was now a "family man," the British must have categorized him in the "theory group" instead of the "action group." Consequently, he was harmless. They were however worried about the "young radical—A. M. Nair."

I said to myself that if the superintendent's guess was good, the British Secret Service must be a rather dim set of people. However, there was nothing to be gained by prolonging the argument with my kind visitor from the governor's office. Our conversation ended on a cordial note, and from then on, the governor's men, especially the chief of the foreign section, were extremely good to me. I was given the privilege of a pass for free travel anywhere in Japan, and a special identity card entitling me to sit in enclosures reserved for important guests like princes and princesses on important occasions.

These came as an anticlimax to the previous week's ordeal.

In the relaxed atmosphere which returned to Kyoto after the great ceremony, I was able to reflect on the events of the past few days with some sense of detachment. I concluded that the episode, terribly unhappy when it occurred, had nevertheless served as a kind of challenge and a trial. Troubles would come, sometimes unexpectedly as they did indeed in my case, but they must be overcome. There was no question of running away. The greater the challenge, the better the experience. A Malayalam proverb had declared that a plant grown in fire would not wilt in the sun.

But I had not reached anywhere near a state of total unconcern or nirvana, and therefore the thought that I had been unnecessarily harassed, kept nagging me. If there was any valid reason, I had failed to discover it. It was after many years that I came to know the truth: it was revealed to me by a reliable source that wished to remain anonymous from others. The fact was that the British intelligence in Japan had sent to Delhi (and perhaps to London) via their Shanghai establishment a totally mischievous report on my meeting with Rash Behari Bose in Tokyo earlier in the year. The report said that Rash Behari and I had conspired to perpetrate a bomb attack on the Duke of Gloucester, like the one which Rash Behari had organized against Lord Hardinge in Delhi in 1912. So, I must be placed under constant surveillance during the period of the duke's stay in Kyoto.

A more irresponsible and fraudulent piece of reporting was impossible to imagine. My meeting with Rash Behari was nothing but a courtesy call. It was true that, even though he had adopted Japanese citizenship in order to protect himself from the British, he remained every inch an Indian patriot and was absolutely anti-British throughout his life. But only a mad man would regard Rash Behari to be prone to cause, whether through me or otherwise, the slightest harm to any guest of the country which had given him shelter from his persecutors.

However, such was the result of the mischief of the British Secret Service that surveillance of me was not confined to the occasion of the Gloucester visit to Kyoto. The Political Department of the government of India in New Delhi issued instructions to police all over India, especially Travancore, to detain me if and when I reentered India because I was supposed to be in collaboration with Rash Behari Bose, and hence a potentially dangerous anti-British terrorist like Bose! My family in India was spied upon for any clue as to whether I was returning, and our correspondence was subjected to censorship.

As it happened, it was all a waste of time and effort on the part of the

British. "There's a divinity that shapes our ends / Rough-hew them how we will." My first visit to India (and I was then accompanied by my wife Janaki Nair and my second son Gopalan Nair) took place on September 18, 1958, exactly thirty years after I had boarded the *Suwa Maru* from Colombo for Kobe. By then India had entered the second decade of her independence. The sun had set on the British Empire in August 1947.

CHAPTER TEN
Student Days in Kyoto

Professor Sakakibara was not only a highly gifted teacher but a most hospitable person. His family was equally friendly. I recall with much regret an incident where I momentarily harbored some ill will towards them, purely due to a misunderstanding on my part resulting from ignorance of Japanese custom. Fortunately, I had stopped short of offending them.

After my language sessions, Mrs. Sakakibara would offer me some refreshments, often Japanese sweet cakes and some tea to go with it. One day I was not hungry and therefore could not eat all that had been given me. I left nearly half of the cakes behind on the plate. The housemaid wrapped that up in a piece of paper and said, "Please take this with you; you can have it later at home." Since in India "aristocrats" like me would not partake of any leftover food, I was annoyed when I was given the packet but controlled my temper as long as I was still in the house. Soon after leaving it, however, I threw the package into the nearest waste bin, vociferously damning them!

I related the episode to the Taguchis when I reached home, but to my surprise, instead of showing me any sympathy, everyone appeared highly amused. Mrs. Taguchi told me, "Mr. Nair, you are mistaken: the maid reminded you about the cakes not to denigrate you but as a mark of the family's regard for you. It is part of our custom." I felt quite sheepish, besides being sorry for having misunderstood my kind professor's family. The thought of it disturbed me for a long time. Fortunately, I had not acted offensively in the professor's house itself and that was a consolation. It was sheer misunderstanding and not any ingratitude.

But I should have known better and cursed myself that I had not cared to study Japan's customs and manners fully. I decided to be on my guard against any further faux pas. In fact, on reflection, I realized that I had no excuse even if I were to think of my Indian "aristocracy." I should have known that the remainder of the cakes given to me by the house maid was not really leftover food in the Indian sense. In India, leftovers would be those items of which a part might have been eaten by *others*. Here it was only a case of my having been given in a package part of what had been served only to me and what I could not fully eat immediately. So, there was in fact no justification for my conduct, from the viewpoint of the so-called Indian custom either. Indeed, in my own home in Kerala there was a rule that food should not be wasted. Buddhist culture also exhorted: "Do not be careless about food; do not throw it away." Thus, on all counts, I was wrong, and I felt truly and properly sorry.

I was glad that I had before long established a good reputation in the campus and outside it for my proficiency in Japanese. Even much later in my life, friends would ask me whether I had any special gift for languages. I could not pretend to answer such a question with any certainty, but it would be correct to say that I had not found much difficulty with any foreign language to which I was exposed for a reasonable period. I could also manage a few of the many different languages of my own country, besides my mother tongue. During my travels in Manchukuo, China, Mongolia, Malaya, and Southeast Asian countries, it did not take me too long to acquire a working knowledge of the respective languages so as to be able to conduct my work satisfactorily.

Regarding my Japanese, I recall a not-too-important yet interesting incident. During the "occupation" years, the Nippon Hoso Kyokai (NHK; i.e., the Japan Broadcasting Corporation) often requested me to give radio talks on a variety of subjects (restricted mostly to economic and cultural matters since political discussions were not encouraged) from their Tokyo station. K. K. Chettur, who was head of the Indian Liaison Mission towards the closing stages of the occupation and was later the first Indian ambassador to Japan, was always keen to know what the Japanese language broadcasts were saying, especially in programs related to India. Besides the usual translation service, which of course he had, he was himself gifted with a flair for languages and could understand a little Japanese. (He always kept on his large desk in his office in the Naigai Building a diary with a cover marked in hand *A Japanese Notebook*, in which he would write down some Japanese words or sentences every day and learn them by rote.) I believe it was in 1951 that he was listening

STUDENT DAYS IN KYOTO

in to one of the NHK programs on India in which I was the speaker. He had missed NHK's introduction of me but kept listening until the end when my name was announced again as the author of the broadcast. He could not believe it because it sounded to him as though a Japanese gentleman was speaking, and he was anxious to know who had such intimate knowledge of India. He asked one of his aides to check and was surprised when NHK confirmed that the speaker was A. M. Nair. This was mentioned to me by the very aide who had done the checking. I was of course pleased, but I think the credit should really go to my teachers.

Japanese is a rich language of great elegance. There are many persons in India and elsewhere who erroneously think that it is similar to Chinese. The fact is that these are two different languages. Although Chinese culture generally influenced Japan in the early days, the Japanese have from the beginning had their own indigenous language. Until about the fourth century, it lacked a system of writing. This was remedied by borrowing from the Chinese system but adapting it to serve the needs of the separate linguistic heritage of the Japanese people themselves.

The modifications brought about over the centuries and the various indigenous devices adopted in the process are complicated, and it is not my purpose to discuss them here. Briefly speaking, after learning Chinese, the Japanese substantially used Chinese ideograms, called kanji, to write their language, but retained their own pronunciation instead of the Chinese sounds. As a simple illustration, the ideogram 水 means "water" both in Chinese and Japanese, but whereas the Chinese will read it as *sui*, the Japanese expresses by it the word *mizu*, an entirely different sound. Chinese sounds of particular words may be used in certain phonetic contexts in Japanese as well, but both the sound and the meaning of the borrowed Chinese character are put to totally separate purposes.

Besides, two sets of syllabaries, called katakana and hiragana, with about fifty sound symbols each, are indigenous inventions, the phonetic arrangement of which is believed to bear the direct influence of Sanskrit. These syllabaries are said to have been composed by the Buddhist sage Kobo Daishi, founder of the Shingon (True Word) sect and who had also introduced the Vajrayana cult into Japanese Buddhism. Thus, although Japanese contains numerous Chinese characters, the two languages as such are quite distinct from each other.

Even though one of the most complex of languages, Japanese is marvelous in its delicacy of sound and politeness of expression. The vocabulary is vast, and its vitality is maintained by a constant process of updating so as to include, as and when the need arises, any new words which may be required to express fresh concepts. A major characteristic of the language is its system of honorifics which traditionally grew along with the society's hierarchical structure. There are special vocabulary repertoires where the presence or absence of honorifics would reflect the nuances of social rank. Such conventions of speech, peculiar to the Japanese people, render the language somewhat difficult to translate or interpret with exactitude.

While on the subject, I would like my readers to know that excepting India, there is probably no other country in the world where the learning of Sanskrit is pursued by so many students and with so much enthusiasm as in Japan. I have mentioned Professor Sakakibara's respect for the Indian scholar of Sanskrit, Ganapati Sastri from Trivandrum. Both of them of course belonged to a high plane of erudition, but there are thousands of Japanese who know at least rudimentary Sanskrit, and also Pali. All major Japanese universities have a department of Indian philosophy engaged in the study of mainly these two languages. They have published several books of high quality on various aspects of India's culture and civilization. Unfortunately, because of their ignorance of the Japanese language, very few Indians seem to know how much work on Indian philosophy is done by Japanese Indologists. For instance, Professor Kogen Mizuno of Komazawa University has published many valuable works on Buddhism from the original Pali, and Professor Akira Hirakawa of Tokyo University is a specialist in the study of the Vinaya Pitaka. In Kyoto University, in recent years, Professor Ashikaga has edited a portion of the Sukhavativyuha Sutra, based on the discovery of a unique manuscript.

In my college classes, all the lectures were in Japanese, except that many of the technical words, and also the roneoed material distributed to the students, were in one or another of a number of foreign languages also, e.g., German, English, or French, depending on the linguistic attainments of the professor concerned. I always used the Japanese versions of the lectures, combined with technical words in English.

The university curriculum was heavy. There was much work to do, and there were no shortcuts; every credit had to be earned with the sweat of one's brow. During my "breaking-in" period, when lack of knowledge of the Japanese language was a handicap, I had to keep my nose really down to the grinding wheel. But once the language barrier was successfully crossed, life became much easier. From then on, I was able not only to get into the mainstream of the academic routine without slogging, but also to find time to feel my way around in extramural activities. A superficial adjustment to the environment and a mere skimming of the surface no longer provided satisfaction.

The urge to get behind the scenes and to understand in fuller measure what made this nation what it was, was irresistible. Here was a country that, in a matter of about a mere half-century, had progressed from a basically feudal setup to the status of a great economic and political power. How did it achieve the transformation? Surely here was an extraordinary national psychology at work, producing rapid results. If Japan could do what she did, why should India at least not be able to break free from its colonial shackles?

The teacher-student rapport at the university was fully in tune with the *guru-shishya* relationship of the old days in India. Unfortunately, the concept had begun to fade in India, but it remained abundantly in evidence in Japan. It was like the bond between parents and children. The teacher regarded it as his duty to see that when the student finished his studies he went out into the world as a complete person, well disciplined, with a strong awareness of civic duties, and eager and confident to do a job of work with a sense of pride in performance.

Within the student community, a strong spirit of camaraderie prevailed, and it outlasted the campus life. The "old-school tie" would normally remain intact for a lifetime, regardless of the vocation which the students took up and of even the different political ideologies they might individually follow. It is this bond which is implied in the Japanese expression *gakkobatsu*, and which in its broadest sense also covers the alumni's permanent affection for their alma mater. I still remember vividly every one of my thirty-six fellow students in the engineering faculty of the Kyoto University of my days. Unfortunately, some of them are no more, but those of us who are still alive remain in touch with one another.

The university atmosphere was peaceful and congenial to serious academic study, but that did not mean that the students pursued no other interests. In fact, there was a good deal of political awareness among them, although they generally felt hesitant to voice their views freely except during intimate and personal get-togethers of close friends. The inhibition was due to the increasing control of civilian life by the military which was undoubtedly becoming stronger.

Moreover, the people, whether students or others, were (and to a great extent still are) by nature rather taciturn, and it took time to get them to speak out their minds. But once mutual confidence was established, an abiding rapport followed. I was fortunate to be able to develop lasting personal good relations not only with my fellow students but also with many persons of importance in the political field. I would associate myself with all groups, without regard to their particular ideological persuasions. My relationship

CHAPTER TEN

with them was what might be called "vertical," as distinct from "horizontal," the latter being always fraught with the risk that one might unwittingly tread on the toes of someone or other. My purpose was to steer a completely unbiased course as far as Japan's internal politics was concerned, and yet avail myself of every opportunity to convert as many of the Japanese people as possible to an anti-British and pro-Indian persuasion which I felt was my main extracurricular duty.

I had however to be careful. For instance, "colonialism" was not quite a popular expression in Japan. After emerging as a major power in the world, Japan itself had started entertaining expansionist ambitions, having already annexed Korea and also some islands in the Pacific, notably Formosa. To get over terminological difficulties arising from such realities, I would speak of British "exploitation" instead of colonialism. Such a distinction, which was indeed very subtle, and really did not amount to any difference, seemed nevertheless to have a more favorable psychological impact on the listeners.

Besides serving as Japan's cultural capital, Kyoto has seen the origin and growth of various important shades of sociopolitical thought. The rightist movement and its influence were naturally predominant, but there were minority leftist groups as well, including communists of the "theorist" category. For instance, the famous Hajime Kawakami, professor of economics at Kyoto University just before my time, was a proponent of Marxist theory. And the late prince Fumimaro Konoe, a former prime minister—who committed suicide on hearing the emperor's announcement of Japan's unconditional surrender—had enrolled at Kyoto University in order to study under Professor Kawakami, to whom should be credited the late prince's socialist molding.

Eminent university professors enjoyed high public prestige, and they were practically immune from the pressures which the military authorities brought to bear on lesser persons. These professors were by and large "theorists," but a number of their students were potential activists. Many of them had quietly joined together and founded the Japanese Communist Party in 1922, to the consternation of the central government in Tokyo. The latter's anxiety appeared to reach a near-panic point in the wake of the general elections of 1928. Voting rights for these elections were far more broad-based than the franchise system which had existed until then, and the result was the surfacing of a number of previously dormant differences of political views among the people. Even the rightist groups were more or less evenly split, the ruling Seiyukai securing only a marginal edge over the opposition Minseito. It was evident that there was a polarization of party affiliations. The non-rightist parties were not able to secure any significant number of seats, but it was of interest that almost half a million votes had been cast in favor of leftist candidates.

Within weeks of the election, Prime Minister Giichi Tanaka of the Seiyukai Party ordered the arrest of practically all the leading communist leaders, about one thousand in number. Those who were arrested included men like Kyuichi Tokuda and Sanzo Nosaka who were to play an important part in the frontlines of the post-World War II history of the Japanese Communist Party. I mention this episode not so much because of any intrinsic importance of it at that time as an isolated event, but because it is reminiscent of the age-old mistrust between Russia and Japan. Russia had turned communist in the wake of its revolution of 1917, and the expansion of its new ideology was one of the fears entertained by several countries, including Japan.

It is also interesting to note that Prime Minister Giichi Tanaka, who decided to detain the communist elements after the election, was a retired army general. He had conducted the Siberian war in which Russia was defeated. He was also the founder of the Tokumu Kikan, the branch of the army engaged in intelligence operations. It was not surprising in the circumstances that the government was anxious to nip in the bud any potential large incursion of leftist philosophy into its system. To this day, Russia and Japan, despite the existence of a state of "normal relations," unfortunately do not see eye to eye on many issues, political and otherwise.

Military training was part of the university life of all Japanese students, but as a foreign student I was not under any such compulsion. I never took part in the drills or allied activities. The training unit, of which every educational institution had one, was normally headed by an officer of the rank of colonel. The head of the unit at Kyoto University was one Colonel Terada. Although these army officers were expected to be under the administrative control of the president of the institution concerned, it was not unusual to see them in practice functioning as though they were responsible only to the military high command. Some of them would tend to be arrogant and to throw their weight about, a natural human weakness under the circumstances. A number of my fellow students attributed a similar quality to Colonel Terada as well. But I, at least as one not involved in military training, always found him and his staff to be pleasant and friendly. We would often have useful discussions where my main subject of conversation would be India and the injustices my country suffered under alien rule.

There was no doubt that the army was rapidly gaining more and more control in Japanese administration at all levels. But as far as I was concerned, the military units, whether engaged in training duties in educational

CHAPTER TEN

institutions or otherwise, could well be a fertile field in which to sow seeds of anti-British propaganda in the cause of India's freedom struggle. Rash Behari Bose knew how to utilize his opportunities with the higher civilian echelons where he was well-known and highly respected. I decided to follow suit to the extent possible vis-à-vis the circles easily within my reach. For the time being the military units provided favorable ground for my propaganda and publicity work. Among those with whom I was in close association was General Yamamoto, commander of the 8th Division of the army stationed in Fushimi, a suburb of Kyoto.

My efforts soon began to yield agreeable results. Demands from various quarters for lectures on Indian affairs progressively increased and took up practically all my spare time. Since I was fortunate to enjoy robust health and the capacity for sustained work for long hours, I was able to go through every one of the engagements. And I tried to create more opportunities whenever possible, taking pains simultaneously to gather information on India from all possible sources for use during my talks. These brought me a good deal of popularity as a student seriously involved in the Indian freedom movement. My background in India, where the British had unsuccessfully tried to arrest me, became increasingly known in Japanese political circles. News of my encounter with the Japanese Tokko (special police task force) during the coronation ceremony also began to spread, evoking much general sympathy for me.

Seeing Japan's preeminent position in Asia, my mind would continually dwell on the sorry plight of my own country, which was still groaning under foreign domination. There was no doubt that Japan's growing power was leading her to an expansionist policy, but recalling my own thinking during those days, I must say that I was less concerned about such a situation than with my desire to utilize what I felt was an opportunity to mobilize Japanese sympathy for India's freedom movement. The work which Rash Behari Bose had already started in Japan was a source of constant inspiration. Although my first preoccupation had necessarily to be with my classroom work, the desire to emulate Rash Behari in his work for India progressively became intense.

From my second year at the university until the end of my studies there, I missed no meeting where Asian or Indian affairs were discussed. Those occasions not merely served to enlarge my sphere of friendship with my contemporaries at college, including teachers, but helped me to come in contact with a number of Japanese organizations engaged in vigorous pursuit of their own nationalist policy. It must be obvious to anyone who has participated in freedom movements that patriotism, wherever it may originate, has a snowballing effect. The impact of the environment in such cases is invariably strong.

The more I saw of the nationalist spirit of the Japanese people, the more I felt inspired in my activities in the cause of India. There were several Indian patriots living abroad yet working for their country's liberation. I viewed my propaganda and other work among the Japanese circles as a similar contribution to the common purpose.

From the sixth year of Showa (corresponding to 1931) when I was in my third year at the university, I began receiving more and more invitations to speak at gatherings of various organizations, particularly those specializing in the study of Asian affairs. To be able to utilize these opportunities to good effect, I tried my best to keep in touch with happenings in my country and abroad, and also had occasional contact with Rash Behari through whom I could obtain much valuable material as well as guidance. Within the campus, it was of course necessary to keep my anti-British propaganda relatively low key in order not to violate the university discipline. But I conducted my campaign more vigorously whenever venues were available outside. Among them were the military establishments.

There was no racial or other type of discrimination in the university or elsewhere in Japan during my college days. Yet, where Koreans were concerned, whether in the student circles or elsewhere, some psychological barrier seemed to exist that could be noticed by anyone who cared to observe closely. This was a byproduct of Korea's status as a dependency of Japan, and human nature being what it was, both sides exhibited the kind of complex that was inherent in such situations. I had a number of very close friends among the Korean students, some of whom were brilliant. There was a certain sense of nervousness among them, and some of them would warn me against speaking anything about Japan's relationship with Korea. It was easy to understand their anxiety. I have already referred to the practice I had learned to adopt of avoiding the word colonialism during my talks before Japanese audiences. Discretion was always the better part of valor.

Another memory of my university days does not pertain to the student world but is related to a Japanese business house with which I happened to have contact under an unusual circumstance.

There was a standing arrangement for me to receive twenty US dollars every month from my home in India for my expense in Kyoto. That was equal to about 70 yen monthly, which was ample. For unavoidable reasons, the remittance would occasionally get delayed, and my friends would help me out temporarily until my money came. There was no opportunity for students during my time for part-time remunerative work to augment their financial resources. It occurred to me therefore to try to build up some reserve against

CHAPTER TEN

unexpected contingencies by attempting some commercial trade. My brother, Narayanan Nair, had become director of fisheries in Trivandrum and was anxious to try out Indian trepangs (sea slugs) in the Japanese market, since he had established that the two varieties were of equally good quality. He sent me a sample consignment, and I gladly agreed to promote sales. A first-rate trading company in Kobe to whom I showed the specimen liked the quality and ordered some large quantity on promise of a reasonable price.

Accordingly, I imported some tonnage of trepangs from Travancore. But suddenly the firm went back on its price quotation and offered about one-tenth of what had been agreed. I reliably learned that it did so because in its view I, a mere student, and therefore a novice in commercial deals, could easily be exploited. In my youthful spirit I felt this to be an affront to my national pride and self-respect, and in a fit of anger, dumped the whole consignment in the sea, incurring a heavy loss. I informed my brother about what I had done. It could not have pleased him, obviously, but I did not feel sorry. Conceivably, some others might have thought and acted differently, but my reasoning was that since I had never gone back on my word with anyone, there was no reason why anyone should do so towards me.

All my friends to whom I narrated this story appreciated my action and agreed that I had done well to adhere to a point of principle, even though by doing so I had suffered financially. The episode served me as a further step in understanding human psychology. There were always persons trying to take undue advantage, but one had to stand up to them without fear of the consequences. The firm which had let me down apologized eventually, but it was too late to make good the damage.

Generally speaking, the enduring memories of my life at Kyoto University are all happy ones. Even to this day I feel that I was fortunate to have had the opportunity to be an alumnus of this great institution. To start with, I had the privilege of enjoying the personal care and attention of the great Dr. Sakakibara, the affable Taguchis, and the rest of the teachers. Towards the end I became an intimate friend of the highly rated army divisional commander General Yamamoto. Through the latter, I was able to evoke among a good cross section of the Japanese elite a keen awareness of conditions in India under the British, and consequently enlist their sympathy for India's freedom struggle. Because of my friendship with General Yamamoto, who practically treated me as a brother, I was, I should like to think, able to secure much moral support from the armed services, especially the younger groups in them. I felt elated when General Yamamoto insisted, as he always did, that I should sit next to him during the meetings which I had been invited to address.

In the seventh year of Showa (corresponding to 1932), I graduated as a civil engineer from Kyoto University. As practical experience was essential in order to round off my studies, I joined an engineering firm in Osaka called Kurimoto and Co., and worked with them for nearly a year, before coming to yet another major turning point in my life.

CHAPTER ELEVEN
1932–33, A New Turning Point

After leaving university, the constraints invariably applying to campus life no longer inhibited my political activities. I could express myself more freely, more openly, and, what was perhaps most important, more boldly. My circle of Japanese friends, both in the armed forces and among civilians, became far wider. Anti-British propaganda and publicity work was shifted into a higher gear. I met larger numbers of people, addressed meetings more often, and wrote articles on India for various Japanese magazines. One of such journals was the *Aryan*, published by the Hindustani faculty of the University of Foreign Languages at Osaka. I toured the country as much as possible in pursuit of my campaign of mobilizing Japanese opinion behind the freedom movement in India.

My memory often goes back to some of my public lectures during 1932–33. I was of course employed as a responsible engineer, but that was so recently that I thought I could for the time being still pass off as a student—or in any case, as a student apprentice. During my public lecture meetings, therefore, I put on a student's uniform, intuitively feeling that by being so attired, I could expect greater sympathy from the audience than by appearing before them as a company employee. The result, I must say, was as I had expected. The audience would generally express astonishment at the audacity of a "student" openly conducting frontal verbal attacks on British domination of India. In bewilderment, some of them would remark, in characteristic Japanese fashion, "Here is a *real* man!" Needless to say, I would feel happy about such compliments, and to a certain extent even proud, although never to the point of any vanity.

I think the Japanese traditional trait of self-discipline and modesty in public behavior had so "infected" me during my university days that I could shield myself from self-adulation or any boastful posture. It was important to do one's duty, but there was no need to show off or appear to do so. In retrospect, I believe that I chose the right approach. The friendships developed during those days between me and important personages among the Japanese people were strong and enduring and have stood the test of time even until this day. A particularly happy memory is that of my close association with one of the greatest Shinto high priests of the period, by name Sengei. He held a high Order of Merit conferred by the emperor. Shintoism, which was the state religion, had a powerful influence on political life. The Venerable Sengei and I were often invited to conduct lecture meetings together, and we addressed the audience from the same platform in Nakanoshima where he lived.

In India, events on the national front had gathered momentum. I have already referred to the nationalists' decision to boycott the Simon Commission on constitutional reforms, established in 1928. The commission plodded on without making any worthwhile progress. By 1931, the congress had called for a nationwide boycott of the British-controlled provincial and central legislatures. Simultaneously, a program of civil disobedience had been launched. Gandhiji and other leaders were imprisoned, but the viceroy, Lord Irwin, realized before long that repression would no longer improve matters for Britain in India. The détenus were soon released from jail, and an agreement was reached between Gandhiji and Irwin to discuss issues of constitutional reforms at a round table conference in London. Pending the result, the congress stayed its program of defiance of the British-made laws.

But the roundtable conference was not a success. Britain rejected Gandhiji's demand for *purna swaraj* (complete independence). Indian nationalism began burning again, and in retaliation the British officers reverted to a reign of repression. The congress leaders were again jailed. The India League in London sent a delegation to India, and it included Bertrand Russell who, after studying the situation, made the vitriolic observation that while there had been "no lack of interest in the misdeeds of the Nazis in Germany... [f]ew people in England realise that misdeeds quite as serious are being perpetrated by the British in India."

I had an abundance of material to publicize India's pathetic plight, and there was much sympathetic response from the Japanese public. On one occasion I gave my audience at a public meeting the gist of an article I had read in an English magazine. It had said that the agricultural production of the British Isles was only enough to meet the needs of their people for 41 days in a year. For the remaining period they depended on food imported from their colonies, especially India, at unfair prices for the producers. Also, when several Indians were starving for want of wheat or rice, English families were growing roses in their gardens, with income extorted from India. Moreover, British rule in India was the rule of the bayonet. Some 1,500 Englishmen rolling in luxury controlled millions of starving people in India by means of terror and repression channeled through an army and a police force whom they treated as their slaves.

Meanwhile, Sino-Japanese relations were worsening rapidly. There were disputes relating to leases of land between Chinese and Koreans (who were "Japanese-protected persons"). China revived anti-Japanese boycott, and her relations with Japan touched a new low when in July 1931 Shintaro Nakamura, a Japanese army captain travelling incognito in China was killed by some Chinese soldiers. Before the end of the year, a state of crisis had been reached, sparked by the Mukden Incident of September 18, 1931. A bomb explosion took place on the South Manchurian Railway line, and Japanese troops—whom some sources blame for having themselves engineered the blast—at once moved against the Chinese troops, on the plea that it was a move calculated to undermine their security. Soon afterwards the Japanese army, headquartered in the leased territory of Kwantung, occupied various strategic points in Manchuria, even without any prior authorization from the Minseito government in Tokyo headed by Prime Minister Wakatsuki.

It is not my purpose in this book to go into the details of the pros and cons of the Japanese army's actions in Manchuria, nor into the merits of the Battle of Shanghai of January 1932 which was essentially a bid by the Japanese navy to emulate the victories of their army counterpart. Suffice it to say that there was much confusion in China, especially Manchuria, during the period. Japanese belligerency in relation to Manchuria had a background of considerable encouragement from the supporters of a policy of promoting military power. Among them was the famous Cherry Blossom Society founded in 1931 consisting mainly of army officers. The political parties, the zaibatsu, and the civilian bureaucracy were all blamed for the people's hardships, which were especially severe in the wake of the world recession of 1929. The depression of 1926 and the unprecedented catastrophe of the earthquake of 1923, when a near-famine situation gripped the country, were still in many people's memory. These, combined with a bulging population, had created a general tempo

1932–33, A NEW TURNING POINT

of extreme dissatisfaction among the masses, which the militarists exploited to their advantage.

In foreign relations, the government resented the framework of the Washington Conference of 1921–22 and the London Naval Conference of 1930, both of which were regarded as unfair to Japan. There was also serious protest against the United States immigration policy, which was discriminatory against Japan. Altogether, the feeling had been gradually building up among the Japanese people that they, although in no way inferior to the Western nations in progress, were being unfairly treated due to racial prejudice. There is no doubt that the Japanese action in Manchuria was preplanned and that it reflected the expansionist policy on which Japan had clearly embarked by the end of the 1920s. But the military's propaganda machine had succeeded in indoctrinating the people into believing that in entertaining extraterritorial ambitions, Japan was in no way wrong when compared with Western countries. It was not for the pot to call the kettle black.

* * *

I had intended to return to India at the end of about a year of work with the Osaka firm, but before the period was through, I received information from my home in Kerala and from other sources, that every bit of my anti-British work was being promptly reported to India by the British intelligence organization in Japan and that I stood a real risk of detention the moment I set foot in my country. I have mentioned earlier that correspondence between me and my family was being censored. In one of his letters, my brother Narayanan Nair had told me that my letters were being delivered to him by police constables, instead of by postmen.

It was by no means a comfortable position. Luckily my brothers had so much personal influence with the authorities concerned that the latter would unofficially tip them off beforehand whenever the dewan in Trivandrum received instructions from the Political Department in New Delhi to search their homes for any incriminating clues about me. Once, a date had been fixed for a raid on the houses of all my family members in Trivandrum and Neyyattinkara. My brothers and uncles, having had prior information from the officers themselves, quietly hid all evidence: letters, photographs, or whatever, so that the police would have no difficulty in reporting that they found nothing. In fact, a photograph of mine was in one of the rooms that

CHAPTER ELEVEN

was searched: it had merely been placed behind a mirror. The police officer looked into the mirror, but did not look behind it. My brother was obviously playing a practical joke on the good police chief. An expert in psychology, he rightly assumed that a person seeing a mirror would ordinarily be interested only in its front!

While on this part of my story, I must record with regret that in December 1939, when my mother died, the then dewan—Sir C. P. Ramaswamy Iyer—was said to have advised my brothers, Kumaran Nair and Narayanan Nair, that they and their relatives should cut off all connections with me. After the partition of my *tharavad*, I had some properties in Neyyattinkara in my own name, and when my mother died, a part of her property also fell to my share. If I were declared dead, all those would belong to the "surviving" members of the family. Some members of my house, whose evidence was apparently acceptable to the authorities, gave signed statements that I had died: accordingly, all my belongings in India derived from my *tharavad* and from my mother, were in fact distributed among the "living" members.

I have difficulty in believing that a person like Sir C. P. Ramaswamy Iyer, reported to be a good administrator, would have given any such advice. If he in fact did, I am at a loss to see why. Had I chosen to do so, I could have probed into this matter and instituted punitory proceedings against the culprits, but to this day I have taken no action against anybody on this account. It was however something of a shock to know that there were persons in my own family who could descend to mean levels. Human nature is sometimes unpredictable.

* * *

Before the end of 1931, virtually the whole of Manchuria came under Japanese control. World reaction was generally unfavorable to Japan. Nationalist leaders in India were among those who disapproved the Japanese action: quite naturally, because they were fighting British colonialism in India and viewed distastefully any signs of imperialism or expansionism elsewhere too. The Kwantung Army however was unconcerned about criticism. It decided to establish Manchuria as a state independent of China.

Puyi, the last emperor of the Qing dynasty who had been deposed in 1912, was living in Tientsin (Tianjin). Under orders from General Shigeru Honjo, commander of the Kwantung Army, Colonel Seishiro Itagaki went there and managed to take Puyi to Changchun (later renamed as Hsingking, or "New

Capital") in Manchuria. The conquered territory was proclaimed as a new state by the name of Manchukuo, on March 1, 1932. Puyi was made the regent. On March 1, 1934, he was invested with the title "emperor," and the Republic of Manchukuo was transformed into a monarchy.

These developments undoubtedly perturbed the USA as well as other western nations, but the former chose to do no more than adopt a policy of "nonrecognition." In China, violent demonstrations took place, and the Japanese community in Shanghai, numbering some 30,000, anticipated danger to their persons and properties. At the request of Mamoru Shigemitsu, who was then minister there, War Minister Yoshinori Shirakawa in Tokyo dispatched to Shanghai a force of three army divisions and a naval fleet under Admiral Kichisaburo Nomura. After a few days of severe fighting, the Japanese forces drove the Chinese troops out of Shanghai.

An aircraft, supposed to be Chinese, was shot down by the Japanese. It was discovered later that it was an American plane painted with the Chinese flag and piloted by an American. When this news was published, I was sitting in the house of Mr. Franklin, an American Presbyterian missionary, in a place called Tanaka near Kyoto University. Mr. Franklin, a pacifist by his own reckoning, was surprised, and said that it was the first time that an American was shot down by an Asian. I replied that it was also probably the first time that an American had died for trying to deceive Asians, and that every time such deception was practiced in future, the result could be the same. Mr. Franklin remarked that the American government was not involved, and that the pilot was only a volunteer. I ended the conversation by saying that in wars there could always be any number of excuses, and that anything could happen.

Meanwhile, on December 10, 1931, the League of Nations had appointed a commission to enquire into the Manchukuo episode, with the Earl of Lytton of Great Britain as chairman, and a member each from Italy, France, the United States and Germany. The Japanese government extended facilities to the commission to carry out the work entrusted to it, but there was a large cross section of rightist elements in Japan which opposed the very appointment of the Lytton Commission. Among the prominent leaders of such opposition was Dr. Shumei Okawa of the Jinmukai, the famous ultranationalist who had, it was said, organized the May 15 Incident in which Prime Minister Tsuyoshi Inukai was assassinated.

It was a remarkable feature of Japanese politics of the time that many of the extreme right-wing nationalists, who were determined to preserve the concept of the emperor's divinity and Japan's military strength and were

CHAPTER ELEVEN

considered dangerous, were men of great learning and personal integrity. Shumei Okawa of the Jinmukai, whom I knew very well and who had taken a liking to me, was one of such people. He held two doctorate degrees from Tokyo University, one in philosophy (including Indian philosophy) and another in politics. He was a friend of India. He and Rash Behari Bose were associates in the Indian freedom movement, and it was in this context that my relationship with him became close.

Similar was the backdrop to my intimate friendship with Mitsuru Toyama who had established the Genyosha (Dark Ocean Society) in 1881, and with Ryohei Uchida, founder of the Kokuryukai (Black Dragon Society) in 1901. They were the most powerful leaders of Japanese belligerency, but there were several others heading organizations dedicated to the same cause. I kept in touch with all of them since opposition to Britain was a strong link amongst all of them and I could profitably utilize that common denominator for my own work for the Indian freedom movement.

The appointment of the Lytton Commission to enquire into the Manchukuo problem was one of the occasions when the right-wing organizations, especially those of Mitsuru Toyama and Shumei Okawa, let loose a campaign of agitation against the Western powers in the League of Nations. They held them responsible for interference with Japan's affairs in Asia, where western powers, who were mostly colonialists anyway, had no business to investigate anything. Few may agree with their thinking, but no one could doubt their sincerity of conviction.

The anti-Lytton Commission agitation launched by Shumei Okawa was the biggest exhibition of anti-West feeling witnessed in Kyoto up to 1931–32. I joined several demonstrations against the Commission and spoke at a large number of meetings to encourage the agitations. The thrust of my speeches was not calculated to lend any support for Japan's conquest of Manchuria but was related to the futility of countries represented on the commission trying to resolve a problem which had best be settled by Asian countries themselves. And I emphasized that Lord Lytton, chairman of the commission, was from the country that was holding India in bondage. Such a man was unsuitable to deal with the Manchurian problem. My theme, "Asia for Asians," went down very well, not only among the right-wing organizations but with other sections of the Japanese public as well. Of course, I was aware all the time that my stocks with British intelligence were rapidly sliding lower and lower.

* * *

A few prominent Indian revolutionaries, besides Rash Behari Bose, had visited Japan after the First World War relatively briefly and done much good work for the Indian independence campaign. Among them were Barkatullah, Lajpat Rai, and Raja Mahendra Pratap. I had no opportunity to meet the first two, but I came in contact with Raja Mahendra Pratap in 1930 when I was still at Kyoto University.

Mahendra Pratap had the reputation of being the first Indian to organize a provisional government of independent India in Kabul, in 1915. He was among the early Indian patriots who worked for Indian independence from outside the country. He was in Europe in the early stage of World War I, and later went to Afghanistan where he was given protection and also Afghan citizenship. It was a matter of faith with him that, whenever he appeared in public, he would stress the fact that he was an Afghan citizen, obviously to express his gratitude to the country which had sheltered him from British reprisal. During my initial acquaintance with him in Kyoto, we had several long discussions mainly dealing with Indian problems, and with his own program of mobilizing support for Indian independence through extensive tours which would enable him to tap many sources.

He was a great traveler, and his amiable personality won him many friends. Often his background as an erstwhile Indian prince was of help. I had serious doubts about the practicability of his program for the mobilization of a world army or even an Asian army to fight Britain; however, no one could doubt Mahendra Pratap' sincerity of purpose and courage of conviction. Although expediency had forced him to adopt Afghan citizenship, he was, in his heart of hearts, a true Indian and a genuine patriot. He had fairly good contacts among the Japanese leaders and did his best, in spite of his lack of knowledge of the Japanese language, to promote Japanese interest in the Indian independence movement. His occasional attempts to use broken Japanese sentences during his lectures were brave and well intentioned. The errors he invariably made were pardonable when viewed in the light of his enthusiasm to get his points across to the Japanese public.

It was during the anti-Lytton Commission agitation in the Kansai region that I met him for the second time. Some Japanese and Indian friends had organized a large meeting in Osaka's Nakanoshima Hall, which had the most spacious auditorium in western Japan. A vast audience had gathered, and it was difficult to recognize the faces of even friends and acquaintances. But I noticed Raja Mahendra Pratap among the audience easily, because he was one of the few Indians and his impressive black beard could not be missed. I was to be the main speaker, and as usual, my subject was British-exploited India.

CHAPTER ELEVEN

I think I was in my full element. With my fluency in Japanese, and the excellent audience response, I let myself go. I was never at a loss for verbal broadsides against the British. Surely British intelligence was watching, but I did not pause to worry about it. Many Japanese leaders and friends congratulated me; so too did Raja Mahendra Pratap, with whom my contact thereafter became more frequent. A bond of personal friendship developed between us, even though in our approach to the conduct of work for the liberation of India there was a fundamental divergence of views.

At a meeting related to the Indian independence movement. Front row, from left: the author, in student uniform; A. M. Sahay; and Raja Mahendra Pratap.

Mahendra Pratap, I felt, was an idealist, without a sense of realism. A good man, and indisputably sincere in his anxiety to see India free, he was nevertheless a dreamer with a penchant, as Jawaharlal Nehru is said to have once remarked about him, "to build castles in the air." He would hold forth vehemently on the merits of his theory of liberating India from the British with the help of a voluntary Asian army which he was sure he could mobilize during his tours in Japan, Southeast Asia, China, Mongolia, Tibet, and so on. I could never find myself in agreement with him on such a scheme. In my view, Indians should fight their battles with their own manpower, although, from the nature of the handicaps, it was necessary to obtain help from all possible sources.

I recall in this connection some of the frank talks I had with fellow students from China and Korea and even with Japanese friends. None of them had anything but friendly feelings for India and sympathy for the sorry plight of my country; yet it was my firm conviction that the prospect of an armed fight against British imperialism by overseas Indians, whether on their own or with men of any other nationalities, was not merely conceptually wrong but unworkable. In fact, some of my Japanese fellow students themselves used to caution me about Japan's potentiality for aggression if her military policies of the time proceeded unchecked. And, surely, India did not want British imperialism to be replaced by any possible Japanese expansionism. When Raja Mahendra Pratap spoke about an "Asian army," he had really no clear perception as to the shape it would take. Yet, as I said, I admired him for his patriotism.

CHAPTER TWELVE
In Manchukuo

Both the Manchurian episode and the Lytton Commission were in a sense tests of the system of collective security which the League of Nations was to protect and preserve. Japan's action in Manchuria and the creation of Manchukuo were, of course, not indicative of much strength for the League of Nations. The commission, undoubtedly, did a great deal of work, although the result of its toils did not fulfill the league's expectations. As I have already mentioned, agitation against it began in Japan almost simultaneously with its creation. The commission visited Japan and had meetings with Foreign Minister Kenkichi Yoshizawa and War Minister Sadao Araki, thereafter it went to Manchukuo for discussions with Puyi and the Kwantung Army chief, General Shigeru Honjo. It also had a stint in Peking.

A remarkable feature of the commission's report was that while in the main it virtually accused the Kwantung Army of aggression in Manchuria and China, it recognized that Japan had certain special prerogatives and rights in the territory. Nevertheless, in the final analysis, the commission did not recommend acceptance of the status of Manchukuo as an independent state outside the suzerainty of China. Japan objected to such a finding, and when the League of Nations Assembly voted for the adoption of the report, the Japanese delegation headed by Yosuke Matsuoka staged a walkout. On March 27, 1933, Japan pulled out of the league.

Another significant aspect of the Manchukuo story and the deliberations on the Lytton Commission's report was that those countries that condemned Japan for her action were mostly the smaller ones. The United States which was not a member of the league, made a show of staunch opposition, but apparently was not particularly worried about Manchukuo. It was perhaps more interested in her own interests in China and in the erstwhile Manchuria. France and Britain, with substantial stakes in China, more or less adopted a similar stance.

In fact, Britain's attitude was ambiguous, an understandable position when one remembers that with what she had done in various parts of the world, especially in India, she could possibly not have a clean conscience when considering Japan's action in Manchuria. On September 16, 1932, a few weeks before the League of Nations Assembly was to discuss the Lytton Commission's report, the London newspaper *The Times*, an acknowledged mouthpiece of the British government, virtually absolved Japan when it said editorially that

> What Japan did in Shanghai found little support in this country; but her position in Manchuria is very different. Her economic interests there are vital to the prosperity of a rapidly increasing population; she saved the country from Russia at the beginning of this century; she has since protected it from the chaos and anarchy which have beset other parts of China. She legitimately acquired economic rights, which were illegitimately obstructed by the Chinese; and she failed through long, patient means to obtain redress by diplomatic means. It can be argued with some force that the rules of conduct which the League lays down are not equally applicable in every part of the world; but the point is apt to be ignored in the Assembly, where all states are in a general way presumed to be equal, and all members are assumed to have reached approximately the same stage of evolution.

Even during the discussions in the league's meetings, the British secretary of state, Sir John Simon, and the delegate from Canada criticized China more than Japan.

Meanwhile, in April 1932, there was trouble in Tokyo. On the 29th of that month, which was Emperor Hirohito's birth anniversary, a Korean hurled a bomb against the dais where Admiral Nomura (commander of the Shanghai action), Shirakawa, and Shigemitsu were seated. While Nomura was unhurt, Shigemitsu was injured in his right leg, which had later to be amputated, and Shirakawa died in May.

CHAPTER TWELVE

In the summer of 1933, I received a message in Osaka from Gunta Nagao, who had been my contemporary at Kyoto University in the political science faculty. We had graduated in the same year and were close friends. Nagao had been given an important assignment in Manchukuo, along with some of our other fellow students of the same year (in different faculties) to assist in the setting up of the new Manchukuo administration, based on the principle of *gozoku kyowa*, or "Five Races Under One Union." The five main "races" living in Manchukuo were: Japanese, Koreans, Chinese, Manchus, and Mongols. The government was to be backed by an organization of representatives of these five races, formed into an association called the Kyowakai (Concordia Association). Nagao was one of the chief architects of this party structure and was an ardent opponent of the Lytton Commission. He had, even at the time of his appointment, asked me to go with him and collaborate in his work, but I had preferred to stay in Osaka and conduct my anti-Lytton agitation from the Kansai region. But when he asked me again in 1933, I decided to accept his invitation.

My status in Manchukuo was that of a state guest. I could stay in Hsinking (Changchun) or any other place I chose. I would not be subject to any specific work schedule and would only help and advise the Manchukuo government whenever needed. For the rest, I could function howsoever I wished and carry on my anti-British activities in whatever manner I thought appropriate. Even though the Lytton Commission had nearly completed its work by the latter part of 1933, and it was becoming clear that Japan was going to withdraw from the League of Nations in protest against the commission's report, Nagao thought it would be advisable to have me in Manchukuo, particularly to organize a large Asian conference in Dairen (Dalian).

* * *

The purpose of the conference was to mobilize Asian support and serve as a counterpoise to the continued anti-Japanese activities of the major Western countries, who were interested in augmenting their strength in China to the detriment of Japan's. Shumei Okawa encouraged me to go, and I decided to do so. Raja Mahendra Pratap, who heard about my program, told me that he was keen to visit Manchukuo also, and sought my assistance. Through Nagao I secured an invitation for him and was happy that on my recommendation he too was offered state-guest treatment.

My first action in Hsinking was to establish an organization there to do publicity for India by means of pamphlets, newsletters, etc., and to conduct propaganda against Britain for its crime of holding India in slavery. Both Mahendra Pratap and I also undertook extensive tours to strengthen the campaign through public meetings and contacts with the various nationality groups. We took care not to rub the Japanese up the wrong side; in fact, we had no intention to interfere with the work of the Japanese or the other participants in the Manchukuo administration. Our concern was strictly limited to that of promoting the Indian freedom movement.

At Harbin, Manchukuo, in 1933. From left: Colonel Lee of Korea, attached to the Manchukuo Army; Raja Mahendra Pratap; and the author.

There was general sympathy for our cause from the Kyowakai. The Mongols, we noticed, were rather noncommitted; but eventually we secured their support also. I was able to acquire an adequate knowledge of Mongolian dialects, in addition to Chinese, and that helped a great deal. Mahendra Pratap too attempted to learn, but, as it happened, I had greater success, presumably because I was much younger.

For our travel by the South Manchurian Railway (SMR), we had free passes in the highest class. Whatever special arrangements were needed for our journeys to remote areas would also be taken care of by the Manchukuo government authorities. In Hsinking, I stayed in the palatial house of Yuzao Homma, a cousin of Shumei Okawa, and in Dairen I was a guest of Shuzo Okawa, Shumei's younger brother, who was an expert in Russian affairs and knew the Russian language. He was also one of the pioneers who helped me to set up a publicity organization in Dairen to promote the cause of Indian freedom.

All the financial support we needed was provided by the SMR, without any strings attached, on the recommendation of Shumei Okawa. In addition to being the live wire behind the work of the Jinmukai, he headed the economic center of the SMR. Next to the government, the SMR was the most powerful organization in Manchukuo. It had multifarious establishments, covering not merely operation of railway lines but extending its influence effectively into almost every other field of activity, such as health, education, economics, research, etc. The Japanese government was the largest single shareholder of the company; the appointment of the president of the SMR had therefore to receive the prior approval of the cabinet in Tokyo.

Japan had formally recognized Manchukuo on September 15, 1932. De jure recognition came from El Salvador on March 3, 1934. The USSR, while withholding formal diplomatic recognition, acknowledged the creation of the de facto new state with the establishment of consulates in the respective territories reciprocally. For some time, there was a stalemate in responses from other countries, but de jure acceptance was given eventually by Spain (December 1, 1937), Poland (beginning of 1938), Hungary (January 1939), Wang Ching-wei's government in China (November 1940), Romania (December 1940), and Thailand (August 1941). Meanwhile, commercial transactions, sometimes clandestinely, at other times openly, were being carried on between Britain and Manchukuo, even though the former was unprepared to recognize the new state formally.

I know that even the United States was conducting trade with Manchukuo, indirectly through certain other countries, perhaps the Central American state of El Salvador. In fact, I had a part in bringing to the notice of the Manchukuo authorities the type of activities that the British and the Americans were indulging in with Chinese help because I came to know some of these collaborators. In the course of my own work, I had built up a wide circle of contacts among various cross sections of the races participating in the government or otherwise important in their own respective spheres. I often got to know about the activities of Western secret agents before the Japanese or the Manchukuo authorities did.

The British naturally disliked me intensely. But I had the strong support of not only the administrative authorities of the Manchukuo government in Hsinking, but of the Kyowakai to which also I was affiliated, and of the Kwantung Army. Lieutenant General Seishiro Itagaki, vice chief of the army, was a personal friend of mine; I had known him in Japan even before his transfer to Manchukuo. He was friendly to India and was greatly interested in her freedom struggle. In 1934 when he was leaving Japan on a world tour and I was seeing him off at Yokohama, he placed his arm on my shoulder and said

> Please go back and carry on the good work in Manchukuo; I hope and pray that I shall see India free from British rule when my eyesight is still good (the typical Japanese way of saying that he hoped he would be able to witness the happy event before he became very old).

My position in Manchukuo was in some ways extraordinary. I was not any office-bearer in the government: yet, being convinced of my bona fides as an impartial observer, the senior authorities would seek my advice on several matters. I always adopted a totally unbiased line in my recommendations and never failed to tell the government what I honestly felt. It was not always palatable to many, but those who really counted within the establishment respected my views.

The Japanese administrators were not free from imperfections, but they must be given credit for the manner in which they tried to keep the country unified. Although there was no doubt about their experts' superior ability in all spheres, especially technical, they took pains to ensure that other segments of the population had equal opportunities to progress. Several highly skilled Japanese personnel were officially placed under the administrative control of Chinese, Mongols, or Manchus, and they carried out their duties without resentment.

The description of the Kyowakai by some Western writers as an organization totally dominated by the Japanese with no voice for the other races is therefore not correct. Japan did make an earnest attempt to preserve the spirit of the *gozoku kyowa* principle. That the other races were not in practice able to pull their weight effectively was a different matter.

* * *

Manchukuo, prior to the control of it by the Japanese, was practically a barren territory, although vast in area and rich in mineral and other natural resources. It was Japanese enterprise which made its remarkable industrial development possible. In this process, the greatest part was played by Showa Steel Works, whose president was Yoshisuke (Gisuke) Aikawa, another of my good friends. The chief city planner was Professor Takei, who was one of my professors in Kyoto University and was reputed to be among the best in the world in that line. The chief engineer of Showa Steel Works was Professor Taguchi, whose houseguest I was during my student days in Kyoto. Under the leadership of these very able persons, and of Juji Yamaguchi, who was head of the Kyowakai for some time in its formative stages, developmental work in Manchukuo was efficient and rapid.

The SMR, initially constructed by Russia, was vastly improved by the Japanese. The super-express train "Asia" between Dairen and Hsingking was the fastest in locomotion in the orient. Cities like Port Arthur, Dairen, Hsinking, etc. were reconstructed to high standards of excellence. Progress in agriculture and allied operations, and in heavy and light industries, was phenomenal. It is important to emphasize that whereas raw materials from Manchukuo were being extensively used for industries within Japan, exports of goods were not at the cost of Manchukuo's economy. It was not like Britain fleecing India.

British policy was to manipulate any industrial growth of India in such a way that it would remain perpetually dependent on its colonial base. Japan's effort was to enable Manchukuo's industry to stand on its own legs. Moreover, unlike England in India, Japan did not try to divide Manchukuo to rule it; her attempt, on the contrary, was to retain the cohesion of the country on the Five Races Unity principle, which was by and large successful. The backward sections of the people were encouraged to come up to progressively higher levels. Relief programs for the underprivileged communities were systematically implemented.

The Indian community in Manchukuo was not large; it consisted only of about 15 or 20 families, mainly of Sindhi businessmen, who were doing well. The most prominent of such houses were those of the Bhoolchands and the Dolathrams. They had both wholesale and retail establishments covering a large variety of consumer goods, with branches in various centers including Mukden (present Shenyang) and Hsinking. Some of them were operating in north China as well. Besides, there were two or three Marwari firms doing gunny-bag trade. If I remember well, one of them was a branch of Marwar & Co. of Calcutta, and another was Walia & Co. They were shrewd operators and had a good hold on the stock market. A few Tamils from Ceylon were in the jewelry business. After the arrival of Raja Mahendra Pratap and myself, all these establishments felt considerably more confident than earlier. I was the main troubleshooter for them whenever they were in difficulty with the local authorities.

They were a closely knit group. Besides joining us to organize our own setup, they worked among the racial associations in the state, often on their own initiative. Most of them spoke Chinese fairly well. However, we had greater scope and resources because of our contacts with those in authority in the government.

Among the areas particularly selected for our anti-British propaganda were parts of northern China and Inner Mongolia. Once Mahendra Pratap and I had together toured these regions, but subsequently, after he had returned to Japan I remained in Manchukuo and undertook further and more extensive journeys to Inner Mongolia and China.

Mahendra Pratap's interest and my purposes were different. His only objective was to explore the possibilities of recruiting personnel for his favorite "Asian Army." There were, surprisingly, a few volunteers for it from China and Mongolia, but altogether his concept was a waste of time. For my part, study of the political and economic situation in the region and its potential as a field for anti-British work was my main concern.

At a later date, the Japanese government in Tokyo found that Mahendra Pratap was proving to be a liability to it. He would seek its help in the impossible task of translating his eerie dreams into realities. In the initial stages of Japan's involvement in World War II, he attempted to launch an Indian independence organization of his own, with headquarters in the Imperial Hotel in Tokyo. The military high command, with whom I was in close contact, consulted me as to what to do with the fantasies of the good raja. He was utilizing his earlier connections with certain groups of important personalities, some of whom even included members of the imperial family. He would keep pressing for various impractical facilities for his nebulous movement.

The Japanese authorities who had various urgent problems connected with the war to deal with, found my friend to be somewhat of an obstruction to their normal work, and wanted to get him out of the way. I was afraid that they might harm him; even deportation could not be ruled out. On my assurance to them that Mahendra Pratap was a good man, deeply interested in promoting the Indian freedom struggle, the military high command desisted from troubling him.

But in return for such a "favor," a compromise had to be made. Mahendra Pratap had to leave not only the Imperial Hotel but the Tokyo city itself and take up residence in a suburban town. The raja, with whom I discussed the problem, was initially unwilling to leave the metropolis, but I convinced him that it was no use arguing with the military authorities. Ultimately, he wound up his office in the Imperial Hotel and moved to Kokubunji. There was no further difficulty for him. He left Japan after India had become independent. I remember him affectionately. Although often mentally living in the clouds, he was, without doubt, a sincere patriot and a courageous man. I had learned

CHAPTER TWELVE

much from him. He was adventurous, self-sacrificing, and hardworking, with the staunch faith that whatever be the difficulties, India would before long be free from the British yoke.

In Dairen, 1934. In the center sits Rash Behari Bose, flanked by Yoshiaki Kakei of Hiroshima's Honshoji Temple (Nichiren sect) on the left and the author on the right.

After setting up branches in various important centers in Manchukuo to pursue publicity work for India and propaganda against the British, I set about organizing the Asian conference in Dairen, for which Gunta Nagao had asked for my help. Almost all the preparatory work was entrusted to me.

I chose the Yamato Hotel, the largest one in Dairen at the time, as the venue. I did so deliberately because opposite to the hotel was the British consulate. Britain should know that a large Asian conference was being held; especially that an Indian was in charge of the arrangements, not as one working under the Japanese or the Manchukuo governments but functioning on his own, although, inevitably, with Japanese support.

The conference took place in the autumn of 1934 and was attended by over 100 delegates from various Asian countries. Among the Indians who took part, besides Mahendra Pratap and me, were A. M. Sahay from Japan, D. N. Khan from Hong Kong, and O. Asman from Shanghai. The delegates included representatives from various parts of China. Several came from Japan, many of them on behalf of right-wing organizations.

The conference served its purpose of enhancing a sense of Asian solidarity. Also, Manchukuo came to be better known to the world. The British were naturally highly peeved. In their prolific reports to the Political Department of the government of India about my part in the conference, their intelligence had painted me with some of their blackest brushes. They had charged me with inciting the Japanese as well as the "puppet" Manchukuo regime to challenge the Western powers' special interests in the region. These reports would

In front of the Yamato Hotel in Sinkiang (Xinjiang), 1933. In the center, in Chinese dress, is Mr. Chang, representing Emperor Puyi of Manchukuo. Left of Mr. Chang is the author; right is Raja Mahendra Pratap.

On the rooftop of the Yamato Hotel in Dairen (Dalian), 1934, during the Conference of Asian Peoples, where ethnic flags were raised under the author's direction.

have surely led to my detention if I had reentered India during the British rule, but as I have already stated, I remained outside my country until after India had become independent.

CHAPTER TWELVE

Group photo with officials of Manchukuo in Sinkiang, 1933. The author is fifth from the right in the front row, with Raja Mahendra Pratap second to the author's left.

* * *

At the time of the partition of India and the formation of Pakistan, several secret records of the then undivided government in New Delhi were to be bifurcated for the benefit of both the countries. During that exercise, the authorities concerned in New Delhi apparently decided that it was no longer necessary to retain many of the sensitive files of the sections which dealt with X (External) matters and consigned them to the incinerator. Among the mass of papers so destroyed was the "top secret" dossier on me. Thus, it was after the Second World War and on the eve of India's independence that my name disappeared from Britain's blacklists of "dangerous Indians."

The British Secret Service had branded me as "Manchukuo Nair," the intention being clearly mischievous: to imply that I was working for the Manchukuo government. The fact was that I was never in the employ of any government, although it was true that I had considerable personal influence with the governments in Tokyo and Hsinking, and also received various facilities from both of them for my work for the Indian freedom movement in the East. Oddly enough, the gratuitous title given to me by the British somehow stuck. Many of my Indian friends also began calling me by the same name, of course goodhumoredly. For some of them I am still Manchukuo Nair, even though Manchukuo died with the end of the Second World War.

IN MANCHUKUO

In September 1934, Rash Behari Bose visited Manchukuo on a lecture tour at the invitation of Ryomei Kazami, president of the Association of Japanese Advisers to the Prefectural Governors (who were Chinese) of the new state. Ryomei was an intellectual with a deep interest in India's freedom. He had organized an Asia League in Japan with a branch in Manchukuo, to promote the concept of "Asia for Asians." He ran a good magazine, for which Rash Behari Bose was a regular contributor of articles on Indian affairs. I was happy to help Ryomei look after Rash Behari's program. I met him in Hsinking, on September 4, and was with him throughout his two-week tour, which ended in Dairen.

The visit led to a temporary setback to Rash Behari's popularity with the Japanese authorities in Tokyo. Firstly, he lectured solely to Japanese audiences, instead of multinational gatherings as his sponsors had hoped. But another action of his was amazingly bold. He openly criticized some of Japan's policies. A little before boarding his ship at Dairen for his return to Japan, he wrote out a telegram addressed to the war minister in Tokyo, General Araki, strongly condemning what he said was Japan's ill-treatment of the Chinese in Manchukuo. And he put down the name of the sender as "Indojin Bose" (i.e., "Bose, Indian"). He gave the telegram to me for dispatch. Somewhat taken aback, I asked him whether it was all right for him to say "Indojin Bose" when he was a Japanese citizen. His firm answer came pat.

"My Japanese citizenship is for my survival. In all my thoughts and actions, I am Indian. I take the responsibility. You make sure you go to the telegraph office yourself to send the telegram as it is."

General Araki naturally did not like the message very much. But Rash Behari's overall image with Japanese authorities was such that the government's annoyance in this instance did not cause him or India any real harm. The telegram was forgotten in course of time. But it was a big lesson for me. It was once again a case of practicing the message of the Gita: *anasakta karma*. Here was a man, technically a Japanese citizen, but an intensely sensitive Indian patriot and unafraid to call himself "Indojin Bose." This incident has lingered vividly in my memory. It was uppermost in my mind when, soon after Japan's entry into the Second World War, I obtained the Japanese high command's approval for Rash Behari's election as president of the Indian Independence League (IIL) and of its first conference in the Sanno Hotel which was attended by Indian delegates from all over Southeast Asia.

During one of my visits to Japan from Manchukuo in 1934, I met (in Tokyo) Mr. Chamanlal, then a special correspondent of the *Hindustan Times* of Delhi. He was on a world tour to write some articles for his newspaper. He

CHAPTER TWELVE

had been in touch with Raja Mahendra Pratap, and both of them were staying in a western-style medium-class hotel in Tansumachi, Azabu. Mahendra Pratap sent word to me, and when I met him, he requested me for two things to be arranged for Chamanlal if possible. The first was an exclusive interview with the war minister, General Araki, and the other a visit to Manchukuo on a sponsorship basis, with an opportunity to meet Emperor Puyi also. These were not easy matters to manage at short notice, but I promised to try.

I came to know that General Araki's office had a long waiting list, going back to over two months of foreign journalists and others seeking to meet him. It was necessary therefore for me to adopt a shortcut for the sake of Chamanlal. I contacted Colonel Iimura, who was chief of the 8th Section of the 2nd Division (Intelligence Organization for Asian Affairs and Russia) at the military high command and told him that a leading journalist of a prominent Indian newspaper supporting Indo-Japanese good relations would like to interview General Araki early, as he would be staying in Japan only briefly. I suggested that it would be good if the war minister could spare some time for him, since that would enable him to exchange views on India. Colonel Iimura asked me to wait a minute, took the phone in my presence, spoke to General Araki, and told me that Chamanlal could meet the general the next day, at 11:00 a.m. It was a surprise to everyone how the Indian journalist managed to secure an appointment so soon when numerous others were waiting for weeks or months.

General Araki was very cordial, and instead of the few short minutes he ordinarily gave his foreign visitors, held a three-quarter-hour discussion with Chamanlal, answering questions clearly and frankly. He told him in reply to one query that Japan had to move into Manchuria to save itself from various hardships, especially a great economic depression, shortage of raw materials, and above all, an unmanageable population problem. He said that Japan was not going to colonize Manchuria. With the consent of the people there, a new independent state had been created, and Japan would ensure the unity and prosperity of Manchukuo for the equal benefit of all the races. Chamanlal sent off a long cable dispatch to his paper. He had no money to pay for it (at least so he said), nor a press credit card. So, I had to manage to meet the cost of the telegram.

For his visit to Manchukuo, the high command agreed to make arrangements and to meet all the cost, up to Hsinking. From Hsinking, the Kyowakai would take care of all further expense to visit Dairen, and then to return to Tokyo. I took Chamanlal with me, and he was satisfied that he had a successful visit. Among his important meetings was the one with Puyi, which I had arranged. The discussions essentially centered on enquiries by Puyi about conditions in India, especially the work of Mahatma Gandhi, about whose health he was highly solicitous. Chamanlal prepared a telegram, highlighting Puyi's concern for Gandhiji, and as on the occasion of his interview with General Araki, sent it at my expense. That was his last engagement, and I saw him off at Dairen where, at the insistence of Gunta Nagao, the Kyowakai provided him with a ticket for Tokyo via Kobe.

I met Emperor Puyi twice during my time in Manchukuo for private discussions on various matters connected with the administration of the country on the basis of the Five Races principle. My opinions were, of course, given purely in my personal capacity, but they were always accorded positive attention and consideration by the authorities, both of the Manchukuo civil government and the Kwantung Army echelons.

As everyone knows, many Western countries called Puyi a "puppet" of the Japanese. It is a fact of history that the Japanese were responsible for bringing Puyi back to power after he had been forced to abdicate in 1912, and for making him head of state in Manchukuo. But Puyi himself did not exhibit any unhappiness about his position. It seemed that he was quite satisfied with his situation and considered himself the proper ruler of Manchukuo.

The Japanese did give him the respect due to a constitutional monarch, devoid, of course, of the concept of divinity, which was reserved strictly for their emperor. At both of our meetings, Puyi enquired about Mahatma Gandhi and the Indian freedom movement. He was a pleasant man to deal with. He congratulated me on my work for India and my activities calculated to undermine British power.

Itagaki and Puyi were on good terms. It was surprising to many who had known of their relationship in Manchukuo that during his testimony before the International Military Tribunal for the Far East (IMTFE) set up by MacArthur to try the so-called war criminals, Puyi did nothing but pour abuse on Itagaki in particular and the Japanese in general. It was a kind of double-cross which I had not thought he was capable of. Obviously, opportunism is sometimes boundless. When the Manchukuo government fell to the Soviet Union in August 1945, Puyi became a prisoner of war and was lodged in a concentration camp by the Russians. It was from there that he had been summoned to give evidence before the IMTFE. He must of course have guessed that the safety of his skin would depend on his testimony at the trial.

CHAPTER TWELVE

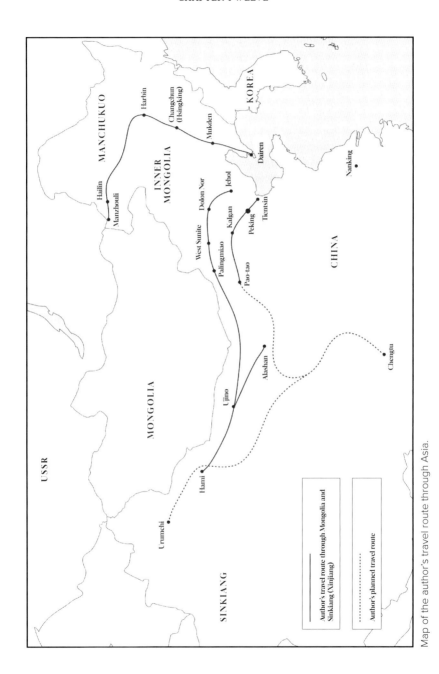

Map of the author's travel route through Asia.

CHAPTER THIRTEEN
In Mongolia and Sinkiang

I have mentioned that I had visited Mongolia briefly in 1933 in the company of Raja Mahendra Pratap. He wanted my moral support, and also to utilize my knowledge of Chinese and Mongolian dialects. In spite of basic conceptual differences about his scheme of an Asian army, I was anxious to cooperate with him to the extent possible. The tour, which lasted about six weeks, was also useful to me; it was inspiring to watch Mahendra Pratap's capacity to face hardships, and his limitless optimism. As far as he was concerned, his projects could never fail, whatever be the flaws that others might find. For me, the journey was an opportunity to observe the lay of the land, mix with the people, and understand something of their work, customs, manners, and religion.

An important economic activity in the region could not escape anyone's attention: the vast caravan trade in wool coming from Tibet and the interior of Mongolia into China and going to the port city of Tientsin (Tianjin), which the British had secured on lease from China.

There were mainly three important caravan tracks: one coming from Tibet and merging with the Sinkiang (Xinjiang) route, another from Alashan (Alxa League), and the third from places fairly deep inside Mongolia but all of them converging at Pao-tao (Baotou). These caravans were amazingly long, consisting of some hundred thousand or more of animals, mostly camels, but including a good number of mules. They would traverse anything up to a few thousand miles before delivering the consignments at Tientsin. My enquiries

CHAPTER THIRTEEN

had shown that this wool was not for use in China but for transshipment to England, for the benefit of the textile mills of Manchester and Lancashire.

The author engaged in activist efforts with Raja Mahendra Pratap. The background in the photograph on the left shows the flags of Manchukuo and Japan.

Mahendra Pratap was not particularly interested in what we saw of these caravans, but I continued to reflect on them. I was anxious to visit the regions where this wool originated and to know more about the trade.

After Mahendra Pratap's return to Tokyo, I stayed back in Manchukuo and contacted my friend, Lieutenant General Itagaki. I told him that I wanted to visit China and Mongolia once again. He felt that I was exposing myself to serious risks, but I had gained enough confidence during my first tour, to be able to persuade him to let me go. He eventually agreed, and after obtaining Tokyo's clearance, was prepared to order elaborate arrangements for my journey. I, however, decided that I would avail myself of only the minimum of requirements: just a few animals that would be adequate for the transportation of myself and a servant, and for the movement of camping equipment and foodstuff from one provisioning stage to the next.

I had, on the previous occasion, seen several European, especially British, missionaries in the area doing medical work among the people. Through such charitable service they had built up considerable influence among the population. There was probably one missionary to every twenty-five or thirty miles of territory. They did not appear to have had much success in religious conversions but had gained much goodwill through their medical service. They had learned the local dialects and made themselves as comfortable as anyone could in such terrain: many of them had their wives with them and some had even motor vehicles. I had, however, the suspicion that they included spies supplying information to various countries, particularly England. Perhaps some of them were helping the supply of fur from the Inner Mongolia region to the Chinese merchants operating the trade routes.

The Japanese had voluntary organizations (*zenrin kyokai*) capable of taking up medical and other social work on the same lines as the Christian missionaries, but since the Kwantung Army was still heavily involved in military and political consolidation of Manchukuo, I gave up my initial idea of asking Itagaki for a medical unit to accompany me. Moreover, on second thoughts, I concluded that I had better confine my visit to serve my limited objective; that is, to assess how best to prevent the vast quantities of wool from being sent to England.

It seemed to me that if the shipments from Tientsin could be stopped, the British textile industry would feel the pinch, and at least to that extent the British economy could be weakened. I recalled the movement launched in India in the latter part of the 1920s and in the early 1930s by Gandhiji to boycott British cloth and other foreign goods. I myself had joined in the burning of Lancashire mill cloth on the beach in Trivandrum in 1925. The ruthless repression against the boycott was indicative of Britain's fear of the likely damage to its textile business. And now I was undertaking a major adventure on my own in remote Mongolia and China to see what could be done to weaken it further. Speaking to me about Tokyo's reactions, Itagaki once told me that the military high command in Japan, while agreeing with my proposal, was nevertheless surprised at the meagre nature of the resources I had asked for to set out on my mission.

The regions I was proceeding to visit were politically as well as economically important. Taking advantage of the age-old enmity between the Chinese and the Mongols, Japan had acquired an unusually strong position in northern China, especially after the creation of Manchukuo. Strategically, the Japanese army wanted to secure a buffer between Manchukuo and the Soviet Union. The government in Nanking (Nanjing) had virtually carved out a large part of the Mongol territory adjoining north China and called it Inner Mongolia. It comprised the provinces of Ningsia (Ningxia), Suiyuan, Chahar, and certain other areas. From Jehol (Rehe), the Japanese had managed to maintain close connections with a number of Mongol princes who were already seeking autonomy from Chinese control. They exploited their anti-Chinese sentiments. The most important among these Mongol chiefs was the energetic Prince Teh Wang (Prince De).

During my earlier visit to Mongolia in Mahendra Pratap's company, I had met Prince Teh at a place called Sunite, which could be reached from the Manchukuo border in the western part, in about ten days. He had been consolidating his leadership among the autonomous Mongolian provinces by establishing a federation of them and setting up a new capital for his "kingdom" at Pailingmiao. It was hardly a capital in the usual sense of the term: there were no buildings but only a number of igloo-shaped tents and a few mud huts. This was the typical living complex for a Mongol community: it would comprise several *gers*, collectively known as *ails* in Mongolian, and normally be located in valleys. It was here that I met Prince Teh a second time. He was surprised to see me again but was as warm as before in his welcome and hospitality. He allotted a tent for my use, and I found it more comfortable than I could really expect. It had even a fireplace and an oven for cooking food. Dried animal dung was the only fuel, as is the case in most of the areas of the region (and even in India in several places) still. There was no vegetation, and hence no timber or firewood.

Our discussions were held in the Mongolian dialect, in which I had managed to acquire fair proficiency. Prince Teh was an intelligent man but virtually ignorant of the outside world. I felt much sympathy for him, for he was in an unenviable situation. He had three powers around him. One was of course China, which was in a state of confusion with several military chieftains, each wanting to treat the area controlled by him as his own province. Chiang Kai-shek at Nanking was not particularly effective in unifying the country. Russia was exerting pressure through Outer Mongolia. And Japan, after consolidating Manchukuo, was in fact extending her influence and had come right up to the border of Mongolia.

An additional problem was the guerilla activities of the communist troops in various adjoining Chinese provinces, under the leadership of Mao Tse-tung. Feng-yu Shan, in charge of one of the border provinces, was establishing contact with the Sinkiang military establishment, across a part of Mongol territory. In the midst of all this, the autonomous government of Prince Teh found itself in the situation of an anthill surrounded by rocks. There was much mistrust of the Chinese on the part of Mongols, and Russia was feared because it might destroy the religious faith which was dear to the Mongolian people.

When I explained to Prince Teh the situation in which he was, he asked me for a way out. I told him that however anxious I was to help him, there was no way I could readily think of as entirely safe. It would be dishonest for me to pretend that the Japanese themselves did not have expansionist tendencies. Moreover, I was, in principle, averse to proffering any advice that could appear as interference in the internal affairs of the countries concerned. My task was to try to weaken the British, without intruding into the affairs of any other country.

Yet, I told Prince Teh that I could introduce him to Lieutenant General Itagaki, chief of staff of the Kwantung Army, who was a good personal friend and whose bona fides I could vouch for. I could not say what the Japanese government's policy towards Inner Mongolia would be, but I felt that Itagaki would give no trouble to the prince. He had no doubt been deeply involved in the creation of Manchukuo, but that was under compelling circumstances not of his making: he was only acting under orders. Basically, he wanted all Asian countries to remain free, although for the Western imperialist nations he had no sympathy.

I made it clear to the prince that my function would be only to secure an introduction for him to General Itagaki. Discussions and decisions would have to be strictly between them. I cautioned him that the general could conceivably be influenced by his staff officers. In any case, the prince should realize that important diplomatic issues should be carefully thought out. Other autonomous units must be consulted. As chairman of the federation, he should carry the various units with him in the decision process. Prince Teh said that he understood my point. At the end of the conversation, I gave him a letter of introduction to Lieutenant General Itagaki.

* * *

Equipped with an official directive from the prince to all the Mongol chiefs of the areas concerned asking them to give me all facilities—camels or horses, shelter, foodstuff, security, etc.—I set out from Pailingmiao for Ujino (Ejin), the last Mongolian kingdom on the western border of Inner Mongolia with Sinkiang in China. After camping briefly in various kingdoms, I reached Ujino in about four weeks' time. Like the previous "capitals," it comprised a cluster of tents. The governor however was a remarkably lovable person, and I enjoyed his company. My stay of about 10 days in Ujino was pleasant.

Both on the way to Ujino and while staying there, I tried to collect a good deal of information about the Mongolian wool trade but was still not sure of the overall volume of it and the sources. Enquiries at Ujino seemed to reveal that the most abundant source was Alashan, one of the bigger Mongol kingdoms, on the border of Chinghai (Qinghai), which was Chinese territory. Anxious to study the situation myself, I requested the King of Ujino for facilities to travel to Alashan. He was perturbed and warned me of the dangerous route which lay across vast stretches of sheer desert, and of the very long

CHAPTER THIRTEEN

distance to the administrative center. I appreciated his concern but pleaded nevertheless for the minimum facilities to get there. He was good enough to agree and provided me with a lama guide, an attendant, three camels and the essential travel equipment. I started for Alashan.

Knowing that the Mongols in general were deeply religious, I decided that it would be helpful in various ways to fit myself into the religious lifestyle of a Mongolian lama, which was similar to that of a Tibetan monk. It would still be better to adopt the ways of that category of lamas known in Tibet as *rimpoches*, who were highly venerated since they were regarded as incarnations of renowned monks who enjoyed the status of living buddhas. During my Kyoto days, I had studied enough of Buddhism, including its Tibetan and Mongolian variations, to know the ways of *rimpoches*.

My posture as a high lama had many useful aspects. Firstly, it entitled me to put a respectable distance between myself and the people around me. I wanted to do so not because I was a snob, but merely since it was prudent from the point of view of my health. The living habits of the local population, I regret to say, were not quite hygienic. It was said that generally Mongolians, as also Tibetans, bathed or changed clothes only once or twice a year. That might be an exaggeration, but it could not be denied that their ablutions were few and far between, and that the disagreeable smell emanating from their bodies was strong. Climate, shortage of water and a number of other reasons could of course be extenuating factors, but none of them rendered the odor any the less offensive. There was a joke that one of the ways in which the people kept warm was by getting themselves bitten by lice which they would shove into their *del*, the flowing robe which is the usual Mongolian dress, similar to the Tibetans' *baku*.

Then there was a danger I had been warned against. Although lamas were expected to be strictly celibate, it was said that the local women would offer themselves to them for sexual pleasure at the slightest indication of any latitude they might notice. The women would consider acceptance in such cases to be a privilege because of their belief that their offspring from a lama would be handsome and highly intelligent. A small lama might fall for a temptation of this nature and get away with it unobserved by the public, but a *rimpoche* had to maintain his prestige all the time since he would be under constant view by everyone, and as a corollary, the women would also be wary about approaching him for the type of favor in question.

As an incarnate lama, or a living Buddha, I could easily prevent women from coming near me, and of course there was no question of their getting into my tent. Thus, there was no risk of my straying from *brahmacharya* (celibacy) and getting into trouble. The incidence of venereal diseases among the local women (and men also) was said to be alarmingly high. A Swedish missionary had told me in one of the camps in Mongolia earlier that probably the whole Mongolian people might be wiped out in a couple of generations due to VD if nothing was done to control these diseases.

I also decided not to have any bodyguards to accompany me. Some of the high lamas used to insist on being heavily escorted during their journeys. I thought it to be incongruous that I, a living buddha and therefore the embodiment of compassion and peace, should allow myself a retinue of burly soldiers for my protection. I had a garland with large beads (like a rosary), which I would keep counting when murmuring Buddhist prayers even if I myself did not understand what I was saying. I told my friends that for a real lama, that was the most potent weapon to protect him from all dangers and to ward off all evils.

I practiced curing many ailments among the people. If they had a headache, I would pray for their recovery. They would recover in due course and thank me. When mere prayers did not work, I would administer some of the patent medicines I had in stock, and it was amazing how many patients quickly regained normal health through my quack treatment. If cure was not achieved, failure, alas, was due to the unfortunate persons' karma (fate), as they should know from their own religion. It had been ordained that they must suffer for their sins. Needless to say, such interludes served to relieve the tedium and thoughts of the dangers of my tour in hazardous terrain, besides helping to acquire much local goodwill.

To many persons, even today, Mongolia is a land of mystery, remote and out of the world like the fictional Shangri-la. Others think of it as the land of Genghis Khan who, seven centuries ago, struck terror in about four-fifths of the then known civilized world, covering Central Asia, China, Europe, etc. Together with his sons and grandsons, he built up the largest empire in history. Thereafter, for some six hundred years, Mongolia declined and remained isolated, before coming out into the mainstream of the world. This Central Asian tableland, which is like a wedge between the USSR and China, now stands divided into two political entities; one, the former autonomous region known as Inner Mongolia now integrated into the Chinese People's Republic; the other, previously called Outer Mongolia, being a sovereign state but remaining within the orbit of Soviet influence.

Kublai Khan, a third grandson of Genghis Khan, had ambitions of conquering Japan in the 1270s but failed due to what the Japanese believe was the intervention of the kamikaze (divine wind), which swept all his ships away

CHAPTER THIRTEEN

from the Japanese ports. Later he embraced Buddhism under the influence of the great Tibetan monk Phagpa Gyaltsen. In the sixteenth century, Sonam Gyatso, the third in the series of the "grand lamas" visited Mongolia at the invitation of the Mongol King Altan Khan and converted him into the "Yellow Sect" of Mahayana Buddhism during their meeting at Koko Nor. Altan Khan conferred on his guru (teacher) the title of "Dalai Lama Vajradhara" ("All Embracing Lama, the Holder of the Thunderbolt"). The word "Dalai," meaning "ocean," has its origin in the Mongolian word *thale*. Thus, the religious culture of both Tibet and Mongolia has its roots in India, from whence Buddhism spread to other countries.

Being from the land of the Buddha, I was naturally at a great advantage. The Mongols with whom I came into contact were impressed by my credentials as a lama and acknowledged me as "Dharm Rimpoche," the very incarnation of all virtue and therefore a VVIP. Even before my arrival at the next stage, news would have reached there that Dharm Rimpoche was on his way and should be afforded all assistance. It was surprising how quickly news could travel in areas where no postal or telegraph facilities or radios existed.

My journey to Alashan was of the most fearsome kind. The estimated travel time from Ujino to the capital of the kingdom, also called Alashan, was two weeks. Throughout that period, there was nothing to see except a limitless expanse of sand. Even to know that you were going in the right direction, you had to depend on the guide. These guides were remarkable men. With mere intuition, they could navigate the deserts in the same way a captain of a ship or an aircraft sets his course on the high seas or in the high heavens with the aid of compasses and computers. Perhaps the camel, aptly called the "ship of the desert," also has a built-in automatic guidance system working on instinct! As for the guides, they could even predict the winds—the direction, velocity, and duration, so as to avoid shifting sand dunes.

The most difficult problem was that of locating the one and only source of water, a well, situated somewhere about midway between Ujino and Alashan. We had necessarily to reach that spot and find it on the eighth day, by which time all the water carried from the starting point would have been exhausted. The camels' reserves must be replenished, and our pitchers refilled to last for another week's journey. If the midway well were missed by any misfortune, the animals and the men would surely die of thirst before reaching their destination. So, on the crucial day, like all other travelers on that route, I and my guide and the attendant all prayed to God, whether in the form of Allah, Krishna, Buddha, or any other power, to lead us on the right path to the water source.

And we really thanked the Almighty when our prayers were answered. In the evening, we hit the right spot, removed the wooden planks covering the well (such protection being essential to prevent it from being filled by sand), saw the lifesaving liquid, and pitched camp. Replenishment done, we set off again the following day and, in another week of correct navigation, reached Alashan.

Fifteen days in the wilderness, in the Land of the Blue Sky that was once Genghis Khan's. During day, the sun and the sand kept us constant company; during nights, the moon and the stars in all their beauty. But our greatest sustaining force was undoubtedly our "hearts within and God overhead."

I stayed in Alashan for ten days. It was easy to get all the information I wanted. In a way there was not much that was new, but it was confirmed that an incredibly large quantity of wool was being sent from Alashan by camel caravans to Pao-tao from where, as already stated, it would go on to Tientsin and then be shipped to England.

I met the local king several times. He was wonderstruck by the audacity of an Indian lama braving a fortnight's journey across a terrifying desert. He was, however, a delightfully friendly person, and at my request provided me with a fresh guide, this time a local chieftain, and a new set of camels for the return journey. Retracing the way to Ujino was as hazardous as the onward trip, but we returned safely after another two weeks.

From rumors I have heard in recent years, it would appear that one of the nuclear weapons-testing sites of the Chinese government possibly lies within the desert region across which I had travelled in 1935.

* * *

The king of Ujino was more surprised than his Alashan counterpart but seemed relieved that I was alive and intact. He insisted that I should relax for a few days, playing mahjong with him. I was used to the game, a popular one in Japan, China, and Manchukuo also, and had acquired a high level of skill in it. The king was not a particularly able player, and I could beat him every time if I so chose. But you should not defeat a king always. You must lose most of the time; otherwise, it would be discourteous. Now, to lose a game without giving the impression that you were deliberately giving it away also needed a good deal of expertise. But I employed the proper tactics, the right gestures and sounds, and ensured that the king won the vast majority of the games. He was pleased.

CHAPTER THIRTEEN

I greatly wished to visit Sinkiang, particularly Hami (Kumul) and Urumqi, for two reasons. Firstly, I wanted to discover more about the wool trade, for which this Chinese province was said to be an important region. Secondly, I was anxious to see the lay of the land in the area, by way of which there was obviously a route to India across the Himalayas. In my youthful enthusiasm, I wistfully thought of the Buddhist pilgrims Faxian and Xuanzang of China, and explorers like Marco Polo of Venice, Sven Hedin of Sweden, and others. They had done it; why couldn't I?

I spoke to the king: he was aghast at my optimism, but was good enough to provide me with the necessary animals and a servant, provisions, etc. He asked me to be careful since it was going to be a dangerous journey. He wanted to arrange an armed escort for me, but I preferred to remain a lama and declined any special protection. Later I was to regret my overconfidence.

This time the route was mostly over plateau land. But there were also the high mountains, some of which rose to 15,000 feet or more. Sinkiang, although mostly barren, had much to offer by way of majestic views. It was a great contrast to the oceans of sand of the Gobi Desert or Alashan. The caravan route wound through rugged terrain, sections of which passed below awesome rock cliffs where the wind would rush through gorges as though it were compressed air let off from huge tunnels. And at such places your voice would produce an echo that you thought could well be heard a hundred miles away.

The track was highly treacherous in a number of places, but the camels are amazingly sure-footed animals. My own caravan was small, consisting of only three animals. Sometimes it would be two days before we could come to any village with human habitation. We went on and on in stages of about 12 miles per day like any other travelers on such routes, and it was about two weeks by the time I thought we were near Hami, which was my first point of interest in Sinkiang. There, for the first time, we ran into trouble.

* * *

My journey across Mongolian territory had been peaceful. There appeared to be no robbers or bandits to harass traders or lamas travelling by the caravan routes. But in Sinkiang, banditry was not under any strong control. Security for travelers unaccompanied by armed bodyguards could not be taken for granted. Obviously, some robber had noticed my small caravan, which had no protection.

Soon after my party had pitched camp on our first evening in Hami, a Chinese carrying a gun with fixed bayonet entered our tent and asked my servant to follow him. Surprised, I asked the intruder what it was all about. He merely stared at me and did not reply but ordered my servant to go with him. The servant became panicky, began to cry loudly, and asked for my help.

During the past three months of travel, I had not come across any situation of this kind, but here, I knew from the look of the gun-toting Chinese, that something was wrong. An hour later, another Chinese came and introduced himself as Fu Low-ping. He was unusually tall and fair and spoke English. He said he was a layman traveler going to Tibet, although I began to wonder whether he could be some security wireless operator or mechanic of the kind I had come across on some occasions in Mongolia. There was no means by which I could learn who he really was and could only go by what he said. He told me that a notorious bandit had captured my servant and would be executing him the following day. And tonight, he (the bandit) would be coming to get hold of me to decide my own fate.

It was puzzling. Who could this Fu Low-ping be and what was he up to? And how did he know of the so-called bandit, the proposed execution of my servant, etc.? Somehow the idea that he might be a wireless *technician* and not an operator (because I did not notice any antenna anywhere) persisted in my mind for some more time, but soon afterwards I began suspecting that he might be in league with the bandit who had taken away my servant. Mr. Fu casually asked me, during our conversation, how many yuan (Chinese silver coins—the value of each was about three rupees those days) I carried with me. I told him that I had 50 coins; it was only after giving him the figure that I began wondering why he had asked me. He went out and returned shortly thereafter to tell me that since he was interested in protecting me, he would negotiate with the bandit chief and arrive at a settlement. It would be a pity, he said, if "a precious lama" like me was harmed by bandits, so he would take risks on my behalf if I could give him all the money.

I thought for a moment, and remembered the words of a famous Malayalam poet who had said that much of man's trouble was due to money and women. No woman was involved in my situation, but I had some money. Agreeing within myself that it was better to remain alive than to perish in Sinkiang and consoling myself that in the circumstances discretion would be the better part of valor, I made over all my money to Mr. Fu. When I asked him for assistance to proceed further into the province, however, he refused and said that I must go *back* and not forward. At that point I was quite certain that Fu was himself the so-called bandit chief. As a last bid I pleaded with him to restore to me my Chinese servant; but this also he declined. With a heavy heart for my faithful servant whom I could not get back from the clutches of his tormentor, I retraced my way and got back to Ujino.

The failure of my project to visit Hami and Urumqi in Sinkiang and possibly proceed further to Tibet, was a great disappointment. I mentioned this to the king of Ujino. He was sympathetic and was sorry that I had not heeded his advice about security. Indeed, I was sorrier: I had placed too much reliance on the prayer beads, which, I discovered to my cost, had no power in Sinkiang!

But the king had news for me of a nature I had hardly anticipated. During my journey into Sinkiang, a small Japanese army plane had arrived in Ujino with an officer who was enquiring about my whereabouts. The king could only inform him that I had left for Sinkiang. The plane went away. I was naturally puzzled but could learn nothing more for the time being. It was after my return to Hsinking that I came to know the details, but I shall narrate them briefly here, in the interest of sequential presentation of events.

What happened was that the Kwantung Army was getting worried about the delay in my returning from tour, and the lack of any news of me. A rumor spread that I was "missing." General Itagaki who was particularly anxious, decided to send out a fighter aircraft to search for me. Since the army had a report that I had left for Alashan, the crew of the plane decided to look for me there. That was about the time when the Kwantung Army had decided also to set up a Tokumu Kikan (intelligence outpost) at Alashan to serve as a listening post as far to the west in Inner Mongolia as possible. A reserve officer, Major Yokota, brother of an army general by the same name, was nominated to take charge of the post, with the help of three or four staff members. The station would also have a wireless set which would be linked to other outposts and the headquarters.

It so happened that before the Tokumu Kikan at Alashan was actually commissioned, I had already started off on my return journey to Ujino. In order not to publicize the fact that a search for me was on, the army put out a story that a plane was going to Alashan with some officers to inspect the new outpost there. But the small (two-seater or three-seater) aircraft had onboard General Itagaki in addition to one or two junior officers. It was most unusual that a general should set out on a tour to inspect an outpost. The fact was of course that he was so concerned about me that he himself decided to join the search party. He was taking an undue risk.

When it was discovered at Alashan that I had left it on my way back to Ujino, General Itagaki stopped over at the Tokumu Kikan and sent the plane, with Major Yokota, to Ujino to make enquiries there. This was the plane about which the Ujino ruler was speaking to me. He naturally could tell the officer concerned only what he knew at that time. It transpired that although the search party would have liked to fly over Sinkiang in an attempt to trace me and my small caravan, the plane was getting low on gasoline and could not possibly do so. Therefore, it went back to Alashan to pick up General Itagaki and returned to Hsinking via Kalgan. Since no definite information about me could be obtained, I was put down in the list of the "missing." Lieutenant Colonel Ryukichi Tanaka, the Kwantung Army's section chief dealing with Mongolian affairs, took this to mean that I had died. He and some of my Japanese friends got together and held a "sake party" to condole my death.

* * *

To revert to the subject of the wool trade. I had observed that although the bulk of the commodity came from Mongolia, the traders were all Chinese, particularly Muslims. There was no money currency exchange: the trade was on a barter basis. The Mongolians would sell the wool against a variety of articles like wheat, millet, cotton cloth and yarn, sash, chopsticks, butcher's knives, daggers, etc. Wheat and millet were luxury items for the Mongolians, whose staple food was meat. Other purchases popular with them included Chinese fur caps, mirrors, brick tea, and salt.

But by far the most important article was tobacco. The Mongolians bought it in amazingly large quantities. They used it in various ways: for chewing, smoking, and preparing snuff. Exchange of snuff was a mark of mutual salutation among both Mongolians and Tibetans. That in turn produced a great demand for Chinese-made snuff bottles or boxes. I also saw vast lots of inferior English-made cigarettes being sold to the caravan people. British traders in Tientsin were doing a roaring business in these with the Mongolians. One of the brands was marked "Hatoman," which I tried out and found to be hopelessly bad. The prices of these cheap cigarettes, in terms of the quantities of wool exchanged for them, were exorbitant. Obviously, the British merchants were cheating the simple and poor Mongolians in a big way. I was reminded of the opium trade which many Western countries conducted successfully with China (and unsuccessfully with Manchukuo).

CHAPTER THIRTEEN

From Ujino I returned to Pao-tao on my way back to Manchukuo. Here also the traders and the numerous innkeepers were well-to-do Chinese Muslims, depending for their income mostly, if not exclusively, on the wool business. After being robbed in Sinkiang, I was an "honorable beggar," barely eking out a living on other people's charity, and was reconciled to remaining so until getting back to Manchukuo.

At Hsinking no one could initially believe that I was my real self and not my ghost, because they had given me up as lost and held a condolence party. But I had not died, and the only significant difference in my appearance was a good growth of beard on my face. Before long, the military authorities and other friends were convinced that I was alive. They were profusely warm in their welcome. In compensation for the earlier condolence party, they celebrated my return on a grand scale.

When I was in the wilderness, an important political development had taken place in Hsinking. I have already referred to my talks with Prince Teh, at Pailingmiao on my way to Alashan. Some time thereafter, the prince came to meet General Itagaki and stayed at Hotel Kokuto, which was also my favorite place in Hsinking. Japanese assistance for the establishment of an independent Inner Mongolian Federation with Prince Teh as the chairman had been negotiated during the visit and eventually it led to the proclamation of the state of Mengkukuo (Mokyo according to Japanese pronunciation; Mengjiang). Earlier, General Kenji Doihara, the then chief of the Kwantung Army's division dealing with "special services," had managed to arrange for the virtual control of Suiyuan by the Mongols. The new state included parts of Ningsia and had Kalgan as its capital.

I was surprised to know that Prince Teh had agreed to these arrangements. They were unnatural. Kalgan was a Chinese city with an economy different from the pastoral base to which the Mongolians were accustomed. In such a situation, the contact between the rulers and the ruled was bound to be weak and unreal. Mokyo had been practically created with the help of the Kwantung Army, without considering the true geographic interests of the Mongolian states involved. Strategic importance of it to the Japanese regime appeared to have been the primary concern that weighed with the Kwantung Army. I gathered that the agreements reached between Prince Teh and the Japanese negotiators aided by representatives of the Manchukuo government were heavily loaded against the Mongolian constituents of Mokyo. I also learned that during the crucial stages of the negotiations, General Itagaki was not present in Hsinking and that the architect of the decisions which were finally accepted by Prince Teh was really Colonel Ryukichi Tanaka.

I always viewed Colonel Tanaka with suspicion because his sincerity was in doubt. He could hoodwink a good man like Prince Teh, just as he eventually let down his own erstwhile chief, General Itagaki. He was a double-dealer. When General Itagaki was chief of staff of the Kwantung Army, Tanaka was his "right-hand man," and the general trusted him completely. But during the "war crimes" trial, Tanaka switched loyalties and betrayed him. He gave wrong evidence in many matters with which Itagaki had had nothing to do and went over to the side of the chief American prosecuting counsel, Keenan, providing him with fake material that ultimately led to the death sentence on the general.

In Kalgan (Northwest China), 1935. Sitting: the author as a Buddhist lama (left) and Mr. Kuroki. Standing: Mr. Tokoto (left) and Mr. Ozeki, both of the Manchukuo government.

My Mongolian trip, including the brief excursion to Sinkiang, took nearly six months. I was back in Hsinking towards the end of the winter of 1935, and decided to visit Tokyo early in 1936 to meet senior officers of the Japanese government and of the military high command, apprise them of what I had observed with regard to the Mongolian wool trade, and discuss the possibility of any positive follow-up action. I arrived in Tokyo in February of the new year, 1936.

CHAPTER FOURTEEN
Visit to Tokyo

Early in 1936, Tokyo was in a state of confusion. The city was virtually under martial law administration. The government was passing through a critical period. On the one hand, there was much pressure from the army for control of the administration. On the other, the army itself was riddled with indiscipline from a section of the ranks. There was a wave in favor of a return to the samurai spirit and much talk of a "Showa Restoration," meaning basically an upsurge of expansionist tendencies.

Internal trouble in the army had been brewing for some time. On August 12, 1935, a young officer, Lieutenant Colonel Saburo Aizawa, had killed, with his sword, the director of the Military Affairs Bureau, General Tetsuzan Nagata, in his office. In what was known as the 2/26 Incident (February 26, 1936), certain extremist elements in the army had attempted a coup d'état to get rid of all those top government leaders whom they did not like. Victims of attempted assassinations were many. Those killed included Finance Minister Takahashi and the inspector general of military education, Jotaro Watanabe and also a former prime minister, Admiral Saito. There were attempts on the lives of Prince Saionji and the grand chamberlain, Admiral Kantaro Suzuki. Prime Minister Okada was saved only because he was mistaken for his brother-in-law, who was done to death.

It was significant that barring one or two isolated and minor cases of personal ambitions, there was no indication that the mutiny among the army ranks was motivated by self-interest on the part of the really powerful rebels. It was no attempted coup in the normal sense. Everyone who revolted was as totally devoted to the emperor as ever before. Indeed, the grievance of the disgruntled officers was that a general situation of "drift" (at least what was so in their view) and apathy in the government was eroding the prestige of the emperor! Some historians discern in this the traditional character of the Japanese nation.

Koki Hirota, who replaced Admiral Okada as prime minister, forced the retirement of many generals responsible for siding with the young rebels and placed the War Council under General Jiro Minami, who was transferred to Tokyo from Manchukuo. Hideki Tojo, serving in Japan as a brigadier and known as a stern disciplinarian, was moved to Manchukuo in the rank of major general, to head the Kwantung Army's detachment of gendarmerie, the Kempeitai. General Itagaki was the commander of the Kwantung Army and was apprehending trouble similar to the problem faced earlier by the imperial army high command in Tokyo. There was a certain amount of unrest, but Tojo's Kempeitai restored complete control.

Further potential insubordination within the Armies was rooted out, but that did not substantially curb the increasing domination of the government machinery as a whole by the military.

Manchukuo figured predominantly in the calculations of the army. They wanted the new state to be rapidly developed since close links with it were vital for Japan's national defense, especially as a safeguard against possible aggression from the USSR. Simultaneously, British and American interests in the Pacific were to be weakened and Japanese naval strength increased. Army expenditure had risen to almost half of the total national budget. The Hirota Cabinet consisted of only men who were acceptable to the war minister (General Hisaichi Terauchi). Among the favorite general staff officers was General Tomoyuki Yamashita.

* * *

It was during this period that British Intelligence in Japan, apparently noticing that I was spending a good deal of time in Tokyo and often meeting high-ranking military officers, sent a totally false report on me to the government of India. They said that the Japanese government and the Kwantung Army had jointly proposed to appoint me as a high-level civilian intelligence officer with the personal rank of a major general in the Japanese army.

CHAPTER FOURTEEN

It was a malicious report. The Japanese knew me well enough to be sure that I would never agree to be on their rolls, even if they had wanted. The British agents were perhaps the only persons who did not know it; or it could well be a case of their being aware of it and deliberately misleading their higher authorities. It was true that I was cooperating with the Japanese in various ways in order to secure facilities for my own anti-British work, but that was quite a different matter from being in their employ. It was an article of faith with me that I would not allow any part of my activity in the Indian freedom movement to be subject to interference by Japanese or any other quarters. I could maintain my right to independent action, only if I were not in anyone's employment.

What prompted the wrong report was probably that, for facilitating my dealings with the Japanese and the Kwantung Army headquarters, I had been equated in rank to a major general. I was also given, for my travels anywhere, a special pass entitling me to demand the priority facilities admissible to an officer of such a rank. One of such facilities was the right to requisition an aircraft in emergencies. In actual fact, I used the concession only once. Ordinarily I had no problem travelling to and from any place without using my pass, since I knew almost all the officers concerned personally. As for my other work, my army equation in rank was really not of much consequence. I dealt with a wide range of officers, from majors upwards to lieutenant generals and full generals, the last two categories being in practice the ones with whom I was in contact for the purpose of all important discussions.

* * *

The disturbed conditions in Tokyo delayed the work I had gone there for, viz. to obtain a decision on what to do about the Mongolian wool trade. However, I decided to stay on in order to secure a clear response. I found that the Japanese government was very keen to stop the trade, but the officers were too much preoccupied with other matters. They would be happy if I could handle the matter all the way. Necessary facilities would be arranged through the Kwantung Army.

I was delighted at the opportunity and agreed to work out a practical scheme. However, I should have a free hand and no needling from any source. In return, I would expect no reward for myself. Also, my requirements would be the minimum. Tokyo accepted my conditions.

Action to tackle the problem had to be basically two pronged. The shipments to England of course had to be stopped, but at the same time it was necessary to ensure that the wool trade as such did not suffer, since the livelihood of so many Mongols and Chinese depended on it. There could therefore be only one foolproof solution: Japan must buy up all the wool and use it to its own advantage without letting it go to England. Moreover, to foil the British merchants, who were strongly entrenched in Tientsin, it was necessary that the purchase must be made at a center where they were either absent or at least not present in force. The obvious alternative place was Pao-tao, the marshalling yard where all the important caravans converged. In other words, the trade should be terminated at Pao-tao, and the British merchants or their agents should be bypassed.

But it was important that the traders should be paid at Pao-tao the same price as they were getting in Tientsin; otherwise, there would be trouble all round. The Japanese government would naturally have to meet the extra expenditure on account of the onward transportation. Such a policy frame was agreed to. The modus operandi was left to be worked out amongst myself, the Kwantung Army, and the Mokyo, or any other authorities whose help might be required.

* * *

In June 1936, when I was still discussing my program with the Japanese government, I received information from my elder brother Narayanan Nair, who had completed his science master's degree course in Canada, that he was shortly returning to India via Japan. He would stop over for a few days to see me. I was naturally anxious to meet him.

We spent a good deal of time together. I was perturbed to learn that he was quite unhappy about my career in Japan. Indeed, he knew that there was danger for me if I got back to India because I was on the blacklists of the British authorities. At the same time, he was greatly concerned that I was getting deeply involved in political work. To make matters worse, some of his old Japanese friends told him that I was well on the way to becoming a ronin,[*] and that unless veered away into some other occupation, I might soon reach a point in politics from whence there would be no turning back.

As a solution, he suggested that I might leave Japan and go either to

---

[*] See Appendix 1.

CHAPTER FOURTEEN

America or Canada. I could study there if I wanted; but if I did not want to study, I could enjoy myself. He would be prepared to meet part of the expenses and hoped that I would mobilize the rest on my own. I could not think of displeasing my brother. I told him that while I would like to honor his wishes, I had to complete my unfinished work in Manchukuo and Mongolia. Therefore, I would go there once more, and on return to Japan I would leave for America or Canada. I knew what my brother's intention was. By moving to a Western country, I could perhaps shed my anti-British image and thus cease being a marked man for punishment on my entry into India. In the circumstances I explained, he agreed that I could go just once more to Manchukuo and Mongolia, but he desired that soon thereafter I should proceed to America.

At a welcome party for the author's brother Narayanan Nair in Osaka, 1936. Front row, from left: the author and Narayanan.

During his stay of a few days in Japan, I introduced him to many of my friends, including Colonel Iimura, chief of the 8th Section of the 2nd Division of the military high command, and Dr. Shumei Okawa. In Osaka, a large number of industrialists, educationists, and cultural leaders organized a large dinner in his honor. The occasion was graced by High Priest Sengei (to whom I have referred earlier) and by Koichi Fukuda, the foremost Chinese scholar of the time. I was often a house guest of Mr. Fukuda, and my brother also stayed with him. The gifts presented to my brother during the function, and even before, by high-ranking public men acquainted with me were so numerous that my brother felt overwhelmed. He was satisfied that I was moving in high social circles and was maintaining my prestige and moral principles according to the best standards. In a couple of days, I said goodbye to him at Kobe, with tears welling up in the eyes of both of us.

As the ship moved away, I was overtaken by a conflict of emotions. When I promised my brother that after completing my work in Manchukuo and Mongolia I would go to America, I was quite certain that it would be impossible for me to back away from my work connected with the Indian freedom movement. I felt guilty that in telling my brother that I would go to America after some time: I was not honest. I gave him a promise in order to avoid hurting his feelings, but that did not reduce my sense of guilt. It was a difficult moment for both of us. My only consolation was that, as far as I knew, he had gauged my mind correctly and known that I said what I did only to please him and that I was not likely in fact to become a turncoat. Of special satisfaction was my brother's assurance that he would report to my mother, who was nearly 80 years old then, that my character and my associations were completely above board.

CHAPTER FIFTEEN
To Mongolia Again: My "Economic War" with Britain

I returned from Tokyo to Hsinking in the autumn of 1936 and began discussions with Colonel Ryukichi Tanaka. He had already received instructions from Tokyo. I set about organizing what I regarded as my economic war to stop the wool trade with Britain.

The first step was, naturally, to get a purchasing mission to take up position quietly in Pao-tao. This was achieved with the active support of nine large trading firms in Japan, among them Kanematsu of Kobe, the largest wool buying company with a wide network (particularly in Australia); Mitsui; Mitsubishi; etc. Kanematsu had all the knowhow for grading the wool and determining prices. The purchase mission was a composite unit with every branch a specialized one. No British merchants could excel it.

For myself, I wanted from the Kwantung Army, apart from the minimum travel arrangements, only one piece of help: the loan of the services of one of their officers, Colonel Kuo, a Chinese who was then working with the Manchukuo Army.

I told Colonel Tanaka that I wanted Colonel Kuo because I had heard about him when he was studying at the Army War College for a graduate degree. He was a Muslim, and it was necessary for me to have the help of such an officer for my work among the Chinese Muslim traders engaged in the wool business. Moreover, his family was one of the most aristocratic in the South Manchukuo area and he could therefore expect VIP treatment there. The Kwantung authorities in general had no perception of the importance of such factors; I had therefore to do a great deal of talking to get them to understand the methods of operation I intended to adopt.

The first requisite was of course the maintenance of utmost secrecy (*bocho*) about the proposed work. Top secret instructions should be sent to all the Tokumu Kikan and other Japanese authorities in the Mokyo and the Inner Mongolia regions involved, asking them to provide me and my associates security, board and lodge, and other essential facilities. They should also be informed secretly that I would be conducting my work in the guise of a Muslim mullah (priest) from India, but this should not be divulged to any unauthorized person under any circumstances. Colonel Tanaka agreed to all my conditions.

In China, the name of a person hardly gave any clue to his religion. A Lee Kang-kuo, a Wang Chou-men, or a Tung, Kung, Ming, or whatever, could be of any religion: Buddhist, Muslim, Confucian—he could even be an atheist. I had thought of changing my name but decided not to. I was young and optimistic and was prepared to take calculated risks. The possibility that someone or other among the Chinese traders might discover my real religion did not worry me; I thought I could cross that bridge if I came to it. I grew a beard of the kind that a Chinese Muslim normally did, and equipped myself with the cap, cloak, and other paraphernalia that went with the image of a typical priest among them. When everything was ready, Colonel Tanaka arranged an introduction for me with Colonel Kuo at the Army Club. All necessary details were explained to him according to the principles of *bocho*. He was most understanding and cooperative.

It was arranged that Colonel Kuo would be on special duty with me for a period of four or five months, accompany me or travel alone, if necessary, to Pao-tao or any other place. He was indeed pleased to have an opportunity to meet some of his friends, especially Muslims from the aristocracy. We struck up a good rapport with each other. It was good to see during our journey to Pao-tao, and in Pao-tao itself, that Kuo was held in high respect by the local people. In his company, "Maulvi" or "Mullah" Nair could also expect VIP treatment. Kuo was always deferential when introducing me, thus boosting my status in the eyes of the Chinese Muslim community still further. That I could speak their language reasonably well was an added advantage.

* * *

CHAPTER FIFTEEN

We left for Inner Mongolia in the summer of 1937. The Japanese Tokumu Kikan at Pao-tao was helpful in all respects. It arranged for our stay at a leading Inn, owned and operated by one of the best-known Muslims in the area. With Colonel Kuo, I would converse in Japanese, which was a more natural thing for me to do than strain my brain for Chinese words. Kuo had learned Japanese fairly well during his training at the military academy in Tokyo. He was a good man, also shrewd and discreet. He decided that I must be given proper introductions to suit my high status as a Muslim priest. "How exciting!" I told myself. Some time ago I was Dharm Rimpoche, a living Buddha, and now I was a Muslim maulvi. I remembered that in the latter capacity, I must naturally pray in the local mosque the next day which was Friday.

Send-off party at Hsingking on the eve of the author's second tour to Mongolia in 1936, hosted by the Kwantung Army under Lieutenant General Itagaki and Manchukuo government representatives. Sitting, from left: the author, Colonel Tanaka (representing Lieutenant General Itagaki), and Mr. Tokuto of the Manchukuo Cabinet. Standing, from left: Yuso Honma and an officer of the Manchukuo government.

Kuo took me to the mosque and secured a front-rank position for me befitting a high priest. For a moment I was a little uneasy because I was an "imitation" Muslim. It would be a tragedy if anyone discovered the truth. But that was only a fleeting thought, and I resumed my stiff upper lip posture and a "never say die" sangfroid. I even began to believe that after all I could pass for a genuine Muslim priest—why not: I had seen mosques in India and had sufficient knowledge of Muslim customs and manners to do what was expected of a priest of that community. There could be minor variations in practice between Indian Muslims and Chinese Muslims, but those would be tolerated because I was, after all, a newcomer from another country and the congregation would understand. But the nagging worry was that although I had seen mosques from outside, I was entering one for the first time in my life; and that too as a high priest. There was some obvious difference in the situations.

I knew I had to pray. After all, I was in the biggest mosque in Pao-tao, and it was Friday. What was still more important, I had been introduced to the chief priest by Colonel Kuo as an eminent Indian Muslim priest and also as one who had high connections with the Manchukuo and Japanese military authorities. When the chief priest invited me to the first row, I was a little nervous. It was no doubt prestigious to be there, but in my situation, it had some disadvantage too. If I could be a little to the rear, I could watch what the men in front of me were doing and perform likewise. The front row was thus a handicap. However, difficulties of this nature should not come in the way of important tasks. I had one purpose, and that was to break the British monopoly on the wool trade from Pao-tao and Tientsin. For that, I should be prepared to go through whatever hazards came in my way!

Soon it was prayer time. I remembered what I had read long ago about the practices to be observed on such occasions. First there would be a washing ceremony. The particular parts of the body to be washed were the hands, the mouth, the nose, the eyes, the ears, the anus, and the penis. I went through all this quite "religiously" in the washing place of the mosque. Ordinarily, the particular part of the anatomy last mentioned would have caused a non-Muslim some concern if someone was looking during the wash time, because the foolproof identification of a man as a Muslim was the mark of circumcision. Any uncircumcised person would have difficulty in posing as a Muslim, not to speak of acting as a mullah!

Due to a fortuitous circumstance, I did not have to worry about this. When staying in Manchukuo in 1934, I had developed a wound on the skin of my penis, and Dr. Omori, a famous surgeon at the hospital there had done a circumcision to rid me of an abscess. It had never occurred to me then that Dr. Omori's operation would stand me in good stead in Inner Mongolia's Pao-tao mosque. As it happened, I now had a perfect set of credentials as a Muslim. I could well discredit anyone who might dare to question them.

I would ordinarily consider it to be a sin to play fool with any religion because all religions are sacred, but I consoled myself by recollecting the proverb: "All is fair in love and war." Since I was engaged in an economic war with Britain, the religious sin I was committing was conceivably permissible under a wider philosophy.

The washing finished; but there was still the problem of going through the right motions at the actual prayers. With the grace of Allah, I managed a sufficient number of unobtrusive side glances at my fellow worshippers to be able to do what they were doing. Perhaps the imitation was not as perfect as I could have made it from a rear row; but, let the Lord be Praised, I came out unscathed.

The prayer itself was not difficult. I knew how to repeat

la `ilaha il`lelaho
(Allah is very great)
ma`hom'd-ur-ra `suli 'la
(And Mohammad is his Prophet)
a'lahu akbr
(Allah is the greatest of all)

Since there were so many persons praying at one and the same time, my lip movements could easily synchronize with those of them. I had only to keep repeating in soft murmur: *la `ilaha il`lelaho . . .*, and no one would be the wiser, even if my Arabic pronunciation happened to be imperfect.

Outside the mosque, matters were easier. I would greet all with the traditional Muslim salutation:

a salam a `aleikum
(May you live, be happy and may all be well with you)

And receive the reply:

`walekum a`salam;
(And may you also live, be happy and may all be well with you)
wa rehmatu 'lahu
(And may all good things from Allah be with you)

Without my knowing it, there must have been something in the way I put on my acts that appeared natural. I could see before long that the Muslim traders and the inn owners accepted me as one of their own community. We got along very well. I had certainly the need for a favorable atmosphere, in order to make the next move: to persuade the traders to sell their wool at Paotao to the Japanese-cum-Manchukuo purchase mission, instead of sending it on to Tientsin. Achieving such a turnabout was bound to be a somewhat time-consuming process. In consultation with Colonel Kuo, I decided that giving any impression of rush could become counterproductive. We set about doing a good deal of propaganda, surely but patiently.

TO MONGOLIA AGAIN

* * *

During our period of outward hibernation, I was observing the psychology of the Chinese Muslims and other communities. From talks with various persons at different social levels, I gathered that there were Muslims in almost every province of China. They were of course a minority, but not so small as I had thought. In the northwestern provinces they accounted for almost 40 per cent of the population. But politically they did not have the same awareness as followers of Buddhism or Confucianism. Their lives centered more around their religion and their trade than on political activities.

Most of them, I noticed, had the habit of referring to themselves as "Muslims" rather than as "Chinese." Religious fervor sometimes assumes strong tinges of fanaticism in various countries, including India, but probably due to lack of political interest, Chinese Muslims were a docile people. Early in the thirteenth century, Genghis Khan was feared not only in Mongolia but in North China, but after the death of his grandson Kublai Khan, Muslim power declined, giving place to Buddhist influence.

The Muslims with whom I came in contact in Inner Mongolia were dignified and cultured men. I found them cleaner and more hygienic than the other communities. In their religious faith, they were more orthodox than their compatriots in certain other countries. This was often reflected in their food habits. Of course, no Chinese Muslim would frequent any restaurant that served pork; at the same time, it must be said to their credit that they were tolerant of other religions. There were no quarrels on grounds of culinary and dining differences.

I did not see any Muslim who drank alcohol or smoked tobacco or narcotics. I was told there was no womanizing among the community either. The Koran, of course, permits four wives, and most of the Chinese Muslims availed themselves of this luxury. Some of my Muslim friends sympathized with me because I, a bachelor, did not have even one wife, which in their opinion was a great pity. Of course I would not dare to go anywhere near a woman, since I had to maintain my prestige as a priest, known locally as an *ahom*. The term was used occasionally even to show respect to important persons other than priests. Even those who did not know that I was a priest regarded me as an important person; I had in any case to be on my best behavior.

When I felt that the propitious time had arrived, I told Colonel Kuo that it would be good if there was a strong Muslim organization in Pao-tao—there could be frequent get-togethers and exchange of views on matters of common

CHAPTER FIFTEEN

interest, to promote social as well as economic cohesion. And by working in harmony as a united body, they could make better profits in business. Why should the merchants take all the trouble to send the wool to Tientsin when they could sell it to the new purchase mission in Pao-tao at a price no lower than what they would get in Tientsin? And the Pao-tao Muslim Association could give similar advice to their communities in neighboring areas as well. All the inn owners could also cooperate, without any loss whatsoever to their income. Colonel Kuo was in entire agreement with me and actively promoted the idea among the Muslim populace in the areas. It caught on remarkably well, and within a few months' time Pao-tao became the terminal point of the wool caravan. The British found their Tientsin source for wool completely cut off.

It was not possible to estimate accurately the amount of damage which this must have caused to Manchester and Lancashire, but it was bound to be considerable. The Chinese Muslim traders and innkeepers had given me much support. One of the richest of them had given for my use a whole building, which I utilized as an office during my five months in Pao-tao. I succeeded in getting him nominated as the president of the association.

At Pao-tao (Baotou) Mosque in 1937 as a Muslim priest. From left: Lieutenant Nanashima; the author, disguised as a mullah; and a news reporter.

I must acknowledge the yeoman services rendered for the progress of the association's work by Mr. Nanashima, a graduate of Waseda University and native of Fukuoka who had joined me within a few months of my arrival in Pao-tao. He was a sincere friend. A lieutenant in the army reserve corps, he could work as a civilian except when called up for specific military duty. He had therefore enough freedom to move closely among the Muslim traders.

Nanashima was an intellectualand at the same time very good in the martial art of fencing. He held the eighth grade in it, which was quite high in the fencing hierarchy. Such a qualification helped him to avoid conscription into the regular army, because he could often get away with the plea that he was useful in training new candidates in fencing lessons.

Under my advice, Nanashima kept urging our Muslim brothers to unite and consolidate their association so that in due course they could demand their legitimate political due. Of course, I took care to see that we were not interfering in China's internal affairs, but only giving personal advice of the right kind to our friends.

The month of Ramadan came during the early period of my stay in Paotao. Colonel Kuo and I took part in the special prayers and fasted just like the other Muslims. We never cheated in this. In fact, I felt better for this fasting. I think that apart from its religious significance, fasting for given periods is highly beneficial to health. Of course, the danger of overeating after the fast should be avoided; otherwise, there can be stomach trouble.

Colonel Kuo left Pao-tao and returned to Manchukuo soon after the Ramadan month in 1937. I returned together with Nanashima in early 1938, after being reasonably satisfied that the organization we had built up would function well on its own. We hoped that 1936 would remain the last year of shipments of Mongolian and Chinese wool from Tientsin to England. The news spread without much delay to Japan and other countries.

In Tokyo, the British embassy had an intelligence officer called Figges, who, I gathered, received in due course a knighthood from the British king, George VI. He had a network of spies and a special budget to watch on me and my activities. He also used to refer to me as Manchukuo Nair, following the description conferred on me by his spy predecessors. For aught I know, he might have shifted my name in his books, from the list of the "dangerous" Indians, to that of the "most dangerous," and perhaps bracketed me with Rash Behari Bose. It may seem odd, but I have never had any *personal* ill-feeling against Figges (or any other British intelligence officer or functionary for that matter). My anger was, as I analyzed my own mind, solely against the institutionalized slavery of Indians that Britain was practicing in India, and my energies were devoted only towards the process of ending it, in whatever way I possibly could. I believed that whether big or small, my Mongolian interlude was a contribution in that sense.

The net effect of my work was that the wool which used to be shipped to England until 1936 was shipped to Japan thereafter. Mahatma Gandhi's campaign in India for the boycott of British textiles and other goods from England was the inspiration for my efforts to prevent the shipment of Tibetan

CHAPTER FIFTEEN

and Mongolian wool for use in Manchester and Lancashire. I was happy that I could achieve the purpose almost singlehandedly.

∗ ∗ ∗

There was a reserve officer by the name of Lieutenant Yamamoto, who had a brainwave that it would help Manchukuo's and Japan's expansion into Inner Mongolia if a Japanese military outpost (Tokumu Kikan) were established at Ujino. He approached Colonel Ryukichi Tanaka for money and other necessary help to go there together with half a dozen Japanese staff on a reconnaissance tour to investigate the feasibility. Tanaka swallowed the idea and provided Yamamoto with all the assistance he asked for. Carrying the Hinomaru (the Japanese national flag), Yamamato and party went to Ujino on horseback, returned, and reported to Tanaka that the place would be ideal for setting up a Tokumu Kikan.

Some friends in the Japanese army told me about this, and I was shocked at the foolishness of the proposal. I knew Ujino well and had studied the lay of the land. Chinese presence there, although unobtrusive, was strong. If the Japanese were to maintain an outpost there, good security arrangements must be a precondition. There was none in existence, nor was action taken to provide any. I warned Tanaka of the grave danger involved in accepting Yamamoto's proposal, but he, like one whose feet were a little too big for his shoes, and whose mind was somewhat unstable, felt that the Hinomaru was all powerful. He sent one Major Ezaki and a staff of fifteen to open a Tokumu Kikan at Ujino. There was also a wireless set and an operator.

Within a month, the Chinese army wiped out the outpost, killing its entire Japanese personnel. As far as I know, this tragic episode was never revealed to the public by the media or any other source. Probably, even in the army, only a very few knew of this "Ujino Ezaki Kikan Incident," which was kept top secret. After the Second World War, the American army conducted some marathon investigations into the affairs of the Kwantung Army, with the help of persons like Major Fujiwara (of dubious fame in connection with his alleged claim to have helped to create the Indian National Army in concert with Captain Mohan Singh, initially a prisoner of war of the Japanese), but I doubt whether even they discovered anything of the Ujino massacre.

Another mishap to the organization I had built up in Pao-tao with the help of just two officers, Colonel Kuo and Lieutenant Nanashima, occurred when one Colonel Nakamura was posted to the Economic Department of the Japanese army high command in Kalgan. I have mentioned before how I had arranged that the Japanese mission stationed at Pao-tao must pay for the wool the same price that the traders would receive at Tientsin. That principle was in fact the backbone of the whole scheme. When Colonel Nakamura came on the scene, he had a bright idea that since Japan was so powerful, there was no need to be lenient to the Chinese caravan operators or the wool traders. He allowed, or perhaps ordered, prices to be reduced to levels which were uneconomical to the traders. The latter felt that they were being exploited.

My friend Nanashima who came to know of this through a staff member of Kanematsu of Kobe was very disturbed and told me about this. We met Colonel Nakamura and cautioned him about the dangers of his policy. But he was as swollen-headed and power blind as Colonel Tanaka. We reminded him of the story of the Ujino Tokumu Kikan. But he said that Ujino was an outpost without an army, whereas Pao-tao was very strongly protected by Japanese soldiers.

Having failed, in spite of much argument with the Kalgan army, to persuade Nakamura to be reasonable, I went to Tokyo in the spring of 1938, to complain to the army high command there. I was shocked to hear from them that about a month after I had left Pao-tao, the Muslim association I had helped to create had broken up due to various misdemeanors of Japanese agents, and perhaps mismanagement by the purchase mission itself. The people had become discontented, as a result of which the Chinese authorities regained control of the area and massacred all the Japanese, including the commander of the Japanese army there, a lieutenant colonel. The Japanese military police command at Pao-tao was also totally liquidated by the Chinese.

This episode, called the Pao-tao Incident, was also hushed up by the Japanese army, like the Ujino incident. The traditional Chinese traders suffered much at least for some time, and many innocent Japanese lives were lost due to criminal neglect on the part of the authorities concerned. The Kwantung Army became so overconfident as to forget elementary realities. These events, unfortunately, were not within my control. My work had ended with the stoppage of the shipment of wool to England, but I felt sorry that some officers could not see things beyond their nose. I returned to Manchukuo with much sorrow at what had happened. But fresh fields and pastures new were waiting.

CHAPTER SIXTEEN
Manchukuo Again

On my return from Tokyo to Hsinking in the middle of 1938, I was hoping to concentrate on the Indian freedom movement's publicity and allied tasks more intensively than I could during the previous year. There was also much to catch up with in respect of my advisory functions vis-à-vis the Kyowakai and the Manchukuo Administration. I devoted considerable attention to these but was involved at the same time in political developments newly taking place.

The Army Ministry in Tokyo and the Kwantung Army headquarters were operating in high gear. The Japanese forces were heavily committed in China, where their presence was growing increasingly unpopular. There were frequent clashes between them and Chiang Kai-shek's army. In December 1937 they had defeated the Chinese forces in Shanghai and captured Nanking, where they indulged in terrible atrocities. But Chiang Kai-shek, after moving his capital to Hankou, began resistance with greater vigor. The Japanese troops were under pressure. The Kwantung Army was vastly expanded to cope with the situation.

An additional concern for the Japanese government was the possibility of Russian intervention in China or Manchukuo, or perhaps both. Tojo, when he was chief of staff of the Kwantung Army in 1936–37, had warned Tokyo that such a contingency could not be ruled out. In such a context, attention had also to be given to the situation in Korea. Korean nationalism had become a force to reckon with. Since three enemies would be worse than two, Japan was inclined to adopt a soft posture towards Korea, at least as a means of playing for time to decide its moves in the face of possible threats from China and Russia.

Manchukuo affairs, in the circumstances, assumed high priority in the Japanese scheme of things. Tokyo decided to step up both economic development of the new state and its preparedness for military defense.

On the economic front, a variety of large, heavy industrial projects were started with the assistance of the Japanese zaibatsu. This provided increased employment opportunities not only to the people in Manchukuo but for Koreans who were recruited and sent to the new sites in large numbers. It was a calculated move, since improvement of Korea's economy could hopefully keep the country politically quieter. Korean labor was even taken to Japan for work in various fields, particularly coal mining. For expansion of the defense forces, several additional army divisions were brought in from Japan. Many of them were posted in areas close to the Chinese border.

A sad part of these activities, particularly increasing the Japanese military presence, was that these were accompanied by large-scale degradation of Korean women. The red light districts filled with Chinese girls in Japanese-controlled areas in China were already a scandal. In Manchukuo, it was the plight of young Korean women to be recruited in alarmingly large numbers for the entertainment of frontline Japanese soldiers. There were Japanese girls too, but relatively few.

Part of the defense effort consisted of maintaining buffer zones between the Soviet Union and Manchukuo and other Japanese-controlled regions. Inner Mongolia was already such a zone, but the army high command in Tokyo had a secret plan for the creation of another. It was quite a novel idea.

There were large numbers of Korean exiles spread over an area within Soviet territory lying immediately across Korea's border with it. The scheme was to penetrate into this population, indoctrinate them and provoke them to agitate against Russia for political autonomy for the region where they formed the majority of the residents. The plan might have appeared to some as rather farfetched, but the Japanese military were quite serious about it and wanted it to be launched quickly. If it succeeded, the Korean exiles were likely to remain loyal to Japan, providing it the second buffer it was looking for.

* * *

CHAPTER SIXTEEN

It was undoubtedly a delicate task. Korean cooperation was unavoidable, which naturally meant the enlistment of a Korean leader. The Japanese government thought of Lee Kai-ten, one of the foremost Korean patriots of the time.

The question would at once arise: why Lee Kai-ten? The reason was his popularity among the Koreans on the one hand and his diplomatic approach to the Japanese on the issue of Korean freedom on the other. To the run-of-the-mill politicians or bureaucrats, Lee Kai-ten was somewhat of an enigma; they of course knew that he was a nationalist but were not sure to what exact degree. But to those who knew him intimately, it was obvious that he was one who burned with patriotic fervor, determined to see his country free from Japanese domination. He would not take any action that was likely to go against such a sentiment. But there were very few who knew him well enough. He was such a shrewd and diplomatic operator that he had made a fine art of promoting the Korean freedom movement most effectively through secret work while giving a wrong outward appearance of being a moderate who was ready to sit down and "negotiate." In some circumstances, therefore, he was an "acceptable" nationalist Korean in the books of the Japanese government. The plan to use the Korean exiles was, in the Japanese view, one such circumstance.

I was one of Lee's best friends who knew his real character and methods of operation in the cause of Korean freedom. We became close to each other through our association with Ryohei Uchida, founder of the Black Dragon Society, and his right-hand man Mitsuru Toyama. Both of these famous Japanese ultranationalists favored us in many ways. They were remarkable men. I have referred to Toyama earlier, in the chapter on Rash Behari Bose. I knew him personally in Kyoto during my university days, and it was there that I came in contact with Ryohei Uchida also. Ryohei died of tuberculosis in 1933. I saw him a few times even in his sickbed and was amazed at the way he kept working hard until his very end. He was a man of iron willpower.

The reason for the affection Ryohei and Toyama had for Lee and me was the patriotism of each of us for our respective countries, which in their judgment was in tune with their own sentiment for the Japanese emperor and for their country as a whole. Some persons might tend to see some contradiction in this. Whereas there was nothing to inhibit the Japanese leaders' minds as far as I was concerned, it might seem rather strange that they showed equally sympathetic consideration to Lee, who came from Korea, which was under Japanese domination. The general impression would be that they would not want to have anything to do, except what might be harmful, with a Korean who was working for the riddance of Japanese authority from his country. But human psychology can operate in strange ways indeed in different persons.

Whatever their critics might say against their right-wing extremism, these leaders of the Black Dragon Society were men of culture. They were so impressed by the sincerity of Lee's patriotic feelings that they would not do anything to prevent him—the easiest thing for them if they so chose—from working for the liberation of his country, even though it was Korea! An unusual kind of approach, but entirely true.

Nationalism, therefore, was what formed a common denominator for the four of us. There was however the strict understanding that none amongst us would tread on the toes of any of the others. Each would work in his own way. If anyone so desired, he might even refrain from telling any of the rest about his movements or activities, and he would not be asked. Still the common friendship would remain absolutely intact and sincere. But Lee and I, of our own volition, invariably shared our thoughts and news of our actions. On a number of occasions, we traveled together in Manchukuo and Korea. I was always greatly impressed by Lee's efficiency in undercover work.

* * *

Lee Kai-ten belonged to South Korea. He was a born nationalist, and was an angry man when Japan annexed Korea in 1910. When we were together in Manchukuo in 1938, he was about 65 years old, almost twice my age but with energy no less than mine—perhaps even more. He had also a razor-sharp brain and a steely physique. He belonged to a rich family, and while staying in Seoul in South Korea would outwardly maintain the trappings of a luxurious lifestyle, but personally was of very simple and austere habits. A firm believer in herbal tonics, his own health was the best illustration of their efficacy. Lee was a nonsmoker and partook of alcohol only very rarely—that too in strict moderation. The disparity in age between us did not affect our sincere friendship which was based on an identity of motivation in the freedom movements of our respective countries. For obvious reasons, his mode of operations was more dangerous than mine.

Lee's son-in-law, Kin, was also a good friend of mine. He was a graduate of Tokyo Hitotsubashi University (THU). A brilliant student, he graduated in 1935 or 1936 at the top of the list in his faculty of economics. THU's economics faculty was a famous one: one of Japan's postwar prime ministers, Mr. Ohira,

CHAPTER SIXTEEN

and a famous journalist of the *Asahi Shimbun*, Ryu Shintaro, and several other prominent economists had graduated from it. Kin was of about my age. He also, like Lee, was a nationalist to his marrow. The father-in-law and the son-in-law made a wonderful team of freedom workers.

It would be incorrect to think that the Japanese had any illusion that Lee Kai-ten could be bought over or persuaded to function as their agent. Nor could they have considered him completely safe for operation amongst Koreans, whether exiles or others. But they had necessarily to take some risk. The buffer zone operation could not be carried on without the help of a known Korean nationalist. The Japanese apparently hoped that the prospect of a Korean autonomous region in Russia and a show of willingness to ease their hold on Korea might constitute reasonable attractions for Lee to take up the project.

Lee Kai-ten, the great Korean patriot.

Han Wakabayashi, also connected with the Black Dragon Society, was the intermediary whom the Japanese government utilized to put the idea across to Lee, through the Kwantung Army. Lee agreed to handle the scheme, on his terms.

He would head a secret movement of revolutionary Koreans in Korea, Manchukuo, Shanghai, and other parts of China, besides those in Russian territory. This organization would run a school in Hsinking to teach the techniques of *boryaku* (espionage) to Koreans of his choice, in collaboration with Japanese officers of the Kwantung Army. The curriculum would be in two parts: one would consist of "spiritual and political teaching," which Lee himself was to handle; the other, involving the theory and practice of "field spying," should be the responsibility of Japanese instructors. The shrewdness of Lee was such that the controlling strings were all entirely in his hands. First and foremost, he was the one to select the "students." He would make sure that every one of them was properly imbued with the determination to work for Korea's freedom, while ostensibly training for penetration into the Korean exile community in Russia.

The scheme was to be financed entirely by the Japanese government. Funds were to be handed over, whenever demanded, jointly to Wakabayashi and Lee. Part of what Wakabayashi received could be used for entertaining Kwantung Army officers, as was the general practice on such occasions; the rest could be utilized by Lee in the manner he thought best. Wakabayashi was eligible for a large commission separately each time for his "liaison function."

Lee invited me to join him as an instructor. Considering my friendship with him, I could not say no, although I made it clear to him in all honesty that I would only teach the broad techniques of espionage, without taking sides either with the Japanese or the Koreans. In other words, I would be an "uncommitted" adviser on the principles of *boryaku* and would not concern myself with the actual implementation of the project. This was acceptable to my friend. Since enlistment of help from an "outsider" like me involved policy, approval of the authorities in Tokyo was necessary. Lee had no difficulty in obtaining it. I was happy to help him since I was all in favor of freedom for Korea by any available means.

With a group of Japanese experts who would provide the necessary camouflage as instructors, Lee Kai-ten started an espionage school in Hsinking with thirty Koreans of his choice and launched a three-month training course for them. At the end of it a second batch of the same strength was put through a similar program. I was the course coordinator and honorary adviser-cum-guest instructor, and also the chief warden.

After the trainees had graduated and were ready to start work, Lee Kai-ten dispatched them to Siberia via the Manchukuo-Korea-Russia border. Later, in early 1940, he himself crossed over to Siberia when the whole area was in deep snow and travel conditions were incredibly hard. I had seen him off at the border township of Konshun (Hunchun). The Kwantung Army and the Japanese military high command in Tokyo were expecting to receive important reports from the party, but no news ever came. And no one heard anything more about the agents or their leader. After World War II, I was informed that some of the Koreans whom Lee and I had trained in Hsinking were prominent in North Korean politics. But, to my regret, I could not gather any authentic news as to what happened to my friend Lee himself.

CHAPTER SEVENTEEN
My Marriage

In the autumn of 1938, while still engaged at the Korean espionage center in Hsinking, I paid a brief visit to Tokyo. It was at the request of the Japanese high command to attend a series of meetings to discuss the situation in Manchukuo. I took the opportunity to meet some of my old friends outside the government as well. Among them was Risuke Fuwa, a businessman in Tokyo, who had an abiding interest in matters concerning India.

Fuwa was a son-in-law of Imagoro Asami, a highly respected village chieftain in Saitama Prefecture, acknowledged as head of the most aristocratic family in the area. During dinner at my friend's house one evening, I met his wife's sister, Iku Asami, who was temporarily staying there as a guest. There was hardly any conversation between us except the usual exchange of polite niceties, but I found myself exceptionally attracted to her.

While I was in Tokyo, I kept my feelings strictly to myself. There was a conflict in my mind on the wisdom of falling in love, which was something which might not mix quite well with my life pattern of the time. I was like a ronin, moving from place to place without any fixed headquarters for my work, or any permanent home. I had so much to do politically that I was unsure whether I could manage to settle down at all to a married life. I therefore tried to put all ideas of marriage behind me, but they would come back continually. Fairly soon after my return to Hsinking, I shared my feelings for Iku Asami with an intimate Japanese friend, Mr. Kori.

MY MARRIAGE

This being the first time he had ever heard me talk on this subject, Kori was highly excited. He took upon himself what he decided to be his duty, viz. to pass the word round that A. M. Nair was willing to get married to Iku Asami. It was a rather daring move on his part, but no one could stop him.

Kori sent telegrams to various dignitaries in the Japanese military high command, including the war minister, General Itagaki, previously chief of staff of the Kwantung Army. Among the Indians in Tokyo whom he informed was Rash Behari Bose. In Manchukuo the news spread rapidly and reached Emperor Puyi through his chief aide, Lieutenant General Kudo. Lee Kai-ten was among the first to be told. The message, which Kori composed all by himself, virtually read as though my marriage to Iku Asami had already been decided upon and that the only step remaining was to determine the date. Although still somewhat at odds with myself on the subject of marriage, I did not object to Kori's bold initiative and was ultimately relieved that I had someone to attend to a matter I realized I really desired but was not quite willing to admit in the beginning.

Kori, of course, was discreet enough to word his communication to Imagoro Asami somewhat differently from that to others, and also to make sure that the message was not dispatched directly but was sent through Iku's brother. It was a request as from me for his consent for me to marry his daughter.

Matters moved quickly. Objections were raised by several daughters of Mr. Imagoro; it was virtually unheard of that a foreigner should be allowed to marry into a Japanese aristocratic family, especially that of a village chief. In the case of Indians, Rash Behari Bose's was the only instance of a marriage to a daughter of an important and well-known Japanese family, and that had taken place at the insistence of no less a person than Mitsuru Toyama. Mr. Imagoro himself, however, kept his mind open. He had heard about me and was not opposed in principle to having me as a son-in-law, but wanted to think things over for a while. In the meantime, congratulatory messages began to pour in. The situation was such that in spite of my work at Lee Kai-ten's school, I thought it necessary to make another brief visit to Tokyo to settle this personal matter one way or the other without delay, instead of allowing needless speculations to develop.

Waiting for me at Tokyo, among various other communications, was an envelope from General Itagaki, with his name franked on it in his own hand. The envelope contained a warm message of good wishes, and a cash "marriage present" of 3,000 yen. For a moment I could not believe that I was counting rightly, because 3,000 yen those days was an enormous sum of money. But, that apart, Itagaki's message itself provided me with the best of credentials that anyone could hope for. I had heard of the objections from Mr. Imagoro's relatives; so, I decided to send him, through a friend, Itagaki's envelope (minus the money, which I kept back for myself, of course) and the message, so that he could decide about my acceptability into his family. The effect, as I had more or less expected, was speedy. Resistance ended, excepting from the two eldest sisters. The latter were reconciled to the fact of my marriage only after Japan had suffered defeat, India had become independent, and I had acquired my own house in Tokyo.

Mrs. and Mr. Imagoro Asami, parents of the author's wife.

Mr. Imagoro had one question to be sorted out: what would be his daughter's *koseki* (family registration) if she married me? At that stage I sent word through her elder brother that India was unfortunately still under British colonial rule, but I was confident that it would become independent before long. When that happened, I would like his daughter, if she married me, to become an Indian citizen. He thought for a while, and with tears welling up in his eyes, placed General Itagaki's envelope in front of the family altar.

I knew that it signified his approval of the marriage proposal. He informed me through his son that he fully agreed with what I had said. He was happy to give his daughter Iku in marriage to me. To change her nationality, I could wait until India became a free country, because he also did not wish to see his daughter becoming a "subject of Britain." I was deeply touched. My father-in-law was in the forefront of those Japanese dignitaries who sincerely believed that India would be free before long. Unfortunately, he did not live long enough to see the happy event. But I tell myself often that he must be feeling happy about it in his abode in heaven.

* * *

MY MARRIAGE

According to my own family tradition, I wrote to my eldest brother Dr. Kumaran Nair about my proposal to marry Iku Asami, giving him, for his information and that of my mother, her family background and seeking the consent of my mother and himself. I was not sure that my letter would reach him, but it did, although delivered by a policeman instead of a postman. His reply came quickly: my family had no objection. My mother, while giving me her blessings, added her hope that I would be able to support my wife (and children in course of time) well, both economically and socially: I should also remain a loving husband and father. She had one more wish: to see me and my family at least once before the time came for her to leave this world. I was overwhelmed with emotion. I wrote to my mother to say that she should not worry about her youngest son: he would remain a good man, even if he did not become a great man. I believe my assurance consoled my mother.

I was married to Iku Asami on February 6, 1939, at a simple ceremony in Tokyo attended by close relatives and friends of the Asami family including Mrs. Imagoro, and some of my intimate friends. The whole group consisted of

The author before his wedding in Tokyo, 1939.

Wedding photograph of the author and his wife, Iku Asami, February 6, 1939.

CHAPTER SEVENTEEN

about twenty persons. My father-in-law sent his blessings through his wife.

On February 7, my wife and I left for Kobe, and we sailed from there the following day for Dairen, where we arrived on February 11. After a few hectic days of celebrations arranged by my friends, I settled down to my normal political activities, the main item on the agenda at that time being completion of the ongoing course at Lee Kai-ten's school. The Korean leader was happy to see me back. I must not omit to record here my deep sense of gratitude for his financial support for my special trip to Tokyo for my marriage and for my return journey. He presented me a sizeable sum of money. Although I had received handsome gifts from several other well-wishers, and the gift from General Itagaki was large indeed, I could well do with Lee Kai-ten's present as well. Even austere weddings were not exactly inexpensive.

I had much to do all the time, including frequent travels within Manchukuo. My wife and I had a good house in Hsinking, and a comfortable life. Our first son, Vasudevan Nair, was born in Hsinking on December 4, 1939. I had never failed even for a day to remember my mother's wish to see me and my family, but unfortunately her hope (and mine too) did not materialize. Five days after the birth of Vasudevan, my mother passed away. Although she was in her eighties at that time, the news caused me profound sorrow. And it still makes me sad when I think of her, as I often do.

CHAPTER EIGHTEEN
Last Spell in Manchukuo

After marriage, it is perhaps natural that most persons, including many who had been active in public life earlier, should want to settle down to a quiet, or at least quieter, life as "family people." In fact, many friends who thought that I had had enough of the role of a ronin and of the dangers attendant on my political activities advised me to take up a "steady," and probably highly lucrative, nonpolitical job. I had no lack of opportunity for such a position, whether in Manchukuo or Japan. It was only in India that I would have had to face unemployment, since the British authorities were itching to get me behind bars in my own country.

But I did not feel in any way tempted to change my workstyle. My marriage had indeed added to my personal responsibilities, but that was no reason why I should stage a volte-face. As for my wife, her background was such as would have normally attracted her to an affluent life pattern rather than to the stresses and strains of the life of a revolutionary who was constantly exposed to danger. But she was not only content, but eager, to fit into whatever field of activity I chose for myself and to help me in it all the way. She was entirely in sympathy with my concept of my life's mission, which was that I should remain part of India's struggle for liberation from colonial rule. I was fortunate in my marriage.

Early in 1939, the Manchukuo government wanted my services in a number of new administrative measures they were introducing in the state,

CHAPTER EIGHTEEN

out of necessity. The government in Tokyo was in full support of the plans, since improvements achieved in Manchukuo would assist them in easing the ever-growing tensions in Japanese controlled areas in China. I said "out of necessity" because Japan, after a fairly easy conquest of Manchuria and conversion of it into an independent state, was facing problems with regard to retaining its control over it. Administrative reforms were a vital need.

* * *

The first requisite in this context was of course the creation of a good cadre of administrators. For this purpose, the Manchukuo government decided to establish at Hsinking, in the early part of 1939, a *kengoku daigakko* (National Construction University). It would run a four-year course for high-grade candidates specially selected from all the five races. There were specialist instructors from various faculties, including military science and techniques. General Itagaki from Tokyo, and also General Ishihara, Colonel Tsuji, Lieutenant Colonel Kataoka, and Major Mishina were sponsors of the new institution, and they invited me to join its teaching faculty dealing with national and international psychology. The institution was under the control of the Manchukuo government's Ministry of Education, but technical support came from the Kwantung Army. I accepted the position of a visiting professor.

One of the ways of teaching I adopted was to hold frequent get-togethers of my students in my house, mostly every Sunday, so that the students from the various "races" would first of all get to know one another well. Those were days when ordinarily no one would dare to express his views freely lest he should be spied upon and reported against. Even a whisper by an independent thinker could result in the military police swooping down on him. Students were terrified of them. But as far as their meetings in my house were concerned, they had nothing to worry about. The Kwantung Army's chief of staff had placed my house off-limits for the military police. Therefore, the students could open out their minds without any fear. It was interesting to watch how in a free atmosphere they ventilated their individual opinions and often clashed vehemently on matters of principle.

The Korean students would generally disagree with the Japanese and the Chinese. But it was noteworthy that there were several among the Japanese students themselves who were liberal-minded and opposed to all colonial expansionism anywhere, although they were all generally agreed that in creating a new Asia, Japan had to play the leading role. I made it a point to ensure that while the students must have a free rein to express their views, their discussions should never descend to the personal level. They should never start quarrelling, nor come to blows. Whatever be the provocations, there must not be any feelings of personal enmity towards anyone. Debates should be well-informed and maintained at an intellectual plane. If one could not see eye to eye with another's point of view, he should agree to disagree. A piece of advice I gave all of them was that they should cultivate one common sentiment: opposition to all types of Western colonialism in Asia.

These meetings, intellectually stimulating, were nevertheless not inexpensive. Our house did not have adequate facilities to feed my student guests properly. My wife therefore would arrange sumptuous meals for them from nearby restaurants at substantial cost.

* * *

Even as efforts were being made to create a better class of Manchukuo administrators, the Kwantung Army was going through a difficult time. Throughout 1939, it was getting more and more bogged down in China. The situation on the Manchukuo-China border was becoming critical. The Japanese found that they could no longer retain their image of invincibility. In some of the border clashes, the opposite side was made up of Russian troops, and the Japanese soldiers took quite some beating. The Soviet Union reportedly had about 250,000 men concentrated in Eastern Siberia for action against the Kwantung Army in the event of any big flare-up.

It was in the summer of 1939 that the so-called Nomonhan Incident took place, with its highly damaging repercussion on Japanese prestige. For the Kwantung Army, it was a great loss of face. Nomonhan was a small village near a stretch of grazing ground on the boundary between Outer Mongolia and Manchukuo. What began as a border skirmish there developed into a major war between the armies of the Soviet Union and Japan. There were massive attacks and counterattacks with large numbers of tanks and aircraft supporting the respective ground forces. The Kwantung Army was badly mauled: casualties in its ranks were estimated at about 9,000 dead, with almost an equal number wounded. It was said that the local Japanese commander had blundered. But Lieutenant General Rensuke Isogai, chief of staff of the Kwantung Army, accepted the blame. He was recalled. Following the

CHAPTER EIGHTEEN

Russo-German nonaggression pact of August 1939, there was a lull on the Manchukuo-Soviet border, although Japan never really ceased viewing Russia as a source of danger.

Summer, 1940. I was still engaged in Hsinking with my normal activities: publicizing the Indian freedom movement and teaching at the *kengoku daigakko*. After the Nomonhan Incident, General Yoshijiro Umezu was appointed commander of the Kwantung Army in place of General Ueda. Reports from Japanese-occupied or Japanese-controlled areas in China were of an alarming nature, indicating that the administration in those regions was far from sound. General Umezu decided to look into the cause of the troubles and held several meetings with his aides to discuss the problem. One of the decisions during the meetings was that I should be requested to visit some of the Chinese centers in question on a fact-finding mission and to report the result to General Umezu.

* * *

I accepted the assignment since it also gave me an opportunity to study what was being done by the British and other Western powers in those areas where they had certain leased territories. I told General Umezu about my special interest, which would be in addition to the work he wanted me to do for the Kwantung Army. I informed him that to carry out my own counterintelligence work vis-à-vis the intelligence operations which Britain was surely conducting in places like Shanghai, Tientsin, Peking, etc., I might have to pose as anti-Japanese on occasions. Therefore, advance intimation should be given to all the Japanese authorities or agents concerned so that they would not mistake my posture but afford me necessary protection and assistance. General Umezu agreed that instructions would be issued immediately. I, of course, would operate strictly according to the code of *bocho*.

I spent altogether nearly five months in Peking, Nanking, and other areas. The cause of trouble was practically the same everywhere. There was no rapport between the Japanese military commands and the local Chinese or other residents. The Chinese did not understand the Japanese methods of work and the Japanese did not try to make them clear. For instance, if a Chinese had to contact the Japanese army authorities for any help, he did not know which particular office to approach. There were too many organizations functioning in the same center: one would deal with what was called "occupation affairs," another would be a prefectural office, a third department would consist of "advisers to the prefectural governments," and so on. And there would be subsidiary units like the supplies and services offices, the military police administration, etc., most of which the local people found highly confusing.

To complicate matters further, there would be nebulous bodies called by names such as Shinminkai (New Peoples' Association) or other "-kai." The net result was altogether chaotic administration. The economy was neglected, and since there was no proper control of the operation of the Japanese business entrepreneurs there was much exploitation of the local people by them.

Briefly, it seemed to me that the Japanese army was trying to govern their occupied areas in China as though they were prefectures in Japan, a system which the Chinese could not comprehend. There was hardly any coordination among the various departments. It was like too many cooks spoiling the broth.

* * *

During my own "counterespionage," I discovered that both the Americans and the British were actively encouraging disaffection among the Chinese people, against the Japanese. The American ambassador had a seemingly innocuous but effective method of "brainwashing" Chinese youth. He would invite small groups of 10 or 15 young Chinese men and women for dinner at his residence almost every evening, ply them with liquor and subtly lecture them about the "evils of Japanese expansionism in China." These persons would soon turn pro-American and anti-Japanese. The British establishments had a similar way of operation. Through their extraterritorial rights in Shanghai and other areas in China, their presence was still effective. The Japanese had no proper organization to neutralize Britain's Secret Service.

Eric (later Sir Eric) Teichman, who was the British consular representative in Peking, was a competent intelligence expert. He had designs which even went beyond promoting anti-Japanese sentiments amongst the Chinese. He planned to map out an overland route from China via Tibet all the way to India across the Himalayas. He once actually set out on such a "pathfinding" journey with a number of motor vehicles and other equipment mobilized with surprising efficiency. It was a grand and bold design, but at least in the initial stages he could not go through with it. I tried to cause as much inconvenience to his expedition as possible within my limited resources. I could not do much,

CHAPTER EIGHTEEN

but at least at three stages (that is, over a distance of about 40 or 45 miles) from the starting point, I managed to have all his gasoline supplies en route set ablaze with the help of Chinese agents whom I recruited for sabotaging the project.

But the British consular service consisted of tenacious officers, and apparently, they were operating deep into Sinkiang and other Chinese areas and beyond. Teichman was reported to have proceeded at least up to Urumqi, which was much farther than I was able to get. As I have said, I was stopped by a Chinese bandit even before Hami. I do not know whether Teichman was able to go beyond Urumqi, but I was told that the British consular officers did chalk out an overland route all the way from China, partly traversing the Gobi Desert, and then via Hami, Urumqi, Kashgar, and Gilgit, and across the Karakoram mountain range into Kashmir in India. They had offices permanently established at all the important points on the way. It is one of my regrets that my ambition to do such a journey never fructified. I sometimes curse that Chinese bandit, even today.

* * *

On my return to Hsinking, I gave a three-page report to General Umezu. He and his staff were surprised at the ineptitude of their China Command offices. Their administrators were totally ignorant of Chinese psychology. Umezu held a private meeting with me at the Army Club for detailed talks on my report, and I gave him full justification for what I had said. I told him that however unpalatable my observations might be to the army or others, I wanted to be thoroughly honest in my statements to them.

I think it was this candidness that enabled me to enjoy the confidence of the Kwantung Army commander. I had the same kind of good relations with General Ushiroku of the China Command, besides General Itagaki (the then war minister), General Ishihara (ex-chief of staff of the Kwantung Army) and several others. Among my friends at the middle levels of the army was one who deserves special mention. He was Lieutenant Colonel Maeda who, despite his relatively junior position in the overall hierarchy, held the very important post of director of naval affairs.

I told General Umezu that some of the deficiencies and defects I had observed were fundamental and related to national psychology. I had noticed a "blinker-eyed" approach on the part of several Japanese officers. Good leaders must be adaptable. They might have to bend certain things without necessarily breaking them. But many of the Japanese who were in control appeared to prefer first breaking the objects they were handling, and then trying to patch up the pieces.

The Kwantung Army appreciated my views. The high command in Tokyo went to the extent of circulating my report ("brutally frank," as they called it) to their military attachés in all the Japanese diplomatic missions abroad for their information.

Many of my friends from Tokyo wrote to thank me for the investigations and the "short report." Conditions were, however, generally such that remedial measures in respect of the administration of Japanese-occupied Chinese areas were not easy to implement. The strain of the never-ending China war was telling on the Army Ministry in Tokyo. With the increased muscle provided to Chiang Kai-shek by the British and the Americans, Japan was getting deeper into the China quagmire. Its effort was confined to maintaining the status quo, rather than attempting to work any administrative wonders. Moreover, World War II had started in Europe, and Japan was heavily engaged in planning ways and means of utilizing the situation to its own advantage.

At the insistence of the emperor, in July 1940 Prince Konoe formed what was called in certain select circles the "war cabinet." Matsuoka was made foreign minister, and Lieutenant General Hideki Tojo became war minister. Admiral Zengo Yoshida was appointed minister for navy. It became clear that there would be no accommodation with the United States. A military pact was concluded by Matsuoka in Tokyo, with the German representative Heinrich Stahmer, on September 26. It was undoubtedly calculated to be operated against America.

Matsuoka scored what was perhaps his most prized diplomatic goal when he succeeded in concluding a five-year neutrality agreement with Stalin on April 13, 1941.

My own gain during my China tour was the knowledge of the devious espionage measures conducted by Britain and the USA. However, with practically no financial resources or manpower, there was hardly anything that one could do by way of counterintelligence work on any systematic basis.

* * *

CHAPTER EIGHTEEN

My last major activity in Manchukuo was, rather strangely, centered on an offshoot of the war in Europe, which had begun in September 1939.

Manchukuo had a sizable population of White Russians who had fled from their country during the Bolshevik Revolution of 1917. The largest concentrations were in Harbin, Hailar, Hsinking, and Dairen. There were also smaller numbers of them in Shanghai, Tientsin, and other areas in China. This community was not a component of the "Five Races" polity (Kyowakai), but the Japanese had encouraged them to form an association of their own. To placate them, they were offered special concessions by Japanese industrial houses engaged in large projects such as conversion of various centers in Manchukuo (Hsinking, Dairen, etc.) into highly modern cities. But there were setbacks in the development programs due to Japan's heavy commitments in China. These in turn caused an unemployment problem among the White Russians.

The Russo-German nonaggression pact of August 21, 1939, had surprised the world. Even though it led to a lull in the Manchukuo-Soviet border, Baron Kiichiro Hiranuma's cabinet in Tokyo was shocked. It viewed it as a violation by Germany of the Anti-Comintern Pact which Japan had concluded with it in November 1936. Japan always regarded the Soviet Union as the greatest danger for it.

Bolstering its defenses in Manchukuo to counter any threats from Russia continued to be an obsession with the Kwantung Army. Among its efforts in this direction was the raising of a volunteer force of several units, comprising nearly the strength of a division, from among the White Russians. It was expected that, being Tsarists, they would be a bulwark against potential aggression from communist Russia. As a spin-off, the jobs created would alleviate the community's economic difficulties.

These White Russians were given military training. The army units raised from among them were also assigned a separate flag with an emblem similar to the German Nazi Party's swastika. The 4th Department of the Kwantung Army headquarters was placed in exclusive charge of the affairs of these units, although Russian affairs in general were being handled by the 2nd Department.

Hitler's initial successes had greatly impressed Japan. When France and Holland fell to the German forces in early 1940, efforts by Japan to penetrate into the colonies of those countries in Southeast Asia were evident. It concluded a friendship treaty with Thailand on June 12, 1940, and used it to secure positions of vantage to begin evolving what eventually came to be called its "Greater East Asia Co-Prosperity Sphere."

When Germany abrogated its nonaggression pact with the Soviet Union and attacked Russia on June 22, 1941, the world was stunned even more than it had been at the news of the conclusion of the nonaggression pact. And what caused immediate consternation in Manchukuo was that as soon as information came in about the German attack on the Soviet Union, it was discovered that all the White Russian units of the Kwantung Army had switched loyalty and reported to the nearest available Russian consular representatives, volunteering their services to fight the Germans. The Kwantung Army commander, General Umezu, was flabbergasted.

One morning in the last week of the same month I was surprised to see Major Matsumura of the Kwantung Army staff's 4th Department driving up to my house in Hsinking. As he was in his army uniform, I could at once guess that it was not a purely private visit. Without much delay he came straight to the point: the army commander would appreciate it if I could see him urgently. I went with Matsumura and met General Umezu. The short point of our conversation was Umezu's enquiry whether I could do him a favor by making a quick investigation into the circumstances in which the White Russian units of his army had defected to the Soviets. He had to send a report to Tokyo on the subject.

I was not keen to take on such a task at that time. It was only a short time ago that I had returned after a strenuous tour in China. Moreover, I was not happy to leave my wife and our baby once again alone in Hsinking. General Umezu however kept pressing me for help. After thinking it over for a couple of days and receiving my wife's assurance that I should not worry on account of her and our son, I agreed to the assignment and set out on my investigation work. Almost subconsciously I was also allured by the opportunity for a further look at what the British and the Americans in China were doing in Manchukuo through their agents.

I asked for special facilities similar to those given me during my previous tour. These were quickly arranged. This time the Kwantung Army went farther than before: they gave me a personal status equivalent to a lieutenant general, and an identification card accordingly. All the Japanese offices concerned were suitably briefed.

Penetrating into the White Russian community was more difficult than infiltrating into Chinese circles. I soon discovered that to get any White Russian to talk, he had to be started off on large doses of vodka. I necessarily to drink with him but must not get drunk as in such an event the whole purpose will be defeated. Enquiries showed that there was a way one could out-drink a White Russian and yet remain sober. A good quantity of olive oil

CHAPTER EIGHTEEN

should first be consumed in order that the intestines would be well lined to prevent alcohol from getting into the blood stream too quickly. That would enable one to keep alert when the other party loosened his tongue. The long-term effect on health would still be bad, but then: no pains, no gains. I had to do my job properly; so, I collected a good stock of olive oil. There had of course to be an antidote ready for use after the party: for this, grated apples with milk was a very good prescription. I partook of it always at the right time.

Over a period of about a month, I got to know the White Russian leadership quite well. That was enough time to establish the reason for the new army units' action. It was simply a matter of national psychology. These Tsarists were undoubtedly anti-communist. In any civil commotion within Russia, they would continue to oppose communism. But in the event of an attack on Russia *by any other country*, they would sink their ideological differences and be Russians first and anti-communists next. Tsarists though they were, the territorial integrity of their motherland was sacrosanct for them. It was clear that in the event of a clash between Russia and any other country, including Japan, the Japanese could not rely on these White Russian units.

I came back and gave a one-page report to General Umezu and substantiated it later during personal discussions with him. It was surprising that the Japanese had not made any attempt to study the psychology of the community before raising a number of army units from their midst. It was the same blinker-eyed approach that was causing them much trouble in China. By ignoring psychology, they had, for all practical purposes, raised a fifth column in their own establishment!

My report was transmitted to Tokyo, but, once again, it was hardly possible to do anything positive. The damage had already been done. Moreover, the government machinery in Tokyo was fully preoccupied with the wider issue of determining its strategy vis-à-vis the Second World War.

In that context, I should like to record a fact which is probably not quite well-known. In the inner circles of the cabinet in Tokyo, there was a serious divergence of views. There were the Hoppo-ha, who favored an initial attack on Russia, and the Nampo-ha, whose preference was for a first strike in the south. The two groups could never arrive at a consensus. Eventually the decision to strike at Pearl Harbor was taken under pressure from General Tojo, against whom the prime minister, Prince Konoe, was helpless. Tojo was then the war minister. He was able to obtain the concurrence of the emperor to the view of the Nampo-ha which, basically, was his individual view. Tojo, nicknamed "Razorblade" to indicate his "sharp brain," adopted the position that with nearly a million Japanese troops stationed in the Manchukuo-China-Russia border regions, an invasion from Russia would be unlikely.

When Germany attacked Russia, the Hoppo-ha were apprehensive that as a measure of spite against Japan, which was not only Germany's ally but Russia's age-old enemy, the Soviet Union might strike out into Manchukuo or even into the Japanese home islands. But the Russians were not in a position to do so even if they had wanted, as they had to throw everything they had into the battle against Germany. Meanwhile the Nampo-ha's contention that moving into the ready raw material resources of the southern regions would be more advantageous, prevailed. The die had been cast.

CHAPTER NINETEEN
The Second World War and the IIL in Southeast Asia

Towards the end of November 1941, I received a message from the Kwantung Army headquarters requesting me to remain in Hsinking until further advice.

It was not difficult to guess the reason. For several months past, the military high command's office had remained in a state of emergency. The communications room was being manned round the clock. I and many of my friends knew that Japan was going to enter the Second World War, but no one had any inkling that the point of attack would be Pearl Harbor. The exact date was also top secret. It was doubtful if the Kwantung Army commander (General Umezu) himself knew, since the details of the strike could have been divulged even to the forces deployed for the purpose, only at the last minute. But on December 8, 1941, all the world heard the news about the attack on Pearl Harbor.

It was Japan's blitzkrieg, executed to a fine degree of precision. At 12:32 a.m. on December 8, Tokyo time, which was 7:52 a.m. on Sunday in Hawaii, navy commander Mitsuo Fuchida led the bomb raid on the American Pacific fleet which had been harbored in the waters of Hawaii like sitting ducks. Several hundred aircraft had taken off from Japanese carriers. Four American warships, besides more than a dozen other ships and over 200 planes were destroyed. American casualties exceeded 2,000. At dawn the same day, Radio Tokyo broadcast the emperor's rescript:

> Patiently have We waited and long have We endured, in the hope that Our Government might retrieve the situation in peace. But our adversaries, showing not the least spirit of conciliation, have unduly delayed a settlement; and in the meantime, they have intensified the economic and political pressure to compel thereby Our Empire to submission. This trend of affairs would, if left unchecked, not only nullify Our Empire's efforts of many years for the sake of the stabilization of East Asia, but also endanger the very existence of Our nation. The situation being such as it is, Our Empire for its existence and self-defense has no other recourse but to appeal to arms and to crush every obstacle in its path.
>
> The hallowed spirits of Our Imperial Ancestors guarding Us from above, We rely upon the loyalty and courage of Our subjects in Our confident expectation that the task bequeathed by Our forefathers will be carried forward, and that the sources of evil will be speedily eradicated and an enduring peace immutably established in East Asia, preserving thereby the glory of Our Empire.

The Greater East Asia War had begun.

On December 9, I received a telephone call from the Kwantung Army general staff asking me over to their office. I soon found that the purpose was to inform me that the Japanese navy had launched its action against Singapore that very day and that the British battleships *Prince of Wales* and *Repulse* had been sunk. To celebrate the occasion, there was a champagne party. The officers, while thus sharing their jubilation, regarded it as the beginning of the end of British colonialism and said that the opportunity had arrived for me to embark on "direct action."

It was significant that during the party, there was no talk, in my presence at least, about the attack on Pearl Harbor. Obviously, the army officers had guessed that Pearl Harbor would not be a subject of any particular interest to me, since India was not an enemy of America. She was only fighting British imperialism.

At long last, colonial Britain was taking a heavy beating from Japan. The time for me to change the nature of my work had indeed come, and I decided that I must move to the scene of the war. The welfare of my wife and young

CHAPTER NINETEEN

son was a matter of great anxiety for me, but my wife, of her own accord, helped me to overcome the mental conflict. She understood the situation very well, and like a samurai's wife, emboldened herself to tell me that I could leave Manchukuo on any mission I might choose in the furtherance of the cause of India's freedom and that I should not have any worry on account of her and our son. I told her that the struggle required immediate reorientation in the light of the latest developments, and that I must do all that might be possible.

It was clear that Hong Kong and other centers would soon fall to the Japanese. They did so by the end of December 1941, and Singapore surrendered formally on February 15, 1942. I informed my friends in the Kwantung Army before the end of the day of the champagne party that I must proceed urgently to the south. At my request they sent wireless messages to Japanese establishments in Tientsin, Shanghai, Nanking, Hong Kong and other stations, asking for all necessary facilities to be extended to me. After bidding my family and friends farewell at the Hsinking railway station, I left for Tientsin the same day and from there flew to Shanghai. General Ushiroku, commander-in-chief of the China Command of the Japanese army in Nanking, had been notified about my movement from Hsinking. He issued instructions to the Shanghai Command which detailed Major Mishina to look after me. The message had also said that I could visit the general at Nanking whenever I wished.

I spent two days in Shanghai, mainly to establish an Indian independence center there formally, to be funded and maintained by the local Indian leaders. Shanghai had a well-to-do Indian population, mostly engaged in trade. There were also fairly large numbers of Sikhs employed in the police. The entire community was extremely helpful, and fully cooperated with me in setting up an organization to conduct effective publicity for the Indian freedom movement. I met several of the Japanese army officers too, to ensure proper protection for all the Indian residents. There was a great deal of disturbance to the normal life in Shanghai because of the sudden developments. I arranged with Major Mishina for his good offices to see that, since Indians were still British subjects technically and therefore liable to be categorized by the Japanese forces ordinarily as enemy nationals, special care should be taken to treat them as a favored community entitled to safety. Through these local arrangements, soon followed by instructions from Tokyo, all the Indians were given due protection. There was a large British presence in Shanghai. A few of those families managed to leave, but the majority were held as prisoners of war.

Escorted by Major Mishina, I went to Nanking to meet General Ushiroku. In spite of his heavy preoccupations, he was good enough to give me a good lunch at his headquarters and talk to me at length about the desirability of Indo-Japanese collaboration in eliminating British power in India, Burma and elsewhere in the east.

From Nanking I made a hurried visit to Hong Kong via Shanghai. Colonel Hara, the area commander, provided all necessary facilities for the inauguration of an Indian office there on the lines of the one already set up at Shanghai. Hong Kong was a nerve center of Indian trade. It was also the best listening post to obtain information on happenings in China.

* * *

After handing over the new office to be run by competent local Indian leadership, I went to Colonel Hara's office to pay him a courtesy call and to thank him for his cooperation. I was accompanied by Lieutenant Colonel Okada of the Ushiroku Command in Nanking. He had come on other duty as well as to meet me. Unexpectedly, however, an unpleasant episode occurred. Hara and I had a quarrel. He patronizingly told me that whereas I was free to do whatever I wished, I must do it all in the name of the Japanese emperor. I thought that was gratuitous advice I did not need, and instinctively reacted sharply against it. I asked him in a stern voice:

"What do you mean, Colonel Hara? Why should I conduct my work in the name of the emperor? I was handling essentially the Indian freedom campaign, and I would do so in India's name."

Hara did not cease his provocations, and I found his manner highly offensive. Nearly losing my temper, I said, "To hell with you; I will do what I think right."

Lieutenant Colonel Okada had kept his two-seater plane ready for his journey with me to Shanghai, but due to the argument between me and Hara, the flight was delayed. I was still angry about Hara's conduct and was not quite sure whether to complain to General Ushiroku or some other senior officer before leaving Hong Kong. However, the situation was saved by Okada, who somehow brought about peace between Hara and me.

During our flight, both Okada and I were rather tense, and remained silent. We were thinking about Hara's performance. On reaching Shanghai, however, we felt relaxed.

Lieutenant General Kasahara, vice-chief of staff in General Ushiroku's China Command, an old acquaintance of mine, and Major Mishina were waiting for us in a luxurious Japanese restaurant. Okada narrated to them the Hong Kong episode. To my surprise, they burst out into a hearty laughter. When I asked them why they were treating such a subject so lightly, Lieutenant General Kasahara said that no one could expect anything better from Colonel Hara who was a "half-crack."

It was then that I learned about Colonel Hara's "reputation" among his own colleagues in the army. He was obviously a competent officer: otherwise, he would not have been placed in charge of an important command like Hong Kong. (He was the officer to whom the Hong Kong garrison of the British army had surrendered.) I was told that he was basically not a bad man; his problem was that as a follower of extreme *kannagara* (emperor worship) he was at times liable to go off balance and become a little mad. That was apparently what had momentarily happened at Hong Kong when he was speaking to me. Lieutenant General Kasahara told me that Hara had created similar difficulties in Korea earlier. If I had known all this background beforehand, I would perhaps have dealt with him differently and avoided the unpleasant interlude.

The Shanghai office of the Indian freedom movement was functioning well. It was the last week of January 1942, and I arranged with Osman, a prominent businessman, for an Indian flag-hoisting ceremony to be conducted on the 26th of the month. A group of Punjabi ladies sang "Vande Mataram" in chorus. That was the first time Shanghai had witnessed an Indian ceremony of this kind in an open ground. Nearly 500 members of the community were present.

I sailed from Shanghai for Japan the next day. Before leaving, I was pleasantly surprised when Major Mishina came to see me off and handed over a gift of 6,000 yen in cash, which had been sent by General Ushiroku with a message that I should use it for my expenses as well as for strengthening the work on behalf of the Indian freedom movement according to my discretion.

On reaching Tokyo I proceeded to the Sanno Hotel Akasaka and booked two rooms, numbers 301 and 302. I needed the extra room for use as an office where there would be much correspondence work to do, besides meeting visitors. I kept for myself a small part of the money given by General Ushiroku and deposited the rest with the hotel management for safe custody. The management was impressed to see my wealth! I must confess that I was myself elated for a while. What a contrast between the penury I went through when I was on my way back from Sinkiang to Hsinking after having been robbed by a Chinese bandit, and now when I had money enough to keep in safe-deposit and thus could establish my creditworthiness at the Sanno Hotel!

My first task in Tokyo was to contact the military high command, especially the 2nd Bureau's 8th Section at the armed forces headquarters in Kudan Hills. The large complex of offices there, the imperial headquarters and the general staff, was collectively called, in Japanese, the Dai Hon'ei. The general headquarters' 1st Bureau, which had four sections, dealt with operational matters. The 2nd Bureau had four branches, indicated for the sake of continuity from the four parts of the 1st Bureau, by the numbers five to eight. The primary concern of the 2nd Bureau was the collection of intelligence, both domestic and foreign, and it was also in charge of *boryaku* (espionage), an activity unavoidable during war. It held the key to various processes in the decision-making machinery and worked in close association with the 1st Bureau. The 5th, 6th and 7th Sections covered European, American, Russian, Chinese, and Southeast Asian affairs. The 8th Section had a large sweep, particularly clandestine penetration into hostile territories, publicity and propaganda, both undercover and open. Supplies and services and transport were the responsibility of the 3rd Bureau.

* * *

The Japanese military high command had, of course, been preparing for war for quite some time. It had also planned to secure the goodwill of the large Indian community in Southeast Asia. As early as September 1941, it had begun to organize a liaison group to be in touch with this community, numbering almost two million. Among them were many recognized supporters of the Indian independence movement. In the context of the Greater East Asia War, their cooperation would be valuable in a variety of ways.

The chief of the army staff, General Sugiyama, was a man of political foresight, although he also, like his colleagues, had overrated Japan's military strength vis-à-vis that of the combined forces of the Western powers. Initial Japanese victories were sensational. It was General Sugiyama who supported the idea that an office should be established for handling matters relating to the Indian community.

He decided to have such an office on a regular basis in Bangkok under Colonel Tamura, military attaché in Japan's diplomatic mission there, since it was a central place from where work in respect of the Indians in various parts of Southeast Asia could be effectively coordinated. A major by the name of Iwaichi Fujiwara and a staff of about twenty persons experienced in intelligence work were deputed to assist Colonel Tamura. Some of them had a fair knowledge of English, and a few could even speak a little Hindustani. I was chosen as the link between the high command in Tokyo and the new establishment in Bangkok which was referred to as Tamura Kikan ("Tamura's Office").

The Indian community in general presented a request to the Japanese authorities, through me, that Rash Behari Bose should be recognized as their leader in Japan and all the Southeast Asian countries. The Japanese government agreed. Here again, it was decided by them that I was to be the channel for discussions and communication of decisions on action programs between the two sides. My official designation for the purpose was chief liaison officer for Indian affairs.

The concept of the "Greater East Asia Co-Prosperity Sphere" (Dai Toa Kyoeiken) was being promoted by the Japanese government even before 1939. Its main purpose, at least initially, was to create a counterforce against Western pressures on Japan as witnessed by the various restrictive measures adopted by them, e.g., the control on immigration to the United States, and the ABCD (American, British, Chinese, and Dutch) economic blockade (sometimes referred to as the "ABCD Encirclement") to weaken Japan. It was in 1940, during the prime minister Prince Konoe's time that the idea took shape within a specific framework. India, however, was *not* included in the scheme. According to the directives of the Konoe Cabinet, the "Sphere" included only the Philippines, French Indochina, the Dutch East Indies, Thailand, Malaya, Hong Kong, Singapore, and Burma. Australia, New Zealand, and New Caledonia were to be brought in at a later date.

* * *

Colonel Tamura had instructions that Fujiwara and his staff should try to study the British military setup in India, Malaya and other places in Southeast Asia. But there was no brief for him or Fujiwara to engage in any direct dealings with leaders of the Indian community in these regions, except that general relations should be maintained in a cordial manner. Fujiwara, however, functioned from the beginning beyond the scope set for him by the high command in Tokyo. Without any sanction, he took upon himself the planning of an eventual expansion of Japanese military authority into India. He sought to do this with the help of the Indian prisoners of war in Malaya. Without any consultation with anyone, not to speak of approval from higher authorities, he chose to place these prisoners of war under the control of an Indian captain, Mohan Singh, who belonged to one of the early British Indian Army units which lost to the Japanese in their Malayan operations in Jitra in the northern region of the Peninsula. After the surrender of Singapore, when large numbers of Indian as well as British soldiers were seized, an alliance took place between Fujiwara and Mohan Singh. Both of them caused a great deal of problems for the Indian Independence League (IIL) in course of time. I shall return to this subject later.

Several books have been written on the Indian independence movement in Southeast Asia: on its leadership initially under Rash Behari Bose and later under Subhas Chandra Bose. A number of them contain errors of facts and distortions of truth, either intentionally or through ignorance. One of the purposes of my memoirs is to set the record straight where it has so long remained misrepresented. As an on-the-spot participant in or an eyewitness of the events, I believe I have a moral duty to inform the public where I think they have been misled.

At the time of its entry into the war in the East, Japan had no clear-cut policy for the handling of matters concerning an India-Japan relationship. Rash Behari Bose was very active in Japan, I was in Manchukuo, and both of us were doing anti-British work in our own ways. There were Indian freedom fighters in Thailand, Malaya, Burma, Hong Kong, Shanghai, and other centers also. But what came eventually to be known as the Indian Independence League, which gave a formal shape to the Indian freedom struggle in all these areas in a coordinated way, came into existence under Rash Behari Bose after Japan's entry into World War II. This happened after several discussions with the Japanese high command in Tokyo by Rash Behari and myself.

I can say this authoritatively because in all those discussions I was the link between Rash Behari and the Japanese military authorities headed by General Sugiyama. Why Rash Behari chose me for such a role in preference to all other Indians, even though several of us were involved in the independence movement, was that whereas he had important contacts with the higher echelons on the civil side, I was the only Indian with easy access on a basis of intimacy to the military, especially with the 2nd Bureau of the Dai Hon'ei. In fact, the first meeting between Rash Behari and General Sugiyama was arranged by me through the officers directly concerned with Indian affairs.

Our effort was to evolve a proper organization of the Indian population in the whole of Southeast Asia, besides Japan, and to introduce workable guidelines to determine how the suddenly changed situation could be utilized to the best advantage of the cause of furthering Indian freedom.

CHAPTER NINETEEN

As I have mentioned earlier, the struggle for India's independence had been vigorously under way for a long time under the stewardship of various leaders outside, besides those inside India. Some of them worked individually, and others as heads of associations with different names. The time had now come to consolidate all those scattered elements into one integrated machinery under a centralized leadership. Rash Behari suggested in consultation with me that the proposed organization should be designated as "Indian Independence League," and General Sugiyama agreed. In the first week of February 1942, it was announced over the radio from Tokyo and in the newspapers in Japan that the Indian Independence League had been established with its headquarters in Room 302 in the Sanno Hotel. We set about chalking out ways and means to embark on a cogent and effective action program.

* * *

I met Rash Behari daily for detailed discussions. Of immediate concern was the safety of the lives and properties of the nearly two million Indian nationals in the areas either already occupied or were likely to be soon overrun by the Japanese forces. I was in constant touch with the military headquarters on the situation in the area most vitally affected at the time, viz. Malaya, where practically half the total Indian population of Southeast Asia had been living. The bulk of them were simple laborers working in British plantations or were engaged in trade, although there were substantial numbers of other categories like lawyers, doctors, technicians, and white-collar workers. The Japanese forces had started to sweep through the Malay Peninsula from the Thai border and to march towards Singapore. With British resistance completely broken, Singapore was bound to fall very soon. Besides the safety of the civilian Indian population, there was the question of the welfare of the Indian soldiers. I requested the military high command in Kudan Hills in strict confidence to issue urgent instructions to their Malaya Command to ensure that their troops would not harm any of the Indians.

It was gratifying that orders accordingly were issued immediately. The effect was remarkable. Except for a few unfortunate isolated cases of ill-treatment, and even killing, the Indian civilian community was spared the dire fate which befell most of the other nationals, especially Chinese. The Indian POWs were also unharmed, unlike the British, Australians, and New Zealanders. Few people in Malaya, India or elsewhere, including those who have written books on the war or on the Indian independence movement, were aware of the fact that it was the orders from the military high command in Tokyo that saved the Indian nationals. The Malaya Command was even told by Tokyo how to distinguish Indians from others, a process in which many Japanese soldiers, particularly those conscripted from the countryside, could not be expected to be adept. A simple method was devised. The signal from Tokyo required Japanese armed men to identify the Indians, whenever in doubt, by asking the question, "Gandhi?" If the answer was in the affirmative, even if it be in the form of a mere nod, the persons were to be well cared for. If orders not to treat Indians as enemy nationals had not gone out in time from Tokyo, the community might have suffered indescribable horrors.

As soon as announcement was made of the opening of the league's headquarters in the Sanno Hotel, thousands of Japanese young men began pouring in as volunteers to join the organization. Rash Behari Bose and I had anticipated such a possibility and were prepared for it. In the earlier stages, even prior to our discussions with General Sugiyama, we had, between ourselves, agreed on a set of fundamental principles which would govern the working of the league.

These were (i) the organization would be based at all levels on the concept of *anasakta karma*, i.e., nothing should be done solely for any individual's personal benefit or for any group's self-interest, (ii) there should be complete unity of purpose amongst the various associations, by whatever cultural, political, or other names they might have been known until the formation of the league, (iii) the league should act in support of the leaders of the Indian National Congress in India and not do anything to oppose or denigrate them, (iv) no non-Indian nationals would be eligible for membership of or active work in the league, (v) although cooperation from the Japanese authorities would be needed and be welcomed, the framing of policies and their implementation would be entirely by the league, with no interference from anyone.

The issue relating to Japanese participation had thus been considered and determined already. I had to sit in the corridor of the Sanno Hotel for several hours daily over a period of some two weeks to meet the large numbers of volunteers and explain why we could not enroll them. I thanked them all, but with a *namaste* (i.e., salutation with folded hands in the traditional Indian style) would tell them that while we were grateful for their touching gesture, our policy required that the league members should all be Indians. We needed the help and cooperation of Japanese friends, but regretted that we could not formally take them into the organization.

It appeared to me that most of the persons who came were sincerely motivated by the desire to help India, but it was possible that some of them might have viewed the league as a means of avoiding conscription into the Japanese armed forces. In any case, it was of importance that we should keep the league completely Indian, both in composition and control.

Soon afterwards, NHK (Japan Broadcasting Corporation) opened a shortwave station for daily broadcasts by us to India. Rash Behari Bose used this facility to address practically each of the important Indian leaders in India to explain the nature and purpose of the league and to inform them that it was a united body of Indians in Southeast Asia and the Far East, determined to support them to the maximum in their struggle for India's independence. In one of his broadcasts, Rash Behari made an impassioned appeal for the preservation of India's unity. He voiced his distress at the news that Mr. Jinnah had been working for the creation of a separate state for Muslims: Pakistan. He pleaded over the radio that even if Jinnah wished to become the president of India we would all be with him, but he should refrain from any action leading to the dissection of our motherland. "Let us all struggle together and have a free India which would remain united forever," he declared.

We were clear in our minds that the Indian freedom campaign could be sustained in Japanese-occupied or Japanese-controlled territories, only with the cooperation of the authorities in Tokyo and their regional commands. That was logical, since Japan held all the power in these areas, and it was no use trying to ignore realities. We, however, never accepted any idea of Japanese *control* of the league. The situation was delicate and needed to be negotiated judiciously and diplomatically with the Japanese high command so that the league could function effectively without compromising its status as an autonomous Indian body. We noted with satisfaction that in Thailand and Malaya the local Indian leaders had already started off on the right lines. In order to infuse confidence among the community, they had established branches of the league in all important centers.

At mass meetings, the Indian population was told that the opportunity to fulfill everyone's aspiration for India's freedom had arrived. Action to strengthen and enlarge the work should be the responsibility of the Indians themselves, but naturally the help of the Japanese was necessary. This should be channelized through programs devised from time to time by the central organization headed by Rash Behari Bose. For the purpose of leading the people in various countries suitably, national councils should be set up. In Malaya the immediate frontline leadership was entrusted to Pritam Singh, and in Thailand, to Swamy Satyananda Puri.

Pritam Singh was a missionary Sikh who had initially gone to Thailand for work there but whom Major Fujiwara took to Malaya in order to call upon the Indian soldiers in the British army to lay down arms and go over to the Japanese side. Swamy Satyananda Puri had been a member of the Greater Indian Society in Calcutta and went to Thailand in 1930 to study Thai culture and language. He stayed on and involved himself in the Indian freedom movement. The Indian population in Burma unfortunately lacked proper leadership. When the war began to intensify there, a large number of them crossed over to India. Many managed to reach safety, but many others were ill-prepared for the difficult journey and perished on the way.

* * *

On the fall of Singapore to the Japanese forces (February 15, 1942), General Archibald Percival surrendered himself and his troops to Lieutenant General Tomoyuki Yamashita of Japan's 25th Army. The prisoners of war included about 45,000 Indian soldiers. They were handed over formally to Major Fujiwara by Lieutenant Colonel Hunt of the British army at the Farrer Park on February 17. Among them was Colonel Niranjan Singh Gill, a highly rated "King's Commission" officer belonging to the aristocratic family of the Majithias of the Punjab. One of the members of this family, Sundar Singh Majithia, had been conferred a knighthood by the British king.

Major Fujiwara accepted the surrender of the Indian POWs with much melodrama, addressing them as "beloved Indian soldiers." He promised to work for good relations between them and the Japanese forces. There was a secret collaboration arrangement between him and one of the POWs, Captain Mohan Singh, whom I have mentioned already. He had been with the 1st Battalion of the 14th Punjab Regiment stationed near Jitra on Malaya's border with Thailand. It was said that he had defected to the advancing Japanese army. There is no authentic account as to what actually took place: according to some sources, he joined the Japanese *after* he had been captured as a prisoner of war, but others say that he had been planning desertion even earlier and decided to give himself up as soon as an opportunity arose.

Mohan Singh had joined the Indian army in 1907 as an ordinary infantry soldier and worked his way up to a commission from the Indian Military Academy at Dehradun. He was made a captain at the age of about 32. Fujiwara was apparently impressed by him and hoped to use him for his own purposes. In any case he seemed to have given Singh much latitude to deal with the rest

CHAPTER NINETEEN

of the Indian POWs so that he would be relieved of the duty of looking after them.

Mohan Singh probably entertained high ambitions when he decided to collaborate with Fujiwara. According to one speculation, he believed that if the Japanese won the war, he could, by virtue of his having been the first Indian army officer to join them, hope to become the military dictator of India. There were others who thought that there was something highly abnormal and suspicious in the Fujiwara-Mohan Singh relationship. For, if it was a matter of looking after the Indian prisoners of war, the services of a senior officer would ordinarily be sought, and there were several among them who were far higher in rank than Mohan Singh.

Apparently, Fujiwara's choice of Mohan Singh was based on the latter's qualification as the first Indian officer to switch allegiance. In any case, it was a comic denouement when Major Fujiwara conferred on Captain Mohan Singh the rank of a general and gave him the command of the POWs with the avowed objective of turning them in due course into the Indian National Army that would eventually try to invade and liberate India. A more absurd plan, and one that was guaranteed to demoralize the senior officers seems to have remained unknown in any military annals. High Japanese army commanders perhaps had no time to look into a strange situation of this kind created by one of the majors. Even if they knew of it, they probably ignored it as a queer thing to be relegated to the bottom of their list of priorities. The highest-ranking Japanese officer whom "General" Mohan Singh was ever able to meet was a colonel, and that too only when he was "sent for." Ordinarily his contacts were with majors and officers of still lower rank.

* * *

On the day following the fall of Singapore, General Tojo made a statement in the Japanese Diet (parliament). He stated that Japan did not consider the Indian people as enemies and that the Japanese government would extend help to Indians in their effort to gain freedom from British rule. Tojo said that it was now time for all Indians to rise and drive the British away from India. He added that Japan's assistance in this would be in the spirit of nonattachment, i.e., Japan had no designs for the conquest of India. The Japanese phrase which he used in order to convey the idea of nonattachment was *mushuchaku no enjo*. There was an interesting background to this.

Some time before General Tojo was scheduled to announce the British surrender of Singapore and to make his reference to India, there was a conference in the military headquarters where I was present. Dr. Niki Kimura was an adviser to the high command on Indian affairs. He was a professor of Indian philosophy at Rissho University and had spent a good deal of time at Tagore's Visva-Bharati University at Santiniketan. He was a scholar of Sanskrit. For convenience in maintaining close liaison with the IIL, he had taken up residence in Room 415 at the Sanno Hotel. Since the league's basic principle was *anasakta karma* (action without attachment), I suggested to General Tojo's briefing officers that it would be good if, in the prime minister's speech in the Diet, the same concept was emphasized as applicable also to Japan's approach to the Indian question.

Both Professor Kimura and the briefing officers agreed. But it took some time for the former to determine the correct Japanese equivalent of the Sanskrit phrase. Eventually he produced the right expression as mentioned, but in the process some forty minutes had passed, and Tojo's announcement had to be postponed by the same period. It was, however, worthwhile. During earlier discussions, I had reminded the Japanese army authorities about the importance of an unequivocal declaration of their intentions in respect of India. Their defective policies and methods of work in China had aroused much distrust, and consequently created several unmanageable problems, as I had myself stated in my report from Manchukuo on the study I had done at their request. It was important to eliminate, ab initio, any cause for Indian suspicion of Japanese motives. India, struggling to rid herself of British imperialism, would never want even the semblance of any colonial approach from Japan. And all possible doubts should be preempted not only among Indians in Southeast Asia but within India itself.

We also used this opportunity to repeat an earlier advice to the Japanese government that, in order to avoid any misunderstandings, all discussions and action on Indian affairs should be coordinated between the IIL on the Indian side and the military liaison group on that of the Japanese.

CHAPTER TWENTY
The Tokyo Conference of the IIL

Soon after General Tojo had announced in the Diet the Japanese government's approach to the Indian freedom movement, Rash Behari Bose and I felt that it was necessary to organize in Tokyo a conference of all the important regional leaders of the league to exchange views and chalk out a clear-cut action program. The meeting was initially set for March 10, 1942, but owing to transportation difficulties, the date was changed to March 28.

During one of the important meetings between Rash Behari and myself, he decided that whereas he would continue as the founder president of the league and would be chairman of the proposed Tokyo Conference, there should be a cofounder and an alternate to him to take on his responsibilities in the event of any emergency. He decided that I should fill both these roles as and when occasion might arise. I felt highly honored by the confidence which Rash Behari placed in me as his number two colleague in the whole establishment of the league. In addition, I was to be the chief liaison officer for dealings on all important matters between the Indian Independence League (IIL) and the Japanese government authorities concerned with Indian affairs, and generally with the military high command in respect of any issue that might come up from time to time affecting the Indian community in the Far East and Southeast Asia.

For the proposed conference, it was agreed by all the Indians in Tokyo that the community in Malaya would be represented by N. Raghavan, a leading lawyer of Penang who was president of the Indian Association of Malaya; K. P. Kesava Menon, a barrister practicing in the supreme court at Singapore (prior to the Japanese occupation); and S. C. Goho, also an advocate in Singapore, besides being head of the youth league and certain other associations in the same city. Burma and the Philippines could not send any representatives, but delegates would come from Hong Kong, Shanghai, and a few other areas.

From among the residents in Japan (besides Rash Behari of course), the participants selected were D. S. Deshpande, V. C. Lingam, B. D. Gupta, S. N. Sen, Rajah Sherman, L. R. Miglani, and K. V. Narain. Although I had been away in Manchukuo for fairly long periods, I had not shifted there permanently. I therefore continued to be part of the Indian resident community in Tokyo and was included among the delegates from Japan. In fact, my role in the conference was multifaceted. Apart from filling the positions already mentioned, I was also to represent Manchukuo's Indian freedom movement centers and the Indian community there. In China there were Indians living in various cities, but the centers other than Shanghai were not in a position to detail representatives. I therefore was to represent the communities in those places as well. Additionally, I was responsible to Rash Behari as the chief convenor-cum-secretary and for all such work as he might entrust to me as the league's cofounder and alternate president.

At the Tokyo Conference in March 1942, at the Sanno Hotel, Akasaka, Tokyo. Rash Behari Bose is in the center; the author sits behind him, third from the left.

CHAPTER TWENTY

Rash Behari Bose speaking at the Tokyo Conference. Seated opposite is K. P. Kesava Menon, and seated center back, wearing glasses, is Colonel Hideo Iwakuro.

The Hong Kong delegates were D. N. Khan and M. R. Mallick, and the Shanghai Indians were represented by O. Asman and Piara Singh.

Before the completion of arrangements for the conference, it had come to our notice that Major Fujiwara and Captain Mohan Singh had been working among the Indian POWs, trying to create an organization out of them to be called the Indian National Army (INA). It was surprising that such an important issue was being handled by two junior army men with hardly any experience in such lines. Rash Behari and the rest of us were concerned about this; so were the civilian leaders of the Indian community in Malaya.

We heard that the Indian army officers, a number of whom were senior to Mohan Singh, were generally resentful of Fujiwara's choice of him to create a new organization. But the situation was rather nebulous since we learned that a nucleus of an INA had been decided to be established, and some officers and other ranks had indicated willingness to join it.

In accordance with the advice of the Tamura Kikan in Bangkok, under which Fujiwara was working in Singapore, we suggested to the military headquarters that a couple of representatives of the Indian POWs might also be allowed to attend the conference since that would be helpful in maintaining the morale of the men who had had to surrender, and in utilizing them in any suitable future activity. Under Fujiwara's arrangements, two representatives came: Captain Mohan Singh and Colonel N. S. Gill.

The opening of the conference was preceded by a tragic event. The aircraft carrying the delegate from Thailand, Swamy Satyananda Puri, besides three others from Malaya, viz. Giani Pritam Singh, Captain Akram Khan, and K. A. Neelakanta Iyer (honorary secretary of the Central Indian Association of Malaya and Kuala Lumpur), as well as some Japanese military officers, had crashed somewhere in Japan, presumably on Mount Fuji.

It was said that due to bad weather en route to Japan the pilot had proposed to delay his takeoff from the previous base, but he was forced to fly according to the initial schedule under the orders of a senior military officer aboard who was anxious to get to Tokyo for a meeting and commanded the crew to disregard the weather. The aircraft was not seen any more; nor were there any survivors. The catastrophe cast a pall of sorrow over the conference, and the meeting's first duty happened to be the agonizing one of condoling the death of the incoming delegates concerned and their companions on the ill-fated plane.

About 25 delegates met at the Sanno Hotel for the conference: the hotel was practically fully utilized by the league for the purpose for a couple of days. Rash Behari Bose was unanimously elected president. I do not propose to detail all the difficulties I had to overcome in organizing the conference. There were many problems, one of which, strangely enough, was related to a request from the Japanese military authorities to hold the meetings at the Imperial Hotel instead of the Sanno Hotel.

There had already been a few brushes between me and the Japanese high command before the provision of certain minimum facilities requested for and by me was settled. I was not prepared to yield in regard to the new and unnecessary proposal. I disagreed with it, pointing out that there was no need for a change of venue. Moreover, we did not like the word "Imperial" for a hotel that was to accommodate a conference of the Indian Independence League. In Tokyo, of course, we understood it in the proper perspective and in the local context, but amongst our compatriots elsewhere we could not anticipate a similar appreciation. Indians unfamiliar with Japan would find the word objectionable because of its association with colonialism and therefore its unsavory flavor. They would think that we were under the "Imperial" control of Japan. It took quite some argument, but ultimately I managed to convert the high command's officers to my viewpoint and got them to agree to our holding the meeting as arranged, at the Sanno Hotel itself. The storm in the teacup was unpleasant.

CHAPTER TWENTY

M. Sivaram, in his book *Road to Delhi*, has given me a great deal of compliment for the organization and management of the conference. He has said, *inter alia*, words to the effect that everything that was achieved during the meeting was due to me. It was gracious of Sivaram. He has also spoken of various aspects of my career as an Indian freedom fighter and my involvement in political activities of various kinds. I should normally have returned to India to take up work as an engineer, but there were serious difficulties since I was in the bad books of the British authorities. I was therefore in a position where I could do only from outside India the work which I had wholeheartedly wished to perform as my contribution to the freedom struggle of my country.

It is true when Sivaram says that I had involved myself in a number of activities in Japan and elsewhere: I had functioned as a ronin, and in Mongolia had travelled as a "living Buddha," a "camel dealer," etc. It is also a fact that the Mongolian prince Teh's contact with the Japanese was due to me and that I had a liaison function between Chinese political leaders and the Japanese. His other references include my associations with the Black Dragon Society and other right-wing political organizations in Japan, in collaboration with whom I was anxious to do everything possible to put an end to British domination in Asia. Sivaram has also mentioned me as the man behind Rash Behari Bose, and my connections with the Japanese military echelons. He has also called me a "man of mystery" with vast energy and much "hidden power" and influence!

* * *

But everything that took place in the conference was not smooth sailing. There was suspicion among the delegates from Malaya, both civilian and military, about the Japanese offer of friendship and promise of help. There were moments when Rash Behari Bose and I found it an exasperating effort to make the delegates see things in the proper light in the extraordinary circumstances of the time.

The Malayan Section adopted a highly legalistic approach to the question of Indian cooperation with the Japanese and the latter's promise of assistance to the cause of India's redemption. They often looked at these as though they were arguing in a court of law. As for the representatives of the POWs, Mohan Singh was all the time reticent during the meetings. Outside, he seemed mostly preoccupied with Fujiwara, but never shared his thoughts with us or any of the other delegates. He was the proverbial "dark horse" among the members of the meeting.

Gill went about as though he had his legs in two boats, unsure as to which one to settle for. He had the temerity to seek out Raja Mahendra Pratap to hold discussions regarding the league's relations with the Japanese. He ought to have known that Mahendra Pratap was out of favor with the Japanese authorities and that contacts with him could land him in the hands of the military police. In fact, matters very nearly came to such a pass until I intervened with the 2nd Bureau in Kudan and saved him from harm.

Rash Behari and I wanted to give a fair chance to Gill to shed what we felt was his amateurish approach to political affairs and to develop into a useful member of the league, for which we noticed he had the potential. He was a man of impressive personality and of basically high caliber. Molded properly, he could be of much help to the league. After some advice from us he appeared to change over to our way of thinking, but Mohan Singh, in Fujiwara's shadow all the time, seemed to be invariably truculent and noncooperative.

One feature of the conduct of the two representatives of the POWs was that there appeared to be deep suspicions between themselves. Gill did not leave anyone in doubt that he had a poor opinion of Mohan Singh and his ability to raise an INA.

Rash Behari often shared his anxieties with me. He wished that the delegates from Malaya were a little more helpful. He had hoped that everyone in the conference would be able to think unitedly. It was a pity that they displayed an amazing degree of heterogeneity in outlook. Some of them had totally misplaced doubts about the nationalist credentials of the "Tokyo group."

Their feeling, nonvocal though it was, that Rash Behari, being a Japanese citizen, could not be an authentic leader of the IIL, was grossly irresponsible. One should have expected men of good sense, as they were supposed to be, to have known Rash Behari better. He was a Japanese citizen because he had to be so for his very existence. But he was, in every drop of his blood, an Indian; perhaps even more so than some of the delegates whose training and upbringing had all been under the British, whom Rash Behari disliked from the bottom of his heart. These are not pleasant reflections, but facts cannot be brushed under any carpet.

Rash Behari Bose conducted the conference with great dignity and ability. No one could have done any better. Despite some discordant notes struck by the representatives from Malaya, the delegates generally got to know one another, and we in Tokyo were benefited by our contact with them. Many of us were worried about their rather "bookish" stand on issues which, during

CHAPTER TWENTY

wartime, could not be wrapped up in legal tomes; but Rash Behari's tact was such that a consensus resolution was adopted emphasizing the league's determination to contribute with redoubled vigor towards the cause of Indian freedom.

It was also decided to have further discussions in a plenary session of the league to be held in a more central place than Tokyo, so that as wide a section as possible of the Indian population in Southeast Asia could be involved in the deliberations. Bangkok was chosen as the venue for such a meeting, which would take place within the next six months. The appointment of a Council of Action—with Rash Behari Bose as president, and N. Raghavan, K. P. Kesavan Menon, S. C. Goho, and Captain Mohan Singh as members—was also approved provisionally, subject to confirmation by the Bangkok conference.

In the garden of the Sanno Hotel, after the Tokyo Conference, March 1942. In the center is Yoshihisa Kuzu, right-hand man and representative of Mitsuru Toyama and alternate leader of the Black Dragon Society; on his right is Rash Behari Bose; to his left are N. Raghavan, K. P. Kesava Menon, and the author.

At the end of the Sanno Hotel meet, which concluded after three days, followed by a courtesy call on General Tojo by Rash Behari Bose and all the delegates, it was good to see that the participants from Singapore and Penang were in a more relaxed mood. N. Raghavan later declared that during the Tokyo Conference the delegates from Malaya were very unfair initially in suspecting the "Tokyo Indians" as potential "stooges" of the Japanese government. It was decent of Raghavan to offer a public apology in mitigation of his initial error—and that of his comrades.

I had, in later days, occasion to advise Raghavan and others who had begun their work with us as doubting Thomases, about the differences between the normal ways of thinking and acting of civilians, and those of military men operating under conditions of emergency such as wars. I also told them that it was not good to assume that only they were wise and that everyone else was otherwise. What I said was briefly this:

> We have two eyes with which we see others, but to see our own face we have to use a mirror. In the absence of a mirror, we should trust someone to tell us how we looked. Those who distrusted everyone other than themselves without some good reason, could possibly be of unsound mind. Any Indian who suspected the bona fides of Rash Behari Bose as an Indian patriot could not call himself a patriot. Moreover, during situations of general disturbance, verbal discussions and understandings on the basis of mutual trust and faith, and on the principle of *bocho* among friends, were potentially more fruitful than the use of pens and hidebound notebooks.
>
> In wars, if a powerful ally went against a written contract and chose to turn against you, what could you do anyway with your documents? On the other hand, if there was mutual goodwill, a verbal understanding was as good as a written one. Few soldiers fighting armed battles had time to do any voluminous paperwork as in law courts. I had certainly many disputes with Japanese authorities, but still we could work together because basically we had mutual confidence and trust. Nobody had to be anybody's "stooge"; what was needed was the courage of one's convictions on the one hand and the grace to allow the same privilege to the other side.
>
> Differences in outlook were bound to exist, but friends with a common aim could certainly resolve them. And even if some problems could not be settled, friendship could still be preserved. In other words, if necessary, two parties could "agree to disagree" (as I used to tell my students in Manchukuo). Also, if one truly believed in *anasakta karma*, it would often be possible to convert the other party to the same philosophy.

CHAPTER TWENTY

Speaking for myself, I believe that from my boyhood, I have always tried to adhere to those principles which I cherished as right. Even in big-time politics, which became part of me (or, perhaps more correctly, of which I became a part), after my graduation from university, this trait remained in me. There were some who, out of ignorance, thought that I was collaborating with the Japanese military forces for the latter's benefit. Others like Colonel Figges of the British embassy in Tokyo were plainly vicious in their efforts to get me detained in India as a dangerous anti-British activist. The truth is that I had several "agreements to disagree" with the Japanese authorities, but still was able to maintain excellent relations with them in furthering the cause of India's freedom.

Just as in the case of Rash Behari Bose, it would be blasphemy to say, or to suggest, that I, even infinitesimally, ever departed from my primary objective of helping the Indian independence struggle. It would be more correct to say, if say one must, that I was able to get a large number of Japanese at the highest levels to agree to work for the Indian cause along with me. In that sense, many of my close friends used to whisper in my ears, after the war, that for fighting against Britain and encouraging my Japanese friends to do likewise, I should have been booked as War Criminal Number One, and that MacArthur somehow missed out on me!

CHAPTER TWENTY-ONE
The Bangkok Conference

Preparations for the large conference slated for Bangkok, in accordance with the decision at the end of the Tokyo meeting, were also entrusted to me by Rash Behari Bose. These had to be more elaborate because of the very nature of the proposed gathering. Infrastructure arrangements presented several problems. I was also anxious to advance the schedule as much as possible since important and far-reaching decisions were required. The publicity campaign organized in Tokyo by means of radio must continue, and additional propaganda work should be undertaken from Bangkok. Both Rash Behari Bose and I practically worked round the clock between April and June 1942.

Meanwhile, the war was going well for Japan. After the surrender of Singapore in February 1942, Rangoon fell in March. The same month witnessed the conquest of the Dutch East Indies. Bataan and Corregidor collapsed soon afterwards, and Guadalcanal was under heavy pressure. (It was eventually captured in August.)

Early in June, we reached Bangkok, accompanied by Deshpande, A. M. Sahay, V. C. Lingam, Rajah Sherman, and a few others, and soon afterwards started preparations for the big meeting. First of all, Rash Behari decided to hold a press conference. Among others, there were two particularly important pressmen. One was M. Sivaram who, until Japan's entry into the war had represented the Associated Press and was since then editor of the *Bangkok Times*. A close friend of the king of Thailand and prime minister, Marshal

Pibulsonggram, and a recipient of the Thai "Medal for Home Defense" (equivalent to the British "George Cross"), he was a highly respected and competent journalist.

I had heard about him earlier, although we met for the first time in Bangkok. I told Rash Behari Bose that Sivaram would be a great asset if we could get him to work for the league. Rash Behari at once agreed and decided to nominate him as the IIL's spokesman and publicity officer. Sivaram, captivated by Rash Behari's charming personality and persuasive manner, discarded all other activity and joined the league heart and soul, to handle its publicity portfolio.

The other well-known Indian journalist in Bangkok was S. A. Iyer, representing the Reuters news agency, which had commissioned him to cover the East Asia War. Sivaram initially tried but failed in his efforts to get him over to the side of our freedom struggle, but eventually Iyer joined, although rather half-heartedly. According to Iyer's own story, Rash Behari, in his inimitable manner, asked him to be not merely the Reuters correspondent but to lend his talents to the Indian freedom struggle as well. He could not resist Rash Behari's magnetic personality and burning patriotism. He joined us, but yet remained rather unpredictable.

Group photo taken in Tokyo before departing for Southeast Asia, May 1942. Front row, from left: the author, A. M. Sahay, Rash Behari Bose, D. S. Deshpande, and V. C. Lingam. Standing third from left is B. D. Gupta, and two to the right is S. N. Sen, followed by Rajah Sherman.

The multiplicity of problems to be overcome before the conference could begin, became evident very soon. Firstly, the number of delegates to be invited from the different national councils had to be decided; also, where and how to find accommodation and other facilities for the participants. And what about the Japanese role? Certainly, we had to have their help, otherwise nothing could take place. But should they be represented, or allowed in as observers? Or excluded from the deliberations of the conference? If they were to be involved, how should the invitation to them be phrased? To what extent could the conference discuss confidential matters during open meetings? Indeed, what exactly were the items which the meeting was expected to debate? Who should prepare the agenda? And on and on. The most ticklish question was that of representation of the military wing. After much thought, we set up, to start with, a preparatory committee to go into all these and allied matters in detail.

* * *

Meanwhile, after Mohan Singh's return from the Tokyo Conference, he set about in earnest enlisting men for his projected Indian National Army (INA). He was only supposed to ask for volunteers, but information reached us that he was employing coercion. Estimates given by various persons as regards the number of volunteers varied considerably.

Initially there were very few officers willing to join him, and the number of other ranks was also no higher than four thousand or so. Eventually the number was said to have increased to some 12,000, but no accurate lists seemed to have been maintained. There were complaints of high-handedness on the part of Mohan Singh. He insisted on oaths of loyalty personally to him by name, an entirely unusual practice in any army.

The conference of Indians in East Asia and Southeast Asia was set for formal inauguration in Bangkok on June 15, 1942, with Rash Behari Bose as its president. There was quite an awkward episode on the preceding day.

At the eleventh hour, some of the lawyer delegates from Malaya suspected that the Japanese army authorities in control of the Silpakorn theater, where the conference was to be held, had secretly arranged for "tapping" the proceedings. Therefore, they wanted the venue to be shifted. I thought this was an amateurish way of looking at things.

There was nothing to show that any eavesdropping had been thought of or arranged for; it was merely some vague suspicion. Secondly, if the Japanese really wanted to know what was happening at the conference, they could employ a vast range of methods even other than "wiretapping." For instance, it would be very easy for them to infiltrate their agents into the conference, and if they chose such a course, no one was likely to know. All the logistics and other arrangements for the conference had to be organized with their help; there was no alternative resource. They could, if they wanted, insist on their presence during the proceedings, or even ban the meetings. But they attempted nothing of the sort. In fact, they were anxious to see that the function was successfully conducted and thereby the solidarity of the Indian community strengthened.

However, when the subject was brought up by Raghavan with the suggestion that there should be a change of venue, Rash Behari readily agreed. Even though he was not convinced of the need to do so, he decided that since Raghavan feared some potential security risk, his wishes should be respected. He asked me to make alternative arrangements. It was all amusing to a point, but last minute changes of this kind were never easy. However, I managed to get another suitable hall in the same theater released, and the conference opened at the appointed time.

Raghavan, subsequently, mentioned this episode as evidence of his conviction (in modification of his suspicious approach in Tokyo!) that Rash Behari was a true Indian patriot who would not allow even the slightest risk being taken where the secrecy of the conference's deliberations, and consequently the interests of the country, were concerned.

Soon after the Tokyo Conference, the military headquarters in Tokyo established, in a portion of the Sanno Hotel itself, a special office to work in close liaison with the IIL on matters relating to the forthcoming meeting in Bangkok. The Tamura Kikan was understandably inadequate, from its location point of view, to handle matters connected with the arrangements for the conference speedily where decisions were required to be taken in consultation with the authorities in Tokyo. The head of the new office was Colonel Hideo Iwakuro, a highly rated officer who was previously a commanding officer of the Imperial Guard. He also had high political connections and a wide range of experience. The appointment of such an officer of proved ability was an index of the importance which the Japanese government attached to the successful organization of the Bangkok meeting. They knew that the outcome of the conference would be vital for evolving a pattern of good relations with the Indian community in Southeast Asia, a matter of considerable importance to them.

When arrangements for the Bangkok Conference were nearly complete, the IIL decided that it should shift its headquarters to Bangkok. That would be a logical step, since Bangkok would be the best center from which follow-up action on the decisions to be taken at the conference could be most conveniently launched.

In consultation with his government, Colonel Iwakuro also moved his establishment to Bangkok. The Tamura Kikan was wound up and replaced by the Iwakuro Kikan. A little later, it was proposed by Colonel Iwakuro that his office should not be described by the name of any particular individual but should have a different name. It was accordingly renamed Hikari Kikan.

Assigned as the Hikari Kikan's principal adviser was Mr. Senda, who had lived for about 25 years in India, mostly Calcutta, engaged in the jute business. He knew India very well indeed and was a good friend of our country. He was really rich but preferred an austere lifestyle.

* * *

The exact organization of the Hikari Kikan was not revealed to the public, for obvious reasons of security. But Iwakuro had personally briefed me in detail on all aspects of it for the information of Rash Behari and myself in our capacity as the chief organizers of the IIL. He did not want us to feel that he was withholding from us anything of importance.

The Hikari Kikan had a department for political affairs, another for military matters. There was a third one for intelligence and counterespionage, publicity, and propaganda, with a sub-office located in Singapore. Administration was the concern of the fourth department. There was an unwritten arrangement under which all details of information relevant to the promotion of good relations between the Japanese authorities and the Indian community would be exchanged between either Rash Behari or me on the IIL's side, and Colonel Iwakuro personally on that of the Hikari Kikan, on the basis of *bocho*. Confidential matters and issues involving policy were to be discussed only amongst the three of us. The oral agreement worked well and avoided the kind of irritations our lawyer friends from Malaya always tended to cause by asking for written communications from the Japanese.

There were several inquisitive members of the Indian community who would keep asking me about the work of Colonel Iwakuro. He appeared to be a powerful man, although affable to everyone. The community noticed that he was, however, officially dealing only with me. Many persons were curious

CHAPTER TWENTY-ONE

to know what was being discussed between us. I of course kept Rash Behari fully informed each time but could not possibly divulge the contents of our talks to others. I had to be careful and would generally give them evasive answers. One particular set of friends became insufferably persistent, and I felt frustrated. When pressed hard, I told them, with affected seriousness, that the Hikari Kikan was a gasoline station. Indeed, we got our petrol for the IIL vehicles from there; so no one could say that I was wrong. In any case, I was spared from further enquiries.

* * *

The conference commenced on June 15 as scheduled. It was a simple inauguration. Rash Behari presided and conducted the proceedings with his characteristic dignity (see Appendix 2). A message of good wishes had been received from General Tojo. There were about 120 delegates in all, the largest number being from Malaya, which accounted for nearly 50, including representatives of the Indian army personnel who had surrendered to the Japanese. Rash Behari's presidentship of the IIL was confirmed, as was the membership proposed during the Tokyo Conference for the Action Council. Burma had sent about 10 delegates, and the remaining numbers, in different proportions, covered Japan, Thailand, China, Manchukuo, the Philippines, Borneo, etc.

The proceedings of the first day were marred due to arguments on certain points unwarrantedly brought up by Captain Mohan Singh representing the army group in Malaya. He was, from the beginning, a source of much annoyance and irritation to the majority of the delegates. His attitude was haughty, and his manners highly supercilious. He made two proposals: (1) that the INA that was proposed to be raised should be entirely his concern and not subject to any control by the IIL, (2) that all officers and men joining the force should take an oath of allegiance to him personally and not to any commander by designation, nor to any organization.

There was general commotion and adverse comment on these totally unacceptable suggestions, the purport of which could only be that Mohan Singh wanted to be a dictator answerable to none. The delegates generally resented them, but the person who stood up and strongly criticized them at once was N. Raghavan, the delegate from Penang and one of the members of the Action Council. He opposed both the proposals of Mohan Singh and stated that they were wholly undemocratic and therefore undeserving of consideration. The

THE BANGKOK CONFERENCE

INA should be fully subject to the control of the IIL and its members should owe their allegiance to it and not to any individual commanding officer by name as though it was a private army. Mohan Singh created a certain amount of loud and undignified noises, with wild gestures, against these very valid objections, and at one stage Raghavan announced to the president that if the proposals as mooted were going to be debated, he wanted to be excused from the meeting. Rash Behari observed that much confusion was likely to take place. He adjourned the meeting and declared that the time for reopening the discussions would be communicated later.

Mohan Singh, in his book *Soldiers' Contribution to Indian Independence,*[*] refers to various matters concerning the Bangkok Conference, but makes no mention of this episode. Incidentally, his statement in the same book that he "was heard with rapt attention for seven-and-a-half hours" on the first day, is a piece of falsehood.[**] He spoke for hardly half an hour, and that too to put forward the two fantastic proposals I have referred to above. The audience was angry.

There is yet another incident which Mohan Singh does not mention. The bad taste of his confrontation with Raghavan during the early part of the conference was aggravated by an amazing piece of indiscretion on his part. He could have tried to sort matters out in a friendly manner, directly with Raghavan or through either Rash Behari or me; but he chose, instead, to contact the Hikari Kikan's junior-most liaison officer, Lieutenant Kunisuka. Through him he sought the support of the Japanese army for his own ideas of organizing an Indian National Army.

Kunisuka's authorized role was merely that of a link on routine matters of logistics between those delegates to the conference who did not know Japanese and the Hikari Kikan's Administration Department. Anything of importance for discussion between the IIL and the Hikari Kikan had to go either through Rash Behari or me, to Colonel Iwakuro. Kunisuka's qualification to be in the Hikari Kikan was merely that he knew some English. He was a clerk in the office of the large wool trading firm of Kanematsu of Kobe. Since he had basic military training (a compulsory part of all high school education in Japan during the prewar decade), he was drafted into the army and posted to the Hikari Kikan.

It was strange that Mohan Singh, who had assumed the rank of a general, should have chosen to deal officially with a lieutenant to enlist the Hikari

---
* Mohan Singh, *Soldiers' Contribution to Indian Independence: The Epic of the Indian National Army* (New Delhi: Army Education Stores, 1975), 122 et seq.
** Singh, *Soldiers' Contribution to Indian Independence*, 122.

Kikan's help in a vitally important matter. A more irresponsible action would be difficult to imagine. And it was stranger still that Kunisuka should have taken it upon himself to try to settle Mohan Singh's score with Raghavan. But facts can be stranger than fiction, as proved by Kunisuka's decision to go to Raghavan's room in the hotel and to start arguing with him against his stand on the INA issue.

When I was passing by Raghavan's room at about noon on the day of the altercations between Mohan Singh and Raghavan at the conference, I heard some loud and angry voices. I recognized Raghavan's voice at once but did not know who the other party was. I entered the room and observed that a full-scale argument was going on between Raghavan and Kunisuka. I was astonished, to say the least, and enquired, as though of both of the persons jointly, "What is all this going on here?"

Raghavan then told me that Kunisuka had come to object to his protest during the morning meeting, against Mohan Singh's proposals, and that in this sort of situation he was preparing to leave Bangkok and return to Penang.

I turned to Kunisuka and said, "Lieutenant, this is a matter which is not for you to handle. I shall take care of it; please go out of this room."

The lieutenant appeared taken back. I was satisfied that he got the message clearly. He stood to attention, saluted, and left the room. I do not know whether he was aware that for the purpose of my dealings with their army the Japanese military high command had decided to treat me as equivalent in rank to a lieutenant general. I had never advertised that fact, and it was possible that a man like Kunisuka did not know. Nevertheless, it was clear from his demeanor that he recognized in me at least a status superior to his, and that was good enough for the occasion.

As soon as Kunisuka left, I picked up Raghavan's telephone and spoke to Colonel Iwakuro at the Hikari Kikan. I told him that I had something urgent to discuss with him personally; could I come over? Perhaps I could see Mr. Senda also? It was nearing lunchtime, and I suggested that, if possible, I should like to see him before he left for lunch. "Yes, Mr. Nair, please come quickly; both of us will wait for you," said Iwakuro. I went over to his office without delay and told him what I had seen and heard a little while ago in Raghavan's room, and also about the confusion during the morning meeting of the conference. I informed Iwakuro that Raghavan was so unhappy that he was packing for Penang.

Iwakuro consulted Mr. Senda and took a quick decision. He said that the action of both Mohan Singh and Kunisuka was objectionable. He would put Kunisuka wise to his legitimate duties and see that he did not repeat his mistake in any form in future. He also said that I should convey his apologies to Mr. Raghavan and request him to stay for the full period of the conference. Iwakuro also wanted me to report everything to Rash Behari Bose, and to plead with him to reconvene the meeting at which he could, if he so desired, issue a clear ruling in the form of an order that the INA, if and when organized, would be fully under the control of the IIL.

My meeting with Iwakuro ended with a clear and emphatic declaration by him: "If it comes to a question of cutting out one of the two parties, I would suggest packing away Mohan Singh. Mr. Raghavan should please be requested to remain with the league. Kindly convey this to Mr. Rash Behari Bose. Once again, I request him to proceed with the conference."

I did not care to have lunch. Going directly to see Rash Behari I gave him a report on all that had transpired. He agreed to reconvene the meeting in the afternoon. I made necessary arrangements accordingly, practically going round all the rooms of the hotel to inform the various delegates and to assure them that the conference was not breaking up but was continuing.

* * *

When the delegates met after lunch, Rash Behari opened the proceedings by stating that he had an important announcement to make and that the announcement would in fact be in the form of a ruling ("Or, I would even say, an order") from the chair. It was with reference to the discussions of the morning on the issue of the INA's organization. He said, "I hereby announce the decision that as and when the Indian National Army is formed, it will be the military wing of the Indian Independence League. It will function entirely under the control of the league in all respects. I hope there will be no further talk on this subject."

However, there *was* some further talk on the subject. Captain Habib ur Rahman, a delegate from the POWs but also a potential INA officer like Mohan Singh, stood up and said, "Mr. President, I would like to support Captain Mohan Singh's proposals. I think Mr. A. M. Nair is creating difficulties for Captain Mohan Singh. Unless Mohan Singh's proposals are accepted, it will be difficult to raise the Indian National Army."

Although some of my friends used to tell me that at times I looked "stern," no one had told me that I ever appeared "angry." But I must confess that when I heard Habib ur Rahman, I really felt furious. Even before he had finished his

CHAPTER TWENTY-ONE

speech, I got up from my seat and for once (unintentionally) departed from the normal decorum of addressing only the chair. I pointed a finger at Habib ur Rahman and said, "Look, Captain, you are a prisoner of war whom the Indian Independence League and the Japanese authorities have been trying to help. But a POW you are, and do not forget that. Your allegiance was to colonial Britain. We thought you wanted to change over to the status of an Indian officer; that was why you were allowed into this conference. I strongly object to your insinuation against me. I am an Indian patriot, and I am now beginning to think you will perhaps never become a true Indian freedom fighter. You shall not defy the chairman's order. If you do, walk out; if you accept it, sit down."

With that, I sat down. So did Habib ur Rahman.

To say that there was a state of consternation in the hall, would be putting it modestly. The tension of the occasion is difficult to describe in any precise terms. There was, however, one desire that was uppermost in everyone's mind; viz. that the subject for discussion during the meeting should at once be changed. The wish was fulfilled. After Habib ur Rahman and I had resumed our respective seats, the chairman immediately took up other matters on the agenda.

* * *

Luckily, the conference faced no further heavy weather. After deliberations spread over nine days, during which a wide range of matters of policy and practice was debated, it adopted a number of resolutions, mainly the following:

(i) The IIL would be guided by the principles that (a) "Unity, Faith, Sacrifice" would be its motto, (b) India should be considered as One and Indivisible, (c) all activities of the movement must be on a national basis and not on any sectarian or communal or religious consideration, (d) the Indian National Congress was the only political organization which could claim to represent the real interests of the people of India and therefore must be acknowledged as the only body speaking for India in all final international negotiations, (e) the framing of the future constitution of India would be by the people of India, (f) the objective of the IIL was the achievement of

India's complete independence, (g) the understanding, cooperation, and support of Japan would be invaluable in securing the objectives of the IIL, (h) all help received from foreign sources should be free from any control, domination or interference of whatever nature from those sources,

(ii) The IIL would consist of (a) a Council of Action, (b) a Committee of Representatives, (c) Territorial Branches and Local Branches,

(iii) All Indians above the age of eighteen would be eligible to be members of the IIL,

(iv) The Committee of Representatives would be constituted by civilian candidates elected by Territorial Branches (a schedule of the numbers from each territory was drawn up),

(v) The Council of Action would consist of the president of the IIL, Rash Behari Bose, and for the time being Messrs. N. Raghavan, K. P. Kesava Menon, Colonel G. Q. Gilani, and Captain Mohan Singh,

(vi) The Council of Action should be responsible for carrying out the policy and program of work laid down by the Committee of Representatives and would deal with all new matters that might arise from time to time and which might not have been provided for specifically in the Resolutions,

(vii) The IIL was authorized to raise an army called the Indian National Army from among the Indian soldiers (combatants and noncombatants) and such civilians as might be recruited for military service in the cause of the Indian independence movement,

(viii) All officers and men of the proposed Indian National Army should be members of the IIL and should owe allegiance to the League, and they would be (a) used only for the purpose of securing and safeguarding Indian national independence and for such other purposes as might assist the achievement of such an objective, (b) under the direct control of the Council of Action and commanded by an officer commanding in accordance with the directions of the Council of Action,

(ix) In the event of any military action being taken against the British or other foreign powers in India, the Council of Action would be at liberty to place the military resources available to it, under the unified command of Indian and Japanese military officers under the direction of the Council of Action,

(x) Before taking any military action against the British or any other foreign power in India, the Council of Action would assure itself that such action was in conformity with the express or implied wishes of the Indian National Congress,

(xi) The Council of Action should make all efforts to create an atmosphere in India which would lead to a revolution in the Indian army there and among the Indian people, and that before taking military action the Council of Action must assure itself that such an atmosphere existed in India,

(xii) In view of the great urgency and imperative necessity of informing and convincing Indians within India and abroad of the meaning and purpose of the movement, immediate steps should be taken to carry on active propaganda by broadcasts, leaflets, lectures, newspapers, and such other means as might be practicable,

(xiii) Foreign assistance of whatever nature should be only to the extent of the type asked for by the Council of Action,

(xiv) For the purpose of financing the Independence movement the Council of Action could raise funds from Indians in East Asia and Southeast Asia,

(xv) The Government of Japan might be requested for all facilities for propaganda, travel, transport, and communications within the area under their control, in the manner and to the extent requested by the Council of Action, and also all facilities to come into contact with the nationalist leaders, workers, and organizations in India,

(xvi) On the severance of India from the British Empire, the Government of Japan would respect the territorial integrity and recognize the full sovereignty of India free from any foreign influence, control, or interference of a political, military, or economic nature,

(xvii) The Government of Japan would exercise its influence with other powers and induce them to recognize the national independence and absolute sovereignty of India,

(xviii) Indians residing in the territories occupied by the Japanese forces should not be considered enemy nationals as long as they did not indulge in any action injurious to the IIL or hostile to the interest of Japan,

(xix) The properties, both movable and immovable, of those Indians who were residing in India or elsewhere (including the properties of Indian companies, firms and partnerships) should not be treated by Japan as enemy properties so long as the management or control of such properties was vested in any person or persons residing in Japan or in any of the countries occupied by or under the influence or control of the Japanese forces,

(xx) The IIL adopt the current national flag of India and would request all friendly powers to recognize it,

(xxi) No unauthorized publicity be given to any of the deliberations or Resolutions of the Conference.

(Note: A record of thanks to various organizations and governments for their help, minor requests made to the Japanese and the Thai governments on certain routine matters, etc., have been omitted in the above list; the Resolutions mentioned are the more important of the ones discussed and unanimously adopted.)

A copy of these resolutions was forwarded by Rash Behari in his capacity as president of the IIL to Col. Iwakuro for transmission to the government of Japan in Tokyo. Within about a fortnight, Colonel Iwakuro informed Rash Behari officially, in writing, confirming that the government of Japan, in the spirit of its policy towards India as had already been announced by the prime minister, General Tojo, supported the resolutions of the Bangkok Conference. As requested in one of the resolutions, the record of the decisions or recommendations of the conference would be kept secret by the Japanese government. Iwakuro requested the president of the IIL to preserve the secrecy of his reply also. Rash Behari told him that he would honor the understanding.

At the end of the conference on June 23, some of the delegates, reminiscing on the proceedings, still felt bitter about the unnecessary flutter which occurred on the opening day on account of the performance of Mohan Singh. But Rash Behari preferred that the issue should be forgotten. Both he and some others, including me, were of the opinion that there should be no publicity of the unpleasant episode. We made personal requests accordingly to all those who tended to remain critical of the Indian army representative. I reminded them of a Chinese proverb, "Convert great quarrels into small ones—and small ones into nothing," and said that we might try that out. My concern really was that if news of the incident leaked out, there would be all manner of speculations. We should not wash any dirty linen in public. To our

CHAPTER TWENTY-ONE

enemy, Britain, we should not exhibit any chinks in our armor. Moreover, nothing should be done to cause nervous apprehensions within the POWs and damage their morale.

But between Rash Behari and me, there was an understanding to leave the league's option in regard to the retention of Mohan Singh in any responsible position open. His activities would be kept under review and suitable arrangements would be made if circumstances should in course of time so warrant.

CHAPTER TWENTY-TWO
The Indian National Army

The Indian Independence League's tireless efforts had succeeded in establishing a proper rapport with the Japanese government authorities. The latter consistently declared that they would not have any designs on India, nor use the IIL for their own benefit.

With the help of M. Sivaram and the support of S. A. Iyer, we organized a good publicity campaign in Bangkok, both in the newspaper media and over the radio. For information about events in India, shortwave news broadcasts from London, New Delhi, etc., were the only source readily available. The political ferment in India was clearly getting stronger. Even before the Bangkok Conference, we had heard that the mission of Sir Stafford Cripps, whom Winston Churchill had sent to India to try to resolve the stalemate, had failed.

In April 1942, soon after capturing Burma, the Japanese advanced into the Bay of Bengal and took the Andaman and Nicobar Islands. The Indian National Congress was totally opposed to any extension of Japan's Co-Prosperity Sphere to India because of the inherent danger involved. On August 8, 1942, we heard Gandhiji's announcement of the famous "Quit India" resolution. All Indians should join to oust the British from India's sacred soil. Britain retaliated by arresting the Mahatma and other leaders. Gandhiji had earlier said that "if the British were to leave India to her fate, as they had left Singapore to hers, nonviolent India would lose nothing, and Japan would

CHAPTER TWENTY-TWO

probably leave India alone." In Gandhiji's view, the British presence would be the only provocation for any Japanese advance into India.

* * *

It was most unfortunate that, soon after returning from Bangkok, Captain Mohan Singh began violating the resolutions adopted by the conference in regard to the raising of the Indian National Army. He started with great vigor to recruit "volunteers" for the army, without any sanction from the Council of Action. There was reluctance from several officers and men, who were suspicious of Mohan Singh's personal ambitions. The methods he employed for enlistment of men generated much protest.

We heard in Bangkok that he was visiting the various POW camps in Singapore and elsewhere and separating the soldiers who were willing to join him from those not prepared to do so. The former would, under various dubious arrangements made by him, receive favored treatment, whereas the others would be harassed, such as being placed on starvation diet. It was said that some were even tortured. According to one report, he placed the officers and men who hesitated to go along with him in concentration camps surrounded by barbed wire fencing and ordered them to be beaten. Another report said that he was employing still harsher third-degree methods. We heard that in a camp called Kranji, where volunteers were scarce, he arranged for machine guns to be installed in order to strike terror among the inmates, and that once or twice firing took place, resulting in some casualties. The Indian POWs were in panic.

On another side, friction was developing between Mohan Singh and the Japanese authorities. The Hikari Kikan in Bangkok told us that Mohan Singh was becoming a hindrance to the development of good relations between the Indian and the Japanese sides.

It was clear that the members of the Council of Action, in Penang and Singapore, viz. N. Raghavan and K. P. Kesava Menon, were unable to restrain Mohan Singh. Colonel Gilani, apparently smarting under the ignominy of having to serve under an erstwhile junior colleague due to the crazy action of a Japanese major who had transformed Captain Mohan Singh unfittingly into a so-called general, nevertheless remained on his side for what could only be reasons of personal expediency.

All this was highly disturbing. If the growing tensions led to any open quarrel, there was no doubt as to who would win and who would lose. After detailed discussions, we decided to request Rash Behari Bose to shift to Singapore immediately to take charge of the situation. He agreed. The Hikari Kikan also decided to move its headquarters to Singapore.

Rash Behari Bose was accommodated in the Park View Hotel. Two young and competent men from among the Tokyo Indians were deputed to assist him. One of them, D. S. Deshpande, besides being well-informed and studious, was also an expert in judo (he had the second grade in it, which was a high qualification). If necessary, he would be competent enough to give physical protection to Rash Behari. The other, V. C. Lingam, was the son of a rich Chettiar in Malaya. His knowledge of Tamil, in addition to English and Japanese, was bound to be of much help.

After an on-the-spot study of the problems, it was clear to Rash Behari that Mohan Singh's high-handedness was going beyond tolerable limits and that, if he did not improve his relations with the Indian POWs and the Japanese, matters would get out of control. The other members of the Council of Action appeared to be powerless. Colonel Iwakuro, a good man, was highly disappointed. Mohan Singh was giving the Hikari Kikan and every other Japanese authority with whom he came in contact an impression that the Japanese presence in Singapore was a favor done to them by him. Of course, no one wanted Mohan Singh to hold any brief for the Japanese, but it was against all norms of common sense and prudence that he should have chosen a path of direct collision with them. Iwakuro found him absolutely impossible to deal with.

Rash Behari tried to smoothen matters and exercised his personal influence and goodwill in dealing with the Japanese, but excepting N. Raghavan, the members of the Council of Action were of no help to him. Everything which they did appeared to be counterproductive.

* * *

Matters went from bad to worse. Serious tension was distinctly building up between Iwakuro and Mohan Singh. The latter, quite contrary to the decisions during the Bangkok Conference, totally ignored the Council of Action. Without any discussions with the IIL or the Action Council, he arranged for the transportation of a large number of INA soldiers from Malaya to Burma, "for training," presumably at the insistence of the Japanese authorities. The IIL headquarters received several reports of serious torture and other atrocities perpetrated against a number of officers and men of the INA, for which Mohan Singh had necessarily to be held responsible.

Raghavan tendered his resignation from the Council of Action to Rash Behari, in a letter dated December 4. He had certain grievances against the Japanese government on the score that the latter were not giving *written* assurances as desired by the Council of Action, but one of his primary complaints was against Mohan Singh, who was acting without any consultations with the Action Council as required according to the Bangkok Conference's decisions.

There would have been no trouble if only Mohan Singh had gone about his work in a responsible and reasonable manner, without posing as a dictator. He was highly insulting to the president of the IIL (Rash Behari). He would ignore him and would not even speak to him on important matters concerning the INA. He was equally bad to Colonel Iwakuro, without realizing that he could not easily get away with *that*. Even so, once Iwakuro called him to his office (the "general" could not but obey the summons of a "colonel") and told him that in the light of the announcement which General Tojo had already made, there was no need for the Indian side to keep on pressing for written replies from Tokyo where everyone was very busy, and that whatever clarifications he wanted should be obtained from Rash Behari Bose, the president of the IIL, under whom he was expected to work. He assured Mohan Singh that it was still possible for the two sides to work together amicably if only he (Mohan Singh) stopped his arrogance.

The only thing which Iwakuro did not tell Mohan Singh was that he had already given a written reply to Rash Behari as early as July 1942 conveying the Japanese government's support, without strings, to the IIL, and also its position of agreement with the stand taken by the IIL at Bangkok. The reason why Iwakuro did not tell him about this was that there was an agreement between him and Rash Behari to keep the correspondence secret. Rash Behari's position in not divulging it was also in accordance with the same. But Rash Behari had given enough indication to all concerned that a good working relationship with the Japanese, within the framework of the policy already declared, was possible without any further paper battle. But, sad to say, three members of the Action Council (i.e., those other than Raghavan) did not show any understanding of realities.

One of Mohan Singh's indiscretions was really shocking to most of us in Bangkok. In spite of the clear resolution of the conference that the members of the INA would owe allegiance to the IIL, he was taking oaths from every soldier joining the force of loyalty personally to him, by name, and to no one else. Many wondered whether a person conducting himself in such a fashion should not at once be removed from all positions of responsibility. In fact, several Muslim soldiers refused to swear allegiance to a Sikh by name, and this created quite a flutter among the officers and men. It was a measure of Rash Behari's tolerance and patience that despite Mohan Singh's unbounded truculence, he gave him every possible chance to improve.

Perhaps Singh, who would constantly engage himself in denigrating Rash Behari and also the Japanese, was deliberately working towards the creation of a crisis, from some kind of sadistic mentality. We could not find any rational explanation for many of his activities.

In the second week of December, Kesava Menon, Gilani, and Mohan Singh resigned from the Council of Action. Their complaint was that the Japanese government were not giving guarantees in writing on various points they had raised demanding autonomy for the INA. All those matters had been really dealt with ad nauseum and, as far as the Japanese government was concerned, been satisfactorily settled. As a last resort, Rash Behari tried to clarify matters personally to Mohan Singh who, enquiries had shown, was the instigator of the joint resignation, but Singh refused to see him. He even declined to send anyone to represent him. It was defiance of authority of the first order.

At that point, Rash Behari found himself with no option but to take disciplinary action against Mohan Singh. He convened a meeting on December 29 (1942) at Colonel Iwakuro's residence. A summons had gone to Mohan Singh, from Iwakuro, to attend the meeting, and he came. Rash Behari told Singh that since he was functioning in a manner detrimental to the interests of the IIL and the Indian freedom movement, he was being removed from the league, and also from the INA command. However, he would be well cared for. He would have a private residence to himself and would not be sent to jail. Besides, he would receive a financial allowance, protection of person, and other facilities. But he would be under house arrest. Colonel Iwakuro agreed with Rash Behari's decision.

Mohan Singh was taken away to an island near Singapore and detained there with reasonable creature comforts.

A day or so earlier to the resignation of Mohan Singh and others from the Action Council, Colonel Gill had been arrested on a charge of spying for the British. It was a sad thing. We (Rash Behari and I) had entertained high hopes of Gill's potential role in the IIL and had arranged to detach him from the rest of the POWs and retain him in Bangkok in order that he might assist the organization in its military liaison work. That, we had thought, would enable him before long to qualify for a high-level position in the leadership of the INA and the IIL. He was arrested while he was on a visit to Singapore from his headquarters in Bangkok, where we had arranged for a good house for him and the services of one Captain Dhillon, a young and bright officer. Unfortunately, both these officers betrayed our trust in them.

We were told that instead of helping the league, they were trying to pass on secret information to the British. There was in Singapore, as well as in Bangkok, a security organization working with the Hikari Kikan. This unit was under Colonel Sakai, one of the most brilliant products of the Nakano Gakko, the military academy which the Japanese government had inaugurated after their involvement in Manchuria. They had found it necessary, on the basis of their experience in Manchukuo, to have a military college which would turn out officers of outstanding quality. The curriculum would be of a high order with emphasis on intelligence training and other specialized fields. Only those who came up to the highest standards of excellence would receive commissions. Sakai was among the first batch of officers to graduate from the Nakano Gakko.

The function of his office was mainly to assist the IIL with information of importance on the military side. At the same time, understandably, he would keep an unobtrusive watch from the security angle on the goings-on within the Indian community and also among the Indian POWs. Since both Colonel Gill and Captain Dhillon had been selected by the IIL, Sakai's office had placed considerable trust in them. They were not only not normally watching their movements and activities but were sending us, through them, valuable secret military documents from time to time.

It was discovered one day that Captain Dhillon had disappeared. As soon as this was known to Sakai's office, it started investigations and began to have doubts about both Gill and Dhillon. I was told that Sakai had reasonable evidence of these two officers having worked as agents for the British. Since Dhillon had already crossed over to India, nothing could be done in his case. But Sakai had Gill detained at bayonet point. According to normal Japanese practice, Gill could have been in serious trouble. Even execution was not improbable. Nevertheless, in view of the standing arrangements between the IIL and the Japanese authorities that no Indian personnel would be harshly dealt with, Gill's punishment was limited to house arrest.

It was a time of extreme anxiety for Rash Behari. Mohan Singh had anticipated, obviously with good reason, that he would be arrested. He had, about a week before his decommissioning and detention, issued an order to his troops that the INA would stand disbanded from the day he was arrested. There was confusion everywhere within the force, since they did not know who was to look after them or command them. The INA disintegrated completely.

There was also trouble in Burma, where the Hikari Kikan was under one Colonel Kitabe, who was previously in Manchukuo. The Indian community in Burma had no proper leadership. A half-hearted organization was functioning under Baleshwar Prasad. We sent Deshpande from Singapore to help him, but certain self-styled leaders had arguments with Kitabe when he decided to seize evacuee Indian properties. The Indian side wanted these properties to be handed over to the group headed by Baleshwar Prasad and Deshpande, but Kitabe was a difficult man: he argued that this was a matter to be decided by the Japanese occupation authorities.

We observed that apart from the general lack of organization in Burma, Baleshwar Prasad and Kitabe were allergic to each other. As the only practical course to reduce tension, we asked Baleshwar Prasad to cease dealing with Kitabe. Matters improved under Deshpande. He was a capable and dedicated man. (Unfortunately, a little before the end of the war, he died in the American attack on the Japanese ship *Awa Maru* near Nagasaki.)

* * *

Sitting in Bangkok, I felt greatly distressed at the various news coming in. Particularly in Singapore, everything seemed to be going wrong. I wanted to go there to see whether matters could be improved, but I could not leave until it was decided to shift the headquarters secretariat of the IIL to Singapore. After the Mohan Singh episode, however, Rash Behari found the task of looking after the affairs in Malaya all by himself too much, especially when his health was not good, and decided to move the headquarters to Singapore. There were several logistic and other problems, but with the cooperation of all concerned, I managed to complete the transfer within a short period.

The immediate task in Singapore was to reconstitute the administration of the INA. There was chaos in that organization. It became clear that several thousand men who had joined the INA had done so under coercion from Mohan Singh and his supporters. Mohan Singh had claimed that there were about 40,000 men in the force. We found the number to be only about 10,000. The rest, if at all enlisted before, had gone back to the POW camps!

CHAPTER TWENTY-TWO

According to our standing arrangements with the Hikari Kikan, however, these men, as well as the earlier POWs, were given preferential treatment. (The British, Australians, New Zealanders, etc., had a much harder time.) Mohan Singh had at one stroke wrecked the organization the IIL had built up to look after these large bodies of Indian soldiers. It was necessary to rebuild it.

A new commanding officer and a team of staff officers had to be newly selected. It was essential to ensure that all of them would willingly work under the control of the IIL. Secondly, the new leadership should be acceptable to the vast majority of the officers and men so that difficulties would not erupt again. Rash Behari had long discussions with me on this subject. We wished we had some good advisers, but unfortunately there were not many available.

K. P. Kesava Menon, whom all of us respected greatly, could have been of great help, but unluckily for us, he was still on Mohan Singh's side and exposing himself to danger as a result thereof. Raghavan was of considerable assistance. Although we did not ask for any specific recommendations from him since he had resigned from the Action Council, we were encouraged by his change of heart and by his new spirit of cooperation with us after Mohan Singh's exit.

Two names were considered for the new leadership of the INA: Colonel J. K. Bhonsle, and Colonel G. Q. Gilani. Rash Behari, I, and Sivaram (who had come ahead of me to Singapore to organize the Publicity Department there) were agreed that between the two, Bhonsle would be more suitable. He would be acceptable to the largest number of officers and men. Apart from his high rating as an officer, he was also probably the senior-most among the commanders, and it was always best to select such a person to head the INA.

We were happy to know that Gilani himself was in favor of Bhonsle's selection as the new chief. Raghavan thought likewise too. After further informal discussions with various cross sections of the army (and the civilian leadership as well), Bhonsle was appointed as the new commanding officer of the INA. He was to be assisted by a staff of able officers, among whom were Colonel A. C. Chatterjee, A. D. Loganathan, M. Z. Kiani, and Eisan Khadir. Chatterjee and Loganathan were medical corps officers. Khadir had experience in publicity work when he was in Saigon and used to broadcast from the Free India radio station there. Kiani had a high reputation as a brave officer and a popular leader.

The new team maintained homogeneity among themselves and good relations with others. Several soldiers who had gone back to the POW camps after the disintegration of the first INA came back and joined the reorganized one. Bhonsle's dealings with the Hikari Kikan were friendly, and the lost harmony was revived.

* * *

There are certain writers, S. A. Iyer being one of them, who have given the public the impression that the INA was created as a cohesive body by Subhas Chandra Bose. That is misleading. The INA was, for the first time, inaugurated as a disciplined, well-organized body of soldiers, by Rash Behari Bose in his capacity as president of the IIL and head of the Indian freedom movement in the Far East and Southeast Asia. He was ably assisted by Colonel Bhonsle and his staff officers. That was in early 1943. On the day the new leadership came into position, there was a large parade held on the grounds in front of the city office, and Rash Behari took the salute from the officers and men of the INA.

He exhorted them to ensure that the organization functioned as a harmonious and efficient body. Speaking with great dignity, and in Hindustani, he told the vast gathering about the importance of the role of the reconstituted INA in promoting the cause of India's freedom. He made it clear that the INA was the military arm of the IIL, which was the supreme body in matters of both policy and direction.

Rash Behari, however, was skeptical about the practicability of building up the INA as an effective fighting force. His reason was simple: everything needed for such a purpose, whether in terms of arms and ammunition, or supplies and services, had to be sought from the Japanese, and that sort of dependence was not a happy situation. As for attempting to liberate India with the help of these Indian soldiers through an armed invasion of India, he had no illusions. If there was any such possibility, he, with his anti-British terrorist background, would have been the first man to take advantage of it. But he saw the realities. India could not be liberated by the INA with weapons to be obtained from the Japanese.

At the same time, it was essential to have a proper organization manned wholly by Indians to look after the Indian soldiers who had surrendered in Singapore and other places in Malaya. The existence of such a setup would also have a salutary effect on the morale of the Indian civilian community. Rash Behari also saw the utility of the IIL and the INA in their role as a great source of moral support for the freedom movement within India. That there was a large body of their compatriots in Southeast Asia solidly behind them and ready to help them in whatever way they possibly could would serve as a source of powerful inspiration to the freedom fighters within the motherland. And that would increase their strength vastly.

Rash Behari's policy produced good results. The IIL secured the Japanese government's undertaking that no Indian army personnel would be required to do manual labor like other POWs. This was no mean achievement. A number of INA men were helpful in various ways in several spheres of the IIL's work. For instance, some of them rendered valuable service in the Publicity Department under Sivaram as translators, announcers, typists, etc. There was yet another benefit, inasmuch as that it gave the freedom movement a homogeneous base in the eyes of Indians both in Southeast Asia and within India, including the Indian soldiers serving under British commands. Enlistment of public opinion in India's favor throughout Southeast Asia was one of the IIL's greatest achievements.

CHAPTER TWENTY-THREE
The IIL's Move from Bangkok to Singapore

I have stated that after Rash Behari shifted to Singapore from Bangkok, the responsibility for the transfer of the IIL's headquarters to the new venue was entrusted to me. Sivaram and S. A. Iyer had been sent by air to Singapore to organize the publicity work in consultation with Rash Behari.

The shifting of the headquarters was fraught with a number of problems, but I had the able assistance of Seshan, an energetic young Brahmin from Kerala who was working in the league's office as Rash Behari's secretary. It is a pleasant recollection that when Colonel Bhonsle was a minister for some time in independent India, Seshan worked with him. He was an excellent man in every respect.

From Bangkok up to the Malay border we travelled in a passenger train, to which were attached five wagons carrying the league's properties: furniture, other office equipment, documents, etc. Seshan and I were given first class accommodation in the officers' compartment of the same train. Before our departure from Bangkok station, a senior officer from the Hikari Kikan had instructed the Japanese officers travelling with us to take care of us and to safeguard the cargo wagons containing the league's goods.

The league's belongings included a very large quantity of money. Bangkok currency was of no use in Malaya, and therefore the Hikari Kikan helped us to convert it all into the Singapore military exchange. Somewhere before reaching Ipoh, we had to transfer ourselves and the wagons containing all our baggage and the office equipment to a cargo train since there were no passenger trains plying farther. We had to sleep in one of the goods bogies.

When we stepped out of our cribbed confines for a breather at the Ipoh station, I noticed that a large staff was working there: Malays, Chinese, Indians and Ceylonese. Almost 80% of the workers appeared to be Indians and Ceylonese. It was a curious sight: a junior Japanese military official, perhaps of the rank of a havildar or even lower, was lining up all the staff on the platform and giving them certain peremptory orders. I enquired from one of the staff who appeared to be a person from Kerala what all this was about. I spoke to him in Malayalam and was pleasantly surprised to hear his reply in the same language, which meant of course that I had guessed correctly. I gathered that as part of the daily routine at the platform, the Japanese expected everyone to "fall in," turn towards the east and, under command from the official in charge, to bow in symbolic obeisance to the Japanese emperor. No one dared disobey, since that would at once attract severe punishment which could even mean beheading.

It was shocking. My mind went back to the experience I had in Hong Kong with Colonel Hara a few days after Japan's entry into the war. He had the vanity to tell me that whatever I did should be done in the name of the emperor. Of course, this was nothing specifically against the Indians or the IIL, but it was illustrative of the type of administration in vogue in Japanese occupied areas. Emperor worship was, of course, compulsory for the Japanese soldiers and they would carry it out sincerely as part of their duties. But the smaller functionaries among them would force all other nationals in their jurisdiction to go through the same motions in the belief that it was necessary.

That was the psychology of the Japanese soldiers of the time, whether there were orders from higher authorities or not. It was a great weakness that they were of a one-track mind. They did not realize the adverse reactions their action generated in many cases. This was a major factor in their general makeup, especially during the war, which eventually contributed to their downfall.

Singapore had already been renamed as Shonan by the Japanese: the implicit meaning of "Shonan" was "Southern Capital of Emperor Showa" (i.e., Hirohito). I got in touch with the Hikari Kikan and set about organizing the league's new offices. The place allotted to us was on the Chancery Lane, off Malcolm Road, in the Bukit Timah area. The Hikari Kikan office was not very far from ours. Rash Behari Bose had a house for himself, and there were a few other residences which the senior officers shared. Colonel Bhonsle and his personal staff were allotted an independent bungalow next to the house of Rash Behari. I had Sivaram and Iyer staying with me, and our house was next to the headquarters office. That was convenient for our work which required attention practically round the clock. Sivaram would listen to all the important radio broadcasts from overseas stations and prepare texts of newscasts to be put out from the league's radio station.

In addition to radio publicity, we undertook the publication of a newspaper in four different languages: English, Hindi, Tamil and Malayalam. The paper was printed under our own arrangements and widely distributed to the large Indian population throughout Malaya. Our radio broadcasts, which on an average lasted about six hours daily, covered about 15 Indian languages, besides English. They would often go on until late in the evening. Sivaram worked like a Trojan, with a very small staff. I used to wonder how, with his frail constitution, he managed to produce so much work. He was a very thin man, and what was worse, a vegetarian. I think he derived all his nourishment from the beer he would keep sipping whenever he was under heavy stress. He was a popular figure wherever he went.

Iyer also did good work, but he had a bad temper which rendered him insufferable to many of the staff. There were occasions when I had to make peace in his office where there would be agitations verging on revolts. Among my various headaches was the responsibility to function like a *tharavad karanavan* holding a joint family together.

One serious difficulty was to secure essential provisions for the league's office personnel during a time of acute shortage. There was practically no rice, sugar, nor even beer for Sivaram in adequate quantities. Fortunately, I had some good Japanese friends. One of them was Mr. Sugawara of Yamagata Prefecture, who was in the business of manufacturing wooden boats up to 500 tons dead weight, for use in transporting goods between Japan and Singapore. He and his associates would somehow arrange to keep us well stocked, free of cost. There were also local friends who helped. "Smuggling" is a bad word, but sometimes (I must confess) I received supplies from certain irregular sources through Sugawara's boats. I knew it was a wrong practice but consoled myself with the thought that small deviations from high principles, not for my personal benefit but to keep the organization going, were reasonably fair in the circumstances.

* * *

CHAPTER TWENTY-THREE

Our mode of work was quite simple. Sivaram, Iyer, and I would go to see Rash Behari every morning and spend fifteen or twenty minutes with him to explain our proposed publicity program for the day and to obtain his approval. Once the broad outline was accepted by him, he would leave the details to be worked out amongst the three of us. Rash Behari had complete trust in us. The policy part of the programs would be according to my direction. I also kept under my control the more cable news receiving and transmitting arrangements because I had the closest association with the Domei News Agency, which controlled these services. It had an office in Singapore linked to its headquarters establishment in Tokyo. This was a very important channel, as efficient, if not better than, the Associated Press or the United Press news systems.

An important feature of the reorganization of the INA by Rash Behari was the induction into it of a large number of civilian volunteers from amongst the young people spread over various parts of Malaya. He had bitter memories of the havoc perpetrated by Mohan Singh, who treated the Indian POWs as his private preserve. Rash Behari felt that it was important to bring in a cross section of recruits into the INA from among the Indian population in Malaya. Training camps were set up for them at Kuala Lumpur, Ipoh, Seremban, and also Singapore. Arrangements were also made for part-time military training for able-bodied Indians who had regular occupations but were prepared to help the freedom movement. In addition, an officers' school was also inaugurated for imparting tactical and other higher training. Providing instructions on general subjects of interest was part of the publicity work under my overall charge.

We would go round inspecting these camps frequently. It is important to record here that on several such occasions we had the benefit of the cooperation of N. Raghavan from Penang who travelled with us. Raghavan associated with us willingly and sincerely, even though he had ceased to be a member of the league's Action Council. Unfortunately, K. P. Kesava Menon kept aloof and gave the impression that he was still on the side of Mohan Singh, who had done his worst to destroy the INA and thereby to jeopardize the welfare of both the Indian soldiers and of the Indian community in general. Many of us were extremely sorry to notice Menon's noncooperation with us, even after Raghavan had changed his attitude from one of unhelpfulness in the beginning to active support later on.

There were some friends of the IIL who thought that Kesava Menon's support to Mohan Singh was the result of his impression that his election as a member of the Action Council was primarily due to the votes of the INA personnel. That was a highly exaggerated, if not altogether mistaken, notion on Menon's part. He was so well known and so much respected in Malaya that, whether there was a Mohan Singh or not, he would have been elected to the Action Council or any other position of responsibility. There was in reality *nothing* at all for which he had to thank Mohan Singh.

The headquarters however received much help from Mr. Yellappa, who was president of the Singapore branch of the IIL. One day, he had a peculiar problem. I was in his office on some work and found him in a state of much tension and confusion. He was unable to concentrate on anything in particular and appeared dazed. I asked him what was wrong. He told me that some men from the local military unit had come and asked him to mobilize some 3,000 Indians to go to Shonan Jinja, the Japanese Shinto shrine which the army had constructed in the outskirts of Singapore, and worship there. They must reach the shrine at 4:00 a.m. the next morning. Many other communities had similar instructions. The Chinese had to send numbers much larger than any other group.

I was amazed and told Yellappa that he should undertake no mobilization as asked by the Japanese officers, whoever they were. I recalled what I had seen at Ipoh on my way from Bangkok to Singapore. Yellappa obviously did not fully know the working of the Japanese army system but I had a fair acquaintance with it. I could guess that the "mobilization" must have been the brainwave of some junior official trying to show off.

Yellappa was surprised, and also worried at my veto of the "orders" he had been given. He feared that not only he, but the Indian community might be in trouble if the instruction was not carried out. The military might even cut his throat. I laughed at this to myself and told my friend not to worry. If any army man or anyone else came to cut throats, he would have to cut mine first. That apparently comforted Yellappa, although his face still appeared creased with anxiety. I stuck to my point and insisted that no one from the Indian community should be asked to go to Shonan Jinja just because someone had come and told him to send 3,000 men. I told him that it was not an Indian shrine, and no responsible Japanese would issue orders of the kind he was speaking about. It must have been the handiwork of some insignificant underling and should be ignored.

No Indian went. The news got round that I had advised Yellappa to disregard the "instructions." As I had anticipated, some small men were trying to throw their nonexistent weight about. The episode was forgotten. Yellappa then began saying that I was a "mysterious" kind of person. It may be recalled that M. Sivaram has referred to me in his book *Road to Delhi* as a "man of mystery." The originator of this phrase was in fact Yellappa of Singapore.

CHAPTER TWENTY-THREE

Sivaram, of course, knew in due course that there was really no mystery or magic about me. The fact was that the Japanese authorities at the higher levels had complete confidence in my bona fides. Being nationalists themselves, they recognized a similar sentiment when they saw it in others. To remain friendly with them, I did not have to be servile. Two persons could have honest differences of opinion and still remain good to each other provided there was mutual respect and genuine goodwill. This was the basis on which I always functioned in my relations with the Japanese echelons, whether civilian or military. I believed that to be the correct basis, and the Japanese side always recognized it as such.

One of Rash Behari's big contributions to the reconstituted INA was the inculcation among its personnel of a sense of India's basic unity despite its diversities. The INA encompassed persons of various provinces in India, of different religions, customs, manners and backgrounds. In such a heterogenous group, Rash Behari succeeded in implanting the awareness that regardless of all the differences, they all belonged equally to one great country, with not only equal responsibility but the same ability to fight against British rule. There were no such things, for instance, as "martial" races and "non-martial" people. These were myths deliberately introduced by Britain for the furtherance of its imperialist purposes. Given equal opportunities, any Indian was as good in fighting or other qualities, as any other. There was no question of north, south, east or west. Rash Behari's exhortations on such lines had a most salutary effect on the morale of not only the personnel of the INA but on the Indian community in general in Southeast Asia, particularly in Malaya where the majority of the Indian population consisted of persons from South India.

CHAPTER TWENTY-FOUR
The Subhas Era and the Second INA

It is not my purpose in this chapter to add to the large volume of literature that already exists in respect of Subhas Chandra Bose's early life in India and England and his rejection of the prestigious Indian Civil Service in order that he might fight for the freedom of India from colonial Britain. It is well-known that he was a great patriot and that he worked for several years in collaboration with Gandhiji, Jawaharlal Nehru, and other great leaders of the Indian independence movement before he had serious differences with them in political ideology.

His dramatic escape from India is legendary. There are detailed accounts published of his daring getaway under a successful disguise. Hoodwinking the British Indian police who were holding him under house detention in Calcutta, he first went to Afghanistan under the assumed name "Ziauddin." Later he got to Berlin via Samarkand and Moscow as "Signor Orlando Mazotta," holding a false Italian diplomatic passport with a fake photograph.

My theme is of limited range: Subhas's role in the Indian freedom movement in Southeast Asia, created during the Second World War by Rash Behari Bose in active association with me, and the leadership of which was passed on to Subhas by Rash Behari when he became too ill.

After breaking with the Indian National Congress, Subhas launched his own political party in India called the Forward Bloc, which was supposed to have been carved out as a leftist group from the main body of the congress.

He did not have much following in it and found himself in a state of virtual political isolation. For a powerful personality like his, that was apparently good enough reason to think of revolutionary measures to achieve India's freedom by working from outside and to shift to a foreign base for that purpose. There are some writers who have tried to compare him with Sun Yat-sen, de Valera, Garibaldi, and Masaryk. I must confess that I am not in agreement with them in such analogies. The situation in respect of India was quite different.

Subhas was undoubtedly a great patriot, and one of the most dedicated of freedom fighters, but anyone who challenged the leadership of Gandhiji or that of his followers of the stature of Nehru, Vallabhbhai Patel, and others in the congress during those days could not really expect to get very far in the independence movement. For the masses, the freedom struggle was represented by the congress.

Be that as it may, Subhas lived in Berlin for more than a year and was unfortunately unsuccessful in achieving anything worthwhile for India during the period. He tried to create an army from amongst the Indian soldiers captured as prisoners of war by the Germans and the Italians but failed. Hitler's priorities were all, or almost all, in relation to Europe. He was hardly interested in India. Subhas, who had gone to Germany with high hopes, was seriously disappointed. It is said that he had to wait for a long period even to meet Hitler. Most of his contacts with the German authorities had therefore to be at relatively junior levels. He found that except for a brief radio program permitted from Berlin, his stay in Germany was serving hardly any useful purpose.

Various stories have been published regarding the circumstances preceding Subhas's arrival in Japan to lead the Indian independence movement in Southeast Asia. Every one of those which have come to my notice is speculative. The stories are either wholly false or composed from half-truths. Some of them might have been written from genuine ignorance, but some others could be deliberate distortions.

Mohan Singh has said that "during his first formal discussion with the Japanese" he "had requested them to bring Subhas to the Far East."[*] That is a delightfully simplistic statement. He does not say with whom he discussed the subject. To the best of my knowledge, there was *never* any formal discussion between Mohan Singh and "the Japanese." The Japanese liaison group always insisted that any official discussions concerning Indian affairs should be held only with the Indian Independence League's president, Rash Behari Bose,

---

[*] Singh, *Soldiers' Contribution to Indian Independence*, 228.

or its chief liaison officer, viz. myself, and with no one else. If Mohan Singh discussed the issue in question with Fujiwara, a discussion which could under no circumstances be "formal," Fujiwara never passed on any message about it to the Japanese government: he would not dare to, considering that he was not supposed to handle such affairs.

However that might be, there is an interesting light Mohan Singh focuses on his own nature, in his book mentioned above, perhaps without his realizing it. It is astonishing to read that in December 1943, when he was still under house arrest but was able to see Subhas once, he told Subhas, in reply to a question whether he would accept him as his leader in India, that he "could not do so at that stage."* His hero in India was Jawaharlal Nehru, whose *Glimpses of World History, Autobiography*, etc. he had read. Bluntly put, what that meant could only be that while Mohan Singh would accept Subhas as his leader in Southeast Asia (during the Japanese occupation, one supposes), he would switch loyalty, ditch him, and go over to Nehru the moment he got to India. What a confession of deliberate intent to double-cross! Opportunism could perhaps be a habit with some persons. It is no surprise that what Mohan Singh claims to be his meeting with Subhas for the first time turned out to be also his last audience with him.

There is a proverb in Malayalam:

Pālam Katakkumpōl 'Nārāyanā';
Pālam Katannētchāl Kūrāyanā'

It refers to a person crossing a dangerous bridge. When crossing it, he is very religious and prays to Lord Narayana (Krishna), but the moment he gets to the other side without mishap, he is a totally different sort of person. In gist, (not an exact or literal translation), it means something like this:

(i) (*While crossing the bridge*)
"Oh God, preserve me, I worship you"
(ii) (*After the safe crossing*)
"To Hell with you!"

* * *

---

* Singh, *Soldiers' Contribution to Indian Independence*, 264.

CHAPTER TWENTY-FOUR

The truth is that the suggestion to have Subhas as an alternate leader was mooted *by me* as early as January 1942. It was done in one of my dispatches to the Japanese government's Army Ministry, for the attention of General Tojo, from Shanghai where I had arrived from Hsinking in December 1941 soon after Japan's entry into World War II.

The gist of my proposal was that Rash Behari should immediately assume supreme control over the Indian freedom movement in Japan and Southeast Asia, but, in wartime, it would always be naturally prudent to have in view, against any contingency, an alternate leader. In the existing context, such a person had necessarily to be one already outside India since it was obviously impossible for any national figure like Gandhiji or Jawaharlal Nehru to come out. Subhas Chandra Bose, who was already in Germany, would thus be the obvious, indeed the only choice in the circumstances for the number two (contingency) position.

As soon as I reached Tokyo from Shanghai and met Rash Behari, I informed him of my action. He fully approved. The Japanese government passed on the suggestion to their military attaché in Berlin and instructed him to maintain contact with Subhas Chandra Bose. For any concrete action, he should await further advice from Tokyo in course of time. It was known to me as well as to Rash Behari Bose that the Japanese military attaché (Colonel Yamamoto) was accordingly in frequent touch with Subhas, but no further action was taken in hand. That was really the inception of the idea that at some date Subhas might be invited to take up the leadership of the Indian freedom movement in East Asia. Every other account on this subject should be discounted as incorrect.

By early 1943, Rash Behari's health was distinctly failing. The heavy burden of work and extreme tension caused a serious setback to his condition. He was suffering from diabetes for a long time and that was aggravated due to stress. Unfortunately, he also contracted pulmonary tuberculosis. By the beginning of 1943, he was a very sick man.

For some time, Rash Behari did not know that he had developed TB. It was Dr. Aoki, a young medical officer of the Japanese army medical corps stationed with the Hikari Kikan who discovered that he was in fact suffering from that dreaded ailment. It was a terrible situation. Rash Behari shared his anxieties with me almost immediately after the medical diagnosis. The need to do something positive to have Subhas brought to East Asia became really urgent.

I was deeply upset to know of the serious condition of our beloved leader. But realities had to be faced. I approached the Hikari Kikan immediately for its good offices to request the Japanese military high command in Tokyo to find ways and means, in consultation with the Germans, to get Subhas over to Japan and then to Singapore expeditiously.

Recognizing the seriousness of the situation, the Hikari Kikan sent an immediate message to Tokyo. Urgent consultations took place between the Japanese government and Hitler's administration. The methodology for transporting Subhas to Japan was worked out over a period of two or three months jointly by the Japanese ambassador (General Oshima) in Berlin, and the German experts. It was decided that the German navy would provide a submarine for the voyage up to a designated place in the Indian Ocean, from where it would be the responsibility of the Japanese authorities to take over.

It was a historic voyage. A great feat of coordination between the German and the Japanese navies, it was nevertheless perilous in the extreme, one which showed the sheer physical courage of Subhas. He had two Indian companions travelling with him: Abid Hasan and Swamy. The route taken by the German U-boat lay via the English Channel and the Bay of Biscay, then along the West African coast in the Atlantic, and traversing South African waters, on to the Indian Ocean, terminating at a point to the south of the island of Madagascar. There Subhas was transferred, at great risk, to a Japanese submarine which took him to Sumatra where he landed on May 1, 1943. On May 16, he was flown to Tokyo.

After staying in Tokyo for some time and paying a courtesy call on General Tojo, Subhas arrived in Singapore on July 2, 1943. The event was warmly welcomed by the Indians all over Southeast Asia and particularly in Malaya because it was an undisputed fact that Subhas had a great charisma, even though, as a radical, he was at cross purposes with the popular Indian National Congress.

The person who was most happy was Rash Behari himself. Despite his poor health and extreme pressure of work, he had gone to Tokyo in order to escort Subhas to Singapore. He was a stickler for decorum and was anxious to see that his successor should be accorded all possible courtesy. Both of them arrived in Singapore in the same plane.

* * *

Two days after Subhas's arrival with him in Singapore, Rash Behari arranged a representative function at the Cathay Hall, where a very large gathering of Indians warmly cheered both the outgoing and the incoming leaders and showed their mixed emotions on the momentous occasion. Rash Behari was most gracious. He told the audience that he had brought them a "very important and precious gift." And pointing to Subhas he declared, "This is what I have brought."

The handing over of the reins to Subhas was one of the most magnificent actions on the part of Rash Behari. He was marvelous on the occasion. I was told that never was there another instance of a great leader cheerfully voluntarily, and with genuine happiness, handing over the vast authority he enjoyed. And Rash Behari had taken the trouble of going to Tokyo to escort his successor all the way to Singapore.

Subhas made a powerful speech impressing upon the vast gathering the need for discipline, unity, and courage to fight the British in India with all the might at the command of every Indian, wherever he might be. He announced, inter alia, his plan to constitute a Provisional Government of Free India in exile, which would eventually move to Delhi.

Immediately after the function at Cathay Hall, Sivaram arranged for a press conference at the Singapore Press Club and invited me also to be present.

We were surprised to see that a number of Japanese press members were perturbed at the manner in which the Cathay Hall ceremony had been held. Subhas had been referred to during the meeting as "Netaji" by some of the speakers. The press men did not seem to like the word, which they equated, however mistakenly, to "führer." Perhaps subconsciously, they regarded it as tantamount to some sort of denigration of Japanese authority.

Subhas was endowed with an impressive personality, and his general approach while dealing with anyone was forceful. These were natural to him and were assets where leadership of Indians was concerned. But it so happened that the Japanese, accustomed to a different code of manners, unfortunately tended to regard Subhas's attitude as one of aggressiveness and condescension that they did not appreciate. Another unhappy impression that somehow stuck in the Japanese mind was that he was highly pro-Germany. Even though Japan collaborated with Germany during the war, there was, among the Japanese, an undercurrent of suspicion of Hitler's policies. Japan was a monarchical state where the people held their emperor as divine. Hitler, for his part, as leader of the Nazi Party, was an altogether different kind of personality. The Nazi system and the Japanese tradition were fundamentally different.

Finding that it was rough sailing for Sivaram, I decided to hold a separate unofficial meeting with the press representatives at the Hikari Kikan. There also it was heavy weather to start with. Somehow the Japanese media had not taken kindly to Subhas. They exhibited a rather strange kind of adverse reflex, although no one came forward with any specific complaint. Gradually, however, the meeting settled down to a calm atmosphere. Sivaram later said that it was my proficiency in Japanese that achieved the change of mood.

There was initially the question of the announcement Subhas had made during the Cathay Hall meeting about the formation of the Provisional Government of Free India. This the Japanese did not seem to worry much about; but it was the word "Netaji" that kept bothering them constantly. They thought that Subhas was trying to assume that he, instead of the Japanese, was the *leader* of Southeast and East Asia. The fact was that he had chosen the epithet for himself during his submarine voyage, and Sivaram had in a way propagated it. It now fell to my lot to get this accepted by the Japanese press.

I lectured a great deal on the innocent connotation of the word. In Hindi, it could apply to any leader, and I explained that the intention was only to describe Subhas as leader of the Indian community. Some of the journalists were not fully satisfied, but eventually none of them pressed his objection.

There was another problem of an internal nature for us. There were large numbers of Muslims in Malaya and also in the INA who were suspicious of anything suggestive of Hinduism. And "Netaji" was a Sanskrit word! But it must be said to the credit of the great stature of Subhas that there was not much of a murmur on this subject among the Muslims after the initial resentment.

* * *

From the day he took charge from Rash Behari, Subhas was totally obsessed with the aim of building up the INA as a force to be launched for the armed liberation of India. His efforts were therefore almost exclusively devoted to attempts to secure training and other facilities and more and better equipment, for the approximately 10,000 men already with the INA, and to increase the numerical strength of the army through fresh recruitment from POW camps and the civilian Indian population in Malaya.

On July 5, i.e., the day following the Cathay Hall function, he discarded civilian attire and changed over to military uniform and top boots

CHAPTER TWENTY-FOUR

(these became his official dress from then until the time of his "disappearance" in August 1945) and addressed a large meeting of Indian soldiers and civilians in the city hall grounds. He spoke passionately and declared that India must be freed by means of an armed attack by the INA, and any others willing to help. He gave the soldiers the battle slogan "Chalo Delhi!" ("On to Delhi!").

And he said, in words reminiscent of Churchill, that for the sake of martyrdom in such a process of achieving independence, he offered his followers "hunger, thirst, privation, forced marches, and death." That speech, alas, turned out to be horrifyingly prophetic in the context of the Imphal campaign which was to take place in about less than a year later.

On July 6, there was a formal parade of the INA personnel, when Subhas took the salute and again addressed them in more or less similar terms as on the previous day. General Tojo, who happened to be in Singapore on an inspection tour of the Japanese-occupied areas in Malaya, also witnessed the function. He had come from Manila in the course of a visit to various territories. He repeated Japan's readiness to help India to win freedom from the British.

A mishap that occurred during the parade greatly upset those among the spectators who were superstitious. A Japanese tank that was in the forefront had an Indian national flag on it. The flag accidentally got entangled in some wires strung across the road, came off its fixture, fell to the ground, and was crushed by an accompanying vehicle. Subhas was visibly angry. General Tojo, like the typical Japanese, exhibited no emotion.

Over a period of about six months, the strength of the INA was "officially" increased to something between 25,000 and 30,000. Unhappily, logistics and other organizational needs for such a force, despite the good work done by Colonel Bhonsle and his staff officers, were woefully inadequate. There were thousands of young and middle-aged civilians in the Indian community who, without knowing anything about wars, simply put on the INA uniform, learned how to salute and swagger, and went about as though they were members of the newly expanded force. They were doing so merely to secure special advantages from the Japanese. The effective strength of Subhas's INA was therefore considerably less than the figure I have mentioned above. No one was sure of the exact number.

When the British recaptured Burma in 1945 and Thailand, Indochina, etc. had fallen to the Allied forces, the number of persons appearing on the INA rolls was about 23,000, including all categories of personnel.

Contact between Subhas and the Hikari Kikan and other authorities of the Japanese government were virtually confined to requests on behalf of the INA. The demands were largely unfilled due to Japan's own difficulties, which were increasing every day as the course of the war was going against it. Yet, Subhas showed admirable tenacity.

What was sad, however, was that all the affairs of the civilian community were neglected by the supreme leader. Dealing with these, in consultation with the Japanese authorities, therefore, became solely my responsibility.

* * *

Rash Behari was persuaded, on medical advice, to spend some time resting in Penang which had a better climate than Singapore. I was with him there all the time. But within a month we returned, and Rash Behari began preparing to leave for Tokyo.

On the eve of his departure, I was at his residence throughout the day. It was a poignant day for all those who had worked with him. Wanting to bid goodbye to Subhas, he asked his secretary, Seshan, to inform him over the telephone that he was coming that evening to his bungalow for a Bengali dinner. Subhas at once said, "No, no, I will come and pick him up. Please request him to wait for me." He came in his luxurious Chevrolet car at 6:00 p.m. and took Rash Behari to his house.

Rash Behari had asked me what advice I thought must be given to Subhas before he finally left for Tokyo. I knew that this was Rash Behari's way. Even when he really did not need any help from anyone (and this was one such occasion) to decide what he should do, he would ask his trusted colleagues for their views. I merely told him, "You know what to tell him; where is the need for me to say anything?" Rash Behari smiled with an air of understanding and remarked, "Yes, that's just like you; I was sure that was what you would say."

Later, he gave me the gist of his conversation with Subhas. He had informed him in detail about the war situation. Japan was in serious trouble: there was a severe food shortage everywhere, and rations had been drastically cut. Emergency war training had been introduced even for women. Arms and ammunition had been running low; bamboo weapons were being used for practice as substitutes for rifles and bayonets. He told Subhas that it would be prudent to give up any idea that the INA could fight Britain and win.

"We should have two sets of eyes," he told Subhas. "One in front and one behind." The eyes behind were expected to see what was happening in the rear (i.e., in the theaters of war and in Japan itself); and the ones in front should look at the present and judge what lay ahead.

Rash Behari also cautioned Subhas that he must remember the story of Manchukuo and other Japanese-occupied territories, especially those in China. There was a great deal of trouble because of the straitlaced psychology of the Japanese. Moreover, if they made any sacrifice in any country, they would lay various claims on such an account. If any Japanese armed force entered India to fight the British, the government in Tokyo was sure to consider that they had established a right to something in return for it. That was natural human psychology, but the point was that we did not want any foreign soldier or civilian to risk his life for the sake of Indian independence. India should be liberated solely by her own people. Whatever material help came could be availed of, but since Subhas seemed to entertain high ideas of preparing for an armed invasion of India jointly by the INA and the Japanese, he was seriously advising him to abandon such schemes forthwith because the INA would never be able to fight effectively—nor would the Japanese succeed if they launched a military action against the Allied forces in India.

I remained silent, so that Rash Behari could continue his talk without interruption. He said that he reminded Subhas about Gandhiji's "Quit India" movement. Britain of course was peeved, but as long as it was the Indian National Congress's policy that India should be rid of British domination, there was no question of any other country being given a chance to come in and take its place. All told, it was Rash Behari's sincere advice to Subhas that whereas the INA should be built up as an effective and disciplined body to look after itself and to extend moral support to the freedom fighters within India, it should never be thought of as a potential strike force to do battle with the Anglo-Americans.

Rash Behari paused for a while, perhaps expecting me to ask him how Subhas reacted, but I deliberately refrained from enquiring. As I had anticipated, soon he himself came out with what I had wanted to know. He said that Subhas made no comments. "He did not put on a cheerful face," he added, in his characteristic style. The implication was clear.

Subhas respected Rash Behari, but did not follow his advice. He certainly worked very hard and very sincerely, but, alas, with a blinkered approach to the situation in hand and with ears not adequately receptive to objective opinions from colleagues who had minds of their own. He went ahead in his own way and within three months prepared a constitution for the Provisional Government of Azad Hind (Free India). That was, at least in spirit, violative of the most important resolution of the Bangkok Conference, which had stated that the framing of the future constitution of India should be by the people of India—meaning the people *within* India.

On October 21, 1943, he announced the gist of it to a large gathering at the Cathay Cinema's auditorium. The formation of a cabinet of thirteen ministers was also declared. Among them were Captain (Dr.) Lakshmi, in charge of women's organizations; Colonel J. K. Bhonsle, chief of staff of the INA; and S. A. Iyer, minister for publicity. Administering the oath of office to himself "in the name of God," Subhas assumed charge of the provisional government as "head of state, prime minister, minister for war, minister for external affairs, and supreme commander of the INA." Rash Behari, although absent in Tokyo, was made "supreme adviser."

My house was the venue for much debate on the new state of affairs. No one had the least doubt about the bona fides or the ability of Subhas, but those who had seen the origin and progress of the IIL and knew the course which the war was taking, considered his obsession with the concept of an armed liberation of India with Japanese help to be fundamentally wrong. His plan could not be implemented. Even assuming that Japanese troops could be used, it was going to be impractical because the war situation was turning gravely to the disadvantage of the Japanese forces everywhere.

Subhas knew our view very well. Sivaram and I had on several occasions tried to persuade him to reorient his ideas, but his nature, sincere though it was, had such an inflexibility and obduracy about it that he would not correct himself even if there were very good reasons why he should. We were reminded of a Malayalam proverb describing a man who insisted that "the horse he had caught had two horns," even if no one could see even one on it.

One day, he suddenly decided to make a broadcast to India on his own. He himself prepared the text of the talk. In accordance with the standing practice of the IIL's Publicity Department, which was still under my control, the text came to me for perusal. I was quite shocked to see certain passages in it attacking Mahatma Gandhi, Jawaharlal Nehru, and other venerated Indian national leaders, in vehement and undignified terms. I could not reconcile myself to such a text which was indicative of some kind of personal vendetta. Without making any fuss that would perhaps mean a confrontation, I merely deleted the objectionable portions and had the paper retyped and sent back to Subhas.

When he was about to start the broadcast, he noticed the changes and was surprised. He asked S. A. Iyer whether there was some omission or whether the changes were made by someone in the Publicity Department. Iyer surely

CHAPTER TWENTY-FOUR

knew and told him the truth: that I had cut out certain passages. Subhas remarked, "Oh! Nair-sahib cut them, eh?" He did not say anything further, and made the broadcast using the text as I had sent him.

The next day he sent word to me through Iyer (somehow Iyer had ingratiated himself to Subhas amazingly closely and was doing practically everything except his legitimate work in the IIL) that he would like to know why I had deleted certain parts of his draft. I told Iyer that the passages in question should never have been included. It was not the policy of the league to attack any of India's national leaders. I also wanted Iyer to remind Subhas that whereas he was fortunate to be staying in luxury, in a palatial mansion provided by the Japanese, the leaders of the Indian National Congress whom he had chosen to abuse were languishing in British jails in India. We must not do anything undignified or unbalanced, nor go against our own country's leadership. The matter was treated as closed.

Subhas's style of functioning was vastly different from that of Rash Behari. The latter, although a strict disciplinarian on serious occasions, was personally informal and would even crack jokes with his colleagues. But Subhas always kept a distance between himself and his coworkers: he seemed to entertain a sort of "master-servant" complex. Moreover, it was unfortunate that he exhibited a vague kind of suspicion towards those who had been in close association with Rash Behari: the list included me and Sivaram.

I had information that the German Secret Service, who had no love for me since I wielded greater influence than they with the Japanese high command, had tried to brainwash Subhas and prejudice his mind against me. At the same time, they had told him that it would be unwise to ignore the IIL's chief liaison officer. Our new leader was thus in a dilemma and was unsure how to handle me. He need not have had any worry. I was with him and the league all the way as long as the league's policies, decided at Bangkok, were adhered to. I was not a competitor to Subhas but a true servant of the organization as built up by Rash Behari and others, including principally myself. I was not a Mohan Singh wanting to usurp any supreme leadership or entertaining ideas of becoming a dictator. It was a pity that Subhas did not get to know persons like Sivaram and me well enough to start with. Eventually he did.

* * *

I and my intimate colleagues in the movement were not adept in the art of flattery. There were some who managed it very well for their own benefit. Among them were S. A. Iyer, A. M. Sahay, and Dr. (Colonel) A. C. Chatterjee. Colonel D. S. Raju had the distinction of being chosen as Subhas's personal physician. Unfortunately, the majority of the newly found confidants filled the role of "yes-men," whose primary function was to please the leader by telling him what they thought he would like to hear. They were not interested in proffering unbiased advice.

The Publicity Department that Sivaram and I had painstakingly organized into an efficient body received a setback. Through our widely distributed news bulletins in various languages and the radio network, we had implemented a systematic scheme of propaganda in support of the Indian National Congress. The position changed under Subhas. He did not seem to want to work according to any policy in respect of publicity. His approach was merely one of bellicosity, exhibited in fits and starts.

Without doubt, his charisma always drew large crowds. The sight of vast audiences and their adoration, however, often excited him and led him to points where he would unknowingly abandon discretion and allow himself to be carried away by emotional upsurges, without realizing the consequences. In one of his public addresses in the autumn of 1943, he declared that the INA would stand on Indian soil before the end of that year. The speech made a great mass appeal but was totally unwise. The INA, for one thing, was in no position to stand on Indian soil before the end of 1943. Secondly, if it was really a question of mobilizing for an attack on India, proclamation of it in advance was not quite the right thing for a commander-in-chief to do. Subhas gave a helpful piece of notice to the enemy, who made full use of it by preparing adequate defense.

Sivaram and I made frantic efforts to stop the story that the press was flashing all over the world, but we did not succeed fully. The damage had been done. Subhas had got into the grip of high emotion, seeing a large and cheering audience, and let himself go on the spur of the moment. By that one outburst of rhetoric, he had unwittingly preempted all prospect (if any there ever was) of success of his favorite scheme of the Imphal and Kohima operations which were to come later. The Allied command in Southeast Asia was overwhelmingly augmented to meet his challenge, and to crush it totally.

Iyer was a competent journalist and publicity expert. If Subhas did not want me or Sivaram, he could well have used Iyer for the good of the organization. We would not have minded it in the least since we wished to have no monopoly on anything. We had plenty of other things also to do. Our interest was only the good of the movement. But, strangely, Iyer, a minister, was being used as an errand-man, called by the high-sounding designation, sometimes, of "first minister," whatever that meant. He did miscellaneous things, the exact nature of which no one clearly knew.

I had a problem with persons trying to nudge me into expression of an opinion whether Subhas was *really* pro-Germany or not. It was often irritating. The truth was that I had a little suspicion that he was, but naturally could not tell anything to those who were likely to misunderstand. Regrettably, Subhas had given an impression, ab initio, of being sold on things German. This applied to Hitler's political, military, and administrative systems. A simple yet significant example was that immediately on his arrival in Singapore, he ordered for himself a military uniform similar in cut to that of a German army officer's. When I and some of my colleagues came to know this, we advised him against the use of such an attire. A few Japanese officers had somehow got wind of it, and the lighthearted ones began referring to our leader as the "neo-führer." The tailor stitched the uniform but, on second thoughts, Subhas decided not to wear it. He chose, instead, something more in tune with an Indian army officer's dress.

Military trappings or other paraphernalia of authority were quite unimportant to Rash Behari. He was a "born leader" who did not need any showmanship, which Subhas liked very much. The latter lived in a large and "posh" house at Katong on the seashore, with a strong bodyguard, and travelled in grand style with a retinue of aides (including a valet). He also secured from General Tojo the allotment of a twelve-seater aircraft for his personal use. An amusing aspect of this aircraft story is that Subhas asked for permission to employ an Indian pilot, but Tojo flatly refused, saying smilingly that he would not like to take the risk of the plane being flown in the "wrong direction"! None of us had any objection to symbols of status on the part of our leader; indeed, he must be comfortable, but why make a fetish of it all and cause uncomplimentary murmurs?

I mention these, not from any sense of recrimination, but merely to highlight what my readers might like to know: the contrast between the personality of the man who self-effacingly but most dynamically built up the IIL and INA on solid foundations, and that of his successor to whom he handed over these readymade and efficient establishments in good condition and without fuss.

* * *

In August 1943, Colonel Iwakuro was transferred from Singapore and was replaced by Colonel Satoshi Yamamoto, previously the military attaché in Berlin whom Subhas had known there. It was a misfortune that even though Subhas had known Yamamoto in Berlin, he could not hit it off well with him in Singapore. The Hikari Kikan's mood was somewhat changing from what it was during Iwakuro's time. The earlier cordiality was flagging.

When Subhas had asked for the Japanese government's formal recognition of the Provisional Government of Free India, Yamamoto simply left the issue to be decided by the government in Tokyo. The 8th Section of the 2nd Bureau sent Colonel Nagi for an on-the-spot study and discussions with Subhas. Nagi was not impressed but adopted a "couldn't-care-less" approach and recommended recognition. Tojo then gave his concurrence, and it was thereafter that Subhas made the formal announcement at the Cathay Hall on October 21.

Meanwhile, reorganization of the INA under Colonel Bhonsle proceeded, although at a much slower pace than envisaged, and with equipment far below standard. This was inevitable since the Japanese were not at all in a happy military or political position. They had started suffering big reverses. Most of the arms issued to the INA were from stocks confiscated from the British and Indian armies at the time of the surrender of Singapore.

The strength of the reconstituted INA could not get anywhere near Subhas's target which he had mentioned on several occasions: 300,000. (On one occasion, in an emotional flight, he actually mentioned the figure "three million," which, of course, he himself acknowledged later as a "slip of the tongue"). The maximum number which could be raised was something between 25,000 and 30,000, and that too largely on paper. The effective strength of persons capable of fighting, if need be, and equipped at least with light weapons of ancient vintage, was not more than between 12,000 and 15,000.

On August 25, 1943, Subhas assumed direct control of the INA as supreme commander. A special set of army rules and regulations had been prepared. However, efforts to secure Japanese recognition for the INA as a separate and "independent" army with a fighting role of its own as distinct from that of the Japanese army ran into heavy weather. Field Marshal Hisaichi Terauchi, commander-in-chief of the Southern Expedition Forces, was unwilling. He considered that the INA was inadequate as a fighting force and that it could only be given subsidiary supporting functions. He even feared that, if it were sent into a battlefield on its own, the Japanese would not have any control over it in the event of its deciding to go over to the side of the British. He therefore declined to part with final Japanese supervisory authority.

CHAPTER TWENTY-FOUR

To go back a little in time, it is well to recall that Subhas had arrived in East Asia at a time when Japan had begun to face serious setbacks in the war. In fact, her initial successes had been halted at Midway. Admiral Isoroku Yamamoto's fleet had suffered a very great defeat at the hands of the American navy. That was as early as June 1942. The losses on the Japanese side were extremely heavy: four aircraft carriers, a heavy battle cruiser, and well over 300 aircraft, as against relatively minor damage to the US fleet.

News of the Japanese defeat at Midway had been kept away from the publi through military censorship. Early in 1943, pressure from the Americans became intense on almost all fronts, both northern and southern. At Guadalcanal in February 1943, the Japanese army was obliged to retreat with heavy casualties. Soon came one of the most serious disasters, when Admiral Yamamoto was shot down on April 14, 1943, by an American aircraft. The United States had broken the Japanese military communication codes and knew the movements of their enemy's army, navy, and air force almost on a daily basis.

In Europe, things were going extremely wrong for the Germans. On the first of February came Germany's sensational defeat at Stalingrad, which Hitler had thought he could capture with ease. Stalingrad proved to be the graveyard of countless numbers of German soldiers and became a legend in the history of Russian resistance.

Despite all this, Subhas was tenacious in his demands on the Japanese for more arms and other facilities to build the INA as a larger group than it was. Sadly, he was giving the Japanese an impression that he was either oblivious of what was happening around, or overconfident. But he had an impressive way about him, and the Japanese did not voice their criticism of him too openly and tried to go along with his wishes to the extent humanly possible.

Internally, Subhas was on an intensive drive to expand the numerical strength of the INA. He even raised a women's unit called the Rani of Jhansi Regiment under Captain (Dr.) Lakshmi. Subhas was a good orator who could rouse his audience to a state of passion. He would go on a fundraising campaign from time to time. "Three crores of pounds" was his target. "And I will get it," he claimed. Indeed, he succeeded in collecting substantial sums of money, mostly in kind: even poor labor-class women would part with what little they had because they felt they were doing a service for their motherland. It was a touching sight when many of them would even part with their Mangal Sutras (called *thali* in Tamil; the small ornament that is the sacred symbol of their marriage) for Subhas's war chest.

But the most regrettable part of his money collection effort was that he took no pains to ensure proper accounting. No one knows how much was misappropriated by the hangers-on who surrounded him. And the irony of it all was heightened by the fact that the rich persons who could afford to give substantially sulked and got away with light donations whereas Subhas would not spare the poorer sections. I once told Subhas that he should collect more from the have's and less from the have-nots. He said he certainly agreed with me and would improve matters. Unfortunately, matters did not improve.

I look back to those days with anguish. There was much talk of large-scale corruption. The pity was that Subhas would not do anything to correct the situation. The poor Indian laborers, most of whom were from Tamil Nadu, gave far more than they could afford, not knowing that someone or other was stealing large chunks of the money earned through the sweat of their brow. Subhas was an intensely patriotic person. But it was sad that he allowed that trait in him to be used by many within the coterie to cover a multitude of their sins. It was generally said that gold jewelry and other precious articles were being mostly stocked under the auspices of S. A. Iyer, who alone knew how much there was and where it was all being stored.

***

In November 1943, Roosevelt, Churchill, Stalin, and Chiang Kai-shek met in Cairo to decide that Japan should be driven out of Formosa, Manchuria, the Pescadores, and all other territories she had acquired by force, including Korea. The leaders later met at Tehran where a secret decision was reached that Russia would join the Americans and the British in attacking the Japanese, as soon as the European war was won.

As a counterpoise to these moves by the Allies, General Tojo held, in the same month, what was called the Greater East Asia Conference in Tokyo.

A fact which did not escape world notice was that whereas the Cairo Conference was amongst leaders of four independent world powers, the participants in the Greater East Asia Conference were all from areas under Japanese occupation. Subhas came from Singapore, Dr. Ba Maw from Burma, Pibulsonggram from Thailand, Sukharno from Indonesia, Laurel from the Philippines, and Wang Ching-wei from China. Another delegate was the prime minister of Manchukuo. General Tojo presided. The decisions taken were rather simplistic: the countries within the Greater East Asia Co-Prosperity Sphere should maintain solidarity and go on fighting against Western imperialism until victory was won.

CHAPTER TWENTY-FOUR

In contrast to the Cairo Conference, which was subjected to a strict news blackout within Japan, the Tokyo Conference was given wide publicity in an effort to boost the people's sagging morale. It must be said that during the conference Subhas was a popular figure, and also received much acclaim in the media reports. He distinguished himself and made a good impression on the other leaders, including General Tojo, although the net value of it all did not amount to much in the general circumstances of the time.

As a political boost to him, Tojo announced at the end of the conference that the Andaman and Nicobar Islands captured by Japan would be handed over to the Provisional Government of Free India. That would provide the organization with a "sovereign territory" as its temporary base. It was of course only a token gesture. Tojo had no intention of giving up control of those strategic islands, but the announcement no doubt had a favorable impact on Indians in Southeast Asia.

An episode preceding the Tokyo Conference, although not highly consequential in itself, is nevertheless worth mentioning since it projects a sidelight on Subhas's relationship with his colleagues who held important positions in the IIL. When he arrived in Tokyo, he found that I was already there. He had seen me in Singapore a couple of days before his departure and was surprised to know that I had reached Tokyo ahead of him. Under the prevalent state of acute transport difficulties, normal curiosity would have prompted at least a casual question as to how I had managed to get there so quickly. But Subhas did not care to ask me anything about the journey.

I had no grievance on account of such neglect, but I could not help recalling the kind of human interest which Rash Behari would never fail to exhibit sincerely towards everyone even when he was under heavy pressure of work. Unfortunately, Subhas often, if not always, gave the feeling to his coworkers that there was a block of ice between him and them.

How I had arrived quickly was quite simple. The Japanese government was keen that I should be available in Tokyo for consultations during the conference and sent me a message directly. I did not have an opportunity to inform Subhas since he had already left Singapore by a plane that was to take a circuitous and therefore time-consuming route. I managed to get on one with fewer stops. I had the facility to secure a seat, if available, on any of the Japanese war planes on a priority basis.

In a large organization such as the IIL, teamwork was most essential. Subhas could have used many of his colleagues to much better advantage than he actually did. Unfortunately, despite his various great qualities as a leader, I was convinced that he was not quite good in the art of man-management.

I must at once add that he never showed me any disrespect. What I mean is that there was an inexplicable and, in any case, quite unwarranted "wariness" on his part about contacts with me, despite my best efforts never to give him any impression that I was seeking any position of parallel leadership with him. Perhaps he felt that the Japanese high command was giving me more respect than he thought they should. Unhappily for him, he had no control over that.

Some of my friends would keep referring to the possible indoctrination of Subhas against me by the German Gestapo. Whatever it was, I did not allow any lack of empathy on an individual basis to come in the way of my doing my duties as I saw them according to my own conscience. I believed that the organization was always bigger than any one individual. I held myself accountable not only to the head of the organization but also to the people in general, who had placed their confidence in me from the days of Rash Behari's direction of the IIL.

* * *

After the Tokyo Conference, Subhas stayed on in Tokyo for some days, pleading with the Japanese authorities for more arms and ammunition and other war facilities to prepare for an invasion of India. He was unsuccessful. On his return to Singapore on November 25, 1943, he prepared, apparently as an office record, a secret note on "Japan's unhelpful attitude." When the paper came to my notice, I reckoned that if it ever fell into Japanese hands, there would be much needless misunderstanding. And if the enemy got hold of it through its spies, it could be dangerous. The document contained a list of the military hardware requested, those few items provisionally promised, and clear indications as to what specific articles the Japanese did not have at all.

During wars, of all times, secrets were to be retained as secrets. The paper in question should not have been where I found it. Without any ado, I quietly arranged for the disappearance of it. In the ultimate analysis in the circumstances, the value of the secret piece of document was perhaps not much. Yet, I wanted to highlight the need for security of classified papers. I destroyed the paper after memorizing it and making sure that I could recall it mentally when required. When at a later date Subhas was looking for the paper, and could not find it, I thought I must tell him what happened. I did so, and was happy that he did not pursue the matter. But Iyer, who was supposed to be in charge of all secret files, felt highly cut up.

CHAPTER TWENTY-FOUR

Send-off party in Nihonbashi Suehiro, Tokyo, December 14, 1943. Front row, third from left is: the author; fifth from left is: Rash Behari Bose.

At every meeting of the Hikari Kikan, Subhas's theme would be the invasion of India. Mr. Senda would invariably oppose the plan strongly. He had no doubt that any armed advance into India by the Japanese or the INA soldiers would be suicidal. But Subhas would not agree. In protest, Mr. Senda left Singapore for Tokyo, informing the Hikari Kikan that any further advice from him would be sent from there on request.

A little earlier, around October 1943, Sivaram and a small group of publicity staff under him had proceeded to Rangoon under Subhas's instruction to reorganize the propaganda work there. Initially, Lieutenant Colonel Kitabe, the head of the Hikari Kikan in Burma, was unhelpful, but Sivaram soon won him over with his tact and managed to set up an effective publicity organization for conducting programs by radio from Rangoon. It was a risky assignment, since the whole area was exposed to British bombing. Sivaram's house was hit during one of the raids. It was a miracle that he survived.

Sivaram remained in Rangoon for five or six months and was with Subhas's headquarters which were moved there in January 1944. During his time with Subhas's office, he had a great deal of difficulty with Iyer, the minister for publicity, whose main function appeared to be to please Subhas and not, as one would normally expect, to offer constructive suggestions, or at least to listen to any good advice from Sivaram about publicity matters.

There was a great deal of internal squabbling amongst the various ministers, and rank corruption on the part of some. One of them was even arrested by the Secret Service of the INA under Subhas's orders, as he was considered to be a security risk. Sivaram told me once that he had not seen such bad administration at any time in his life as during his stay at Subhas's headquarters in Rangoon.

I remained in Singapore, in charge of the IIL's headquarters. My office was still the main channel of communication with the Japanese government in Tokyo. It was also the only means for the league to keep the Indian residents in Southeast Asia informed of developments on the war fronts and within India. The distribution of news and the publicity broadcasts from Singapore were kept up. Subhas, whose attention was confined to military schemes for "Chalo Delhi," had no time to look into the innumerable problems relating to the Indian civilian community's relations with the Japanese occupation forces, a perennial source of potential irritation. I concerned myself to a great extent with resolving the problems, with the help of the Hikari Kikan.

***

The first week of every new year was (and still is) a time of much celebration in Japan. But in January 1944, the people were gloomy and despondent. Despite censorship, shockwaves of Japanese reverses in the war were reaching the home front.

The army and the navy were in retreat in all the war theaters in the Pacific. Supplies and services were difficult to maintain. The air force was taking a terrible beating, and at one stage, aircraft frames were being made of plywood assembled by using a special adhesive obtained from Burma. When the supply of this commodity was disrupted due to Allied mining of the sea routes, the Japanese air arm dwindled to an alarmingly low level. Although endowed with great stamina to withstand hardship, the people found their endurance stretched to breaking point. Every commodity was in short supply.

Moreover, the government embarked on a total mobilization which included all men from 12 to 60 years of age, and unmarried women and widows in the age group of 12 to 40. In a desperate move, Tojo, under the pretext of better "coordination of the war effort," assumed combined charge as prime minister, war minister, and army chief of staff, an unprecedented step for which he earned one more nickname "Total Tojo."

It was clearly at a time of near-total despair that Tojo gave his "nod" to Subhas's persistent plea in favor of the scheme he was obsessed with for a strike against the Allied forces across the Burma border. The Japanese prime minister surely knew that with her communication lines already overstretched and with a critical shortage of supplies and services, Japan had absolutely no means to sustain an invasion of distant India. It appeared therefore to be a case of *obureku mono wa wara mo tsukumu* ("a dying man catching at a straw").

In giving his consent to what, as a military man, he must ordinarily have known would be suicidal, Tojo could have only been motivated by two considerations: (i) an attack on India could probably be the best means of defending Burma, which the Allied armies were preparing to recapture, (ii) the people's morale could perhaps be bolstered by the opening of a diversionary front and creating an illusion that Japan, instead of being on the brink of collapse, was still alive and fighting. There was, *possibly*, also the vague hope that if northeastern India could be overrun and the Anglo-American forces compelled to withdraw from there, the large-scale supplies being airlifted from there to China could be stopped, thereby easing Chinese pressure on the Japanese troops in that part of the world.

CHAPTER TWENTY-FIVE
The Imphal Campaign

Without giving a thought to the overwhelming military demerits of the project, Subhas took Tojo's concurrence in the plan to invade India as a personal triumph. Early in January 1944, he had already moved the headquarters of the Provisional Government of Free India to Rangoon. A little earlier, he had "officially" taken over Andamans. Lieutenant Colonel A. D. Loganathan who was positioned there as chief commissioner of both Andamans and Nicobar Islands found that the "transfer of territory" was merely nominal and that he had no effective control over anything in either of the islands.

Immediately on receiving Tojo's clearance for "Operation U-Go" (as th action into India was codenamed), Subhas held long discussions with Lieutenant General Masakazu Kawabe, commander of the Japanese Burma Area Army, and Lieutenant General Renya Mutaguchi, who was to be in charge of the campaign into India. He proposed that the INA might lead the attack and that the Japanese army might follow it. Kawabe was infuriated. Subhas exhibited a total ignorance of Japanese psychology. It nearly rung the curtain down on the whole scheme. Japanese soldiers were worshippers of their emperor. They would not follow any non-Japanese commander; they would sooner commit hara-kiri (suicide by ripping open the stomach) than do something offensive to their national pride. When Field Marshal Terauchi heard about this, he was as wild as, or perhaps wilder than, Kawabe.

However, the issue died down when Subhas immediately shifted his stand.

The maximum concession Kawabe was prepared to allow was to try out one INA regiment under an Indian commander subject to overall control by the Japanese command. Any further fighting role for the INA men would depend on the performance of the regiment to be deployed on such an experimental basis. For the rest, certain modalities for joint action in subsidiary supporting functions were tentatively agreed upon. But in fact, nothing really worked well.

On the contrary, there was much confusion and mutual recrimination. Eventually, apart from the experimental regiment, all that was accepted by Kawabe and Mutaguchi was the attachment of a few small INA units of 100 to 200 men to the Japanese commands, essentially on secondary duties such as making and repairing roads and bridges, transporting rations, protecting supply lines, putting out forest fires, driving bullock carts, and chores of a similar nature. The "experimental regiment" was hardly used in battle according to any official arrangement between the two collaborating sides.

The military operations undertaken encompassed two sectors: the Arakan Hills and Imphal. The Arakan battle, which was launched on February 4, 1944, proceeded well for the Japanese for some time, but the Allied command soon caught up with it and hit back, forcing the invading force to pull back and confine itself to holding off the counterattack on the India-Burma frontier in the southern sector.

The bid for Imphal began on March 21, but ended in about three months in what some war historians have recorded as the most tragic single disaster in the annals of conventional land war anywhere in the world.

* * *

The Japanese had thrown about 120,000 troops into the battle, but preparations were incredibly inadequate and haphazard. There was no heavy equipment; even supplies of small arms and ammunition were grossly short of needs. For transportation, there were altogether 26 four-ton trucks, most of them in bad condition, some having broken down even before starting. Part of the rations was carried in bullock carts and the rest as head loads by foot soldiers. There were hardly any medical facilities in what was one of the most disease-ridden regions.

The base commanders, including Subhas, were blissfully unaware of the

THE IMPHAL CAMPAIGN

situation on the Indian side. The Allied Southeast Asia Command (SEAC), which had been established under the supreme command of Admiral Louis Mountbatten, had massed a formidable force in a determined bid not only to prevent any successful Japanese advance into India but to recover the whole of Burma, starting with the Arakan and Myitkyina and then moving on to the Chindwin Valley and elsewhere. The Japanese intelligence service was hopelessly deficient. When the Burma Area Army of the Japanese ordered the Imphal campaign, it did not know that the SEAC in the area, armed to the teeth and numerically thrice in strength, was waiting to pounce upon it. The Japanese troops had practically no air cover. The operational aircraft at their disposal were not even one-tenth of the number which the SEAC had mobilized. The terrain was familiar to the Mountbatten command, but strange to the Japanese and the INA.

To us in Singapore, the propaganda work of the Japanese army appeared to be pathetically inane. False reports of Japanese and INA successes were being circulated. A picture distributed, supposedly a photograph of the conquest of Imphal by Japanese soldiers, with INA men carrying a portrait of Subhas and showing them planting an Indian flag in conquered territory, turned out to have been taken in a familiar village in Malaya!

There are different stories about the Imphal operations. Some claim that the Japanese and the INA forces fought so fiercely that the British initially withdrew from Imphal. The township was therefore actually held by the attacking regiments for some time. Other accounts say that just when the invasion was about to succeed, the Japanese army and the INA ran out of all supplies including ammunition. They were pushed back by the British army, especially by the Gurkha regiments. No one can be sure as to what exactly happened, except that ultimately the whole campaign was an utter disaster for the Japanese and the INA.

What I have heard from some of my Japanese acquaintances who were field commanders in the operation is that the Japanese and INA soldiers were miserably ill-equipped and outnumbered. They had no chance against the vastly better provisioned and well-armed British army. The impression that the British forces were under heavy pressure initially was deliberately created by the Allied command. As a clever ploy in both the Imphal and the Kohima sectors, the British allowed the invading troops a free run for a short while, and then encircled, besieged, and destroyed them. The Japanese troops, and also one of the INA units under Colonel M. Z. Kiani, put up a brave fight, but they were hopelessly overwhelmed.

Estimated Japanese losses in the Imphal campaign were staggering. About

CHAPTER TWENTY-FIVE

65,000 men were killed and countless others died of malaria, cholera, typhoid, and other diseases during their retreat through the jungles. It was like a death march and established a gruesome record. The forests were littered with quagmires formed by heavy monsoon rains, and both those morasses and the hill tracks blocked by swollen and treacherous rivers were impassable. An enormous number of men died of venomous snakebites and a variety of other hidden dangers. It was thirst, hunger, disease, and death all the way up to the Burma bases. And several died even after struggling into the headquarters hospitals because they had become irrecoverably sick.

A little-known fact is that all the three field division commanders, Lieutenant Generals Yanagida, Yamaguchi, and Sato, bitterly protested to their superiors, Lieutenant Generals Mutaguchi and Kawabe, and later also to Field Marshal Terauchi, against the total mismanagement of the operations by the base command. Mutaguchi took a tough line and replaced them all, but that did not improve matters. Lieutenant General Kotoku Sato, who lost about 25,000 of his best men, defied Mutaguchi and began his withdrawal with a surviving 10,000, disobeying orders to stay on and fight. Mutaguchi's threat to court martial him was met by Sato's outburst that he disregarded his orders because the whole plan of the operation was "stupid and mad." That was the only instance in the entire Japanese military history of open insubordination by a field commander or anyone else. It was a measure of the enormity of the Imphal tragedy.

The INA's casualties were believed to be about 600 killed and 2,000 dead from starvation and diseases. Those who succeeded in getting back to Burma and into the hospitals numbered only about 2,500. Approximately 2,000 men defected to the British side during the battle. That was a big blow to Subhas, who had proclaimed loudly that the moment the INA men set foot on Indian soil, the Indians fighting under British commands would come over to them en masse and join the march to Delhi. The exodus happened to be in the opposite direction. The defectors no doubt marched, or perhaps were entrained or airlifted, to Delhi, but not the INA just yet. The latter got there after Japan's defeat and the end of the war.

Our hearts must go out to the victims of this terrible catastrophe. Over 70,000 young men had paid with their blood the price for an irrational decision over which they had no control.

It was with utter consternation that we in Singapore heard that, in spite of all this, Subhas was still optimistic and trying to "regroup" and prepare for a second assault on India. When we heard a report that Subhas had told Kawabe that he would send the women of the Rani of Jhansi Regiment also to the frontlines as reinforcements, we feared that he might have gone out of his mind and must be immediately put under medical treatment. Luckily, Kawabe turned down the offer. From my side, I told the Hikari Kikan to pass on an advice to the Burma Area Army that if another invasion was attempted, there would be no survivor at all in his command and that posterity would curse him forever. The entire Burma Area Army was already on the verge of collapse under the pressure of the SEAC's offensive from India, but it was still holding on, and the tenacity of the Japanese was remarkable because for quite some months the British forces were not able to penetrate the main Burma defenses.

* * *

Even as the fateful Imphal campaign was drawing to its calamitous end, a tragic incident had taken place in Singapore. K. P. Kesava Menon was arrested and jailed on April 24, 1944.

Kesava Menon had been unfair to Rash Behari Bose under the mistaken impression that the great Indian patriot's technical status as a Japanese citizen was a handicap to his effective leadership of the Indian freedom movement. Nevertheless, everyone in the IIL, including Rash Behari, respected Menon for his uprightness and integrity. He was a staunch nationalist and a firm supporter of the policies of the Indian National Congress under Gandhiji's leadership. I had known him, and to some extent had dealings with him, even when I was a student in Trivandrum.

He was inclined to be rather rigid when a little flexibility would have been advisable, but that was due to his strong personal value judgements to which he adhered tenaciously, and which were part of his strong personality. Those who knew him well, as Rash Behari and others like me did, understood his goodness.

As far as I know, no one who has written until now about K. P. Kesava Menon or the INA or IIL has recorded why exactly he came to be imprisoned by the Japanese army in Singapore. Apparently, the authors did not know. Perhaps Menon himself was not absolutely sure of the cause, since there is no mention of it in any of his voluminous and highly informative memoirs of his life in Malaya during the Second World War. The truth, which was made known to me in Singapore and to Rash Behari in Tokyo since both of us had access to the secrets of the Japanese army's inner circles, was that *Kesava Menon was arrested at the personal insistence of Subhas Chandra Bose.*

Menon's characteristic tendency to express his views with sledgehammer force, even during the abnormal wartime environment, had often caused me anxiety. He was also inclined to be off guard, not always caring to know well the persons he was speaking to on sensitive subjects. His strong opposition to Subhas's policies, particularly where they contravened those of the Indian National Congress, was well-known. Reports that were coming in of the terrible episode of the invasion of India by the Japanese forces and the INA under Subhas's grand patronage greatly upset him. These added to his bitterness against Subhas's leadership.

During that period, when speaking one day to a visitor to his house, he remarked, among other things, that Subhas, who had appointed himself as "head of state" of the independent India to come, over the heads of Gandhiji, Nehru, Patel, etc., and had embarked on a suicidal course for the invasion of India, needed the "state of his head" to be examined and treated properly. He also said that this "head of state," who had once claimed in India to be a socialist, was really a fascist, as proved by his dictatorial manner of functioning in Southeast Asia.

The visitor, choosing to be a fifth column, reported Menon's remarks to Subhas. In a fit of rage and vendetta, Subhas instigated the Burma Area Army to ask the Japanese military police in Singapore to arrest Kesava Menon as a dangerous man hindering the Japanese war effort and therefore a security risk.

There are some who think that Kesava Menon was arrested at the insistence of the Japanese authorities in Singapore, represented, as far as India was concerned, by the Hikari Kikan. That is not true. Orders for his arrest came from Rangoon as requested by Subhas Chandra Bose, in a signal from the Burma Area Army directly to the military police command in Singapore. The incident came to the attention of the Hikari Kikan as well as to the IIL headquarters office only after Menon had been taken away and locked up.

The message from Rangoon was an "immediate" one, and the military police acted with lightning speed. They went to Menon's house at 4:00 a.m., bundled all the members of his family into one room under guard, and took him away without even allowing him to say a word to his wife and children, who did not know his destination. It was an affront, not only to the norms of common decency, but to the IIL and the Hikari Kikan as well. Kesava Menon was still a member of the IIL at the time of his arrest.

To anyone who had seen the birth and growth of the Indian Independence League under Rash Behari Bose, it was unthinkable that a time would come when his successor would ask the Japanese military police to detain a patriot like Kesava Menon. And absolutely callously, he was treated like a third-class criminal and taken to jail, first for interrogation and later for imprisonment under conditions of extreme hardship. He went through so much suffering that his survival was a matter of wonder to many who knew how much he had borne. Persons who had caused great harm to the IIL, like Mohan Singh and Colonel Gill, although arrested for misbehavior against duly constituted authorities, were treated honorably and lodged in houses with all creature comforts at the insistence of the IIL. And here was Subhas throwing away Kesava Menon to be dealt with like prisoners of the category of murderers and lunatics.

The military police setup was outside the control of the Hikari Kikan, and we were unable to have the orders countermanded. All that I could personally do was to use my influence with some of my friends in the military police establishment and to prevent their men from perpetrating any atrocities on Kesava Menon, as they were in the habit of doing to their prisoners in the ordinary course. Still, no member of his family or any other Indian was permitted to see him. When once his son was allowed to do so, it was to enable him to convey to Menon the news of the death of his daughter who had been with his family in Singapore.

The episode of K. P. Kesava Menon's arrest will remain the blackest spot in the story of the Subhas era in Southeast Asia.

CHAPTER TWENTY-SIX
The Close of the Subhas Era

After the Imphal debacle, Sivaram, who had been quite unhappy in Rangoon, returned to Singapore. He was glad that Subhas had sent him back to function as the League's spokesman and to carry on his previous publicity work together with me. I was naturally pleased to see him back.

But matters started going wrong once again for him. He was given all manner of irksome directives from Rangoon telling him what to do. He was asked to devise programs calculated to condemn Gandhiji's projected talks with Jinnah (September 1944), to describe Nehru as an "ally of the British" and Rajaji as an "agent of the viceroy" (Field Marshal Wavell). Other leaders like Sardar Patel, Bhulabhai Desai, etc. were also to be found fault with in the broadcasts from the IIL radio center in Singapore.

Sivaram was exasperated. He wrote to Subhas saying that he would like to be relieved of his membership of the league and of his position in the Publicity Department. In my case, I did not take similar action. My position was that I would ignore such instructions from Rangoon, if any, as were contrary to the policy of the IIL as established during the Bangkok Conference. I merely prevented Sivaram from preparing the kind of programs which Subhas wanted. Strangely, I was never given any specific directive from Rangoon. Or perhaps not so strangely, because Subhas, Iyer, and company must have realized that I would not carry out any *unreasonable* advice or orders from Rangoon or anywhere else.

Sivaram's letter caused worry to Subhas. He was invited to see the chief at Rangoon. Sivaram went there and had long talks. No reasonable solution of the impasse was possible, and he insisted that his resignation be accepted.

At that stage, Subhas invented a way in which Sivaram could somehow be kept on in the league organization. It was agreed that he might leave the Publicity Department because he simply could not tolerate the kind of interference in work he was being subjected to, but Subhas was prepared to create a post for him in Tokyo. He would go there to study the Japanese diplomatic practice and procedures. Perhaps Subhas hoped that such information would be useful when he became head of state in India and began to receive envoys from other countries and send out ambassadors in exchange. Already, it was rumored that one Mr. Hachiya had been selected by the Japanese government and accredited as ambassador to Subhas's Provisional Government of Free India, although it was never known what work he was doing.

Sivaram thought that it was a good opportunity to get away from Southeast Asia. He returned to Singapore from Rangoon to pack for Tokyo. It was the autumn of 1944—the first week of October, to be more precise.

* * *

By a coincidence, I had a message from the Japanese government at about the same time, through the Hikari Kikan, suggesting that I take over the IIL's publicity work in Tokyo since the previous arrangements had proved unsatisfactory. I also learned that the Hikari Kikan in Singapore was winding up before long.

The decision I had to take was a difficult one. Parting with the IIL, for the creation of which I had labored much together with Rash Behari Bose, was going to be a big wrench. At the same time, it was no use overlooking that under the new leadership, the organization had virtually disintegrated. Subhas had sought to replace the vast network of the league's branches by establishments under the control of the Provisional Government of Free India, manned by INA men recruited from among civilians in Southeast Asia. The result was chaotic. The INA officers had no experience in running such offices. They were going about as though they were part of the Japanese occupation forces. Their demeanor invited resentment from the Indian community who preferred to look after themselves instead of being wrongly cared for by others.

CHAPTER TWENTY-SIX

Subhas would tour various places in Southeast Asia and deliver emotional speeches exhorting everyone to "do or die." He functioned as though the community could be looked after by speeches. Many began to lose interest in the platitudes which were practically all they were getting. Others were confused when they heard different names for what, to them, was ostensibly one and the same thing: they did not know what to make of the new "Provisional Government for Free India" as distinct from the Indian Independence League. In fact, a movement as such had all but ceased to exist. The Indians, either individually or in groups of their own choice, began dealing directly with the Japanese authorities. Subhas, during his whirlwind tours which he continued to perform, would ask for more and more volunteers for the INA since he wanted another attack to be launched into India. But the response began to fade and eventually became almost nil.

Group photo with members of the Provisional Government of Free India and associates. Sitting second from the left in the front row is A. M. Sahay; center is Subhas Chandra Bose. The author stands in the very back row, slightly to the left. A. M. Sahay, who had been a leader since Rash Behari Bose's time, is in military uniform as chief secretary. The author, critical of Subhas Chandra Bose's policies, found himself sidelined from the mainstream movement, reflected in his position in the photo compared to earlier ones.

With a heavy heart I told Sivaram one morning that I was also leaving Singapore for Tokyo, since it was only from there that I could expect to do any more useful work. I suggested that whatever was the work he was being sent there for, he and I could do something to improve the publicity work from Tokyo. Sivaram agreed and set about recruiting a few young men to assist us at the Radio Tokyo and in dealing with the other media in Japan.

I left Singapore in the first week of October and arrived in Tokyo in a few days. Sivaram, together with his publicity assistants, numbering about ten, joined me in the second week.

Immediately on reaching Tokyo, I sought out my wife and child and was relieved to discover that they had managed to move out to the village and were safe. Tokyo itself, like other large Japanese cities, had already become targets of American bombing raids from various Pacific Island bases captured by the Allied forces. From the safety point of view, going from Singapore to Tokyo at that time was like falling from the frying pan into the fire. July 9, 1944, the date on which the Imphal campaign was officially called off (although it had actually ended much earlier), had coincided with the announcement of the American capture of Saipan in the Marianas. 25,000 Japanese soldiers defending it had died there to the last man. Among them was Admiral Nagumo who, over two years earlier, had commanded a task force for the Pearl Harbor attack. With their landings on Saipan Island, the Japanese homeland had come within striking distance of the Americans' B-29 Superfortress bombers. During the same month, Japan had lost New Georgia.

With these great debacles, Tojo's position had become untenable. He and his cabinet were forced to resign on July 18, 1944. Retired general Kunikai Koiso became the new prime minister. He was brought over from Korea where he was governor general. Earlier he was commander of the Kwantung Army. I knew him when I was in Manchukuo.

But the change of prime minister did not improve matters; not even the decision that Koiso would share his powers with Admiral Yonai (in order to placate the navy). Japanese reverses in war continued unabated. By September, the Gilbert Islands also fell to the Americans, and in October, MacArthur's army registered its famous victory in the Philippines, at Luzon, after the bitter battle of Leyte Gulf where the Allied troops made the biggest amphibious landing after the one they had done at Normandy in France in June of the same year. In the Leyte operations, the Japanese navy lost nearly two-thirds of its ships. The country never recovered from the blow.

I and Sivaram, with our small staff, had necessarily to live in Tokyo and face the risks, but I insisted that my wife and child should remain in the village.

CHAPTER TWENTY-SIX

In fact, it was due to my wife that we were saved from possible starvation, which was already stalking certain sections of the Tokyo population. She somehow managed to send me, through various extraordinary and often dangerous means, enough of essential food commodities to enable us to run a common kitchen for our establishment. Sivaram and I did whatever was possible for our office to do. We kept up the broadcasts from Radio Tokyo, covering the events as honestly and truthfully as anyone could during those days. We knew that the end was coming.

* * *

By November 1944, Rash Behari had become critically ill and was bedridden. There was only a maidservant staying in his house, and I saw that she, although conscientious, could not really help very much. I therefore split my time between the Publicity Department, where I would work during day, and Rash Behari's house, where I spent the night. News of the developments since his departure from Singapore distressed him so much that after some time I tried to divert his mind from the war events. Medical attention was difficult to obtain, although my doctor friends, such of those who were available, did their best.

November 1, 1944. Tokyo's skies had just cleared after a severe air raid by waves and waves of B-29's, when a small Japanese plane carrying Subhas and Lieutenant General Saburo Isoda, head of the Hikari Kikan in Burma, arrived in the capital's airport. The two distinguished visitors had come for consultations with the new prime minister and the imperial general staff, on "military matters."

During his stay of a few weeks in Tokyo, Subhas delivered several public speeches predicting Japan's ultimate victory. He also proclaimed that the INA would be expanded by large-scale recruitment of Indians in Southeast Asia and that another attack would be launched into India to drive the British away. One of my friends in the Domei News Agency covering the speeches was aghast and whispered to me that here was one who must be an "incarnation of Alfred the Great." The aptness of his comparison was not quite certain, but one must say that Subhas was an optimist of a rare kind. And whatever might be the opinions about the soundness of his thinking, his abundance of energy which enabled him to go through speech after speech was truly remarkable. I attended some of his lectures but later stopped going because there was no point in listening to talks that made no political or practical sense at the time.

On the occasion of Subhas Chandra Bose's visit to Tokyo in November 1944. He is flanked by Inosuke Furuno, president of the Domei News Agency (right) and Mr. Fukuda, chief of the Southeast Asia Bureau of Domei. Behind them are V. C. Lingam and the author.

The imperial high command was in no mood to discuss Subhas's "military" schemes, or any scheme for that matter. It referred him to Shigemitsu, who was foreign minister. That was perhaps one way of disposing of an inconvenient visit. But Shigemitsu found no time to meet him either. Subhas then wanted to see General Koiso. He could not secure an appointment through his own efforts, and so asked me whether I could help.

I could have spoken to Koiso, using my old Manchukuo days' acquaintance with him, but preferred to work through my close friend, Kono, president of Domei, who was highly influential with the government, as a member of its "brains trust." I introduced Subhas to him and requested Kono that he should arrange a meeting for him with General Koiso.

It was amusing that after I had introduced him to Kono, Subhas suggested that he be left alone with him: in other words, I must leave the room. I almost laughed aloud but controlled myself and slowly walked out.

Kono arranged the meeting Subhas wanted with General Koiso. The discussions, as I soon gathered from Kono, centered on the question of more arms and ammunition for the INA. It was amazing how a great leader could function in a small way by completely ignoring the realities of a very serious situation for his host country. Koiso's reaction was predictable: he cut short the meeting with a quick veto of any further military action by Subhas or anyone else across the Burma border. On the other hand, Koiso asked Subhas to mobilize all available INA resources to support the Japanese defense effort in Burma against the SEAC. Subhas had no option but to agree. There was no scope for any further discussions. The situation was desperate for Japan.

* * *

Before leaving for Rangoon in the last week of November, Subhas went with me to see Rash Behari in his sickbed. During the conversation, Rash Behari gave him what he termed his "last advice." Referring to the IIL's radio broadcasts and other publicity efforts, he told him that the broadcasts from Tokyo were all right, but Subhas, from his side, "should not increase the number of our enemies." The implication was clear to those who knew the scenario. It was a comment on the propaganda programs conducted from Burma under Subhas's direction (with Iyer's help, of course). There was a great deal in them attacking the USA in addition to Britain. Rash Behari was reminding his visitor that our enemy was only Britain.

It must be recorded that Subhas heeded this "last advice." He stopped the propaganda against America.

What he saw on return to Rangoon was surely far from encouraging. Mountbatten's SEAC was preparing to recover Burma. The Japanese 15th Division was putting up a valiant effort to stem the tide, but the odds against it were too heavy. Subhas threw in all that was left of the INA to help the Japanese army. He toured Malaya and tried his best to recruit more men to join the force. But there was, understandably, hardly any favorable response. On the contrary, as I heard in course of time, there was much opposition to him in several centers. That was particularly because it was clear that the recruitment of Indians was really for the purpose of fighting as mercenaries for the Japanese. This was not what the patriotic Indians in Southeast Asia had in view when they joined the IIL under Rash Behari Bose.

In an effort to improve efficiency, Subhas expanded his cabinet. One of the additions was N. Raghavan, who was given the finance portfolio. An interesting sidelight in this context was that, before accepting the appointment, Raghavan sent a cable to Rash Behari seeking his approval. He was doing this because he had earlier resigned from Rash Behari's Action Council, a step which he later regretted. It was decent of Raghavan to consult Rash Behari who, apart from being the previous leader of the IIL, was still the supreme adviser to Subhas's organization. The ailing patriot could not send a telegram himself but asked me to do so on his behalf, agreeing to Raghavan's proposal to join the expanded cabinet. I sent the message. Raghavan became a minister. But a stage had been reached when nothing could help the INA or the Japanese any longer.

* * *

Rash Behari Bose passed away on January 21, 1945. I had continued to spend the nights at his house, and it was my painful duty to administer the last drop of water to him before the end came. When he knew that death was knocking at his door, he told me that he would be born again to carry on the fight for India's freedom. His last look was at the framed tablet which he always had on the wall in front of him with the words: "Vande Mataram."

Rash Behari Bose's funeral altar, 1945. The ribbon and insignia on the left is the Order of the Rising Sun, Gold and Silver Star, conferred on him by the emperor of Japan.

CHAPTER TWENTY-SIX

Prime Minister Hideki Tojo delivers a eulogy at the memorial service for Rash Behari Bose on April 5, 1942.

A great life had ended. India lost one of her greatest sons and one of the foremost leaders of her struggle for independence. To me personally, his demise caused the deepest sorrow. The grief still lingers.

Captain Mohan Singh has descended to a very low and mean level in his book when he says several uncomplimentary things about Rash Behari, who was among the greatest of India's freedom fighters. Among other uncivilized remarks, Singh has called him a "pigmy." There can be no pigmy smaller than anyone who hurls such an expression at Mahanayak Rash Behari Bose, a giant among Indian patriots. Mercifully, Mohan Singh has refrained in his book from comparing his own height with that of Mount Everest or the other way round.

A little before Rash Behari's death, the emperor of Japan had decorated him with a high distinction: the Order of the Rising Sun, Gold and Silver Star. The medal was handed to him on behalf of the emperor, by Lieutenant General Seizo Arisue of the imperial headquarters.

The Japanese people organized a solemn and dignified funeral, which was presided over by Koki Hirota, ex-prime minister, as chairman of the funeral committee. A large number of Japanese dignitaries and the entire Indian community were present. The last rites were performed at Zojoji Temple in Shiba, Tokyo, and among the Japanese leaders who came to pay their last respects were General Tojo and several cabinet ministers, past as well as those in office. The large premises of the temple overflowed with mourners, many of whom had to remain standing outside for want of space within.

THE CLOSE OF THE SUBHAS ERA

Memorial service for Rash Behari Bose. Front row, from left: Senjuro Hayashi, Koki Hirota, Hidezo Toyama (third son of Toyama Mitsuru), Yoshihisa Kuzu. Second row, far left: Prime Minister Hideki Tojo.

* * *

By March 1945, Mountbatten's thrust across Burma had become a serious threat to Japan's westernmost defense line. In April, General Heitaro Kimura replaced Kawabe as the chief of the Burma Area Army. But that in no way resulted in any relief to the harassed Japanese forces. They were in an extremely difficult plight. There was chaos in Burma. Kimura's men fought bravely but were unable to cope with the SEAC pressure. Casualties among the Japanese soldiers exceeded 100,000. Subhas had provided several units of the INA to fight along with the Japanese, and many of these men were killed. But quite a large number went over to the British 14th Army, incurring the wrath of Subhas who swore to deal with those "traitors" when the time came.

Ba Maw, head of the Japanese-sponsored Free Burma, had escaped to Moulmein (present Mawlamyine), and his family had been dispatched to Thailand. General Aung San's guerillas, instead of helping the Japanese as had been hoped by Kimura, were harassing them. Subhas's Provisional

CHAPTER TWENTY-SIX

Government of Free India headquarters, and the INA, were riddled with internal troubles. Defections from the INA continued.

Kimura decided to withdraw from Burma to Thailand. Subhas still was hopeful of mobilizing more INA men and keep fighting and went again to Malaya in a bid to find fresh recruits. But it was all to no avail. Eventually he accepted Kimura's advice to pull back to Bangkok. Along with a few hundred INA men and some women of the Jhansi Regiment, he reached Bangkok on May 7, 1945, one day before the announcement came of Germany's capitulation and the end of the war in Europe.

The Provisional Government of Free India, the IIL, and the INA all disintegrated by about the time Burma was evacuated by the Japanese.

I had reports from friends coming from Singapore that after the fall of Burma and during the impending ouster of the Japanese from Thailand, Subhas went to Singapore again to enlist personnel for the INA to help the Japanese hold on at least to Malaya, which was the last hope they had. He appeared still to be of the view that by some miracle Japan would ultimately win.

And what was more disquieting, he continued propagating the theory that India could be liberated only through an armed revolution spearheaded by him from Southeast Asia. Since there was no other arrangement for publicity, Subhas himself would broadcast from Radio Singapore putting forward his ideas of another armed attack and blaming the Indian National Congress for its "defeatist attitude." Everywhere in Malaya, he would ask for "blood from the Indian soldiers and money and materials from the rest of the community." He worked very hard, but what materialized, basically, was a great deal of discontent and fear among the people who apprehended that they were probably being led into a greater catastrophe than they might normally face, when the Allied armies started the offensive to retake Malaya.

The news was so distressing that at one stage, in May 1945, I thought I should go once again either to Bangkok or Singapore to share the miseries of the Indian community there and see whether it was still possible to do anything to help them. I consulted a colonel friend in the imperial headquarters regarding transport facilities but was told that, while those could be provided if I insisted, Japan was on the verge of total collapse. Efforts were being made to sue for an honorable end to the war.

Such being the situation, I decided to stay on in Tokyo and see whatever remained to be seen and to do anything that might yet be practicable in the circumstances, although the state of affairs frankly looked hopeless.

A piece of news which reached me at about that time was somewhat intriguing. I gathered that S. A. Iyer, who was then in Bangkok along with

Subhas, was in frequent touch with the consulate general of Portugal there. The consul general, although a Portuguese national, was of Goan origin. It was impossible to understand why an Indian who held a high position in the Provisional Government of Free India should be in contact with the Portuguese. It seemed suspicious, but I decided to give Iyer the benefit of the doubt and concluded that it was perhaps merely a personal matter, nothing underhand.

* * *

The rest of the story of the INA is generally well-known. Much has been said by many regarding the impact of that army on the freedom movement that eventually brought independence to India in 1947. The INA and Subhas deserve a place of honor in our freedom struggle, but it was surely not they who played the primary part. In my view, Indian independence was won mainly through India's internal leadership and the self-sacrifice of her own people within the country. There was indeed a great deal of moral support they received from the INA and from Indian freedom fighters in various parts of the world, but we should view the whole scenario in its proper perspective. The fact that the Imphal debacle was a great tragedy that could have been avoided if emotion had not got the better of practical wisdom should not be overlooked.

After the INA's surrender to the Allied forces and the repatriation of its personnel to India, the British conducted a trial of certain officers of the organization on charges of a variety of crimes, such as "waging war against the king, murder, abetment to murder, gross brutality in the methods employed to induce their fellow prisoners to join them," etc. Without their realizing it, the British, by their decision to embark on these trials in public, lent a great fillip to Indian nationalism.

The large-scale recruitment of Indians to fight Britain's war had already vastly increased the numerical strength of Indian nationals in the British Indian armed forces, and these new officers and men, who were seething with discontent against the discriminatory treatment given to Indian soldiers vis-à-vis their British colleagues, could no longer be taken for granted. Britain could not expect to continue holding India in bondage for long, unless they brought in hundreds of thousands of armed personnel from England.

The issue of the INA trials became highly political. The Indian National Congress, under the inspiration of Nehru, Bhulabhai Desai, Tej Bahadur

CHAPTER TWENTY-SIX

Sapru, and many others, decided to defend the accused INA personnel. A great patriotic upsurge was aroused in the country at the national level. The resentment against British colonialism reached its peak. The Indian component of the navy in Bombay mutinied against the British commanders.

The INA emerged as heroes. In the process, however, as often could happen in such cases, several undeserving persons secured recognition. Large numbers of ex-INA men clamored for loaves and fishes of government jobs at the time of India's independence, and Jawaharlal Nehru, in his magnanimity, conferred favors on several without always sifting the genuine freedom fighters from the pretenders. There were some who did not merit any honor: it was thrust upon them. One of such cases, in my opinion, was that of Colonel Shah Nawaz Khan, who secured a minister's position in the Government of Free India under Nehru. Everyone who was in Singapore during the difficult initial days of the war seemed to think that his conduct was highly unhelpful. He was a fence-sitter, undecided as to whether to remain a POW under the Japanese or to join the IIL. (Later, of course, he was shown much favor by Subhas.)

I am not saying this out of any grievance on account of any nonrecognition of my own services. Far from it. In fact, just as a certain number of Indians who were with the IIL and the INA were inducted into the Indian Foreign Service, I was also offered entry into it. There was the promise of an ambassadorship in due course. But I had always thought of my part in the Indian freedom struggle in a different light. One of the fundamental principles of the IIL was the concept of *anasakta karma*. A possible position in the bureaucracy of independent India was not a motivation for me, and when I was being considered for a place in free India's new diplomatic cadre of officers, I did not show any interest. It might have been a different matter if I was being offered a senior head of mission's post straightaway as a political appointee, but the status of a cog in the career diplomatic wheel that some of my friends accepted did not appeal to me.

My observations on the "mushroom" freedom fighters who paraded themselves before Nehru and received favors from him have therefore no relationship to my own career. As far as any diplomatic position for me in Japan was concerned, the government of India would not have succeeded in appointing me as their representative in Tokyo because I was too much on the wrong side of the "Allied powers," at least the British component thereof.

However, I did not feel that my work in Japan as a private individual had ended with the arrival of MacArthur and his contingent at the Dai-Ichi

Building in Tokyo to begin the "occupation." Sooner or later there would be a peace treaty between the defeated country and the "Allies." I somehow felt that I had a duty to perform in that connection. I was anxious to see the shape of things to come and play a useful role in respect of Indo-Japanese relations under the changed conditions.

CHAPTER TWENTY-SEVEN
The Surrender of Japan

By the end of 1944, Tokyo and other cities in Japan had come under heavy American bombardment, and the situation was worsening every day. It was a mark of the great capacity of the Japanese people to suffer calamities that there was still some semblance of normal activity among civilians in the capital and other places. For Sivaram and me, it was becoming more and more difficult to carry on our work, although we did not give up altogether.

Finding it pointless to stay on in Tokyo, Sivaram left for Singapore (under risky conditions), with transport arrangements provided with much difficulty by the 2nd Bureau at my request. His departure was a little before Rash Behari's demise. I stayed on, although there was no doubt that the war was going to end in Japan's defeat. MacArthur's forces had landed in Luzon on July 9, 1944, as already stated, and had started marching into Manila. On February 16, 1945, some 1,500 aircraft from the American 5th Fleet, which had come within 200 miles of western Japan, pounded Tokyo and Yokohama. It was carpet bombing, since there was practically no Japanese air resistance. What was left of the Japanese air force was virtually only its kamikaze wing, which was of no use against the B-29 Superfortresses.

American pressure on Iwo Jima was on and growing. The island's defenses crumbled in March. Casualties on both the Japanese and the Allies' sides were very heavy. The battle for Okinawa had also begun in March and was heating up when General Koiso decided to resign on April 4, giving place to Admiral Kantaro Suzuki. Suzuki, who had earned his fame during the Russo-Japanese War, was reluctant, since he thought he was too old at 77 years, but bowed to the wishes of the emperor. That was apparently Japan's last bid to save Okinawa. But it was of no use. The Japanese navy lost its most prized battleship, the 72,000-ton *Yamato*, the largest ocean liner in the world at that time, and 15 other warships. Over 12,000 men were killed in one of the most savage series of battles. Among those who died was Rash Behari's son Masahide. American casualties were estimated at about 13,000.

Meanwhile, one of the heaviest air raids which Tokyo had gone through had been carried out on March 9. It was an incendiary bomb attack during night and was calculated to inflict the maximum damage to Japan's armament production factories located in the northeastern suburbs of Tokyo. About 350 B-29s flew over Tokyo at an altitude of 5,000 feet and dropped over 2,000 tons of napalm, magnesium, and phosphorus. The Japanese air force had no night fighters, nor any radar control against enemy planes attacking in darkness. Over 100,000 persons were killed in that one night, and over 500,000 saw their houses reduced to ashes.

Raids followed raids at intervals of a few days each, and by May more than half of Tokyo was in ruin. The emperor stepped out of his palace to see what was happening, and he was surely not pleased at what he saw. The average Japanese however showed incredible stoicism. He still bowed to his emperor and voiced no complaint.

With the fall of Okinawa, the Allied stranglehold on the home islands had become an imminent possibility. It could soon tighten to a point of near-death for a choking population. Tokyo was burning, except for the emperor's palace and a few buildings deliberately spared by the low-flying Allied aircraft delivering bomb loads over the city. More than five million Japanese in Tokyo alone were without shelter, besides the incalculable numbers killed. It was a wonder how nearly half the city's population rendered homeless survived—perhaps only because it was summertime. If it were winter, most of those who had lost their houses might have perished from the severe cold.

There was nothing that the Supreme Council for the Direction of War could do except to bid for a negotiated peace. Shigenori Togo, who had replaced Shigemitsu as foreign minister, tried to seek Soviet mediation, but the Russians prevaricated. The Soviet Union had secretly promised America and Britain at the Yalta Conference in February 1945 that it would enter the war against Japan within three months after the end of the European war. In fact, as the Pacific situation developed, Russian intervention had ceased to be relevant for the Americans who were, by July 1945, capable of winning without Russian help. But the Soviet Union obviously was glad to get on to the bandwagon. Eventually came the Potsdam Conference of July 1945 and the American-British-Chinese declaration of July 27 calling for Japan's unconditional surrender. Prime Minister Suzuki rejected the ultimatum, but events were inexorably getting out of control for Japan.

Hiroshima was atom bombed on August 6, 1945, and Nagasaki treated similarly on August 9. The two cities were completely wiped out. There was talk of more atom bombs coming, although America had in fact no more at that time.

Russia entered the war against Japan on the same day that Nagasaki was bombed, and at a time when Japan for all practical purposes had been defeated and was seeking neutral mediation for a negotiated ceasefire.

In the midst of all the air raids, I stayed on in Tokyo, wondering how I was managing to keep my body and soul together. I had to keep shifting residence frequently. I would visit my family in the village as often as possible but spent a considerable amount of time nevertheless in Tokyo, to be in touch with the military high command so that I could remain informed of the developments.

The author, his wife, and their two sons at their evacuation home in Ibaraki, 1946.

While War Minister Anami was still exhorting the Japanese army even as late as the first week of August 1945 to go on fighting, the imperial forces were dying in vast numbers every day, and the same was the case with the civilian population. Wave after wave of American B-29 bombers blasted the cities by pinpoint attacks. There were still efforts by the Japanese to undertake a total mobilization to defend the home islands on land, but that also was becoming a futile attempt.

On the morning of August 15, 1945, radio listeners first heard the Kimigayo (Japanese national anthem) and then their emperor's voice:

> To our good and loyal subjects . . . After pondering deeply the general trend of the world, and the actual conditions obtaining in our Empire today, we have decided to effect a settlement of the present situation by resorting to an extraordinary measure . . . Should we continue to fight, it would not only result in an ultimate collapse and obliteration of the Japanese nation, but would also lead to the total extinction of human civilization . . . It is according to the dictate of the time and fate that we have resolved to pave the way for a grand peace for all the generations to come, by enduring the unendurable and suffering what is insufferable . . . Unite your total strength to be devoted to the construction of the future. . . .

The Imperial Rescript was long, and only short excerpts have been reproduced above. Briefly, the emperor was declaring the termination of the war, with Japan's acceptance of the Potsdam Declaration, which had demanded unconditional surrender.

The Allied powers had their V-J Day on August 14, 1945. A ferocious and tragic war had ended with incalculable loss of lives and untold suffering. A nation had fallen from a great height of power to total defeat and its aftermath of indescribable hardship to its people.

* * *

Although the emperor made his broadcast only on the morning of August 15, his decision to accept the Potsdam Declaration and unconditional surrender had in fact been taken on August 10, the day following the atom bomb raid on Nagasaki and destruction of the whole city. It took four days for him finally to overrule the pleas from various sections of the armed forces that the military be allowed to keep fighting and to annihilate itself to the last man if need be. General Korechika Anami, the war minister, prostrated before him and begged for a change of decision. He wanted the war to go on until the bitterest end. But the emperor remained unmoved. The decision of the emperor that Japan surrendered unconditionally was conveyed to the Allied powers on August 14. Anami, who believed that Japanese armed men must never surrender, had the unenvious task of telling his colleagues that he had failed in his effort to persuade the emperor to reconsider his intention. He informed everyone that, from then on, they must "eat stones."

A group of young officers revolted. Major Hidemasa Koga, son-in-law of General Tojo, and another major, Kenji Hatanaka, went to the Imperial Guard Division and gatecrashed the commander's office. General Mori was there. The rebels wanted him to join them and stage a coup to oust the cabinet of Suzuki. When Mori refused, Hatanaka shot and killed him. Thereafter, with Mori's seal, they forged an order to the Imperial Guard to follow them. They went to the palace to look for the recording of the emperor's surrender broadcast, which they had heard was in custody in the premises. They could not find it. On August 14, they stormed into the broadcasting station in an attempt to get hold of the tape, but again failed. The emperor's speech went on air as scheduled.

On August 14, General Anami, in the tradition of the samurai, composed a letter of apology to the emperor, and committed seppuku (hara-kiri). While Anami was dying, General Tanaka, commander of the Eastern District Army, led a loyal unit of the Imperial Guard and managed to quell the rebellion of the young officers. It is believed that it was he who prevented them from shooting down everyone in the broadcasting station, on which the two majors had been mobilizing a strong force for an attack.

When the people heard the emperor's broadcast, they wept, but still bowed towards the palace.

For the next several days, the youthful groups of the armed forces remained dissatisfied and militant. But soon conditions became normal. Major Koga and his colleague Hatanaka and many others had killed themselves with their guns, and a large number of officers had committed hara-kiri ceremonially at the military grounds in Yoyogi. Several more ended their lives on a hill near the Palace by means of hand grenades in a mass suicide.

Prince Higashikuni succeeded Suzuki as interim prime minister. Other members of the royal family were asked to go to various areas personally to ask the Japanese soldiers to accept the surrender orders, since most of them disbelieved the broadcast.

Admiral Matome Ugaki, commander of the navy's kamikaze wing, flew his own plane in the direction of Okinawa and never returned. Obviously, he crashed himself to death. He had left a message owning responsibility for the death of innumerable young pilots including teenagers under his command, and also for the failure to protect the life of Fleet Admiral Isoroku Yamamoto.

Vice Admiral Takijiro Onishi, "father of the kamikaze," slashed himself to death with a sword. The number of others who killed themselves was very large, including several high officials of the civil administration and, of course, armed forces generals and other senior commanders. The trauma of defeat and the horror and agony which followed so completely overwhelmed them that they wanted to preserve at least the nation's spirit of *bushido* by ending their lives.

American troops had begun arriving in Japan from August 29. General Eichelberger flew in early in the morning of August 30, and General MacArthur's C-54, *Bataan*, touched down at the Atsugi airport in the afternoon of the same day. There was much apprehension among the Americans that there might be a desperate attempt on his life by the Japanese troops in the area or by some of the kamikaze pilots who were living near the airport. But nothing untoward happened. On the contrary, the entire 15-mile road to Yokohama where MacArthur was to stay temporarily in the Grand Hotel before moving to the American embassy building in Akasaka, Tokyo, was well protected by Japanese soldiers who appeared to give him the same respect as they would to their emperor. MacArthur was astonished.

Russia ended the six-week war with Japan on September 2. It felt that it had avenged its defeat at the hands of Japan in 1904. The Soviets annexed south Sakhalin and the Kurile Islands. However, unlike what had happened in Germany, mainland Japan was not allowed to be occupied by Russian forces. The occupation army in Japan was, for all practical purposes, that of the USA, with token participation of the Commonwealth countries.

Mamoru Shigemitsu, leading the Japanese delegation, and Lieutenant General Yoshijiro Umezu, representing the imperial high command's armed forces, signed the surrender document on September 2 in front of General MacArthur on board the American battleship *Missouri* in Tokyo Bay. Umezu was initially very angry and refused to sign, but subsequently bowed to the emperor's wishes.

Speaking on the occasion, MacArthur hoped that a better world would emerge "out of the blood and carnage of the past… Let us pray that Peace be now restored to the world and that God will preserve it always. These proceedings are closed."

CHAPTER TWENTY-SEVEN

An armada of over 400 B-29 planes and more than 1,500 carrier-based aircraft roared past the *Missouri* to mark the end of the ceremony, which filled the whole Japanese population with tears.

On September 8, MacArthur formally moved into Tokyo and established his office in the Dai-Ichi Building. Three days later, on September 11, the American military police went to General Tojo's house to arrest him. Tojo attempted to commit suicide by shooting himself with a pistol. Although he was seriously injured, American doctors saved his life. Eventually he was sentenced to death by the "war crimes" tribunal set up by MacArthur and was hanged on December 23, 1948.

* * *

Before his dismissal in April 1951 by President Harry Truman (for his opposition to Truman's policy vis-à-vis the conduct of the Korean War), MacArthur had said that he had democratized Japan. The emperor was stripped of his divinity. One of MacArthur's predictions was that Japan would become a Christian country within twenty-five years. That did not happen. MacArthur was succeeded by General Matthew B. Ridgway. American help, financially and in various other ways, to rehabilitate Japan, was indeed great. With that assistance, but predominantly by dint of sheer hard and sustained work by its skilled people, the nation made a miraculous industrial and economic recovery. The country remained under occupation for 6 years 8 and a half months, before the San Francisco Treaty came into effect from April 28, 1952. Its postwar growth to the status of an economic superpower has been of a nature never before witnessed in the annals of any defeated country.

CHAPTER TWENTY-EIGHT
The Disappearance of Subhas Chandra Bose

More than thirty-six years have passed since V-J Day (August 14, 1945), when the Allied powers brought Japan to heel and forced it to surrender unconditionally. Subhas Chandra Bose is still regarded in India as the hero of the Indian National Army (INA) and one who, in spite of the Imphal debacle, is credited with having hastened the liberation of India from British rule. He is reckoned as a martyr. There has however been much controversy around his alleged death.

There is no doubt that the Greater East Asia War hastened the process of the emergence of India as a free nation. It also cannot be disputed that Subhas was a great patriot and freedom fighter. Having admitted these, we might pause for a moment to view the scenario in respect of his leadership of the Indian Independence League (IIL) and its affiliated organizations, the most important of them being, of course, the INA. Let us try to cast any emotional overtones aside and to appreciate the situation in perspective with reference to the circumstances of the time when the Japanese empire collapsed.

Subhas was reported to have asked the Japanese military authorities in Southeast Asia for an aircraft to take him and some of his colleagues away from Japanese-controlled areas to a Russian-occupied territory—most probably Manchukuo, which had already partially been occupied by the Russians, who had declared war on Japan on August 9, 1945, a few days before the ceasefire. It is generally believed that he did so at the insistence of his advisers.

The quality of a leader really comes under test during times of emergencies or crises. He naturally ought to swim or sink with his followers. If the story of Subhas's escape from Southeast Asia, whether under advice from his colleagues or on his own initiative, is correct, that would mean that he left all the men (and women) whom he was leading in the lurch at a time when they most needed courageous leadership. I find it difficult to believe that a leader like Subhas would have done such a disservice. Therefore, I am skeptical about the whole story of his escape as seems to have been generally accepted.

There are persons who have tacitly or openly approved Subhas's decision, if he ever took one, to flee from Southeast Asia, on the ground that a precious life such as his should not be exposed to danger from the victorious Allied forces, particularly the British, who would undoubtedly reoccupy the areas and treat the supporters of Japan as their enemies. The same persons also say that Subhas wanted to escape in order that he might be able to continue to fight for India from an alternative base. I find it impossible to accept any such theories because they are not rational. By fleeing from the area of trouble, he was unlikely to achieve anything. It was not like leaving India for another country to join Indian freedom fighters abroad. The situation could not be equated to any that had prompted other freedom fighters to attempt to do from outside what they could not from within. For instance, it was certainly not similar to the escape of Rash Behari Bose or to what prompted others like Raja Mahendra Pratap to get away from India.

**

It is incredible that anyone should consider Subhas as a type of leader who would desert his people and run for safety for himself, under any circumstances. He was much too courageous for any such action. And his alleged destination, viz. Russia or a Russian-controlled area, could certainly not be a congenial place for any renewed work for Indian freedom as far as any sensible person could see. Russia was a friend of Subhas's enemy, Britain, and was also fighting Japan, Subhas's friend. In any plan to set up under the circumstances a new Indian independence center under Moscow's auspices there could therefore be no iota of logic.

Then, it is said that he was arranging with the *Japanese* to have him flown to Russia or a Russian-controlled territory. Anyone with rudimentary knowledge of Japanese psychology would not believe that any Japanese pilot would fly an aircraft into a Russian base or even over Russian-controlled airspace. He would sooner commit suicide by other means, most likely the traditional Japanese mode of hara-kiri or alternatively by crashing into an enemy target like a kamikaze flyer. And a Japanese commander would deploy a plane for such a flight only if he did not want the plane to land or its occupants to survive.

We are told that Subhas was provided seats for himself and one of his aides, Captain Habib ur Rahman, in a plane in which some Japanese officers were also travelling. It is said that the plane was carrying a large number of boxes containing gold and other precious things as part of Subhas's baggage, and that en route the aircraft crashed in Taipei, resulting in Subhas's death due to burns. Habib ur Rahman was reported to have sustained some injury, allegedly while trying to put out the flames on Subhas's clothing. On the other hand, there were persons, at least until recent years, who thought that Subhas was still alive, hiding somewhere. There have been many bizarre conjectures, some of which might make excellent material for sensational movie films.

In my view, every report that has appeared on the subject of Subhas's disappearance is unworthy of acceptance.

I have already referred to the naïveté of theories regarding any Japanese aircraft trying to fly Subhas to Russian territory. That question should be straightaway ruled out. In discussing other points associated with the alleged event, we come across the reported large quantities of wealth the plane was supposed to be carrying. It is said that this was in the form of precious jewelry donated by the people of Southeast Asia, particularly the poor Tamil laborers in Malaya. As I have mentioned earlier, women even parted with their Mangal Sutras and gave them away to Subhas's war fund. What happened to this wealth?

The very supposition that there was a plane crash in Formosa in which Subhas was burnt is open to serious suspicion. It was said that some persons other than Subhas were also killed in the alleged crash, but to the best of my personal knowledge, every one of the Japanese passengers listed as killed was alive for long periods after the reported accident and supposed "deaths." It is not credible that in an aircraft that crashed with a dozen or so passengers plus the crew, just one man, Subhas, was killed. I would regard such a story as a fabrication, whatever be anyone else's view of it.

Some of the "dead" men are probably still alive. Some others in the same category are unfortunately no more. A few of them whom I knew personally

CHAPTER TWENTY-EIGHT

had told me that the "list of the dead" published identically in a number of books was a piece of calculated fraud.

As for the several boxes of wealth in terms of jewelry, there seems to be a great deal of mystery. Nothing that has appeared in any of the records I have been able to find proves anything. Some very small number of gold ornaments and other things, insignificant in value, supposedly the remains from the alleged air-crash losses, were handed over, after the war, by the Japanese government to the government of India through the Indian embassy in Tokyo. Whether these petty items were really part of the war collections from the Indian community is itself an open question. I personally doubt any such assumption. Those articles could have been picked up from anywhere. In any case, what happened to the rest of the jewelry, which according to rough estimates was several hundred kilograms in weight? An answer has not even been remotely established in any satisfactory manner.

* * *

There were some highly suspicious aspects to the whole alleged episode of the aircraft crash, the supposed death of Subhas, and the disappearance of the wealth he was said to have been carrying.

There seems to be general agreement that initially both S. A. Iyer and Habib ur Rahman were to accompany Subhas, but due to lack of space it was decided that only Habib ur Rahman would do so. But Iyer managed to reach Tokyo within two or three days after the alleged plane crash. He was for some days in the Dai-Ichi Hotel in Shimbashi, Tokyo.

Some members of the IIL's Publicity Department who were staying in the same hotel tried to meet him, but he evaded them. A Japanese, Lieutenant Colonel Kadamatsu, was however with him for several hours in his hotel room until late in the evening. What transpired between them was not authoritatively known, but there was a strong rumor that there was much "planning" between them as to how a story should be cooked up about Subhas's "disappearance" and about the "loss" of the bulk of the Indian wealth.

In the last week of August 1945, I met Iyer at the residence of A. M. Sahay, where I saw a very large metal box brought by Iyer. I was intrigued by its size and wanted to have an idea of its weight by trying to move it. It was so heavy that no amount of effort by me—and I was not a weak-bodied man—was of any avail. I was then convinced that the box contained not clothing but something else, most probably heavy metal. I asked Iyer what it was. He was absolutely cagey and merely said: "Something important." That was no occasion for jokes.

Iyer's evasive answer could only mean that there was a secret about that box, which he did not want me to know. His conduct towards me, an important member of the Indian freedom movement and an ex-colleague, was extremely odd.

From Sahay's house, Iyer went to Colonel Figges, the British embassy's chief intelligence officer, and surrendered himself to him. Within a couple of days of that event, Habib ur Rahman also went to Figges and gave himself up. Both Iyer and Rehman were later repatriated to India by the British. I was told that Iyer received all his "arrears of pay" from Reuters, and that Habib ur Rahman was similarly given all his "dues" by the British government, whereafter he opted for service in Pakistan. The most trusted lieutenant of Subhas found it undesirable to stay in India!

Iyer, in his own book, *Unto Him a Witness: The Story of Netaji Subhas Chandra Bose in East Asia, Bombay, 1951*, has stated that when he was in Tokyo, the Japanese foreign office requested him to help them draft a radio news item about the plane crash and Subhas's death. I consider this to be indicative of some conspiracy. In the first place, the foreign office was not running NHK. Secondly, why should the help of Iyer have been sought? If anyone had to be approached for help, Habib ur Rahman would surely have been a more logical choice. How could Iyer be expected to know what had taken place when he was not on the scene of the alleged occurrence?

There were two commissions appointed by the government of India to enquire into the disappearance of Subhas: the Shah Nawaz Khan Committee, and the Khosla Commission. I was personally aware how these commissions functioned in Japan. They went about their work as though their duty was to establish that Subhas had been killed in the reported air crash. And so in their reports they said he had been killed in the crash. They did not examine some of the most important persons who could have given evidence truthfully and who were easily available. I believe most of the witnesses who were questioned exercised their wits rather than their knowledge. The fact was that they did not have anything by way of the latter. In my view, it was shoddy work.

Justice Khosla has said in his report that he did not visit Taipei, where the crash was supposed to have taken place, because the government of India had no "diplomatic relations" with the Formosa government. With all respect to the judge, I say that the argument was naive. I have no doubt that if the

CHAPTER TWENTY-EIGHT

Taiwan administration had been asked, it would surely have extended all possible assistance. There was no diplomatic consideration involved; what was to be attempted was the unearthing of the truth about an important matter of public interest in India. There appears to be no indication in the report that the commission ever approached the Formosa authorities. After all, there are Indians visiting Formosa even now, although there are still no "diplomatic relations" between it and the Indian government. I regret to say that I think very poorly of the performance of the commission.

In 1950–51, I had suggested that the only hope of discovering the truth lay in the appointment of a *joint* Indo-Japanese commission of enquiry. Both Japanese and Indian newspapers were enthusiastically in favor of such a move and some of them suggested, editorially, that it was the only course which could be expected to produce any worthwhile results. Indeed, discovery of the truth could not be guaranteed even by a joint commission because of the long lapse of time, but if anything at all was possible, it could be achieved only through such a commission. H. V. Kamath, MP, an ex-member of the Indian civil service who had resigned from it to enter politics and had been a devotee of Subhas, at least in his early political career, supported the suggestion, in a speech in the Indian parliament. He said that my proposal should be implemented.

The government of India sought the cooperation of the Japanese government. The latter, while promising all facilities to an Indian commission of inquiry, dodged the proposal for a joint commission. The reason was not difficult to guess. They did not wish to stick their neck out if they could possibly keep it unstuck. I think it was a mistake on the part of the government of India not to have pressed the point. The net result was that much money was wasted on two commissions whose reports, in my opinion, could not be relied upon at all.

When the Shah Nawaz Khan Committee was in Tokyo, I was once contacted by one of its members, Mr. Mitra, in my personal capacity, for a private talk on the subject. Shah Nawaz himself did not think of getting in touch with me, and I could easily gauge the reason: in the early days of the INA, he was a fence-sitter, and even for the Indian freedom movement as such, he gave only a small part of his heart. I told Mr. Mitra that the whole manner in which the commission was setting about its business was faulty. No inquiry commission should come with an idée fixe and then try to prove what it had already decided to prove. If they had an open mind, they should begin with a number of hypotheses: for example, (a) alive, (b) dead, (c) captured, (d) missing, (e) suicide, (f) murder? None of these contingencies was improbable; therefore, every one of the questions must be thoroughly investigated. That was not done.

* * *

To some, all that I have said may appear not to add up to much. But if my comments at least provoke some unbiased thinking in responsible quarters, I shall feel satisfied. Personally, I am not at all sure that Subhas did either really try to get away from the organizations which lay around him in shambles at the time of the Japanese surrender, or, if he did make an attempt, that he succeeded. Unfortunately, I have no means now to document my own suspicions, but I think that only an unreasonable mind would rule out any of the possibilities covered by the questions I have posed.

In this connection, I recall clearly that one day in the summer of 1951, the late V. K. Krishna Menon was in Tokyo for a while en route to various places, including Peking as special representative of Jawaharlal Nehru. He was staying in the Imperial Hotel in which Colonel J. K. Bhonsle, ex-chief of the INA, also happened to be residing for the time being. I was at the hotel to meet some friends when Bhonsle, seeing me, came over and introduced me to V. K. Krishna Menon, giving him some detailed background information on my life and work. He told Menon that when he (Bhonsle) surrendered himself and the INA to the British forces in 1945, they did not ask him anything whatsoever about Subhas, and only enquired, "Where is A. M. Nair?" My immediate reaction, which I kept to myself, was one of bewilderment: whether the British had any hand in the "disappearance" of Subhas, either directly or in combination with anyone else.

Answering a specific question from Menon, Bhonsle confirmed that there was absolutely no talk by the British authorities concerned about the alleged plane crash or any other circumstance concerning Subhas's supposed death, which had been announced over the radio all over the world. Both Menon and I, felt that if the British had believed the news of the aircraft disaster and refrained from saying a word about it, that would be thoroughly un-British. (And surely Krishna Menon, who had spent a good part of his life in England, knew the British well.) It was true that the agents of Britain had colonized and exploited India for a long, long period, but it was yet strange that none of the British officers present at the surrender of the INA should say even a word of concern about Subhas, unless they had some top secret information to preserve. If it was top secret, what was the content of it? After all, as many readers may recall, the Japanese had condoled the death of Roosevelt even when the war was still ongoing and the two sides were arch enemies.

If it was a matter of totally ignoring the IIL and INA, why should the victorious officers want to know anything about A. M. Nair? There could be speculations galore, and answers equally plentiful. But I do not think the truth has ever been established. To the best of my belief, the whole story of the plane crash is a fabrication.

Mohan Singh has said, in effect, that he is "strongly of the opinion" that the plane accident took place on August 18, 1945—when, according to his own statement, he himself was in Sumatra—and that Subhas died in it, because Habib ur Rahman told him so, and Habib was a "god-fearing gentleman of noble disposition," etc.* I am afraid I do not at all accept that Habib ur Rahman was what Mohan Singh describes him to be. I have also no faith in Mohan Singh's concern for truthful statements. If one were to make a list of the number of pieces of falsehood, misrepresentations, distortions, and concoctions in his book, it would, I think, be a long list.

There could be various types of espionage or cloak-and-dagger work during wars, by Japanese as well as by any other party. In abnormal times, no one could be quite sure who was dead or who was captured or killed, or was missing, etc., whether an aircraft which was supposed to do X, Y, or Z actually did so or not. One could not be too sure even whether a plane, by whatever name it might be called: 97-2, Sally, or whatever, really existed, not to speak of its having got off the ground.

There were probably a number of persons who were potential turncoats in disguise. They could be friends, enemies, agents, double agents, anything. Wars made strange bedfellows. And if interested organizations with money or other kinds of power influence some persons in certain ways, as they sometimes do, they may find it mere child's play to make a false story appear to be absolutely true.

Some persons are so firm in their loyalties that they would rather commit suicide than turn against their comrades or let them down. Others might not have any such qualms of conscience. These types are not peculiar to any particular country: they may be in any place, including India and Japan. For instance, some persons who were intelligence officers doing counterespionage against Britain and America during the war, are known to have helped the occupation authorities greatly with secret information of various kinds after Japan's surrender.

---

* Singh, *Soldiers' Contribution to Indian Independence*, 347.

To see some such cases, one did not have to look very far in Tokyo, and it is conceivable that similar categories of persons existed elsewhere also. During the late 1940s and early 1950s, there was an office on the fourth floor of the Naigai Building in Marunouchi, engaged in preparing material for use against Japan by the American prosecutors (led by Joseph Keenan) for their work in the International Military Tribunal for the Far East. The Indian Liaison Mission was located on the fifth floor of the same building, but the fourth floor was normally off-limits to anyone other than those working in the secret office there, generally called the War History Office. But serving as an important member of that office was Major Fujiwara Iwaichi, who had been Captain Mohan Singh's patron and who had claimed credit for the raising of the INA. It was, I believe, the same office which helped the Americans to locate something like half a million of the most valuable historical and other volumes of books and other material from Japanese sources, including the government archives and the various universities, and ship them to the USA.

It would seem that for some persons, everything was fair, not only in love and war but in peace as well. They could perhaps even prepare lists of fatal casualties of air crashes or other accidents which might not have taken place at all. Some of them would qualify as super-magicians: they could perhaps make day look like night and vice versa. Who can say that a few of such remarkable men might not have worked on the episode of Subhas's "disappearance"?

* * *

Yet, although I personally would like the story of Subhas's escape to be untrue (because I have never known him to be a coward), I would not quarrel too much with those who might believe it. Human nature could be unpredictable. Different persons might be tuned to different ways of thinking and acting which to them could seem natural, although to others they would seem otherwise. For instance, after his disputes with the leadership of the Indian National Congress, Subhas, in a sense, had "run away" from India (an expression used by a friend quite inoffensively). It is not everyone who does such a thing in political life. Ordinarily one stands up and fights for his convictions, win or lose, within the country itself. The same kindly friend of mine as referred to above observed that when Subhas found himself in Berlin on a wrong wicket, his fortuitous move from there to Southeast Asia, however

CHAPTER TWENTY-EIGHT

welcome in the circumstances for Rash Behari, me, and almost everyone else in the IIL, was also some sort of "escape."

Against such a background, it was not impossible, according to some, that Subhas might have tried to "escape" from Southeast Asia also when the chips were down. Action of that kind could well be in conformity with some ingrained quality. Whether such a quality is good or bad is not a subject of discussion herein. That would be a matter of value judgement which I do not propose to enter into.

Those who accept the "escape" (or "escapism"?) theory—some of them, surprisingly, even considered it to be a wise thing if it actually happened!—probably have also another fact in support of their preference: Subhas having left a family behind in Germany, but not wanting to tell anyone about it. It came to be known long after his "disappearance" that he had married his German secretary by the name of Emilie Schenkl in February 1942, and that they had a girl with the Indian name "Anita." I was told by friends who had seen her and who also knew Subhas well that Anita's face was virtually a replica of Subhas's. Jawaharlal Nehru entertained Anita as his guest in independent India when she was a young lady in her teens. But Subhas had given everyone in Southeast Asia to understand that he was a bachelor.

One fails to see why a married man should not say that he was a married man. There is nothing wrong in a person entering into matrimony; it is a natural thing. And one would normally be proud to feel attached to one's family, despite any kind of political stresses and strains. It may all be very well to say that marriage is one's private affair, but that kind of argument goes only for common people. (Indeed, I am not sure whether it should apply even to such a category.) Great leaders are always in the limelight, and their private lives cannot be totally erased from their public image. But then, knowing is believing, just as seeing is believing.

That, I feel, was another instance of some inherent "escapism," without, of course, detriment to courage and patriotism! I think there is much truth in the adage that the best study of mankind (and its vagaries), is man. It is also said that the dividing line between genius and the opposite of it could in some cases be very thin.

I respect Subhas and regard him as a great Indian, but I would not make a martyr out of him as some others appear to have done. There have been many great leaders in the world, and Subhas was one of them. But all of them are not necessarily martyrs. Some great leaders have made great mistakes; I would say Subhas was one of them also. His first mistake was to leave India in the hope that he could raise a revolutionary army of Indians abroad to fight the British and liberate India by force of arms. His greatest mistake was to think that he could secure independence for India by means of an invasion of it by the Japanese and the INA. Failure was writ large on it even before it was contemplated. But that does not in any way devalue Subhas's patriotism. What it means is only that in his political perceptions and judgements, and in the course he adopted to channelize his enormous dynamism and forceful personality, he was in error. I repeat that this is my personal opinion, for which I take full responsibility. I have no desire to force my view on anyone.

Public memory is proverbially said to be short. In an earlier chapter, I have pointed out that the INA as a well-organized and cohesive body was created by the IIL under the great leadership of Rash Behari Bose. In all modesty, I say that in this, as well as in the whole range of the work of the Indian freedom movement in the Far East and Southeast Asia, I was his closest and most dedicated associate. Subhas inherited a readymade and efficient organization from us.

Rash Behari shunned the floodlights of self-publicity and showmanship, and devoted all his great energies to quiet but dynamic, efficient, and constructive work. Subhas liked not only to lead but to *appear* to do so, with all the elaborate trappings of such a role, and to be in the forefront through high-gear advertisement. Perhaps that is why today, in the public mind in India, the INA and the Indian freedom movement in Southeast Asia as a whole stand identified almost entirely with Subhas.

Subhas's arrival in the Far East and Southeast Asia scene was solely due to Rash Behari Bose. But for Rash Behari, he would not have been able to be in Southeast Asia or the Far East. Let us not make any mistake about it. Subhas knew it in his heart of hearts and respected Rash Behari, although, unfortunately, he almost always allowed his emotions to run away with practical wisdom. His leadership was both heroic and tragic.

Let me hope that before long, the memory of the great part played by Rash Behari Bose in the Indian freedom struggle will be revived and preserved for posterity.

We seem to be tending to forget even Gandhiji, Nehruji, Rajaji, and the countless other luminaries who showed us the way on the long, hard, and harsh road that we had to tread towards our independence. Let us wake from our slumber and bestir ourselves to remembrance of the great men to whom we owe the freedom we enjoy. And let us also not forget anyone in the second lines who sustained the frontlines. Let us endeavor to give the lie to the concept that public memory is short.

I have said a great deal about the Subhas era and allied subjects and seek my readers' indulgence in this regard. I must now conclude my observations by suggesting that we devote no more thought either to the Imphal episode or to the other tragic topic of the "disappearance" of Subhas. Forgetting it all will be the best service we can do to him and to our country.

The late Mitsuru Toyama once told me that for the sake of preserving bigger things, it was not only permissible but necessary to forget smaller matters. In the totality of the Indian freedom movement, I think we can afford to let bygones be bygones in respect of the unhappy interlude centered around Subhas Chandra Bose in Southeast Asia. What is important today is that we should not do anything to drive a wedge into the cause of great national concern to us: the promotion of close and friendly relations between India and Japan.

CHAPTER TWENTY-NINE
India and Postwar Japan: Justice Pal's Dissenting Judgement On "War Crimes"

When Japan surrendered unconditionally to the Allied powers, India was still under British rule. As part of the British Commonwealth Occupation Force (BCOF), there was a small contingent of the British Indian Army also posted in Japan during the early part of the occupation regime under General MacArthur. To look after the interests of the Indian community, the government of British India, in consultation with the British Liaison Office in Tokyo, appointed L. P. Jain as head of the Indian Liaison Mission. The resident Indians, a prosperous community before the war, had, like everyone else, suffered great hardship and severe financial loss during the bombing of Tokyo and other cities by the American air force. They numbered about 750, the majority being engaged in trade. The main concentrations were in Yokohama, Kobe, and Osaka. The number in Tokyo was relatively small. There were a few students who had been studying in Japanese universities but had been caught up in the turmoil of the war and were unable to return to India.

In addition to the immediate question of rehabilitation of the Indian community, the head of the Indian Mission had the responsibility to assist the revival of trade between India and Japan, which was the main source of sustenance for the vast majority of them. For a considerable time after Japan's defeat, there was no international trade with the country because the sea routes had been mined by the Allied navy and no passenger or commercial ships could ply to or from it. It took time before minesweepers could render the routes safe for merchant vessels.

Meanwhile, however, the Supreme Commander for the Allied Powers (SCAP) had an office to deal with policy matters relating to trade between Japan and other countries. Mr. Jain did a certain amount of preparatory work with it to safeguard India's commercial interests, although it was doubtful whether he was as energetic as the other heads of mission in occupied Tokyo. The first head of the Indian Liaison Mission after India's independence was Rama Rau of the Indian civil service.

During his time, K. P. S. Menon, the then Indian ambassador in Peking, made a fact-finding visit to Korea on behalf of the United Nations and stayed in Tokyo for a while en route and met General MacArthur. After seeing the conditions in Tokyo and in Seoul (where Syngman Rhee was president), Menon made a press statement to the effect that he found "Rhee-baiting" in Korea more refreshing than "MacArthur worship" in Japan. MacArthur was annoyed at this and sent for Rama Rau to ask for an explanation of K. P. S. Menon's pronouncement, and an apology.

I was told that Rama Rau informed MacArthur that India was no longer under British occupation but was a free country. In fact, MacArthur had a grouse against India as a consequence of a number of instances in which India adopted a policy of friendship with Japan on terms of equality and nondiscrimination. He felt that India was chalking out a policy of its own in its relations with Japan and not playing second fiddle to the SCAP policies. Indeed, he was right in his assessment!

After Rama Rau, there were one or two others as heads of the Indian Mission, including B. N. Chakravarthy, who was transferred to Tokyo from Peking. That was in 1948 when the trial of the so-called Japanese war criminals by the International Military Tribunal for the Far East set up by MacArthur was in progress. I recall that Mr. Chakravarthy was of considerable assistance to Justice Radhabinod Pal of the Calcutta high court, who was the Indian judge on the tribunal.

**

The arrival of Justice R. B. Pal in Tokyo really marked the beginning of my association with the officialdom of the government of India. In the course of his deep study of background material, Justice Pal wanted to know as much as possible about conditions before and during the war, and also acquire as much knowledge as possible about Japanese customs, manners, national psychology, etc. He was also anxious to have firsthand information about Manchukuo. He had heard about me, my stay, and my work in Japan and Manchukuo, as well as my part in the Indian freedom movement in Southeast Asia in association with Rash Behari Bose and Subhas. My role was to supplement the vast amount of information he had himself been collecting from all over the world for his study.

Justice Pal and I developed much mutual affection. Our meetings, which were frequent, lasted on several occasions for many hours at a stretch. He never tired of asking questions and listening to the answers. Ironically, there was an Indian lawyer who had been inducted on the prosecution side, his duty being to argue against the Japanese. He was P. Govinda Menon from Kerala who was public prosecutor in the Madras government. He had an assistant also to help him to prepare briefs and other documents. After some time, however, Govinda Menon got quite tired of doing a job that he felt was unreasonable. He had no heart to argue along with Britain and America to condemn Japan, and he decided to return to India.

In this connection, a fact which has never been published hitherto either by Indian sources or any other, is that when Govinda Menon decided to go back, he had a personal and private talk with Justice Pal explaining his difficulties in staying in Japan to argue against the Japanese leaders who were in prison, and even enquired from Justice Pal what he felt on the question of his continuing on the tribunal; specifically, whether he intended to stay on. Justice Pal wanted to think about it calmly and not rush into any decision immediately. He, therefore, told Govinda Menon that he would decide his own future position fairly soon.

After careful deliberation, he decided in consultation with Mr. Chakravarthy that it would not be appropriate for India to be unrepresented during the trial and that even though Govinda Menon was determined to go back, he, as a judge, would remain, keeping an open mind just as every judge was expected to do.

Justice Pal was one of the most erudite persons I have ever come across. I was far younger than him in age and experience, and of course was no expert in international law. But I was deeply impressed by his decision to continue to participate in the proceedings of the tribunal and not prejudge the outcome. He once told me that the duty of a judge was different from that of an advocate:

he should not leave the proceedings until they were completed. Accordingly, he sat in along with the other ten judges throughout the hearings. His insight into international jurisprudence, particularly in relation to wars and war crimes, was extraordinarily deep. He also devoted an enormous amount of time studying the backdrop to Japan's declaration of war on America, Britain, etc. His suite of rooms in the Imperial Hotel was practically chock-full of legal documents and various other books. He had virtually no interest other than work.

* * *

The international tribunal delivered its judgement on November 10, 1948. Among the eleven judges, Justice Pal was the only one who fundamentally dissented on the very rationale of the trial. There were a few minor technical objections from two or three other judges, but the total dissension of Justice Pal created a sensation. The more so because among the eleven judges on the tribunal, he was the only specialist in international jurisprudence as distinct from general legal qualifications.

He had made the deepest study of the subject and had come to the conclusion that at no time in the history of the world had it been held that the mere fact of one country going to war against another was in itself a crime. In any case, no one had been tried for such an act.

Another basic objection of his was that during the hearings, the prosecution had gone far beyond its brief. MacArthur had appointed the tribunal for the specific purpose of determining whether the Japanese leaders who had been imprisoned in Sugamo were guilty of war crimes from the time of Pearl Harbor onwards until the end of the war. It transpired during the hearings that the prosecution had started off with a prejudice and was only trying to back it with attempts to produce proof of its fixed stand. It had begun with an indictment of Japan from the time of the Mukden Incident, which led to Japanese occupation of Manchuria and the subsequent creation of the state of Manchukuo.

Justice Pal in his judgement said that the tribunal had no jurisdiction over the Manchurian question or any related events. He did not find any legal justification to doubt the bona fides of Tojo and the other accused when they adduced the discriminatory and hostile treatment by America and Britain and Japan's national interest of self-protection as her reasons for going to war. Justice Pal went on to say that "we may not altogether ignore the possibility that perhaps responsibility was not only with the defeated leaders."

He also said, "When time shall have softened passions and prejudice, when reason shall have stripped the mask of misrepresentation, then justice, holding evenly her scales, will require much of past censure and praise to change places." Proceeding, he stated that the tribunal had asked for several of the defendants to be committed on the basis of charges that they ordered, authorized or permitted atrocities against Allied war prisoners and civilian personnel, but he could not find anything on record to prove that any of the accused who were in prison were, as individuals, actually guilty of such crimes.

The point which the tribunal had before it for decision, had therefore not been proved by the Prosecution. Summing up his review, Justice Pal said,

> I would hold that each and every one of the accused must be found not guilty of each and every one of the charges in the indictment and should be acquitted of all those charges.

Another historic pronouncement made by Justice Pal was the caution that the name of retaliation should not be allowed to be invoked. The world was really in need of generous magnanimity and understanding and charity. The real question arising in a genuinely anxious mind, was whether mankind could grow up quickly enough to win the race between civilization and disaster. "As a judicial tribunal we cannot behave in any manner which may justify the feeling that the setting up of the tribunal was only for the attainment of an objective which was essentially political, though cloaked by a juridical appearance."

Referring to the allegations of Japanese conspiracy to wage war, Justice Pal said, "At least many of the powerful nations are living this sort of life and if these acts are criminal then the entire international community is living that criminal life." He proceeded, "No nation has yet treated such acts as crimes and all the powerful nations continue close relations with the nations that had committed such acts."

He went on to point out that an inevitable concomitant of armed warfare was hatred engendered in the minds of the contestants. The spirit of patriotism that inspired men to answer the call of their country in its hour of need bred within those men the fiercest antagonism towards that country's enemies and the enemy became a thing to be hated. He did not share the common virtues, and his peculiarities of speech, race, or culture became significant as points of difference. With such a state of mind coming as the natural result of the upheaval of the social order war produced, it was not difficult for credence to be gained for stories of atrocities committed. "All the factors that can provoke a propaganda of this character were present in the case before us," said Dr. Pal.

There was an additional unfortunate factor that could not be neglected, he added. The numbers of prisoners in Japanese hands were overwhelming, and this indicated that there was a fight every white man felt was necessary against Japan because Japan was trying to explode the myth of white supremacy. Among other points on the basis of which he dissented were that the actual perpetrators of war crimes had to be dealt with in different forums and not in the tribunal that had been set up by General MacArthur. No one would be able to accuse any of the victor nations of any mistaken clemency towards any of the alleged perpetrators of all those foul acts. But guilt did not reach *any of the present accused.*

What Justice Pal meant was that the function of the tribunal was to assess whether any of the individuals in question, who had been accused of war crimes, had actually perpetrated acts of cruelty or inhumanity of a nature that would come within the definition of war crimes. He was of the view that none of the leaders who were being charged was guilty of any such crimes in their individual or official capacities. Those officers or men of the Japanese army who might have committed atrocities on the frontlines had already been or were being dealt with by local courts concerned or other instruments of the victorious Allied commands. In Tokyo, the tribunal was expected to go into the question of the crimes if any of the specific personalities who had been imprisoned in Sugamo.

He found no proof for any of the charges against them. Summarizing his basic objection, he said "1. That no category of war became criminal or illegal in international life; 2. That the individuals comprising the government and functioning as agents of that government incur no criminal responsibility in international law for the acts alleged; 3. That the international community has not yet reached a stage which would make it expedient to include judicial process for condemning and punishing either states or individuals." Justice Pal also said in the course of his dissension that there was no evidence to show that any of the accused wanted to wage war in a ruthless manner. There was no proof of their having adopted a ruthless policy. If there was anything approaching that, it was the decision of the Allied powers to use the atom bomb.

And the most significant portion of the great Indian jurist's momentous judgement was in these terms:

> Future generations will judge this dire decision. History will say whether any outburst of popular sentiment against the usage of

such a new weapon is irrational and only sentimental and whether it had become legitimate by such indiscriminate slaughter to win the victory by breaking the will of the whole nation to continue to fight.

* * *

According to some extraordinary rules of the tribunal's constitution, no dissenting judgement was to be allowed to be read in the court. Justice Pal wanted at least the gist of his judgement to be made public in court so that everyone would know his position, but this was not permitted by the Australian chairman. The historic judgement, running to over 1,300 pages, was also not (as far as I know) officially published in full. But, of course, the accused knew that Justice Pal had differed from his colleagues, and the media gave fairly extensive coverage. The entire Japanese nation viewed Justice Pal's courage of conviction with deep respect.

General Seishiro Itagaki, who was a good friend of mine and about whom I have written earlier, was one of the accused who were sentenced to death by the majority judgement. When he came to know of Justice Pal's stand, he was happy that there was at least one jurist who had adjudged him and his co-prisoners to be innocent. He was reported to have remarked that Dr. Pal was like a beacon of light in a world enveloped by dark clouds.

It is interesting to note that the position taken by Justice Pal found support later from an eminent British jurist, Lord Hankey.

Soon after the end of the proceedings of the tribunal, Justice Pal returned to India. But it was my good fortune that I was able to keep in touch with him even thereafter.

He visited Japan later, on three different occasions. The first was in 1952, to attend the Asia Congress for World Federation. Dr. Pal lectured at several centers to intellectual audiences, the most prominent of the venues being the universities of Tokyo, Waseda, Hiroshima, and Fukuoka. His subjects covered a wide range, from international jurisprudence to matters relating to the Korean War. It was a matter of distress to him that the USA had used Japan as a base for the bombardment of Korea. He also dealt with Indian philosophy and Indo-Japanese relations, and propounded the lines on which these should develop for the mutual benefit of both these important Asian countries. He discussed Vedanta, Sanskrit literature, the age-old contacts between India and Japan—so on and on.

CHAPTER TWENTY-NINE

Justice Radhabinod Pal visiting Sugamo Prison, November 1952. The author is behind Justice Pal on the right. Sugamo Prison housed not only Class-A war criminals but also Class-B and Class-C criminals.

At the Cenotaph for the Victims of the Atomic Bomb, November 1952. From left: the author; Justice Pal; Mr. Sen, a Bengali interpreter; and Masaaki Tanaka, who translated the published portion of Justice Pal's dissenting judgement.

Justice Pal's thesis for his doctorate in law was *Jurisprudence in Vedanta*, a subject I believe no one else has been able to deal with as effectively as he has done.

His other two visits, in 1953 and 1966 respectively, were also under the auspices of important organizations in Japan sincerely interested in promoting proper Indo-Japanese understanding and goodwill. The great Yasaburo Shimonaka was his principal sponsor during 1953. In 1966, the emperor of Japan awarded him the decoration of the Order of the Sacred Treasure, First Class. Earlier, in 1959, the president of India had bestowed on him India's second highest honor: the Padma Vibhushan.

It was a great privilege for me to be travelling and staying with him throughout his tour in Japan. It was a still greater privilege to be his official interpreter and translator. I was always given a place on the platform along with him in order to convey to the Japanese audience the contents of his speech correctly and in an unbiased manner. I must confess that Dr. Pal's diction was of such a high order that I had to draw on every bit of my resources of knowledge of the Japanese language to do justice to his speeches. I would say without hesitation that during the postwar period, there were only two Indian philosophers of the stature of Rabindranath Tagore. They were Dr. S. Radhakrishnan and Dr. Radhabinod Pal.

Justice Radhabinod Pal giving a lecture, with the author interpreting.

Whereas I interpreted all his speeches on matters other than high philosophy, the philosophical discourses were interpreted by Professor Nakamura of the University of Tokyo, who was a scholar of philosophy and was certainly far more qualified than me for the task of interpreting the high, abstract, and abstruse concepts of Indian philosophy.

It is one of my pleasant memories that in 1957, when my eldest son Vasudevan Nair was on an orientation visit to India, he stayed with Justice

CHAPTER TWENTY-NINE

Pal at his house in Calcutta for nearly a month and was able to learn so much about India and its culture that it was more fruitful than perhaps a whole year of study anywhere else. He still vividly remembers the kindness and consideration Justice Pal showed him. He used to be called "Vasu" as if he was a member of the family. Dr. Pal used to insist on his Vasu eating with him and spending as much time as possible to hear his talks on various subjects concerning India and the world. My son still talks to me about this whenever he visits me in Tokyo from Manila, where he is a senior officer in the Asian Development Bank.

CHAPTER THIRTY
The India-Japan Peace Treaty

When B. N. Chakravarthy had completed his tenure and was posted out in the latter part of 1949, K. K. Chettur was appointed as the new head of the Indian Liaison Mission in Tokyo. Mr. Chettur had visited Japan briefly earlier when he was a senior officer in the Indian Commerce Ministry to conclude a trade agreement between the two countries. His wide-ranging political vision, besides the commercial acumen he displayed, attracted the special attention of Pandit Jawaharlal Nehru who nominated him to head the Indian Mission in Tokyo in succession to Mr. Chakravarthy, even though he was not a permanent member of the career diplomatic cadre. He belonged to a distinguished Nair family in Kerala and was a nephew of the famous Sir C. Sankaran Nair, whom I have mentioned in the opening chapter of this book.

I had not met Mr. Chettur during his first visit and was therefore rather surprised when one of the first things he did after taking charge of his new assignment was to send word asking me to see him for a discussion. I was still more surprised to be told that he would like me to join him as his adviser on political as well as other matters of importance to India-Japan relations. Many new developments were bound to take place: he would need the help of someone who had been through the mill during the war and had the best local contacts. In his view, I was the most suitable person from the Indian community for the position in view.

I felt honored and agreed to be of service to him. But Mr. Chettur did not announce the decision as he was anxious to avoid possible ill-feeling among others about his having singled me out, even though he knew that no one else had any better qualifications for the work envisaged. Human nature being what it was, it was prudent not to cause unnecessary speculations and needless irritations. He briefed me suitably and gave everyone the impression that my visits to him were private and informal, when in fact they were mostly official.

K. K. Chettur (second from right) and the author (third from right) visiting the Asahi Shimbun offices in Tokyo.

During the SCAP regime, most heads of mission were content to conduct their activities within the limited circles of their colleagues representing the victorious countries. And generally, they found their own level, in the backwaters of the ocean that was MacArthur's headquarters. That hardly needed any special official assistance locally, other than what the occupation authorities provided free of cost to all the establishments, whether offices or residences, of representatives of the Allied powers. But Mr. Chettur wished to go beyond such an artificial, and in many respects superficial, environment. He was vitally interested in ascertaining, in depth, what was happening in the inner circles of the *Japanese* echelons, cutting across the barriers which had inevitably come to exist between the victors and the vanquished.

The times were abnormal. Japanese leadership lay low and refrained from being vocal. Understandably so, since there was a political and economic purge in progress at MacArthur's insistence, and no one wanted to be on the blacklists if he could possibly help it. Everyone was extra-cautious and tight-lipped. That, however, did not mean that they were mindless, or inactive. There were several important Japanese of high standing in their respective fields, unobtrusively planning their country's future on the reasonable assumption that sooner or later Japan would once again be a sovereign nation. But they would not talk, except to those in whom they had complete confidence.

Mr. Chettur's aim was to formulate the course which Indo-Japanese relations should take, not only during the occupation period, but in a post-peace treaty era that was bound to follow. Solution of current problems was of course part of the daily routine, and important indeed, but his sights were set on the shape of things as they should develop in the long run. Foundations must be prepared for an enduring relationship, and every current activity should fit into such a wider perspective. Proper planning could be achieved only by acquiring full information about the goings-on in the various inner circles: those of politicians, industrialists, educationists and other intellectuals, the information media, and so on. It was here that Mr. Chettur particularly wanted me to help him.

* * *

My duties were primarily twofold. One, fairly routine, although laborious, was to prepare a gist, on a daily basis, of all the important news and commentaries appearing in the Japanese dailies, magazines and other media, and coming out in broadcasts from Radio Tokyo. Items concerning India naturally needed special attention. To these must be added my assessments, which Mr. Chettur would utilize for the purpose of his own final evaluation.

Secondly, but more importantly, I had the responsibility to arrange meetings for Mr. Chettur with Japanese leaders in different spheres of public activity, sometimes individually, at other times in small groups. The occupation atmosphere was not congenial to free and easy dealings with them for reasons I have already indicated. But Mr. Chettur was avidly interested in getting to know well as many cross sections of the Japanese elite as possible: conservatives, liberals, socialists, and even radicals like communists.

CHAPTER THIRTY

I was to be the contact man. The task, needless to say, was delicate. But it was also exciting because I was perhaps one of the few foreigners, and certainly the only one among the Indians who knew almost everyone whom Mr. Chettur wanted to meet and talk to. I went about my task enthusiastically since I was convinced that it was in the interest of both India and Japan.

During all such meetings, I was the interpreter. Mr. Chettur had a razor-sharp mind that often produced penetrating questions. It was to the credit of his natural dignity, refined manners, genuine hospitality, and friendship for Japan that all those with whom I got him in touch felt entirely free in his company and shared their views truthfully with him. And it was their unmasked opinions and thinking that he wanted to have.

The meetings would very often be in the evenings. Leaving his office or house, as the case might be, there were many occasions when I worked throughout night at my home and prepared notes and briefs covering the talks, together with my comments, to be ready for Mr. Chettur by the next morning.

Discussions were not confined to non-officials. Few officials would mix freely during those days with foreign diplomats, but through my personal contacts I could arrange for Mr. Chettur to meet members of the higher bureaucracy as well. The golf courses, where the head of the Indian Mission could be seen, were quite pleasant venues for exercise and also talks. The hospitable house which Mr. and Mrs. Chettur maintained with much care, was another good place for meetings. Amongst the Japanese officialdom who were friendly and frank, although at times difficult as well, were Bamboko Ono, a leading figure in his own right besides being speaker of the parliament, and Shigeru Yoshida, the prime minister himself.

* * *

Shintaro Ryu was then chief editorial writer of the *Asahi Shimbun*; he later became its managing director. He was profoundly erudite. I had known him intimately for several years as one of the finest of gentlemen. He eventually became a close friend of Mr. Chettur's and the two met very often for detailed discussions on a wide range of subjects. There were also several friends in the Domei News Agency through whom we could receive national and international news more quickly than many others. Tansan Ishibashi, the famous economist who was one of the leaders "purged" by

MacArthur (but became a prime minister in post-peace treaty Japan) was also an intimate friend of mine, and Mr. Chettur had several meetings with him. It was interesting to watch two intellectual stalwarts exchanging ideas on matters of the moment.

Among other frequent visitors were Fusanosuke Kuhara, founder of the Hitachi and Nissan groups of industries; Mr. Katsumata, Masaburo Suzuki, and Asanuma (the socialists); Akira Kasami, chief secretary to the prewar cabinet of Prince Konoe; Aiichiro Fujiwara, a well-known industrialist who took to politics and was foreign minister for several years; and the late Mr. Inukai, who later became justice minister. Most of them were in the SCAP's "purge lists," and we had to be careful.

* * *

Preparations for the so-called San Francisco Peace Treaty were in evidence when John Foster Dulles started visiting Tokyo in 1950. Through a close circle of friends, I kept myself in the know of the major trends of the discussions between him and the prime minister, Shigeru Yoshida. Yoshida had several reservations about the American proposals, but Dulles successfully forced the United States positions down Yoshida's throat.

Yoshida was a career diplomat in his early days and used to be called a "Yellow Englishman"; he admired the British and would even try to imitate them. He was a cigar smoker like Churchill and his general attitude had a Western orientation. The pressure that Dulles put on Japan often took the form of his wanting Yoshida to just say "Yes" to the draft of some of the treaty clauses that were not particularly edifying to Japan; for instance the provision for the retention of Allied forces in Japan even after the treaty. But, of course, one had to recognize that Yoshida was not in any easy position. His infinite capacity for flexibility had to be viewed with generosity. His genuine desire to end the occupation as soon as possible could not be faulted.

During the deliberations amongst the representatives of the US State Department, the SCAP, and the Japanese government on the US-Britain sponsored draft treaty, I used to give Mr. Chettur up-to-date reports of the progress of the negotiations. I was told that the government of India received from Tokyo far more information than from Washington on the subject. They got it more quickly too. Sifting the voluminous information reaching him through me and juxtaposing it with his own knowledge gained independently through discussions with various sources, including General MacArthur himself on a number of occasions, Mr. Chettur came to the careful conclusion that India should not be a party to the joint treaty but must conclude a separate one bilaterally.

When the US government sought the government of India's concurrence in the draft of the San Francisco Treaty, therefore, Pandit Nehru and his cabinet had all the necessary material with them for a decision. In a note dated August 23, 1951, to the US State Department, the government of India regretted its inability to accept the joint draft.

The reasons were in accordance with Mr. Chettur's recommendations. These, mainly, were based on two basic grounds:

(i) The treaty was hedged in by a condition that the US forces would remain in Japan until the Japanese could assume full responsibility for their defence and that no help should be sought from any third power without US permission. Such a provision was violative of the principle of full sovereignty.

(The American argument in favor of the condition was that it was in accordance with Japan's own request, since the country did not wish to be left defenseless. But in Tokyo we had information that this was only an eyewash. The fact was that America wanted military bases in Japan against possible threats from the Soviet Union. This was one of the clauses to which Yoshida had to say "Yes" under pressure from Dulles.)

(ii) Just as Formosa should be returned to China without leaving the timing for doing so indefinite, the Ryukyu and the Bonin islands should be restored immediately to Japan instead of being placed under UN trusteeship. These islands were historically Japanese and were not acquired by means of aggression at any time.

(The American argument in justification of its stand was that the Potsdam Declaration had demanded the confinement of the Japanese people to the four home islands and such minor islands as the parties to the surrender proclamation might determine. India's position, in effect, was that the Potsdam Declaration was not fair in this respect.)

These reasons were announced by Pandit Nehru in the Indian parliament on August 27, 1951. He declared at the same time that India was not asking for reparations from Japan. A White Paper was issued by the government of India on August 30 stressing India's "inherent and unquestionable right not to sign a treaty with which she was not fully satisfied."

A piece of information he had could, however, not be announced by Pandit Nehru from considerations of diplomatic propriety. He had actually seen the text of a US-Japan bilateral security pact America was going to make Japan sign on the same day as had been set for signature of the San Francisco Treaty. Since the text of the security pact had not yet been circulated, and was therefore still a secret, Nehru naturally could not publicize it.

There was perhaps no doubt that many countries knew of a forthcoming US-Japan bilateral security pact and at least some also were aware that the signature of it would take place on September 8, 1951. But I believe very few, if any, other than India, had a copy of the text of the pact in advance. I was able, by a stroke of luck, to get one for Mr. Chettur through perfectly "normal" means.

The Cabinet Press Club in Tokyo had been confidentially told by the government about the security pact and given copies thereof a little ahead of the due date, but instructed to release the text simultaneously with the San Francisco Treaty and not earlier. A close journalist friend of mine had a mind of his own in this matter and decided that there was nothing confidential about the pact—at least as far as I and he were concerned. So, he gave me a copy, which I in turn turned over to Mr. Chettur. And Nehru had it well in time to read it and see that under the umbrella of the San Francisco Treaty, America was going to *insist* on Japan remaining in the US power bloc. Such a situation was unacceptable to India in principle because it did not concede to Japan a position of full "honor, equality and contentment among the comity of nations." It would be a different matter if Japan, *after* becoming a fully sovereign state, decided of its own volition and after careful deliberation to agree to foreign troops being stationed in its country for a short term or even for a long period, but it was not correct that the restoration of independence should be subject, in effect, to such a condition, in favor of a particular country—of course America in this case. I believe that it was the perusal of the text of the security pact that set the seal firmly on India's decision not to join the San Francisco Treaty.

* * *

CHAPTER THIRTY

The joint peace treaty which was concluded with Japan by 49 countries (including Japan) out of the 52 who had attended the San Francisco conference, came into force on April 28, 1952. The separate India-Japan Bilateral Treaty of Perpetual Peace and Amity was concluded on June 9, 1952. It was signed on behalf of India by K. K. Chettur, and for Japan by Katsuo Okazaki, foreign minister, who said in a press statement the same day:

> The spirit of amity and goodwill of India towards Japan is abundantly shown throughout the treaty. It is particularly exemplified by the provisions waiving all reparations claims and returning Japanese property located in India.

The text of the treaty is reproduced in Appendix 4. This short and straightforward document might give, prima facie, the impression of a simple and easy piece of work, but it is needless to say that a great deal of thought and labor over a fairly long period had gone into its making. There were days, weeks, months, of anxiety.

But it is curious how there can also be a lighter side to almost every serious situation. In the present instance there was a kind of coincidence which proves the saying that facts can be stranger than fiction. I have not become an expert in bureaucratic practices, but in the course of my advisership to the head of the Indian Mission, I came to know something of what is called the "decision-making process" in the rather ill-defined body in New Delhi called the "government." (I imagine that mutatis mutandis the practices must be the same in all democratic governments.) Decisions are taken "collectively," which also is a rather nebulous expression. In regard to the deliberations on the San Francisco Treaty and the India-Japan Treaty, the procedure, I was told, was that before each or all of the "problems" went up to Prime Minister Nehru and his cabinet for orders, there had to be consideration by and comments from a group of seven senior officers.

Those seven were: (i) K. K. Chettur, head of the Indian Mission in Tokyo and originator of most of the correspondence; (ii) A. M. Nair, his adviser; (iii) N. R. Pillai, secretary-general in the Foreign Ministry in New Delhi (second only to Nehru in the Foreign Office); (iv) K. P. S. Menon, foreign secretary for most of the time in question (later he was assigned to Moscow as India's ambassador and retired from there after several years of distinguished service); (v) V. K. Krishna Menon, post-independence India's first high commissioner in London and for some time special representative of Nehru and his "roving ambassador" before joining his cabinet; (vi) N. Raghavan, ambassador of India in Paris; (vii) Sardar K. M. Panikkar, ambassador in China.

All these seven happened to be from Kerala. And, as yet another coincidence, the three officers in the Indian Mission in Tokyo dealing with the subject at the grassroots level—K. R. Narayanan, second secretary (at present India's ambassador to the USA), M. S. Nair, third secretary,[*] and P. S. Parasuram, principal secretary to K. K. Chettur (he later chose to leave the Indian Foreign Service and joined the Ministry of Irrigation and Power and retired as its director)—were also all from Kerala.

Thus came about the talking point in certain circles in Tokyo that the Indo-Japanese Peace Treaty was the handiwork of "ten gentlemen from Kerala." How exactly such a situation materialized was unclear. But V. C. Trivedi, the then first secretary in the Indian Mission in Tokyo—who became a vice-minister in the Foreign Office in New Delhi before retirement, and unfortunately died some years ago—had a theory. With his tongue in his cheek, he once told a friend that this was the result of a well-calculated plan by Jawaharlal Nehru. He had heard that John Foster Dulles had engaged twenty experts to try to persuade India to join the San Francisco Treaty. Nehru wanted the subject to be carefully studied. To economize, he chose to have only half the number on the Indian side, but in order to ensure an equal match, he decided to have all the ten from the (then) smallest state in India so that a reasonable ratio could be maintained between the two sides!

Another diplomatic gossip of those days was that Nehru's sister, Mrs. Vijaya Lakshmi Pandit, who was Indian ambassador in Washington at the time of the negotiations connected with the San Francisco Treaty, had wanted to sign *that* treaty on behalf of India in order to add a "feather to her hat" (even though no one had seen her wearing a hat, or even a cap); Nehru, however, vetoed the idea and accepted Mr. Chettur's recommendations. I once jokingly asked Mr. Chettur whether that was a true story. He said it was impossible to verify it.

* * *

A few months after the conclusion of the treaty, Mr. Chettur left Japan on transfer as ambassador to Burma. I continued my association with him until the last day of his work in Tokyo. A little before his departure, he sprang a surprise on me.

---

[*] He eventually rose to the rank of ambassador before retiring.

CHAPTER THIRTY

Neither when he first asked me to be his adviser, nor at any time throughout the period of my work with him had the idea of any remuneration entered my mind. I was happy to keep doing my job without thinking of any pay bill. I was not rich, but had just enough to get by without difficulty, and did not view my work with the Indian Mission as any source of additional income. But then one day, I had a strange experience. Mr. Chettur told me that there was a sum of money sanctioned for me by the government of India in recognition of my services to him and through him to New Delhi; he had therefore asked his office to pay it to me. It was a large amount according to the standards then prevailing. I was embarrassed, and told Mr. Chettur that I would like to decline any payment since I had always viewed my contribution as part of my duty to my country and to the cause of close and friendly relations between India and Japan, which was what I had lived and worked for most of the time. I had grown up in anti-British work and in the cause of the struggle for Indian freedom, in the spirit of *anasakta karma*. I had been fortified in that faith by my acquaintance with the activities of Rash Behari Bose even when I was a student. My intimate association with him during the time of the Indian Independence League in the Far East and Southeast Asia had strengthened it. I was grateful for the government of India's and Mr. Chettur's consideration, but I must be excused from receiving any money. When we parted that day, both of us were a little out of sorts; somewhat puzzled, one might say. I heard Mr. Chettur say softly, "I am going to face some accounting problem!"

Nothing more was discussed about this particular question for some time. But Mr. Chettur had not forgotten it. He was a very shrewd man and was not the type of person who would give up easily anything he wanted to do. He invented a plan which was to be a compromise between the government of India's position and mine.

He called me in one day and said that the government of India wanted to make a *gift* to me for the educational support of my children who were growing up. Soon his attaché walked in with a cheque in my favor and a receipt for me to sign. While Mr. Chettur was still expounding the importance of education and how expensive it was becoming, the attaché virtually "begged" me to take the cheque and give a receipt so that he could close his office's accounts books. For the first time in my life, I accepted a payment from the government of India "in recognition of my services to the country."

After Mr. Chettur's departure, I felt that I had practically completed the work I had wanted to do for India in the political field in Japan. I changed my course of life and became a business entrepreneur. Friends would jokingly speak about my new vocation as a come down from the status of a samurai or a ronin to that of a mere merchant. But I felt that the scope of my political work had narrowed down almost to an insignificant point in the circumstances as they evolved after the peace treaty. I kept in touch with the Indian community and continued to offer my help whenever required. There was no dearth of social work. Opportunities for me to remain in closer contact with my wide circle of Japanese friends also increased. But the major part of my time and energy went into my commercial business.

Full understanding, cordiality and mutual respect have always remained the hallmarks of the relationship between my country's embassy and me, except that a small ruffle clouded it a little at the time when much activity was going on in India and the Indian missions everywhere in the wake of the Chinese invasion of India in October 1962.

That was a period of some confusion in India's relations with China. China, which had been professing brotherly friendship for India, virtually stabbed us in the back. The possible "provocation" India offered by harboring the Dalai Lama and vast numbers of Tibetans who came along with him from across the borders could not be cited as any convincing excuse for the Chinese attack. On the other hand, India could not absolve herself of responsibility for neglecting her defenses in the area and for the great failure of her intelligence service. Based on hopelessly wrong information provided to him, Prime Minister Nehru ordered the Indian armed forces to "throw the Chinese out." He had no idea of the immensely stronger Chinese presence on the other side and how unprepared the Indian forces were. We suffered a humiliating defeat.

During a discussion with some Indian friends on this subject, I expressed my view frankly that this border war was a big mistake. Apparently someone reported my critical remarks to the Indian ambassador, who perhaps presumed that "A. M. Nair was voicing anti-India feelings." Probably at his insistence, Alan Nazareth,[*] second secretary, came to me the following day and had a long and friendly talk on the Indian situation, particularly with reference to the Chinese invasion. I said to him the same thing I had told my other friends: with due respect to Prime Minister Nehru, I felt that he had been badly misled and let down. It was wrong tactics to fight a war when defeat was absolutely certain. The Chinese strength on their side was probably twenty times that of ours at any given point on the borders.

Nazareth understood my stand. He must have reported the gist of the conversation to his ambassador. The next day I was invited to the embassy

---

* Indian high commissioner in Ghana at the time of writing.

for a discussion with the ambassador, who apparently wanted to satisfy himself that my view had been conveyed to him correctly. The subject was the same; my opinion also remained the same as I had given Nazareth. I recommended to the ambassador that New Delhi should be advised not to prolong the war but seek a negotiated settlement. We had better pay greater attention to developing our country economically, in preference to fighting an infructuous war with the Chinese when we were so ill-equipped. Some of the younger embassy officials seemed to like shadowboxing and persisted in their view that India should "put up a big fight." I became a little unpopular with some of them when I advised them that they had much to learn about wars and peace.

A few days later, my old friend Chamanlal suddenly turned up in Tokyo and asked me whether I could undertake a job of "mediation" between India and China. He said that if I agreed, he would inform Nehru who would then probably ask me to go to Peking to talk to the Chinese leaders. It was not at all clear to me—nor, I felt, to Chamanlal for that matter—what kind of "mediation" I was expected to do. I might at one time have been "Manchukuo Nair," but had no reputation as a "China Nair." I told Chamanlal that perhaps the Indian embassy, with its various resources, might be advised to send a delegation to "negotiate" with Peking, and that he had better leave me in peace. This made me a little more unpopular with the embassy for a time. Fortunately, however, the little flash in the pan was over fairly soon and my association with my country's envoys got back to an even keel before long.

* * *

Today it so happens that I am the oldest Indian resident in Japan and have been the president of the Indian Association in Tokyo for the past several years. It has been my privilege to have received much consideration and affection not only from Mr. Chettur but also from all his successors. I have been happy that various opportunities have come my way to help the Indian community in general, and important officials as well as non-officials from India visiting Japan from time to time. In my individual capacity I continue my interest in the promotion of good relations between India and Japan in various forums. Illustrative of this is the establishment of the Pal-Shimonaka Memorial Hall on the shores of Lake Ashinoko at Hakone.

THE INDIA-JAPAN PEACE TREATY

Pal-Shimonaka Memorial Hall in Hakone, 1974.

In front of the Pal-Shimonaka Memorial Hall. From left: Eric Gonsalves, Indian ambassador to Japan; the famous scholar-philosopher Tetsuzo Tanikawa, former president of Hosei University and chairman of the Pal-Shimonaka Memorial Committee; Mrs. Gonsalves; Tomi Kora, president of the Rabindranath Tagore Society of Japan; the author; and Masaaki Tanaka (far right).

I was one of the organizers of this memorial to two eminent personalities. I have already said a great deal about Dr. Radhabinod Pal and need hardly say anything more. My readers will be able to appreciate how great a friend of Japan he was. Yasaburo Shimonaka was a stalwart in the publishing business in Japan and was a great friend of India and of Dr. Pal in particular. Mr. Shimonaka and Dr. Pal regarded each other as brothers. During one of Dr. Pal's visits to Japan, Mr. Shimonaka accompanied him throughout his tour. When they were at Hiroshima looking at the memorial to the war dead, Dr. Pal noticed an inscription to the effect that "We shall not commit the mistake again" (*futatabi ayamachi o okashimasen*). Suddenly he became tense and enquired in the presence of representatives of NHK (Japan Broadcasting Station) who were accompanying him, "Who will not repeat this? Japan or America? Because it was America that dropped the Atom bomb on this city and destroyed the whole of it."

Dr. Pal was visibly moved, and everyone around him shared his intense emotion on the occasion. The news of this was broadcast by NHK in all its transmissions the same day.

While on this subject, if I may digress a little, NHK had an arrangement, for a number of years, to run a special program to mark the tragic annihilation of Hiroshima by the first atom bomb in history. Dr. Pal's comments as I have quoted above formed part of the program of broadcasts. I observe that lately Radio Tokyo has not been putting out any such special feature on August 6. I hope the omission is only temporary, and that reminders of important historical events, which would do everyone a great deal of good, will be revived by the media as a service to the public. Let me also hope that memory will remain in focus on Japan's Treaty of Peace with India, which is the most honorable bilateral agreement two countries could ever conclude in the circumstances.

For brief life sketches of Dr. Radhabinod Pal and Yasaburo Shimonaka, please see Appendix 3.

Epilogue

It has become a fashion to say that Japan is no longer a country, but a phenomenon—an economic wonder. As an overseas Indian who has spent nearly two-thirds of my seventy-six years in and around this country, I cannot find much fault with this seeming hyperbole. It is largely true. Even up to a decade prior to the last world war, the name "Japan" used to evoke in many minds ideas associated with "imitations," Mount Fuji, cherry blossoms, and geisha. The general notion of the country from outside was such that if one saw an item marked "made in Japan," he knew that it would perhaps be the cheapest thing that money could buy. As a psychological corollary, it was also more or less a synonym for "poor quality." Japan today has a totally different image.

It was in 1928 that I arrived in this country for the first time to study civil engineering at Kyoto Imperial University. The year coincided with that of the coronation of the present emperor, Hirohito. He was ceremoniously enthroned at Kyoto on November 10 that year, when he declared that

> It is our resolve to endeavor to promote, within, the education of our people and their moral and material betterment so that there may be harmony and contentment among them and power and prosperity for the whole nation, and to cultivate without, friendly relations with all nations . . .

He was then twenty-seven years of age and had been educated at home during childhood by General Maresuke Nogi, and later toured abroad in France, Belgium, England, and some other Western countries. His divinity however was completely intact, and the enthronement ceremonials included the use of the traditional symbols of the one and only imperial dynasty which has ruled the country: Amaterasu's mirror, the precious gem, and the sword supposed to have been originally held by a dragon in its tail.

It must be said that the country's current leaders are still united in some ways to the legendary days, and we see dignitaries including ministers, and at times the emperor himself, paying homage at Shinto shrines during important national events. But, as an old hand, I notice a quietly decreasing interest in such events and a certain erosion of the ancient values. As a consequence, there appears also to be a weakening of the fiber that held the nation together like one single steel rope in the past.

Although the legendary history of Japan goes back to Amaterasu's grandson Jimmu, who is said to have founded the nation some six hundred years before Christ, its story as a modern state emerging from feudalism begins only from the time of the Meiji Restoration in 1868. But what it did (and for a time undid) during a span of one hundred years has few parallels in world annals. Between 1868 and 1941 the country became very much involved in Manchuria and Korea, got itself inexorably deep into the quagmire of a seemingly never-ending war in China and, to cap all, challenged the combined might of the United States and Britain and several other countries. It made a bid for all-round leadership of the whole of Southeast Asia under a plan which it called the Greater East Asia Co-Prosperity Sphere.

The bid failed disastrously, and Japan, for the first time in her history of 2,500 years, suffered the humiliation of an unconditional surrender to the Allied powers and the occupation of her land by alien forces. Its assets were practically all destroyed by carpet bombing by enemy planes, and two of the cities were wiped out in August 1945 by the deadliest killer known until then to mankind: the atom bomb. Millions perished in the war, and those who survived went through indescribable hardships. The whole country had to go without even a commodity like common salt for a long time until the sea lanes were rendered safe by minesweepers and commercial ships could come and go. The people shivered in the cold and traveled in packed trains like canned sardines.

But their endurance was astonishing. They felt much shame at the calamity they had brought on themselves, but there was no crying over spilt milk or mourning over their fate. The people "bore the unbearable" and went through the trauma of the occupation with much fortitude. In their practical approach to the inevitable realities of the occupation, they had even to lower their traditional social values, as for instance by the kind of fraternization that subsisted between the American soldiers and the Japanese. It should be added however that this was only a temporary phase, possibly calculated to engineer as speedy a termination of the occupation as possible on the "practical principle" that "if you can't beat them, join 'em." Then, within less than six years of regained sovereignty, the nation rose, phoenix-like, from its ashes. It has today attained the status of an economic giant.

During my long stay in this country and elsewhere, I have witnessed a great world drama that on the one hand exhibited the depths to which social degradation of alien-occupied countries could go. On the other hand, I have also observed the heights to which courage, fortitude, and disciplined hard work could rise. In both cases, the biggest Asian role and the largest Asian dramatis personae were provided by Japan.

Thirty-six years ago, when the world war ended with Japan's total defeat and surrender, the average income of a Japanese was only slightly better than that of the average Indian's. About the size of the state of Maharashtra (372,000 sq.km.) in India, the Japanese group of islands has nearly twice its population (115 million). But the same country, which had lost almost all its assets in 1945, and which has still no raw material resources of its own (except an abundance of electricity and a limited quantity of coal), is today economically the second richest country in the world, second only to America. At its current growth, it is reckoned that it will jump to the first position before the turn of the century.

In real terms, Japan's gross national product has been doubling almost every eight years, a rate of progress unmatched in the economic history of the world. Experts estimate that at the current rate of progress, the per capita income of the average Japanese in the 1980s will exceed that of the average American. And if the trend continues, it will be more than double in the 1990s. In industrial power, Japan in 1979–80 was listed as the world's fourth largest. It is believed that by now (1982) it has overtaken West Germany and the USSR and is behind only the United States of America. There have been predictions from several sources that Japan's economy is basically fragile and that it has been brought up to its present gigantic proportion because of its small expenditure on defense. It is also said that it received a tremendous boost from the Korean War of 1950 and the subsequent Vietnam conflict.

It is claimed by some that if the two military superpowers come to a showdown or if the West Asian countries apply an oil squeeze on the non-oil producers, Japan will collapse and starve. Such stories can be highly exaggerated. Japan heavily depends on other countries for its raw materials, but so do many other nations, more or less, not excluding West Germany. It is mostly a matter of degree, and for a country like Japan, with its tremendous skill to improvise, disasters such as apprehended by some need not necessarily take place. Of course, in the event of a nuclear shootout between the two superpowers, nothing will probably be left anywhere, and there will then be no question as to who will be number one and who will be number hundred. The prospect will be that all will come down to zero.

"What is it that makes Japan tick?" is a question which has become almost a cliché. The answers can be long, but there can also be a shortlist of them. In such a list can be found Japan's organizational skill, combined with her collective industrial and fiscal discipline. This is something difficult to understand for persons who have not tried to study Japanese traditional psychology. I should preface what I say in this respect, by the caution that qualities that could be virtues in certain given conditions can become vices when the conditions change, and what happened during the years immediately preceding Japan's entry into the Second World War provides an illustration of the point.

Against such a background, it can be stated that what makes Japan tick is, basically, her people. Here we have a nation fundamentally endowed with a great sense of unity. The people act as one integrated group in all matters which affect their country's collective interest. For the good of his country, the average Japanese is capable of sacrificing his personal comforts and his self-interest. This quality has been ingrained in him over several centuries, particularly during the past ten or twelve decades, and is quite meaningfully related, on a national scale, to the concept of *bushido* (the way of the warrior), the origin of which goes way back to the period of the samurai or the ronin.

The Japanese are sticklers for details, have a penchant for research and innovation, and aim at standards higher than any they have seen in the relevant fields. Some observers have stated that they were always great in small things. But they also had a kind of "blinkered" approach, without their being aware of it, which caused their critics to declare them as capable of being "small in big things." This weakness they seem to have remedied after the war. They do not want another war if they can possibly avoid one.

In their daily life they exhibit an artistic appreciation of their own tradition, and a good taste that make for a high degree of social order. They would deplore any vulgarity of customs or manners. These traits, in turn, are conditioned by a keen passion for the beauties of nature, and for music, painting, and other fine arts.

EPILOGUE

Welcoming Queen Elizabeth II and Prince Philip, Duke of Edinburgh, at a reception in Shinjuku Gyoen, 1974. Mrs. Nair greets the queen; next to her is the author. Standing next to the queen is the Indian ambassador, S. Than.

The author introducing Tetsuko Higuchi (Rash Behari Bose's eldest daughter) to Indian Prime Minister Indira Gandhi at a reception in Tokyo, 1969.

EPILOGUE

The author in discussion with Prime Minister Indira Gandhi in Tokyo, 1969.

For some period now, I have been spending a few months every year in India and residing for the most part in Tokyo. I think therefore that I am in a position of advantage to observe conditions in India, and mentally compare them with what happens in Japan in similar areas of activity. India, a vast country of subcontinental proportion, has an abundance of manpower and a plethora of individual talent of the highest order. In intelligence and capability, the average Indian is next to none in the world. But, alas, where collective effort for national progress is required, we do not seem to "tick" in the way the Japanese do. We appear to lack the kind of self-discipline that must dovetail into national discipline to make a country truly and rapidly great in the modern sense. For instance, look at the scenario on our industrial front.

We waste a colossal amount of energy on strikes, "go slow," and other acts that retard production, slow down progress, and thus negate the very wherewithal for improvement and progress. I do not say that there should be no freedom to strike, nor that there are no strikes or other labor problems in Japan. What I say is that first of all there are fewer such problems because the administrators, whether in the private or public sector, plan better than we seem to have been doing, and avoid situations that can reasonably be anticipated and avoided. For instance, why is it that in India we do not have a national wage policy that ought to eliminate at least to a near-total extent any valid excuse for strikes on grounds of disparities in remunerations? Secondly, if work stoppage in fact occurs, there is a way with both employers and employees in Japan that ordinarily enables settlements to be reached amicably and without undue delay.

And a few things, inter alia, that attract attention there are that (a) during work stoppage, no one would normally destroy any property because preservation of production and ancillary facilities is a sine qua non for return to normal production when a dispute is resolved; (b) as soon as a confrontation is satisfactorily ended, all things fall back into proper positions as they were before, and almost invariably the lost time is also made good by extra work; (c) there is hardly anything known in Japan as "go slow" tactics; (d) punctuality is observed throughout working hours, and there is no idle talk in any office; (e) there is a universal sense of the dignity of labor at all levels; and (f) no papers are held up for want of peons to take them from one table to another because the institution of peons does not exist.

Just as industrial discipline is part of national discipline, so is civic sense inseparable from collective social order. For example, hygiene. Tokyo has a population exceeding 13 million people. There is air pollution, which is of course a terrible thing but which has become an inevitable price for industrial progress anywhere—but there are no stinking rivers or lakes, nor any slums. Why do we have them in India? The reason can only be administrative laxity and bad planning in a country that has no dearth of talent among its people. If there is the will, the task is certainly not difficult. Make every occupant of a house or tenement responsible for the cleanliness of his own premises and of the area immediately surrounding his; make the municipalities remove garbage in time in closed vans and prevent unauthorized squatting, which is what creates slums. Develop the villages so that everyone does not crowd into the cities. Disperse industries and offices to avoid further deterioration and eventual death of saturated cities. Set up municipalities that work.

It is useless to say that the problems are too big for solution. They are not, if the leaders play their leadership role responsibly. Can all our politicians honestly say that they are adequately unselfish? Here again, let me not be misunderstood or misconstrued. I do not say that everyone in Japan or other highly advanced countries is an angel or a paragon of virtue. Such an ideal situation exists nowhere in the world and may be found only in heaven. Nature abhors perfection. But it is seldom, if ever, that one would see in Japan an office holding up a file, or a law enforcement functionary committing, condoning, or abetting a crime for some petty consideration and getting away with it all with impunity.

Such things may appear to some persons to be "normal" or, at worst, "small," but the Japanese as a people do not view them so. They look at them as dangers because, unless curbed, they spread like a canker right down to their marrow so that major surgery, which may mean amputation, might eventually be the only recourse. Indeed, in most cases of that kind, the punitory mechanism is inbuilt in the people's ethos itself. They "lose face," which is about the worst kind of punishment for a people who have developed, over a long period, a certain pride at the national level in good performance.

Many persons in Japan have come under charges of various kinds; they are however brought to book with efficiency and dealt with properly when charges are proved. In India, are we seriously trying to book major culprits against whom reasonable suspicions exist, or is dirt brushed under the carpet? Let all the "leaders" honestly ask themselves these and similar questions. And let them remember that what they do, their underlings are likely to copy. There is a proverb in Malayalam to the effect that if the fence starts eating the crop, you cannot blame the cattle.

A national ethos of the kind I have indicated cannot be brought about overnight. In India, the process has been rendered all the more complex because of the poisonous legacy of a long period of colonial subjugation of our country. It may take long years to overcome its ill effects and to set us all on the right course. But have we begun those years, although we unshackled ourselves over three decades ago? If not, let us begin them at least now so that we shall catch up.

In conclusion, I should like to make a brief mention of the state of Indo-Japanese political and economic cooperation. I had visualized a certain pattern, before and during the war, and also at the time I was working with the government of India on the treaty between India and Japan. What I see today is, however, not quite the same. I think India owed it to Japan to acknowledge that, whatever eventually occurred, the Greater East Asia War that Japan started did hasten the independence of India and other Asian (also African and other) countries under colonial rule. But India did not forget this, as will be clear from what I have said on that subject in this book. At the time of the India-Japan Treaty of Peace, India dealt with Japan gracefully. The Japanese leaders of those days, who belonged by and large to my generation, were well aware of this, and were thankful for India's generous gesture.

However, for reasons perhaps attributable to both the Japanese and the Indian sides, I cannot help feeling that the initial expectations of perpetual cooperation have not fructified to the extent then hoped for. Japan, especially after its phenomenal economic growth, does not seem to have been giving sufficient thought to the importance of promoting cooperative activities to the common good of the two countries in trade, or technical and other areas. It seems to me that the United States umbrella under which Japan has chosen to remain has perhaps created some difficulty for the proper development of Indo-Japanese relations to the requisite extent. Japan takes a great deal of interest in ASEAN affairs but seems to look askance at India. I am not trying to do any fault-finding; it may well be that India is also to some extent responsible for not building well enough on the good foundation which K. K. Chettur had laid at the time of the peace treaty.

There is no doubt that the foreign policies of the two countries have several areas of divergence. Japan clearly is part of the Western power bloc led by America, whereas India is a nonaligned country, together with about one hundred other nations. India obviously has no right to decide Japan's policies, just as Japan should not try to determine India's. But I recall a few instances where I think Japan could have taken, vis-à-vis India, a position somewhat different from what she seems to have done. To the best of my recollection, when India was invaded in 1962 by China, I do not think Japan voiced as much concern as many other friends of India did. Memory of India's friendship toward her could have been a little less hazy on Japan's part. Similarly, when President Nixon moved the nuclear-powered American aircraft carrier *Enterprise* from the United States 7th Fleet (it was rumored that the *Enterprise* was redeployed from Yokosuka in Japanese waters, and that it even carried an atom bomb) to the Bay of Bengal to threaten India during Pakistan's war with India, the Indian people were astonished that no protest came from Japan.

More recently, Foreign Minister Ito, during a visit to India in 1980, appeared to have something to say in New Delhi to the effect that Japan was not in favor of India's policy towards Kampuchea (present Cambodia). Japan of course had every right not to agree with India on any question, but I do not think there was any need for the foreign minister to say in New Delhi what he did, about India's foreign policy. Perhaps there was pressure from other quarters; perhaps, again, it was just a case of a show of Japan's increasing economic power in Asia and the world. A neutral position would have been in order, and criticisms were really uncalled for. At the time of writing, there is a great deal of talk about American efforts to rearm Pakistan. One hopes that Japan would not take sides on the issue to India's detriment.

The government of India's approach to Japan and Japan's attitude to India in matters of industrial collaboration seem to leave much to be desired. Here are two great Asian countries. One (Japan) is technologically highly developed, but without raw materials; the other, with vast natural resources, can do with some import of technology from Japan, for assimilation into its own capabilities, which are potentially great. But things somehow do not seem to have clicked. Friends in India tell me that the lack of mutual collaboration to any great extent is due to Japanese reluctance to part with technology; they want to set up their own plants in India, as they have succeeded in doing in Brazil, Mexico, and even in America and some other countries.

Japan should, I think, remember that India is a developing country that cannot afford to have any predominantly foreign control of production units in it. Japan will not lose by not insisting on such control. She could well afford to be satisfied with fair returns.

I am told that when it comes to any question of Japan's sale of technology alone to India, the price quoted is invariably too high. I hope this is not true; if it is, Japan would not be acting quite in the spirit of cooperation that had been envisaged.

I have wondered on occasions whether India has also not unwittingly failed to do the kind of hard and concerted thinking and planning that are important ingredients in making major Indo-Japanese cooperation continuous and mutually beneficial. It is not enough to receive some Japanese financial grants or loans via the Aid-India Consortium or otherwise. That does not quite amount to a scheme of Indo-Japanese good relations or cooperation that can be regarded as durable. We must do something more, instead of being content with ad hoc and piecemeal action in fits and starts.

But Japan and India should still be able to find a good modus vivendi that would place all their relations on an even keel to mutual benefit, in the way which K. K. Chettur, Dr. Radhabinod Pal, Shintaro Ryu, Yasaburo Shimonaka, and other stalwarts had in view. There are surely enough persons of wisdom and goodwill on both sides who can ensure that leaders such as those I have mentioned do not turn in their graves at anything that happens between the two countries. Let me hope that Indo-Japanese dealings in all matters will be such that the souls of these and numerous other great men on both sides will always rest in peace.

APPENDICES

Appendix 1
Explanatory Notes

Bushido

In simple terms *bushido* means "the way of the warrior." It is a code of conduct, the main ingredients of which are (i) a high sense of personal honor and chivalry; (ii) great love of the country, for the sake of which the individual will be prepared to offer any sacrifice, including his own life if necessary; (iii) repentance for any sin committed and determination not to repeat mistakes, and self-punishment even to the extent of suicide by ceremonially conducted hara-kiri (self-disembowelment) if the sin is serious; (iv) unquestioned loyalty to the master whom the person serves, and of course to the emperor.

The spirit of *bushido* was inculcated in Japanese society over the centuries, from people's very childhood. This led to a certain "regimentation" of the society. Whether it was good or bad is difficult to say: it had both these aspects. The extreme discipline it introduced into the society enabled the rapid progress of the country along modern lines, especially beginning with the Meiji Restoration in the latter part of the nineteenth century. On the other hand it is blamed as one of the contributing factors for the rise of militarism that set Japan on the warpath, because it produced a collective sense of belligerency and expansionist ideas that got the better of individual freedom of thought and action and eventually resulted in the country's great defeat in 1945.

Ronin

A ronin is generally described as a samurai (warrior) without a specific master to serve for the time being. Historically the concept has an association with a famous incident that took place during the Edo Period (1600–1867), especially that part of it when the Tokugawa Shogunate held supreme sway and virtually had unified control over the various provincial feudal lords, who had until then been functioning more or less autonomously in their respective areas. ("Shogun" means a "generalissimo" or "commander-in-chief".) There was political stability in Japan practically throughout the Tokugawa regime, which lasted over two hundred years, but one sensational incident took place during 1701–3, generally known as the episode of the "47 ronin."

Some chiefs had come from Kyoto to meet the shogun at Edo (the old name for Tokyo). Three daimyo (territorial feudal lords) had been detailed to look after them. One of these daimyo, Naganori Asano from Ako, was insulted by a senior officer of the shogunate. In a fit of anger, Asano attacked the officer (by name Yoshinaka Kira) with his sword and wounded him, although he could not kill him as he had probably planned to do.

Whether under provocation or not, it was a serious offence on the part of Asano to have drawn his weapon in the precincts of Edo Castle. The shogun therefore confiscated Asano's fief and ordered him to commit suicide.

Asano accordingly killed himself by seppuku (i.e., hara-kiri or disembowelment), but when the news reached Ako, Asano's samurai retainers were infuriated and wanted to avenge the death of their erstwhile lord. They initially resisted the order to surrender the fief and Asano's residence, but ultimately allowed the shogun's orders to be carried out as advised by their leader, Yoshio Oishi. However, Yoshio planned a stratagem for avenging the death of Asano and the loss of his and his compatriots' prestigious status of samurai which became "reduced" to that of ronin.

Taking a secret oath to wreak vengeance on Kira, these 47 ex-samurai shifted to Edo. To avoid suspicion on the part of Kira or other agents of the shogun, Oishi marked time for about two years, deliberately leading the life of a debauch in order to give the outward impression that he or his ex-colleagues could not be up to any vengeful action. But he was only playing an act to hoodwink the shogunate's spies and other retainers. In January 1703, all the 47 ronin mounted a sudden attack on Kira's house and killed him and many of his samurai.

These 47 ronin had acted against Edo's authority, but at the same time their loyalty to their late lord (Asano) and their spirit of sacrifice created a great impact among the Japanese people who regarded them as heroes. The shogun, although initially annoyed, also eventually took a sympathetic view. His decision in the circumstances was that all the 47 persons should be allowed to atone for their crime by the honorable means of hara-kiri. They killed themselves accordingly.

The dramatic story of these famous 47 ronin is the subject of numerous ballads and other pieces of literature written by several great Japanese authors. The best known of the works is the *Chushingura* by Izami Takeda (early 18th century).

The graves of these 47 ronin are located in the premises of a temple in Tokyo. They are still worshipped as national heroes.

Appendix 2
Rash Behari Bose's Presidential Address at the Inauguration of the Bangkok Conference (June 15, 1942)

Allow me to express my sincere thanks for the great honor you have done me by calling upon me to occupy this chair and guide the deliberations of this historic conference. While greatly appreciating this expression of love and affection for me, I am not unaware of the fact that along with this honor you have placed on my shoulders a great responsibility by electing me the president of this conference. However, if I have obeyed your command and taken this chair in spite of my knowledge of the intricacies of the problems that will come before this conference, I have been prompted to do so by my great faith in your spirit of cooperation and your sincere desire to put your heads together and to come to useful decisions without wasting much of your time on unnecessary discussions and arguments. I am sure I can count upon unreserved help and cooperation in successfully conducting the business of the conference.

As I stand here my thought goes to the unfortunate air accident, last March, that claimed the lives of our four valuable comrades—Swami Satyanand Puri and Gyani Pritam Singhji of Bangkok, and Captain Akram and Mr. Nilakantha Ayer of Malaya, while they were flying to Tokyo to attend our Indian Independence Conference.

We can well realize the great loss to our cause at such an important period of our struggle and we all feel it very deeply. However, brethren, let us take it as inevitable and pray for the peace of their souls. In our grim, final struggle against British Imperialism, we shall have to offer great sacrifices. Many of us will have to lay down our lives before the world can see India free. It can be well said that these four comrades have given us the lead, of which our compatriots in Thailand and Malaya can well be proud.

During and since 1857, when we first revolted against British Imperialism in India, hundreds of thousands of our most respected and beloved compatriots have laid down their lives in their efforts to free our Motherland. We cannot forget the fact that they have nourished the seeds of *swaraj* with their blood, and it is the result of their supreme sacrifice that we are today so near our goal and can hope with confidence to achieve Independence in the near future. The world knows only a part of the long list of Indian victims of British Imperialism. Let us pay our respects to the memory of those numberless known and unknown comrades. Placed as we are today, we can do very little beyond that. But the time is fast approaching when in every city and town in India we shall find a worthy monument erected in their memory and we Indians will pay our homage to them and look upon them with pride.

Our homage is also due to those respected leaders and workers as well as the organizations that have in various ways made untiring efforts since 1857 to liberate our country from bondage. Their list is in no way small and in no way their contributions negligible. Let us pay our respect to that greatest living Indian, Mahatma Gandhi, who, with his magic hand, roused the Indian masses from centuries of long slumber and has created self-confidence in them. We can have no doubt that when the new and true history of India will be written, Mahatma Gandhi's name will have to be mentioned as the savior of India.

I do not want to take your time by going into the details regarding India's struggle for freedom since 1857. Suffice it to say that although the failure of our revolt of 1857 was a great blow to the nation, and although a general depression had overwhelmed the country, our efforts to overthrow British rule never ceased. Under the circumstances prevailing in those days, the activities had to be carried on underground and within a limited scope; and whenever there was an opportunity a revolt was attempted. After minor preparatory stages our first effort on a large scale was made when the war of 1914–18 started. Our workers were active everywhere. The Indian Army was prepared to join the revolt. A part of the army had actually revolted rather prematurely. We thought we were going to succeed. Unfortunately we did not meet with success on that occasion. Thousands were sent to the Andamans and Mandalay and hundreds of them still remain rotting in prisons and concentration camps.

During that war of 1914–18 the British were partially successful in receiving India's cooperation by telling lies and making false promises. Our people were misled by the fine phraseologies of the shrewd British diplomats. They promised us freedom after the war, as they are doing even during the present war. But soon after the conclusion of that war it was realized that they not only did not mean to keep their promises but definitely wanted to take away even the shadow of civil liberties which the Indians were having in prewar days. When they protested against that, the response from the British side was in the form of bombs, bullets and machine guns. Needless to say, the tragedy of the Jallianwala Bagh of Amritsar in April 1919 is still fresh in the memory of every one of us and the wound has not healed. It really cannot be healed until and unless we have completely destroyed the power that was responsible for that great humiliation of our people.

Every tragedy, however, has a lesson, and so has the tragedy of Jallianwala Bagh. The blood of more than a thousand of those innocent martyrs that included even our women and children, cannot go without significant results. The great upheaval that swept India from one corner to the other, and the great movement of noncooperation and civil disobedience that has been carried on by the Indian National Congress since 1919 and that has wonderfully organized the masses of India for political struggle, were undoubtedly the direct result of the massacre of Jallianwala Bagh.

We must all bow our heads in reverence and be grateful to those brothers and sisters who, by giving their lives at Jallianwala Bagh have created a new life for India. As we know today, millions in India are prepared and determined to suffer and sacrifice their all for the cause of their Motherland. When in 1939 the war in Europe started, Britain once again began to indulge in jugglery of words in order to secure Indian cooperation and help. But to the great delight of us all, to this very day the nationalist leaders in India have refused to be misled and have continued to resist all British efforts to drag India into war. Our respect goes to Mahatma Gandhi for the most admirable way he has led the nation clear of all dangers of being entangled in this war.

With this background in India, the Greater East Asia War was declared on the 8th December 1941. No matter in which part of the world he or she might be living, whatever might be his or her attitude toward Japan, I refuse to believe that there was a true Indian patriot who was not extremely delighted and gratified in his heart of hearts when the great news of the declaration of war by Japan against the Anglo-Saxon race reached his or her ears. I refuse to believe that there is any true Indian patriot, whatever be his or her career or conviction, who might not have rejoiced as, from day to day, the mighty Imperial forces of Japan on land and sea and in the air went on administering crushing blows against their imperialism in Asia, and the British Imperialist bases in these parts began to totter one after the other like houses of cards. For is there a man whose eyes can withhold joyous tears when he sees before his eyes the power of the greatest enemy of humanity and peace, the greatest aggressor of centuries, being destroyed? Those of us who were destined to live and work in Japan had particular reasons to be overjoyed at this most welcome happening.

We have been working in Japan for decades and we can see Japan in a position to stand by the oppressed Asiatics and to liberate Asia. We were anxiously awaiting the day when Japan would fully realize the great significance of creating a free and united Asia and would feel convinced that it was in the interest of Japan herself, as also of the rest of Asia, if not of the world as a whole that the octopus grip of the Anglo-Saxon Imperialism in the East must be destroyed root and branch. We all were fully convinced that Japan alone was in a position to take the honor. Thus when on the morning of that most auspicious day, the day of Enlightenment of Lord Buddha, we heard the most auspicious news of Japan's declaration of war against our common enemy, we felt convinced that our mission in Japan was fulfilled. We felt convinced that India's freedom was assured. Being in Japan for decades, I knew well that she was not in the habit of taking any serious step unless she had fully weighed her strength and was convinced of success. I therefore did not share the views of those who thought that due to her continued military activities in China, she was too exhausted to challenge the mighty Anglo-Saxons, or so called ABCD combined forces. I was one of those who had not the slightest doubt that the war in China was a prelude to the real war against the powers who were actually responsible for the continued fratricidal conflict between China and Japan. Happenings on the international chessboard during the past more than ten years have been suggesting that such a worldwide conflict was inevitable. It was also apparent that the question of Indian freedom could be successfully solved only when Japan rose in arms against British imperialism.

Now that Japan and Thailand have taken up arms against our common foe the joint efforts of our worthy allies ensure the doom of the British Empire and our complete victory is assured.

These effective efforts on different fronts to destroy our common enemy bring us a reminder regarding our own duties and responsibilities in this common effort for our common cause. We must ask ourselves what we have done and what we are going to do to contribute to this great cause. Only praising Japan, Germany and Italy will not entitle us to the position for which we are craving. We must contribute our might and must make the greatest sacrifice we can. Then alone can we command the respect and consideration of our worthy allies and then alone can we claim a place worthy of a great nation like ours in future international assembly.

Realizing this very important fact, and our duty towards our Motherland at this most important juncture, we in Tokyo promptly met on the 8th December 1941 at the Rainbow Grill and decided upon a program of action. My compatriots formed a committee and asked me to lead the movement. I gladly agreed to abide by their decision. We at first undertook to consolidate Indian opinion in East Asia in favor of a definite fight from without. Meetings were held in different centers of Japan and resolutions were passed emphasizing the solidarity of our compatriots, the great need of declaring the Independence of India by destroying British imperialism and expressing confidence in our work.

On 26th December 1941, for the first time in the history of Indians in Japan, a Conference of nearly fifty representatives of the Indian residents in Kobe, Osaka, Yokohama and Tokyo—all the four cities where Indians reside—was held at the Railway Hotel at Tokyo to consider the problems. A resolution was passed calling upon the Indians to realize the gravity of the situation and the dangers ahead for India. The resolution read as follows:

> Whereas the continued defeat of the British and their allies in Europe and Africa has sealed the fate of British imperialism in Europe;
>
> Whereas the most decisive destruction of British sea and land forces by Japan in the East has given a death-blow to the power and prestige of British imperialism in Asia;
>
> Whereas the war is fast approaching the shores and borders of India, the British stronghold, the Axis Powers may be obliged to invade India in order to destroy the main source of British fighting strength;
>
> Whereas such an invasion will bring unimaginable and extreme hardships, miseries and suffering to millions of innocent and helpless Indians in cities, towns and villages; and
>
> Whereas the only way to avoid this most unhappy situation is to declare complete independence of India from British rule and to cut off all possible connections with British imperialism in every possible way immediately;
>
> the Indian Nationals residing in Japan assembled in this Conference most seriously and earnestly appeal to the Indian National Congress

and the people of India immediately to declare independence and to capture all power from the British in India, to take immediate effective steps to stop each and every source of Indian aid to the British Imperialist war and to declare on behalf of the people that India has no desire whatsoever to be involved in this conflict and has never been willing to help Britain.

Our representatives were sent to Shanghai, and on 26th January this year a huge gathering of the Indian residents of Shanghai was held in the Young Men's Association hall when similar resolutions as passed in Tokyo were very enthusiastically passed and our movement was given unanimous support.

In the meantime we established contact with the military and civil high commands in Japan and began to impress upon them the necessity of helping India in her struggle for freedom for the very achievement of the great object for which Japan had declared war against Britain and America. We made it clear to them that so long as British imperialism in India continued, Japan could not expect a final victory in this war. At last we succeeded in prevailing upon them: and General Tojo, the Prime Minister of Japan, openly declared before the Imperial Diet that his Government was prepared to help the Indians in our efforts to free our country from the long bondage. In this declaration before the Imperial Diet after the fall of Singapore, he said:

> It is a golden opportunity for India, having, as it does, several thousand years of history and splendid cultural traditions, to rid herself of the ruthless despotism of Britain and participate in the construction of the Greater East Asia Co-Prosperity Sphere. Japan expects that India will restore the proper status of India for the Indians and will not stint herself in extending assistance to the patriotic efforts of the Indians. Should India fail to awaken to her mission forgetting her history and tradition, and continue as before to be beguiled by the British cajolery and manipulation and act at their beck and call, I cannot but fear that opportunity for the renaissance of the Indian people would be forever lost.

The declaration offered us great encouragement and we felt convinced that India could safely hope to be free before the East Asia War came to an end. Counting upon the promises of General Tojo, we established our headquarters at Sanno Hotel and started our activities and preparations in right earnest. We decided that a Conference of the representatives of Indian organizations in various parts of East Asia should be held for exchanging views regarding our future move. With the help of the military authorities, things were conveniently arranged and the representatives of our compatriots residing in Malaya, Hong Kong, and Shanghai along with those of Tokyo, sat in Conference for three days and framed the preliminary constitution for the working and progress of our movement. Those friends from abroad who participated in the Tokyo Conference had occasion to come in contact with responsible members of the Japanese army in Tokyo and to know more and more about the standing of our movement. Discussions at the Tokyo Conference were varied and we did our best to lay down a solid foundation upon which we could base our plan of action in future. We all know that the Conference in Tokyo was held at a time when things were less settled than they are today. Friends from the East Indies were not present. We were deprived of the valuable help and advice of our friends in Thailand due to the unfortunate accident. Burma and the Andamans were still in the hands of our enemies. We therefore were unable to come to a decision that could be claimed to be representative of the views of our compatriots in East Asia as a whole. We therefore decided to hold a large and more representative Conference at a later date when the decisions taken at Tokyo were to be ratified. This Assembly in which we are participating today is the result of that decision.

The responsibility to convene this Conference was placed upon my shoulders and I was asked to hold it in this city. I am sorry that the Conference was delayed by a couple of weeks. We expected to arrive here earlier but due to the extraordinary period through which we are passing, things could not be always done as expected and we have to adjust ourselves according to circumstances.

I know I have exhausted your patience by chronologizing the events and activities during the last more than six months. But it was necessary to acquaint you with what had happened and how we have proceeded, before we sit down to business and work out far-reaching decisions.

Friends, we all realize the gravity of the situation and also the fact that we are passing through the most important period of India's history. I do not want to waste time on long speeches. We had enough of that during the last more than five decades. We really cannot afford to waste our time on meaningless talk and arguments. Those who really want to serve the Motherland, cannot have much time to talk. If we go on talking without coming to any concrete decisions, time will not wait for us and we shall be left only to shed tears at our past folly, and it will be too late to mend things. I know there are knotty problems that will come before you for discussions and will need your must careful consideration. I know you will have to do a lot of thinking and face a lot of doubts from within before you can decide. But, if you have come with a grim determination to thrash out a positive, concrete, and actually useful plan, you will be able to come to quick decisions. Let us all fully realize our responsibilities towards our land of birth and let us realize well that our downtrodden country cannot afford to lose this golden opportunity that comes only once in centuries. Our brothers and sisters have in hundreds of thousands laid down their lives and have suffered and sacrificed for more than a century so that our country may be once again free. Let us rise to the occasion and carry their efforts to success so that the souls of the martyrs in heaven may find peace and be pleased. Let us rise and act so that the great preparations that Mahatma Gandhi has made during the last more than two decades may bear fruit and our children in future may think of us with pride and respect as the members of a free nation.

I know many of you have come with doubts and suspicions regarding the ultimate fate of our country as the result of our activities. I assure you that I can well appreciate your feelings of uncertainty and your desire for security and yet I believe they are based on false premises. Having the bitterest experience of Imperialist exploitation for centuries, we have begun to doubt even our good friends and if we insist on this attitude the world will go on and we shall be left behind to regret our indecision.

I want to sound a note of warning here. Our enemies have always been successful in keeping us divided and in creating false impressions in our minds on such occasions. On many occasions in the past we have missed opportunities to free our country, by being victims of lying British propaganda. I can only hope that we shall not repeat our folly. Our doubts and suspicions are to a great extent the results of shrewd and well-thought-out plans of our enemies to sabotage our efforts. Those of us who have intelligence enough and who are not blind to facts and happenings, can see the way clearly.

We should feel thankful to the Governments of Japan, Germany, Thailand and Italy for the most friendly attitude they have been showing towards our cause. We must be particularly thankful to Japan for the most encouraging, hopeful and definite promise of help in our sacred cause. Let us not forget the words of Pandit Jawaharlal Nehru when he said:

Success Often Comes to Those
Who Dare and Act: It Seldom
Goes to Cowards.

I make an earnest appeal to you all, friends, to see that when you conclude your session you have a most practical and workable plan of action for India's freedom so that we can start our work right after the Conference and march ahead. We are fortunate enough to have the most valuable help of our Indian Army at our disposal. They deserve our great respect for the great service they have already rendered to our cause by refusing to serve the enemies of India. But their greater service is still awaiting our decision. No one can doubt the bravery of our soldiers in a righteous fight for a righteous cause. Our sympathy goes to the families and friends of those Indian soldiers who had, erroneously believing that they have been fighting for a right cause, lost their lives in Europe and Asia. They have been misled by the same propaganda of lies by Britain that is responsible for the unfounded suspicions in the minds of so many of us. I bow my head to the bravery of our soldiers and we should have no doubt that with their wholehearted support we are going to win our final fight against British imperialism. Let us stand shoulder to shoulder and let us march hand in hand to success. Let us remember we have one indivisible nation, INDIA – One enemy, England – One goal, complete Independence.

Source: Shri Rash Behari Bose's archives, in the custody of his daughter, Mrs. Tetsu Higuchi. Reproduced by courtesy of Mrs. Higuchi.

Appendix 3
Brief Life Sketches of Justice (Dr.) Radhabinod Pal and Yasaburo Shimonaka

Justice (Dr.) Radhabinod Pal

Son of the late Bipin Bihari Pal. Born on January 27, 1886, in Salimpur, Nadia District, West Bengal. Graduated in 1907 as a bachelor of science from the Presidency University, Calcutta (Kolkata), with honors in mathematics, and obtained the master of science degree in 1908. Thereafter studied law and received the bachelor of law degree in 1911. Started his working life as a professor of mathematics but joined the bar of the Calcutta high court as an advocate after securing his law degree. Received the master of law degree at the top of his class in 1920. Was appointed professor of law in the University of Calcutta's Law College in 1923 and served in that capacity until 1936. In 1924, the University of Calcutta awarded him the degree of doctor of law; his doctoral thesis was *The Hindu Philosophy of Law in the Vedic and post-Vedic Times Prior to the Institutes of Manu (Jurisprudence in Vedanta*, for short).

Appointed Tagore memorial professor of law in the University of Calcutta in 1925 and again in 1930 and 1938—probably the only person to be thrice honored with such a distinction. Was legal consultant to the government of India over the period 1927 to 1941. Became joint president of the International Academy of Comparative Law and a member of the International Law Association of the UK in 1937. Served on the panel of presidents of the Congress of the World Law Societies during the same year.

Judge in the high court of Calcutta from 1941–43. Vice-chancellor at the

University of Calcutta from 1944–46. Judge on the International Military Tribunal for the Far East in Tokyo from 1946–1948, when he wrote his famous dissenting judgement pronouncing that the so-called Japanese war criminals were guiltless under international law.

Member of the United Nations' International Law Commission from 1952–67, serving as president in 1958 and 1962.

Visited Japan in 1952 to attend the Asia Congress on World Federation and conducted several lecture tours under the auspices of the Japan-India Friendship Association. Developed a lasting brotherly affection and respect for Yasaburo Shimonaka, founder of the publishing firm Heibonsha and a true friend of India. At his invitation, Dr. Pal visited Japan again in 1953 and gave several lectures in various parts of the country to intellectual audiences.

Named national professor of jurisprudence in India, in 1959. Elected judge of the International Court of Justice in 1960.

On January 26, 1959, he was awarded the second-highest Indian honor by the president of India, the Padma Vibhushan, next only to the Bharat Ratna (Gem of India). Visited Japan for the fourth time in 1966 and received the decoration of the Order of the Sacred Treasure, First Class, from the emperor of Japan.

Author of several books on law, particularly Hindu law, in which he is considered to be probably the highest authority.

Passed away on January 10, 1967, in Calcutta. He had four sons and six daughters.

Yasaburo Shimonaka

Born on June 12, 1878, at Shimotachikui, Konda-mura, Taki-gun, Hyogo Prefecture. Teacher at Unchu Elementary School, Kobe, from 1897–98. Joined the *Jido Shimbun* (Children's Newspaper) in Tokyo in 1902. Taught at the Saitama Normal School in Saitama Prefecture during 1911–18.

Founded the publishing firm Heibonsha in 1914. Published a very useful book called *Ya, kore wa benri da: Pocketsu komon* (A Pocket All-Round Handy Book).

Organized the Keimeikai, a reformist association of educators, in 1919 and the Nomin Jichikai (Farmers' Autonomous Association) in 1925. Founded the Shin Nihon Kokumin Domei (New Japan National League) in 1932 and was chairman of its administrative committee. Promoted the founding, in 1933, of the Dai Ajia Kyokai (Greater Asia Association) and the Gandhi Association of Japan.

Founded the Shinmin Inshokan (New People's Publishing Company) in Peking in 1938 and was elected vice president. In January 1947, testified at the hearings of the International Military Tribunal for the Far East as witness in defense of Iwane Matsui. In August of the same year, founded the Tokyo Inshokan Printing Company, Ltd. In association with Toyohiko Kagawa, launched the movement for the establishment of a world federation, in November 1951.

Invited Justice Radhabinod Pal to Japan in October 1952, and both of them travelled across the country giving lectures at various places on important topics of a wide range. In November the same year, he held the Asia Congress on World Federation in Hiroshima, which adopted the Hiroshima Declaration. Invited Justice Radhabinod Pal again in September 1953 and organized a lecture tour for him for the benefit of intellectual audiences and in the cause of India-Japan friendship.

Elected, in 1955, president of Sekai Renpo Kensetsu Domei (Alliance for the Construction of a World Federation). In November of the same year, organized the Committee of Seven for World Peace Appeal and launched it on its work.

Was chairman of the national committee of the meeting to welcome Pandit Jawaharlal Nehru, prime minister of India, during his visit to Japan in October 1957. Was chief delegate from Japan to the Ninth World Congress on World Federation in August 1959. Was acquainted, through correspondence, with President J. F. Kennedy (1961).

Passed away on February 21, 1961.

Leaders engaged in promoting India-Japan friendship formed an association (of which the author is a founding member) and donated generously for the construction of a memorial in honor of Justice Radhabinod Pal and Yasaburo Shimonaka. A monument named the Pal-Shimonaka Memorial Hall, built on the shores of Lake Ashinoko in Hakone, was inaugurated in 1974. It is a dignified structure commemorating a great Indian and a great Japanese personality who regarded each other as brothers.

Appendix 4
The Treaty Of Peace Between the Governments of India and Japan
(June 9, 1952)

WHEREAS the Government of India have by public notification issued on the ninth day of June, 1952, terminated the state of war between India and Japan; AND WHEREAS the Government of India and the Government of Japan are desirous of cooperating in friendly association for the promotion of the common welfare of their peoples and the maintenance of international peace and security in conformity with the principles of the Charter of the United Nations; The Government of India and the Government of Japan have therefore determined to conclude this Treaty of Peace, and to this end have appointed their Plenipotentiaries:

THE GOVERNMENT OF INDIA
K. K. CHETTUR,
Ambassador Extra-ordinary and Plenipotentiary in Japan

THE GOVERNMENT OF JAPAN
KATSUO OKAZAKI,
Minister for Foreign Affairs of Japan

Who, having indicated to each other their respective Full Powers, and found them good and in due form, have agreed on the following Articles:

Article I

There shall be firm and perpetual peace and amity between India and Japan and their respective peoples.

Article II

(a) The Contracting Parties agree to enter into negotiators for the conclusion of treaties or agreements to place their trading, maritime, aviation and other commercial relations on a stable and friendly basis.

(b) Pending the conclusion of the relevant treaty or agreement, during a period of four years from the date of the issue of the notification by the Government of India terminating the state of war between India and Japan:—

1. the Contracting Parties shall accord to each other most favoured-nation treatment also with respect to air traffic rights and privileges;

2. the Contracting Parties shall accord to each other most favoured-nation treatment also with respect to customs duties and charges of any kind and restrictions and other regulations in connection with the importation and exportation of goods or imposed on the international transfer of payments for imports or exports and with respect to the method of levying such duties and charges and with respect to all rules and formalities in connection with importation and exportation and charges to which customs clearing operations may be subject; and any advantage, favour, privilege or immunity granted by either of the parties to any product originating in or destined for any other country shall be accorded immediately and unconditionally to the like products originating in or destined for the territory of the other Party;

3. Japan will accord to India national treatment, to the extent that India accords Japan the same, with respect to shipping, navigation and imported goods, and with respect to natural and juridical persons and their interests—such treatment to include all matters pertaining to the levying and collection of taxes, access to the courts, the making and performance of contracts, rights to property (tangible and intangible), participation in juridical entities constituted under Japanese law, and generally the conduct of all kinds of business and professional activities;

Provided that in the application of this Article, a discriminatory measure shall not be considered to derogate from the grant of national or most favoured-nation treatment, if such measure is based on an exception customarily provided for in the commercial treaties of the party applying it, or on the necessity of safeguarding that party's external financial position or balance of payments, or on the need to maintain its essential security interests, and provided such measure is proportionate to the circumstances and is not applied in an arbitrary or unreasonable manner; Provided further that nothing contained in sub-paragraph (2) above shall apply to the preferences or advantages which have existed since before the 15th August, 1947, or which are accorded by India to contiguous countries.

(c) No provision of this Article shall be deemed to limit the undertakings assumed by Japan under Article V of this Treaty.

Article III

Japan agrees to enter into negotiations with India, when India so desires, for the conclusion of an agreement providing for the regulation or limitation of fishing and the conservation and development of fisheries on the high seas.

Article IV

India will return or restore in their present form all property, tangible and intangible, and rights or interests of Japan or its nationals which were within India at the time of the commencement of the war and are under the control of the Government of India at the time of coming into force of this Treaty; provided that the expenses which may have been incurred for the preservation and administration of such property shall be paid by Japan or its nationals concerned. If any such property has been liquidated, the proceeds thereof shall be returned, deducting the above-mentioned expense.

Article V

Upon application made within 9 months of the coming into force of this Treaty Japan will, within 6 months of the date of such application, return the property, tangible or intangible, and all rights or interests of any kind in Japan or India and her nationals which was within Japan at any time between the 7th December 1941 and the 2nd September 1945 unless the owner has freely disposed thereof without duress or fraud. Such property will be returned free of all encumbrances and charges to which it may have become subject because of the war, and without any charges for its return. Property the return of which is not applied for by or on behalf of its owner or by the Government of India within the prescribed period may be disposed of by the Japanese Government in its discretion. If any such property was with Japan on the 7th December, 1941 and cannot be returned or has suffered injury or damage as a result of the war, compensation will be made on terms not less favourable than the terms provided in the Allied Powers Property Compensation Law of Japan (Law number 164, 1951).

Article VI

(a) India waives all reparations claims against Japan.

(b) Except as otherwise provided in this Treaty, India waives all claims of India and Indian nationals arising out of action taken by Japan and its nationals in the course of the prosecution of the war as also claims of India arising from the fact that it participated in the occupation of Japan.

Article VII

Japan agrees to take the necessary measures to enable nationals of India to apply within one year of the coming into force of this Treaty to the appropriate Japanese authorities for review of any judgment given by a Japanese Court between December 7, 1941, and such coming into force, if in the proceedings in which the judgment was given, any Indian national was not able to present his case adequately either as plaintiff or as defendant. Japan further agrees that where an Indian national has suffered injury by reason of any such judgment, he shall be restored to the position in which he was before the judgment was given or shall be afforded such relief as may be just and equitable in the circumstances of the case.

Article VIII

(a) The Contracting Parties recognise that the intervention of the state of war has not affected the obligation to pay pecuniary debts arising out of obligations and contracts (including those in respect of bonds) which existed and rights which were acquired before the existence of the state of war, and which are due by the Government or nationals of Japan to the government or nationals of India, or are due by the Government or nationals of India to the Government or nationals of Japan; nor has the intervention of the state of war affected the obligation to consider on their merits claims for loss or damage to property or for personal injury or death which arose between the existence of a state of war, and which may be presented or represented by the Government of India to the Government of Japan or by the Government of Japan to the Government of India.

(b) Japan affirms its liability for the pre-war external debt of the Japanese State and for debts of corporate bodies subsequently declared to be liabilities of the Japanese State, and expresses its intention to enter into negotiations at an early date with its creditors with respect to the resumption of payments on these debts.

(c) The Contracting Parties will encourage negotiations in respect to other pre-war claims and obligations and facilitate the transfer of sums accordingly.

Afficle [sic] IX

(a) Japan waives all claims of Japan and her nationals against India and her nationals arising out of the war or out of actions taken because of the existence of a state of war, and waives all claims arising from the presence, operations or actions of forces or authorities of India in Japanese territory prior to the coming into force of this Treaty.

(b) The foregoing waiver includes any claims arising out of actions taken by India with respect to Japanese ships between September 1, 1939, and the coming into force of this Treaty, as well as any claims and debts arising in respect to Japanese prisoners of war and civilian internees in the hands of India: but does not include Japanese claims specifically recognised in the laws of India enacted since September 2, 1945. Japan recognises the validity of all acts and omissions done during the period of occupation under or in consequence of directives of the occupation authorities or authorised by Japanese law at that time, and will take no action subjecting Indian nationals to civil or criminal liability arising out of such acts or omissions.

Article X

Any dispute arising out of the interpretation or application of this Treaty or one or more of its Articles shall be settled in the first instance by negotiations, and, if no settlement is reached within a period of six months from the commencement of negotiations by arbitration in such manner as may hereafter be determined by a general or special agreement between the Contracting Parties.

Article XI

This Treaty shall be ratified and shall come into force on the date of exchange of ratifications which shall take place as soon as possible at New Delhi (or Tokyo).

IN WITNESS WHEREOF, the undersigned Plenipotentiaries have signed this Treaty.

DONE in duplicate at Tokyo this Ninth day of June, 1952 in the English language. Hindi and Japanese texts of this Treaty will be exchanged by the two Governments within a month of this date.

FOR JAPAN,   FOR INDIA,

(Katsuo Okazaki)   (K. K. Chettur)

Text of announcement made by the Japanese Foreign Minister, at the time of issue of the text of the Treaty:—

> *The spirit of amity and goodwill of India towards Japan is abundantly shown throughout in the Treaty. It is particularly exemplified by the provisions waiving all reparations claims and returning Japanese property located in India.*

S/d- Katsuo Okazaki,
Japanese Foreign Minister, June 9, 1952.

Sources: Lok Sabha Secretariat, New Delhi: *"Foreign Policy of India": Texts of Documents: 1947–59*; "The World and Japan" Database, Database of Japanese Politics and International Relations, National Graduate Institute for Policy Studies (GRIPS), Institute for Advanced Studies on Asia (IASA), University of Tokyo: *Treaty of Peace Between the Governments of India and Japan*

About the Author

Ayyappanpillai Madhavan Nair, or A. M. Nair, was born in Kerala, India, in 1905. He came to Japan in 1928, where he studied civil engineering at Kyoto Imperial University. In 1942, he participated in the establishment of the Indian Independence League, and from then until the end of the war was consistently involved in various movements in the cause of India's independence. In 1949, he founded the Nair Trading Company and opened Nair Restaurant in Tokyo's Ginza, which continues to this day. In 1984, he was awarded with the Order of the Sacred Treasure, Third Class. A. M. Nair passed away in 1990 in Thiruvananthapuram (Trivandrum), India.

An Indian Freedom Fighter in Japan: Memoirs of A. M. Nair

2025年3月27日　第1刷発行

著　者　　A. M. ナイル
企　画　　公益財団法人日本国際問題研究所
発行所　　一般財団法人出版文化産業振興財団
　　　　　〒101-0051 東京都千代田区神田神保町2-2-30
　　　　　電話　03-5211-7283
　　　　　ホームページ　https://www.jpic.or.jp/

印刷・製本所　　大日本印刷株式会社

定価はカバーに表示してあります。
本書の無断複写(コピー)、転載は著作権法の例外を除き、禁じられています。

© 1982 G. M. Nair
Printed in Japan
hardcover ISBN 978-4-86658-261-0
ebook (ePub) ISBN 978-4-86658-262-7
ebook (PDF) ISBN 978-4-86658-263-4